MODERN NEWS REPORTING

MODERN
NEWS REPORTING

THIRD EDITION

By CARL WARREN

Radio News Editor of the *New York News* Formerly City Editor of the Winfield (Kan.) *Daily Courier* Reporter and Washington Correspondent for the *Chicago Tribune* City Editor of the *Detroit Mirror* Instructor in the Medill School of Journalism, Northwestern University.

HARPER & ROW, Publishers, New York and Evanston

Library of Congress catalog card number: 58–59883

To Dorothy B. Warren

CONTENTS

ILLUSTRATIONS

PREFACE

This revision of *Modern News Reporting*, like the previous editions, aims at a single target. Its one objective is to launch young men and women into orbit as newspaper reporters.

Every science, art, profession or job changes with the times and the task of gathering and writing news which deals with all of them is no exception. Textbook revisions are required to keep pace with the development of new tools and with the trends of the trade.

Just as reporters of earlier eras learned to use the telegraph, typewriter and telephone, so those of today need to be introduced to the radiophone and tape recorder. They should know how the Teletypesetter has standardized newspaper style and understand the relationship of radio, television, and the other mass communicators to their own practices and future.

As mechanical advances continue, patterns in writing improve. Although there are no substitutes for clarity and readability, there are new ways of attaining them with simpler words and phrases, shorter sentences, better arranged paragraphs, and stronger story structure.

Subtler and perhaps more significant is the current controversy over *objectivity* versus *interpretation* in news presentation. The author attempts to interpret this feud objectively in common-sense terms. Also for the benefit of beginners bewildered by disagreement among editors themselves, he undertakes to assess and explain realistically—rather than judge —crusades and exposés, crime and sex news treatment, and other newsroom issues.

While each of these developments is fully discussed, the fundamental lessons in earlier editions of the text are preserved. The author is convinced that a beginner must understand the principles of the arch and the wheel before building space ships.

Likewise he has firmly resisted the temptation to update the book by wandering into other fields of little or no real value to the cub reporter. *Modern News Reporting* does not purport to cover the newspaper business—only a fractional part of it. Much less does it try to blanket the multiple media of mass communication.

It deals with the work of the general assignment man during his intern period—his first year on a local room staff, that of the mythical Midland *Times*. It enters only into those specializations such as sports, business, the courts and politics which he is likely to encounter at once.

The Midland *Times* is a medium-sized paper in a medium-sized American community. It is in effect a cross or a compromise between a small town paper and a big city daily with the attributes of both. Difficult as it may seem to span the gap, it is well for the learner to do so at the start. He may move from a rural to a metropolitan job or back again, perhaps as an editor or publisher.

Indeed the most promising growth in job opportunities on big city papers in the last decade has been on the suburban sections. Reporting for these zone-coverage and split-run editions—actually hometown newspapers within a newspaper—largely duplicates the methods used on smaller papers.

It has long since been proved that the rudiments of reporting, like those of law, medicine or engineering, can be successfully taught, studied and, if combined with practice, mastered in the classroom. Admittedly advancement comes only with experience but the traditional apprentice with "ink in his hair" almost always is outdistanced by the trained man with a sound educational background.

One temporary advantage of the apprentice is his opportunity to learn by direct contact how to handle the armory of practical devices used by newsroom craftsmen. Too many writers of texts intended to impart know-how on specific journalistic subjects, the author believes, overlook these so-called gadgets and fail to combine cookbook rules with academic theories.

On the other hand, memorizing too many rigid rules may restrict a student so that he freezes up at the typewriter. In writing style, especially, initiative should not be turned into inhibition by a succession of *must* do's and don'ts.

To those trained in reporting some of the advice in *Modern News Reporting* may seem elementary. But this book is planned for the benefit of those with no full-time news experience who expect to step from classroom to city room. It has been written for the students of today who will be the reporters of tomorrow.

The author wishes to acknowledge the able editorial assistance of his wife, Dorothy B. Warren, who has shared in the preparation of this and all previous editions of *Modern News Reporting*.

C. W.

FOREWORD

The lessons in *Modern News Reporting* roughly parallel the progress of a cub reporter in actual work. They move from the simple and basic to the complex and comprehensive.

The book is arranged to meet the special needs of students and instructors in schools and departments of journalism with a course in reporting apart from those in copyreading, editorial writing, radio and television news, public relations, photography and other allied subjects. It consists of:

1. Text—for study.
2. Shop talk—for discussion.
3. Practice—for exercises.
4. Assignments—for homework.

The book provides the basis for a one-year course, the 32 chapters corresponding to the standard 32 weeks in two semesters. The course may be condensed into one semester by using only the first 16 chapters or by combining 1 and 2, 3 and 4, and so on. It can be expanded under the new trimester school-year plan by extending laboratory hours.

A logical plan calls for lecture and practice periods in a one-two ratio. Thus, if three hours a week are devoted to the course, the instructor lectures one hour and two hours are allotted to practice, with discussion during or at the end of each period.

Most of the raw material must, and should, come from newspapers. An instructor with reasonable diligence can clip from papers sample stories similar in content to those found in the text. Current copies for clipping should be available to students. Each should also take at least one daily paper at home. Newspaper reading, marking and clipping is a part of his training. He will be doing them as long as he is a reporter or editor.

By looking ahead in the book a student may anticipate homework assignments and save articles he may use later in the course. It is of special advantage to teachers to collect clips and other lecture and practice material in a future file as well as to preserve in a scrapbook or otherwise data for use when the course is repeated.

MODERN NEWS REPORTING

CHAPTER 1

The Reporter and His Job

OCCUPATION: NEWSPAPERMAN

Will you so designate yourself in the future? That question probably faces you as you start the study of this book. You think you can or hope you may become a reporter.

You can—if you want the job, train for it, work at it, and stick to it until you succeed. The notion that newspapermen are born, not made, is nonsense. They make themselves. The ability to gather and write news is not something you inherit, like blue eyes or dark hair. It's something you learn to do, like swimming or sewing. All you need is average intelligence, energy, study, practice and—to advance—experience.

Few mature students of journalism today are fooled by the false ideas about newspaper work foisted upon the uninitiated by fiction, films, and television dramas. The facts, of course, are that modern editorial departments don't house a brawling bunch of "The Front Page" era rascals who drink up their pay, always wear press cards in their turned-up hats and their hats in the office. True, some reporters wear trench coats, but only when it rains.

Excepting for the chatter of typewriters and an occasional call for a copy boy, a city room is just about the calmest place in town, especially near a deadline. If anyone should shout, "Stop the presses!" he would either be clowning or crazy.

You can go through hundreds of newspaper offices without finding a single man who has been gunned into the gutter on an assignment. Reporters don't roam streets and dark alleys like see-all, know-all detectives, ready to catch a criminal or wipe out a crime syndicate. And a cub seldom scores a sensational scoop, somersaulting himself into headlines and fame on his first day at work.

No, the typical reporter is a solid and respectable citizen. At home or

1

on duty it's hard to tell him from anybody else. He works reasonable hours, usually under supervision, goes home at night, figures out his taxes, writes checks for the laundry and milk, and takes the youngsters for a drive on Sundays.

However, there is no denying that reporting, like show business, is and always will be one of the so-called glamour occupations. Although he scoffs at synthetic thrills, every veteran newsman knows the pleasure and excitement inherent in the nature of the work he does. He is bored less of the time than most other people. Nearly every day he has opportunities to make new friends. He is in touch with men and women of achievement in many fields. His richest reward is the satisfaction of going where things happen, of becoming the first to know, of being an insider, then seeing the product of his brain in print—perhaps under his own name—where it wins attention and moves the minds and emotions of others. It is a kind of satisfaction no other craft can duplicate.

Most newsmen are married to their work and, in a spirit of camaraderie, talk shop eagerly and frequently. And when they talk to their neighbors they are listened to respectfully. They are recognized as men with knowledge and influence.

If you have sensed this feeling of potential prestige and power—the feeling a reporter gets the first time he walks through a fire line or takes his seat at a press table—you already are being drawn into the newspaper business. And if you desire these things above all else, there is no better way for you to earn a living than by entering it. You will never be completely disenchanted.

FIRST, FINISH YOUR EDUCATION

Not many years ago the city editor who could interview a college graduate without wincing was a rarity. Today he is an exception. Half the nation's newspapers make a liberal arts education a prerequisite to employment while more and more employers are looking with favor on men and women with journalism degrees.

The lad who left high school at 16 and can move fast with picture plates or coffee containers is of more immediate value in a newsroom than a young bachelor of science. The former youth may be learning to type an obituary with two fingers but, unless he is an exception, he progresses slowly. A few difficult assignments usually reveal his flaws. Sooner or later he stumbles and stops moving forward. He has reached his limit. Something is missing. That something is education.

A reporter, not content to remain a mere artisan, needs more than good

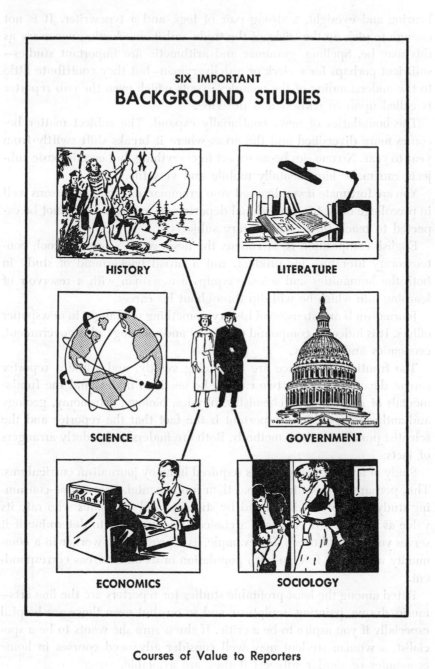

SIX IMPORTANT
BACKGROUND STUDIES

HISTORY

LITERATURE

SCIENCE

GOVERNMENT

ECONOMICS

SOCIOLOGY

Courses of Value to Reporters

hearing and eyesight, a strong pair of legs, and a typewriter. It is not enough to pick up the tricks of the trade and its mechanics, necessary as this may be. Spelling, grammar and arithmetic are important studies—sufficient perhaps for a clerk or a deliveryman—but they contribute little to the understanding of the complex events which even the cub reporter is called upon to witness and describe.

The boundaries of news continually expand. The subject matter becomes more diversified and the areas where it breaks shift swiftly from year to year. No one can be an expert in everything, but certain basic subjects can make him mentally mobile and versatile.

You are fortunate if you learned your grammar and spelling lessons well in precollege days, for professional departments and schools cannot be expected to teach these rudimentary subjects.

English composition is, of course, the news writer's primary tool; contemporary literature his product. But a broad background of study in both the humanities and science equips a newsman with a reservoir of learning into which he will dip throughout his career.

Journalism is an extension of history, something not taught in newspaper offices. It is indeed a compound of history and sociology plus government, economics and the law.

The frontiers of science are advancing swiftly, and while a reporter cannot devote himself to two careers he needs to understand the fundamentals of mathematics, chemistry, physics, biology, astronomy, geology and anthropology. More important is the fact that the reporter and the scientist pursue the same methods. Both are finders and orderly arrangers of facts.

Study of a foreign language is required in many journalism curriculums. This, perhaps, is more traditional than fundamental. It is a time-consuming study most often challenged by students and graduates who rate its value as doubtful. If you have a choice of courses, try to determine if it serves your special needs, for example, as a prospective worker in a community with a big foreign-born population or as an overseas correspondent.

Rated among the least profitable studies for reporters are the fine arts—music, drama, painting, sculpture, and so on—but even these are helpful especially if you aspire to be a critic. If she is sure she wants to be a specialist, a woman student may well consider advanced courses in home economics or similar subjects if they are available.

In campus life, a young person has a chance to learn the amenities of social relations. While he has no monopoly on common courtesy and good behavior, he will have an opportunity to use this training to advantage when he needs to win friends and elicit information. Fortunate is the reporter with a likable personality and the knack of striking up acquaintances, for they often are the sources of news. Facts he knows are important. People he knows are more so.

Education does not end with a diploma. A good reporter keeps up with the times. His curiosity about the past, the present and the future never wanes, but renews itself every waking hour as the years go by. He listens to radio and watches television news programs. He reads incessantly—books, magazines and, above all, newspapers.

A reporter is jealous of his waiting, commuting and even eating time. A newspaper is his frequent companion. He reads avidly, swiftly, skillfully, sometimes marking or tearing out what he reads. He not only is storing away general information but is memorizing colorful words, well-turned phrases and story structures. Tomorrow or the next day they will appear in his own copy.

If he expects to write well, a reporter first must learn to listen and read well. A writer who views the passing scene casually—perhaps only for diversion—is one who has failed properly to fuel his mental missiles. He will find when the countdown comes that they fizzle out on the launching pad.

WAYS TO GAIN EXPERIENCE

Many a June graduate has stared at the *Positions Held* section on an application form and thought desperately: "How *can* I hold a position until somebody hires me?"

There is no substitute for practical day-to-day experience. But the young man who has decided upon a newspaper or any other career should start thinking about it before he finishes his education—the earlier the better. The one who has not tried out his hand or earned a dollar before donning cap and gown is, indeed, at a disadvantage.

Departments and schools of journalism are providing the best kind of vocational as well as professional training for newspaper work. As avenues to entrance they are practical in every sense of the word. However, the student who can combine outside work, paid or unpaid, with his studies does not need to enter a career. Upon graduation he is in it and off to a flying start.

Two kinds of practice opportunities are open to you as a journalism undergraduate. Both will extend your receptivity for instruction in the classroom and laboratory.

First, go to work for your school newspaper. Here you are better off than students of, say, engineering or law, for colleges don't run industrial plants and courtrooms as they do campus publications. Don't demand a title. Earn it. Start writing. Every item, even if it goes in the wastebasket, counts up on the ledger of experience.

Second, try to get a part-time newspaper job while going to school. Send stories to your hometown paper. Go to a nearby newspaper office and offer to work—at almost anything if it opens the door to reporting. Cover and contribute pieces about school sports and other activities. Then ask for vacation or summertime work. Learn and earn, if you can, at the same time.

Internships arranged by some schools of journalism, providing a link between classroom and city room, offer the finest opportunities to gain experience. If you can qualify for one, by all means take it.

Should you go into military service, try to associate yourself with the post newspaper or public relations office. Work with pencil and typewriter as often as possible.

Thus you can prepare yourself for the day in June when you apply for a full-time job as a newspaper reporter. You will carry with you something in addition to a diploma as evidence of your ability to fill it well.

LOOKING FOR A JOB

With or without schoolday experience, the beginner must face the realistic prospect of finding work which will earn him a living and give him at least a reasonable promise of security and promotion in the future.

The job market conforms to the law of supply and demand. It goes up and down with the times. For several years journalism schools with curtailed enrollments may be unable to fill their job offers. In another period positions for starters may slack off due to economic conditions beyond the control of any college or newspaper office.

Newspaper consolidations may diminish opportunities temporarily in one area, but merged papers then tend to increase their staffs. Split-run editions make more openings as metropolitan papers reach out for readers in growing suburbs. And the diversion of students into allied fields—radio and television newscasting, trade magazines and public relations—lessens competition for the available newspaper positions.

The American newspaper business is the world's greatest salesman. It sells automobiles and air conditioners, bath salts and baby carriages, life insurance and lollipops, but does comparatively little to sell itself to its own prospective personnel. Certain other industries, in times of

DATA NEEDED FOR
A JOB APPLICATION

WALTER A. WILSON

Age: 25
Single
No children

723 Parkside Ave.
Clifton, Cen.
Tel: FRanklin 3-6412

Position wanted: Newspaper reporter

EDUCATION

Graduated: Clifton Elementary School
Graduated: Clifton High School
Graduated: St. Anthony's University,
Mercerville, Cen.
BS in Journalism

EXPERIENCE

2 Summers ---- Messenger and clerk for Clifton Printing Co.,
302 Main St., Clifton, Cen.

1 School
year ------- Wrote "High School Notes" column for Clifton
Daily Courier, Courthouse Sq., Clifton, Cen.

4 School
years ------ St. Anthony's U. correspondent for Mercerville
Daily Monitor.

2 School
years ------ Campus reporter, sports writer and editor
of the Saint, university newspaper.

1 Year and
8 months --- U.S. Army. Corporal. Reporter and rewrite man
for Division newspaper. Honorable discharge.

1 Year and
3 months --- Reporter, sports writer and makeup man for
Clifton Courier.

REFERENCES

Dr. Edwin R. Morris, president, St. Anthony's
University, Mercerville, Cen.

George Tremont, manager, Clifton Printing Co.,
Clifton, Cen.

Frederick C. Dorsey, publisher, Clifton Courier,
Clifton, Cen.

A Chronological Résumé

expansion, use newspapers to advertise for recruits. They also send their agents from campus to campus to proselyte candidates with promises of good pay, on-the-job training, fast promotions, and a cultural environment for men and their families.

More and more newspapers are turning their attention to the enlistment problem but by and large only the cream of the college crop is sought out. Many graduates must go after their own jobs.

Employment agencies, psychology experts, successful businessmen and editorial writers press advice on college graduates as to how they can best get on a payroll. No blanket set of rules is offered here, but only one or two suggestions.

Whether applying by mail or in person, always send or leave a physical reminder of who you are—a brief résumé—and where you can be reached. If you do not present a résumé you probably will be asked to fill out a job application form. Few vacancies are waiting for a newcomer to walk in and fill them and few busy editors are willing to ask questions and note down information about an applicant. Most jobs are filled by reference to typed or mimeographed résumés and filled-out application forms on file.

So important are résumés that they are prepared by professionals on a fee basis for job seekers without the know-how to compile them alone. A would-be newsman, however, should be able to compose, type and obtain duplicates of his own.

A résumé should provide the information asked for in application forms—personal data including your name, address, telephone number, age, family and military status; facts about your experience, including your salary on each job held and the reason for leaving it; and references.

A résumé may be chronological or functional. The first sets forth in its body the jobs held by the applicant in the order they were held, while the second gives his background in relation to the duties on the job he wants. In either form a résumé should be only as long as it is likely to be interesting to a prospective employer.

For a young person with slight, if any, experience a simple one-page chronology probably is the most practical. Such a résumé can be presented at the start of an interview or easily be mailed with a covering letter requesting an interview.

If you have clippings of articles you have written, it is well to have the best of them with you when you are interviewed but do not insist that every page of your scrapbook be inspected.

If you are offered a job, don't be choosy. Take a long-range view and be willing to start at the bottom—the deep bottom if necessary—counting out papers as well as writing personals for a small paper or as a copy boy on a larger one if you have to in order to get started.

Too many young men expect to be graduated on Monday, get a job on Tuesday, win a promotion and a raise on Wednesday, rent a home on Thursday, buy furniture on Friday, marry on Saturday, and then start a honeymoon vacation with pay in advance. Others are willing to hold off the wedding date a few weeks if the publisher has a good-looking daughter who can cook.

It doesn't work that way. If you have no advance connections you may have to try and try again before you land the kind of a job you want, meanwhile earning a living and getting more experience on one not so attractive.

After starting, prove your ability. Show your superior, by willingness to do the small chores cheerfully and effectively, that you can fill the bigger job for him better than an outsider. The boss may not be running a school for apprentices, but he is looking eagerly for energetic and resourceful men who do more than they are asked to do—and a little better than expected.

WOMEN ARE WANTED

A few fabulous females invaded the newspaper field in the past, among them Elizabeth Mallet, who edited one of England's first papers; Anne Royall, who interviewed John Quincy Adams; and Nelly Bly, who circled the globe in the late 19th century.

However, at the turn of the 20th century a figurative *For Males Only* sign hung in almost every city room in the land. These signs came down about the time that men stopped giving women their seats on streetcars and taking off their hats in elevators. There may be a few such city rooms left, but not more than a few.

Nearly every newspaper now has its quota of women reporters. The proportion is about one to four or five. Here and there are women editors and executives, but the ratio is smaller in these positions.

The prejudice which still exists against newswomen is based more on the prospect of losing them quickly than on lack of equal ability. Women, in increasing numbers, are combining work with homemaking, but many still treat a job as a stopgap between school and marriage, causing them to desert, whereas marriage rivets a man even closer to his source of income. More women are absent because of duties at home. Further, city editors hesitate to call in women late at night or to send them to cover riots, floods, fires or other developments where there is an element of danger.

Women broke into newspaper offices as society, then food and fashion writers. They still dominate in these departments where there are good positions. But there is no classification of writing which women have not entered. Here and there they even are doing sports and politics but their most significant conquest has been in the field of general assignments, where they have proved to be the equal of men.

As a member of the local staff the feminine reporter receives many assignments rich in romance and human interest, particularly those with a "woman angle." She capitalizes on her natural intuition, inquisitiveness, ability to talk information out of men, and tendency to personalize. These attributes help to give her a "nose for news" with a sensitive two-way mental antenna.

While a woman's writing style, tabbing her in past days as a *sob sister,* may be more emotional and less impersonal than that of a man, good reporting calls essentially for identical training and qualities for both. The woman reporter must not expect to be pampered. She must expect her share of unpleasant jobs and learn to work and fight for her news. She has to display the same "nerve," the same aptitude for sustained work under prolonged pressure, the same willingness to accept criticism without a show of temperament, the same regard for accuracy and fair play, and the same fitness for producing well-ordered and readable copy as the man at the adjacent desk. As a member of the reporting sisterhood she may at times be called upon to express a woman's viewpoint, but she must write with a man's penpoint.

It should be explained here that references in this book to newsmen and similar masculine terms in general usage are meant to include women as well as men.

START AT THE BEGINNING

One attribute of a profession such as law or medicine is that it calls for long preparation on short income. That holds true in some measure for newspaper reporters. At the start they would make as much money driving a truck or operating a switchboard. It therefore behooves the beginner to remember that Rome was not built in a day and that he can hardly hope to become a columnist or an editor until he has gone through an apprenticeship as a cub reporter.

The complaint of cynical executives that students fresh out of college want to be only drama critics, book reviewers or foreign correspondents is exaggerated. Few are so brash. A large majority of journalism graduates are not prima donnas but straight-thinking, levelheaded young people seriously setting out to start at the beginning and willing to win their own way on merit.

Nevertheless, some think they can be byline specialists before they know their ABC's—a distorted perspective which arises from misguided warnings that the general assignment reporter is outmoded and the writer of the future must be an expert on one subject or another to survive.

A majority of successful specialists as well as executives started as general assignment reporters, who are and always will be the backbone of local newsroom staffs. They learn first how to cover and write personal items, obituaries, interviews, fires, accidents and speeches. Usually they are called upon at once to dip into news interesting to large blocs of the reading public, such as sports, news for women, business, labor, crime, the courts, sex and politics. It is the getting and writing of these general kinds of news that is dealt with in this book.

The newspaper business needs and wants young men and women with sound educational backgrounds and the ability to discover facts, penetrate to the heart of a news story, think straight and write clearly. It does not need and will not tolerate fledglings inculcated with an idea that their main mission is to solve—according to their own lights—the problems of diplomacy, race, religion, science and politics.

Once he has mastered the rock-bottom rudiments of reporting and become an expert gatherer of general news as well as a versatile and compelling writer, the newsman is in a position to go on, as his talents and opportunities direct him, into special writing, executive work, or an allied field of communication.

In our final chapter—after a full and intensive study of general reporting—we shall look ahead into these opportunities.

DOES REPORTING PAY OFF?

The answer to this question can be applied to just about any occupation as well as journalism. The newspaper business pays off in proportion to what is paid into it. In America the log-cabin-to-president tradition is as strong as ever. Those who expect something for nothing remain at the bottom. Those with punch and perseverance go to the top, where there always is plenty of room.

Whether reporting is a profession, trade, science, art, craft or game—

the terms are used interchangeably in this book as they seem to fit—
there is no validity to the belief that it is in the same economic class
with the ministry and country school teaching.

Starting salaries vary in accordance with the times and the locality,
but on the average they match those in comparable vocations, ranging
from $60 to $90 a week for apprentices to $125 to $175 for experienced
men on metropolitan dailies. Executives draw premium pay of $10,000
a year or more.

Whether or not he becomes a union member the reporter finds that a
substantial bloc of his fellow workers are covered by contracts of the
American Newspaper Guild regulating job classifications, wage mini-
mums, overtime, dismissals, and other working conditions. These contracts have gone far in shielding newsmen from unfair practices and
providing them with reasonable security.

A majority of newspapers attract and retain employes by providing
such incentives as paid holidays and vacations, maternity and military
leaves of absence, the services of a medical department, disability and
illness payments, group life and health insurance, and pension plans.

While at the start a reporter may have to struggle to make ends meet,
his chances for advancement mount as he produces. He seldom needs
to ask for a raise. His performance and product—news in print—speak
for themselves. He may be confident he will not go long unrecognized.

Within five to six or seven years any self-confident and self-reliant
young man or woman may expect to be fully matured, well paid, secure
in his position, and prepared by experience to move up to the ranks of
the specialists or executives.

SHOP TALK

1. What special aptitudes should a reporter possess?
2. Choose the most important liberal arts courses for a journalism student.
   Rank them.
3. Should the study of a foreign language be required? Which one?
4. Compare the prospective incomes of a reporter, a teacher, an engineer and a
   lawyer.
5. What is the best term to apply to reporting—profession, trade, science, art,
   craft or game?

CHAPTER 2

What Is News and Why?

THE DEFINITIONS OF NEWS

Ask a seasoned reporter or editor what news is and he is likely to tell you it's anything the city editor says it is or something printed in newspapers and suggest that you look at one.

Try the dictionaries. News, according to one, is "a report of any recent event or situation." Another calls it "tidings or intelligence of new or hitherto unknown things." They agree that it is matter of interest to the public.

These definitions are sound. *News*, however, like *art* or *truth*, is a short word with multiple meanings. In a narrow sense it is a product as simple as soap or shoes. In a broad sense it is elusive in quality, endless in variety, and has no limits other than those of life itself.

What is news in Midland may be nonsense in Moscow. What is news to the old may be folly to the young. What is news to a man may be tedium to a woman. What is news to a farmer may be trash to a teacher. What is news to the pauper may be trivia to the prince.

While all news is intended to interest, inform or entertain somebody somewhere—large sections of the public, if possible—no news attracts the attention of everybody everywhere.

Consider the weather—the nearest approach to news with universal appeal—a topic of conversation in every tongue among people of every era, age, sex and occupation. The forecast is standard front page news around the world. Still, outdoor conditions may be of no concern at all to a person in a hospital bed and they certainly do not interest one who has read or heard a weather report just a short while ago.

The people who handle them evaluate news stories in relation to each other. It is necessary at times to discard items, columns and pages in order to make way for material of wider appeal and therefore more

Final Home Edition

Fair Tonight and
Sunday

Details on Back Page.

THE FORECAST

Possibly unsettled at times today and cooler. Temperatures
Friday: Max. 99; min. 69. Sun-
rise today, 5:02; set, 7:43.

THE WEATHER

For Duluth and vicinity:
Local showers tonight or
Sunday; warmer.
Details on page 14.

The Weather

SATURDAY—Partly cloudy.
Friday's high 88, low 61.
Weather detail on Page 17.

THE WEATHER:

Light to locally heavy frost tonight; somewhat warmer Wednesday; fair tonight and Wednesday.

THE WEATHER

Fair, rising temperature today;
Thursday unsettled and warmer.

Weather Today

Showers; Cooler

(Detailed Report on Second Page)
High tide 12:26 p.m., low tide 6:42 p.m.

THE WEATHER

UTAH — Unsettled, little
change.
IDAHO — Cloudy, unsettled,
cooler.
TEMPERATURES

Max. Thurs... 89   6 a.m. Fri... 66
Min. Thurs... 64   9 a.m. Fri... 76
Min. Fri..... 59   Noon Fri... 83
Sunset Fri. 7:48; Rise Sat. 5.01.

THE WEATHER

Fair and Cooler
Today and Tomorrow

Details of Weather on Page 2

Weather:

Showers Monday. Clearing and
cooler Tuesday.
Weather Report on Page 8.

News of Almost Universal Interest

worthy of the limited space available. For everything that goes into every edition of a newspaper something else must be left out simply because there is not room for it. Thus there is no absolute quality in news. Its values are relative.

In order better to understand this intangible and transient substance, let us follow the common-sense advice of the newsroom veteran and look at the papers themselves. On their pages we will find that there is surprising accord as to the nature of news among those who prepare it for publication.

ISOLATING THE NEWS ELEMENTS

Pick up any daily newspaper with pencil and paper in hand. Examine the stories on the first page as though you were a mathematician searching for common denominators or a chemist seeking to separate the elements. As you find a characteristic shared by two or more articles, write down a word or phrase to describe it.

You probably would start with *newness, nowness, freshness, lateness, up-to-date* or *of recent origin*. Next you would note *nearness, closeness to home, localized* or *of personal interest to the reader*. You already have discovered two basic ingredients in the stuff that makes news.

Now try to cut down the list by finding one word to encompass a group. As a start we may call the two qualities found at once *immediacy* and *proximity*, then add six more to make up the following list of eight:

1. Immediacy	5. Conflict
2. Proximity	6. Suspense
3. Prominence	7. Emotions
4. Oddity	8. Consequence

We now have a working list of news elements. Admittedly the terms are empirical and, like the news definitions, general and coextensive. Several usually form a mosaic within a single story and they appear in many disguises. To be meaningful they need to be further broken down and illustrated with examples.

IMMEDIACY—THE FIRST NEWS ELEMENT

The word *news* is not composed from the initials of the compass points—*North, East, West* and *South*. It is simply the plural of the English word *new*. And new it must be.

News is a perishable product, good only when fresh. Its salability diminishes as the clock goes round. Last week's papers are in the furnace

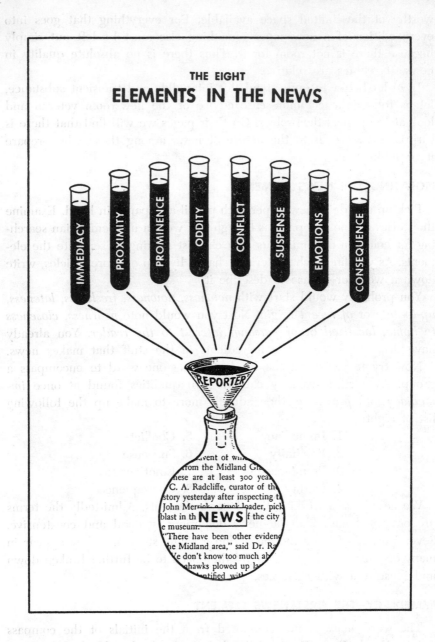

THE EIGHT
ELEMENTS IN THE NEWS

IMMEDIACY

PROXIMITY

PROMINENCE

ODDITY

CONFLICT

SUSPENSE

EMOTIONS

CONSEQUENCE

REPORTER

NEWS

Chemistry of the News Laboratory

or, if kept at all, are spread on shelves, wrapped around bundles, lining the bottoms of bird cages, or waiting for the junkman.

With the primary precept of immediacy in mind, the writer demonstrates in his story that he is reporting something which has just happened or is about to happen. Ordinarily in his opening paragraph he uses *yesterday, last night* or *early this morning* if writing for an AM paper; and *this morning, today* or *this afternoon* for a PM paper, or a day or date in the future, thus:

> Two persons were killed yesterday . . .
> Mayor Nelson announced today . . .
> Three hundred delegates will gather here next Tuesday . . .

So important is the time element that an hour or two often changes or kills the value of a story, particularly if a new angle develops, causing it to be rewritten, or a final deadline passes. For most AM papers the day ends in the early morning and for most PM papers in the late afternoon.

Radio and television, which broadcast instantly, have lessened the surprise value in newspaper news, reducing the frequency of extra editions and shortening the lives of scoop stories, but competition still calls for speed all along the conveyance line. Other elements being equal, last-minute occurrences get the most attention.

Although the writer customarily cites the newness of his wares in his lead or first sentences, the immediacy rule may not embrace the full text of the story, perhaps only its beginning. On a timely peg he may hang a washline full of facts and background data previously pinned up for all to see.

Also it should be made clear that immediacy concerns not only recency —the time of *occurrence*—but also primacy—the time of *disclosure*. Information which is unknown to you but will make you gasp with surprise when you first hear or see it is news to you, regardless of its age.

News has been called history on the wing. But even events of the long ago may become big news. The Dead Sea scrolls and the contents of Egyptian tombs have made many a headline. Every newspaper in the land would print a significant newly found letter written by George Washington or Abraham Lincoln. The telltale time element is found in the words "newly found."

The reporter then gives an up-to-the-minute or right-now touch to his story by the simple process of pointing out that his facts have just become available for publication. He has a hundred handy words and phrases to explain that he is presenting facts only now being disclosed, revealed, announced, divulged, voiced, uncovered, changed, made public or brought to light. Thus the immediacy element is recognized and fulfilled.

Like the distant past, the future often is brought into the perspective of the present. The prediction of experts yesterday or today may well make news of an election months away or of interplanetary travel in generations ahead—again the element of immediacy.

THE IMPACT OF PROXIMITY

To every human being the most interesting thing in the world is himself and after that the things nearest to him in body and mind—his job, health and money, his home and family, his friends and associates, his clubs and church, his hobbies, recreations and amusements.

The reporter therefore strives incessantly to link the lives of others to the lives of his readers—to build bridges into their own experiences, hopes and ambitions.

The person who yawns over a report that famine has swept a million Chinese to their graves will snap to attention if he learns his neighbor's child is in the hospital. And if his own child is hospitalized or, say, wins a prize in school, causing the family name to appear in the paper, that item—from his viewpoint—is packed with interest.

It is axiomatic that your own name in print is the most exciting thing in all literature—especially if it is spelled correctly. It is no wonder that reporters go after names—plenty of names—and get them right.

One person's life can be mapped as a series of concentric circles. The smallest at the core represent his own desires, needs and problems—the objects and events closest to him. These shade off into matters in which he has no interest at all.

It is impossible, of course, to give a news story for general consumption the direct me-to-you appeal of a personal letter, and so the appeal must be to groups of people with common interests.

Outside of his own thoughts and activities and his own home and place of work a man is most concerned with his own neighbors and neighborhood. A traffic accident across the street or a fire in the next block is of more concern to him than if it occurred on the other side of town.

Widening the circles, we still find the personal interest pull strong within the bounds of the community or city. If a famous artist declares that the girls in France are beautiful, the Midland *Times* may carry a paragraph; if he says the girls in America are beautiful, a stickful, perhaps; but if he says that Jane Owens and Mildred Howell, Midland College coeds, are beautiful, perfect types for television, the editor will call for a column with pictures. A new park system for Midland is news in Midland but means nothing in Washington, D.C. The citrus fruit shipment report is carefully read in Florida, which raises oranges, lemons and grapefruit, but not in Kansas, which raises wheat.

Nonlocal news has become a commodity which wire services and syndicated features have made available to all newspapers. But individual papers, especially in relatively small communities, cannot afford to be content with news of such widely diffused interest. A meeting of the local garden club or businessmen's association—even who ate with whom and what they ate at a church social—takes precedence in the hometown paper over a Geneva parley of diplomats to settle the fate of nations.

Editors, reporters and rewrite men continually ask themselves: "If this happened outside my immediate area, would I be interested in reading about it?" Hence they not only concentrate on affairs in their own circulation zones but strive to connect the community with the outside world—to find and develop local angles. In newsroom parlance this is called *localizing*.

The pull of proximity is so strong that news is classified geographically as well as topically. The divisions include world or foreign news, national or domestic news, regional or state news and, finally, local news.

Proximity, as the word is used here, means mental as well as linear—psychological as well as physical—nearness. How things are here may be closely related to things there. For example, the reader may be deeply interested in relatives living abroad or the experiences of his son at an overseas military installation. A crisis in a foreign capital can mean that his son soon may be in battle. If he has toured another land himself he can easily jump the gap from the near to the far. Sarajevo and Pearl Harbor once seemed remote places to Americans but the events which took place there affected all of us. Thus occurrences anywhere which have meaning in the lives of local readers are newsworthy.

In a unique way proximity modifies the surprise quality of news. If you go to a party, a meeting, a play or a boxing bout, the account of it will be the first thing you will look for in the paper. Although you know all about the event, you will check your version against the printed story. For you there is no newness in the account of a wedding you attended. You were there. But you certainly will read the account. If it was your own wedding you probably would clip it out, mail it to a relative, or put it in your scrapbook.

This peculiarity of the proximity element is illustrated by the cub reporter who phoned the city editor: "No use writing about this fire. Everybody in town is here."

THE PULL OF PROMINENCE

Widely heralded persons, places, things and situations, known to the public by reason of achievement, position, wealth or far-flung publicity, possess a strong and recurrent news interest sufficient to command an eager audience whenever they appear in print.

Prominence may be intense but of short duration, like that of a political campaign or a murder trial. Or, like that of Antarctica, space exploration or the segregation issue, it may exert a constant pull on popular attention, showing no abatement month after month and year after year.

Holders of public office, by virtue of power and influence, are highly newsworthy. If President Wrightman, Governor Paulson or Mayor Nelson voices an opinion on a current topic—even if one of them meets with a minor mishap—newspaper readers demand the details. Judges, military officers, police and fire chiefs, professors, union agents, clergymen, all are competent, authoritative and quotable.

Suppose Will Brown, a corner grocer, says there ought to be a law to have juvenile delinquents horsewhipped or put in chain gangs. That's no news at all, for Will Brown is a nobody without responsibility. But let a state legislator or a jurist say the same thing, and the statement becomes news, attributable to him, for he is a responsible somebody who can and may do something about it.

Everyone likes or dislikes heroes, dignitaries and athletes. Few are averse to reading the chronicles of explorers, screen, stage and television stars, and millionaires. Their glamorous and adventuresome doings afford a vicarious escape from the humdrum of ordinary lives. Indeed many a reader is more concerned with what celebrities eat and wear or with whom they romance than in the prospect of a world war. Fame and infamy alike draw public attention. In the news columns the renowned scientist finds his feat of genius printed alongside the exploits of a notorious criminal.

Numbers make news, but prominence as well as proximity bears on their value. An airplane crash killing a dozen persons, especially at the edge of town, is a major story while a distant crash killing one attracts little attention—unless that one is widely known.

Consider the prominence of places. A man jumps from a hotel window. News? Yes, but vastly more so if he leaps from the top of the Eiffel Tower, the Washington Monument, the Statue of Liberty or Niagara Falls. An event in an ordinary house is less likely to see print than an event in the White House. Monte Carlo, the Riviera, Death Valley, Hollywood, Las Vegas, Miami Beach, the Loop, the Golden Triangle, Times Square, Broadway and the Bowery are further examples of places instantly recognized or imagined by everyone.

Similarly, inanimate objects carry headline appeal. A best-selling novel, a popular song, a Stradivarius violin, a Rembrandt painting, the Hope diamond and the Empire State Building are random examples.

You also may apply the prominence yardstick to situations, dates or issues of the day. When the temperature soars, a reporter and photographer visit the zoo to see how the polar bears and penguins are doing on a hot day. On Feb. 2 they'll find out about the ground hog and his shadow. As Thanksgiving approaches, reporters look up the price of turkeys and just before Christmas they interview a street-corner Santa Claus. If the public is concerned over nighttime activities of school children, you will find the reporter carefully covering speeches on that subject or interviewing officials about the conduct of the younger generation if several couples have been robbed on "lovers' lane."

Thus on every possible occasion the city editor aims his assignments and the reporter hinges his story on prominent names, places, events and situations.

ODDITY OFTEN IS NEWS

Paraphrasing Phineas T. Barnum's famous saying, "The public likes to be fooled," we may say that the public certainly likes to be astonished. Anything can win space in the paper if it causes a man to exclaim, "Well, what do you know about that?" while his wife adds, "For heaven's sake!" and the children chime in, "Wow!"

Nobody in particular notices or cares if the sun rises in the east and water runs downhill. But everybody would notice and care if the sun one morning rose in the west and water began to run uphill. The newsworthiness of the odd, rare and strange was recognized about 1882 by Charles A. Dana in his classic remark: "When a dog bites a man that is not news, but when a man bites a dog that is news."

Trains arriving on time, planes landing safely, and rivers remaining in their banks are not news. These are normal and customary occurrences. They happen all the time. Critics of newsmen often say: "Why don't you write more about good people instead of bad people?" The news-

papers print plenty about good people, but goodness is commonplace.
Try to imagine these headlines in print:

> Bank Teller Confesses He Never Stole a Cent in His Life
> Teen-agers Discovered Obeying Teachers and Parents
> Man and Wife Found Faithful for Fifty Years

It is fortunate for society that honesty, virtue and obedience are the
usual while wrongdoing and wickedness are the exceptional, but there
would be an unfortunate end in store for a newspaper that failed
to recognize the difference.

Rarity makes superlative news. Also-rans don't count. The record-
breakers—the fastest—are the ones who break into print. Also the brav-
est, meanest, tallest, smallest, prettiest—in fact, the -est of any kind—
are newsworthy.

Applying the "man bites dog" formula, consider these examples of
oddity as topics for a reporter:

> A chemist makes a purse from a sow's ear.
> Snow falls in south Florida.
> A safety society official is arrested for speeding.
> A wooden leg keeps a drowning man afloat.
> A bridge player with thirteen spades loses the bid.
> A policeman's star stops a bullet.
> A robin attacks his image on a shiny hubcap.
> An ear of popcorn explodes in a field.
> A baby is born in a helicopter.
> A hen mothers kittens.
> A deacon robs a church.
> A "dead" man appears at his own funeral.
> White men outshoot Indians in an archery contest.

Supersonic speed pilots and flying saucers, nudists and voodoo wor-
shipers, ghosts and haunted houses, pirate shipwrecks and buried treas-
ure, coincidences and catchy slogans, the bizarre and the exotic—oddity
in all its thousand and one forms feeds the news gristmill. Concerning
the near-impossible and the near-miraculous human curiosity is insati-
able.

CONFLICT DRAWS THE CROWD

Within every human animal, especially males, lies an emotional chord
which instinctively responds to a fight. Who among us does not in his
secret thoughts yearn to "share the battle yonder where the young
knight the broken squadron rallies," to engage the enemy with the odds
against us, to snatch victory from the verge of defeat?

For good or evil, combat between men or armies, of men against animals, of mind against mind, or of any power against another always has intrigued the multitudes. In prehistoric times the sole male occupations were hunting and fighting, as they are among primitive tribes today. Civilization but thinly veneers the primal instinct for battle.

Look at the sports pages to see the struggle for superiority in unadulterated doses. Boxing, wrestling, football, basketball and virtually every other sport reenact the hand-to-hand, weapon-to-weapon and wit-to-wit combats of our ancestors. Modern contests are less bloody, more sportsmanlike, but in each one the fight and its outcome—victory or defeat—is the news.

Again, in news of violence—war, wrecks, fires, floods and riots—the conflict element is paramount. A street fight, a revolution, a world war—conflict energizes them all. It motivates even stories of the inspirational type—the pilot who saves his plane, the policeman who braves a gunman's bullets, the boy who rescues his dog or vice versa.

Physical struggle represents but a small fraction of the sum of battle. In a sense, all life is competitive, an unending series of mental, moral and physical contests from cradle to grave. A fight therefore spells action which everyone old enough to read can understand.

Two neighbors quarreling over a fence step into print as they enter the courtroom. Two candidates sparring for political office produce columns of controversy and major news on election night. A union on strike, two business tycoons in a proxy battle for control of a company, or two matrons vying for superiority as party-givers and hostesses find themselves in print. Thus conflict rages throughout neighborhood relations, politics, business and social life. Finally it is found in every phase of foreign relations.

Reporters from rural to overseas correspondents know that a struggle for supremacy makes a story where none existed before. Their writing vocabularies are replete with such words as *attack, dispute, clash, defiance, collapse, victim, destroy, defeat, success* and *triumph*. They well understand the conflict element in the news.

SUSPENSE IN THE NEWS DRAMA

All the world's a stage, and all the men and women merely players. The newspaper, holding a mirror to the scene of human performance, catches and reflects the drama of real life, recording the ceaseless tumble of events from entrance to exit.

One of the strongest elements common to the stage and the newspaper is suspense—the piling up of action toward an unpredictable climax. Just as a theater audience puzzles over what will happen next, so the reading public wonders and talks about tomorrow's developments in a continuing news chronicle. Suspense creates and expands news appeal.

Certain fixed events or successions of events, such as a presidential election or a world series, amass headlines as a result of suspense which mounts as a decision approaches. Who will be elected? Who will be the champions? Millions, ready to cheer or moan, await the answers.

Unexpected incidents may spring up at any time anywhere and by sheer suspense become a serial sensation. A Captain Carlsen, fighting alone to save his ship from an Atlantic storm, captured the imagination of the world. Journalism history also has been made by epochal entombments, such as those of Floyd Collins in a Kentucky cave and Benny Hooper in a Long Island well. In the same classification are submarine and mine disasters with life-and-death issues hanging in the balance sometimes for days or weeks.

Suspense as a news element does not necessarily combine with consequence. Men butcher cattle for food and shoot deer for sport. The lives of such animals are of little consequence. Yet a cow caught in a silo or a deer trapped on a mountain ledge may move swiftly from the inside to the outside pages as efforts are made to rescue them. Their ultimate liberation wins space under the day's biggest headlines.

Closely akin to suspense as a news value is mystery. Both heavily flavor stories of crime and punishment. "Whodunit" is a magnet to readers of real as well as fictional crime stories. As long as the police are baffled, news interest blazes high; but when a satisfactory suspect is caught and the enigma solved, the story flickers, smolders and dies out. If the accused person is brought to trial the story is rekindled by the suspense in the court drama. What will the verdict be? That is the question.

The dramatic formula with suspense as the key component may be applied directly by a reporter or rewrite man to the format of a story. In a suspended interest story he deliberately withholds the climax for a surprise finish. This is a favored formula for short, humorous stories. Such a reversal of orthodox structure, however, is seldom used when the consequence element is strong, demanding a disclosure of important news facts without delay.

HUMAN EMOTIONS AND APPETITES

Each of the previously discussed news elements, especially suspense and conflict, grows in the deep soil of our instincts and emotions. In fact they are primary emotions. Therefore we use the term *emotions* as a separate news element only for the want of a more specific word to include in our analysis the gamut of other human responses to outside stimuli ranging from the purely animal appetites to the highest spiritual satisfactions.

Together the emotional elements make up that potent quality in news called *human interest.* Undoubtedly the most powerful of these is sex. To ignore it would be a serious omission, for the relations of men and women form the core of a heavy percentage of the news in all papers. It appears in stories of romance, marriage and divorce. It permeates reports of crime and news from the courts. It even enters politics.

Sex differences are apparent in newspaper departmentalization. Women turn to the pages with articles on society, styles, homemaking and child care. Men reach for the sports and business pages.

In America the beautiful woman, like the successful man, is a symbol of perfection. The actress and the heiress as well as the bandit queen and the woman senator make readable copy. Any member of the fair sex may be a featured player in the drama of the Linotypes—especially if she *is* fair.

The innate desire for food, clothing and shelter brings immediate reader response, especially if a change is threatened or promised. A bread or milk price war, liquor and tobacco lawmaking, styles and fashions, catastrophes that destroy homes, and extreme weather of any kind clutch the attention of all classes of readers wherever they live and work.

Every newsman recognizes the human interest in children and animals. The birth of a baby to prominent parents, a child left on a doorstep, a 4-year-old wandering away from home, the rescue of a little girl from a fire, the escapades of youngsters are of absorbing concern to adults. No less enthralling are stories of animals, especially in cities where few but cats and dogs are seen. Frequently a kitten up a tree, a dog whimpering on his master's grave, a monkey scampering from his cage are placed at ringside while more noteworthy news happenings are escorted to seats in the rear.

The ebb and flow of ambition, hate, fear, love, jealousy, sympathy, vanity, envy, wrath, avarice, generosity and humor in human affairs are reflected in the news mirror. Reader anger is aroused by injustice and brutality. Reader sympathy responds to helplessness, loneliness, and the anxieties of unfortunate folk. Many a tragic story has tugged at the heartstrings of readers as the result of a reporter's descriptive ability.

Comedy plays a diverting role in the drama of the black-and-white columns. A politician who speaks eloquently for an hour into an unattached microphone, a mouse that upsets a wedding, or a professor who nails himself into his attic appeals to the reader's sense of humor.

One more news quality may be mentioned in the emotions category. That is the crowd or herd instinct. In reports of such colorful events as parades, ship launchings and civic receptions the news writer tries to capitalize on this instinct by translating the crowd reactions into his copy. Anything that moves the crowd to laughter, tears or cheers is news. There is no escaping the fact that the public loves a good show, and reading about it is next best to being there.

IS IT OF CONSEQUENCE?

Closely allied to immediacy and proximity as news factors is the one we call *consequence*. By this term is meant import or significance to readers as individuals or en masse.

To give timely information already has been cited as one of the functions of the press. People want to be up-to-date, sociable, creative, efficient, authoritative. They want to gain time, health, money, popularity, advancement, comfort and leisure. They want specific new information about how to attain these goals, and newspapers try to give it to them in palatable form.

From early times the newspapers have been conveyers of data about public meetings, the doings of governmental agencies, politics and international affairs—all informative and of consequence to many.

The story of a duck leading her brood across a busy street or a minister of the gospel running away with a 16-year-old choir girl may be easier to read than one about income taxes, social security, minimum wage negotiations or a local assessment, but the heavier news is sought after and is printed. It is the job of the reporter to find it and make it as easy to read and digest as possible. The actual passage of a law or its interpretation by a court may be a dull and technical procedure. Nevertheless, it may intimately touch the lives of millions.

It may be of slight importance to John Citizen that the bus company and its employes are at odds, but when the reporter tells him that a strike may force him to walk to work tomorrow or that he may have to pay five cents more to ride, the news enters the zone of personal application.

Suppose Midland's waterworks has been put out of operation by a breakdown of machinery. The city editor at once will start asking the following questions: How long will the reservoir supply last? Is cistern water safe to drink? What will the fire department do? Will the swimming pools close? Should garden sprinkling be stopped? His reporters will give the public the answers.

One of the obligations of newsmen in selecting, judging and writing news is to determine what is of real consequence and see that it is reported even at the sacrifice of more entertaining and diverting but less important news.

News of consequence often heralds the march of progress. It is in the news columns that significant changes in the established order of things are first recorded—scientific achievement in the laboratory, observatory, industrial plant and around the council table.

With test tube, microscope and telescope men continue to search the unknown for new truths that will mean a fuller life for human beings. Discovery of new drugs and medicines, flights into space, release of nuclear energy, new methods of transportation and communication, the introduction of automation in industry and business, and experiments in world government typify the progress element in the news. Happenings which are meaningful and indicate trends, as against those which are accidental or frivolous, make news of progress.

Through the release of nuclear energy, forces locked up in nature since the beginning of time are being unleashed and put to work. As a result, our civilization is being thrust into a rapidly changing environment that demands human adjustments on a scale inconceivable just a quarter of a century ago.

Newspapers are the greatest potential force in the scientific and cultural education of the masses. The average reader is hungry for news of progress but he has no appetite for scholastic words and technical phraseology. It is the reporter's mind that must serve as the filter through which hard-to-understand facts reach the mind of the reader. It is the reporter's task to simplify, explain and popularize—to answer the realistic question: "What does it mean to me?"

In our analysis of progress, the last of the news elements, we see again that each of the eight meshes into the others and that all are wrapped together to answer the question: What is news and why?

INSPECTING A FRONT PAGE

As a practical test of the news elements just outlined, choose a paper and dissect the front page. Eight stories, for example, appear on page one of today's Midland *Times,* as follows:

1. President signs income tax bill.
2. Strike violence breaks out in three cities.

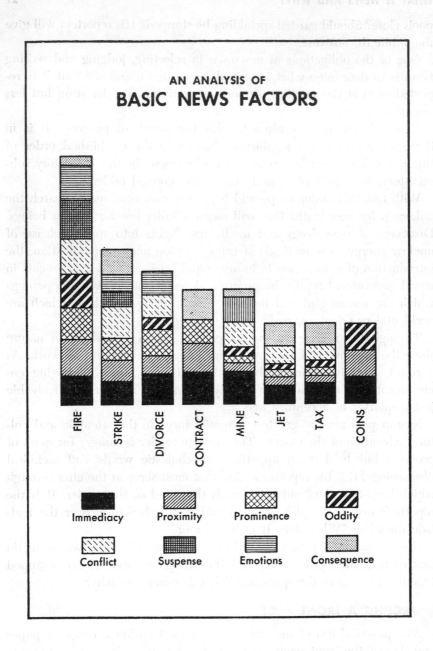

AN ANALYSIS OF
BASIC NEWS FACTORS

FIRE STRIKE DIVORCE CONTRACT MINE JET TAX COINS

Immediacy   Proximity   Prominence   Oddity

Conflict   Suspense   Emotions   Consequence

The Eight Elements Applied

3. Fifty men entombed third day in distant mine.
4. Television star wins divorce.
5. Midland man finds buried box of coins.
6. Contract let for Midland post office.
7. Jet missile reaches record height.
8. Two Midland children die in fire, dog rescues a third.

Now analyze the news factors in each story and tabulate your findings. It will readily become apparent that only one factor, immediacy, is found strong in every story, that at least one other factor is strong in each, and that the articles containing the largest combined portions of all the elements constitute the sensations of the day.

The banner headline in this morning's *Times* appears over the fire story in which the news elements piled themselves up to the summit of interest. An ordinary house burning in Midland at 2 p.m. would have been a fair story. But this one occurred at 6 p.m., too late for the afternoon newspapers, thus intensifying the quality of immediacy. Added to the emotional interest in children and animals was the fact that the children involved were those of prominent parents. This brought in both emotion and prominence. The dog, tugging at the dress of one girl, led her out through the flames, while the brother and sister perished. The rescued girl was critically burned and may die. Conflict, oddity and suspense were thus piled on top of the other elements. No newsman could possibly overlook the appeal of such a combination. The story clamored for attention.

SHOP TALK

1. Compose and compare several definitions of news. Apply them to stories chosen at random from current newspapers.
2. Analyze the elements of appeal in five stories, using as a model the eight elements discussed in this chapter.
3. Which of the eight elements do you consider most important? Cite examples to back up your selection.
4. Select three major events from American history and indicate the elements that would have made them front page stories at the time they occurred.
5. What do newspaper readers want, and why? Should a newspaper give the public what it wants?

CHAPTER 3

Inside the Local Room

YOU ARE ON THE *TIMES*

You may now consider yourself a reporter on the staff of the Midland *Times*, a mythical but typical newspaper in the nonexistent city of Midland in the imaginary state of Centralia, U.S.A.

Midland, a county seat, is the trading center for a score of smaller communities clustered about it in and near Timber County. It has the characteristics of a medium-sized growing city with burgeoning suburbs. It takes pride in its institutions and industries. Its residents are local-minded and absorbed in their own affairs but they readily accept the fashions and practices of New York, Chicago and Los Angeles. They are at once provincial and cosmopolitan.

A drive in and around Midland will carry the visitor through attractive home and apartment areas and a section occupied by lower-income families, many of foreign extraction. Factories and railroad yards lie across the Timber River beyond a bustling business district. The country-side to the north and east is a checkerboard of subdivisions, their new homes and shopping centers alternating with patches of open fields. Office buildings, stores, hotels, courthouse, hospitals, churches, schools, libraries and parks are those of a normal American city.

The varied character of life in Midland is reflected in three daily newspapers. The *Times*, a morning paper, is the most widely read, but closely pressed by its competitors. These are afternoon papers, the *Herald* and the *Gazette*.

The *Times* averages 16 to 24 pages on weekdays and 36 to 48 on Sundays. It is printed in three main editions—Early, Home and Final— on modern rotary presses. Although it specializes in local news, domestic and world news run close seconds. It is a member of the Associated Press. It also receives dispatches from a score of out-of-town correspondents.

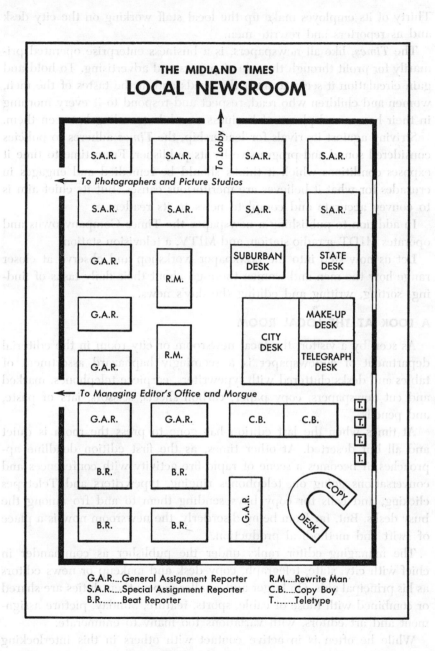

THE MIDLAND TIMES
LOCAL NEWSROOM

To Lobby ↑

S.A.R. S.A.R. S.A.R. S.A.R.

← To Photographers and Picture Studios

S.A.R. S.A.R. S.A.R. S.A.R.

G.A.R. R.M. SUBURBAN DESK STATE DESK

G.A.R. MAKE-UP DESK

CITY DESK TELEGRAPH DESK

G.A.R. R.M.

← To Managing Editor's Office and Morgue

G.A.R. G.A.R. C.B. C.B. T.

B.R. B.R. T.

B.R. B.R. G.A.R. T.

COPY DESK

G.A.R....General Assignment Reporter   R.M....Rewrite Man
S.A.R....Special Assignment Reporter   C.B....Copy Boy
B.R.......Beat Reporter   T.......Teletype

A Typical City Room Layout

Thirty of its employes make up the local staff working on the city desk and as reporters and rewrite men.

The *Times*, like all newspapers, is a business enterprise operated primarily for profit through the sale of papers and advertising. To hold and gain circulation it seeks to meet the needs and fit the tastes of the men, women and children who read, respect and respond to it every morning in their homes and places of business or while traveling between them.

Striving against its rivals for leadership, the *Times* adheres to policies considered sound and progressive by its publisher. From time to time it exposes conditions which it thinks should be remedied and engages in crusades for what it believes are meritorious causes. But its chief aim is to convey accurate and complete news to its readers.

In addition to publishing a newspaper the Times Company owns and operates MIDT, a radio station, and MITV, a television station.

Let us now step into the newspaper workshop and observe at closer range how the men and women there go about their daily tasks of finding, sorting, writing and editing the day's news.

A LOOK AT THE LOCAL ROOM

As seen by a visitor, the local newsroom or city room in the editorial department of a newspaper is a seemingly haphazard assortment of tables and desks cluttered with typewriters, earpiece telephones, marked and cut newspapers, copy paper, carbon sheets, scissors, jars of paste, and pencils.

At times when the last edition has gone to press the room is quiet and all but deserted. At other times, as the first edition deadline approaches, it becomes a scene of rapid-fire activity with conferences and conversations going on, telephones ringing, typewriters and Teletypes clicking, and calls for copy boys sending them to and fro among the busy desks. But, far from being disorderly, the newsroom now is a place of swift and methodical production.

The managing editor ranks under the publisher as commander in chief with city, state, telegraph, copy desk and makeup or news editors as his principal aids. On larger and smaller papers their duties are shared or combined with those of cable, sports, feature, Sunday, picture assignment and art editors, with variations too many to enumerate.

While he often is in active contact with others in this interlocking organization, the reporter is under the direct supervision of his immediate superiors, the men at the city desk.

The city editor of the *Times*, an AM paper, reports for duty at 5 p.m.

after an assistant, the desk or day city editor, during the late morning and early afternoon has handed out assignments and started the reporters on their day's work. On a PM, or afternoon, paper, the city editor works days, with an assistant taking charge after the main editions are out of the way. A third assistant, a suburban editor, is on duty during the day. A fourth sits at the city desk during the lobster shift, 1 to 9 a.m. at the *Times*, while reporters, with the exception of a man at police headquarters, are off duty. Here again the organization varies on different papers. Reporters often refer to the city desk as "the desk," to the city editor or assistant on duty as "the man on the desk," and more loosely to outsiders as "the office" or "my office."

THE TYPES OF REPORTERS

Ask a writing reporter his occupation, and he will say: "I'm a newspaperman." Inquire closer, and the reply will be: "I'm a reporter." You ask again exactly what he does, and he will tell you he is on the street, covers a beat or does special assignments. In other words, he fits into one of three groups into which the gatherers and chroniclers of home-town news are divided. These are:

> *General assignment* or street reporters, who bring in the bulk of the day's miscellaneous news such as speech, accident and human interest stories.
> *Beat* or run reporters, who cover particular news sources such as police headquarters or city hall.
> *Special assignment* reporters, who handle such special categories of news as sports, business, politics or society.

Aside from these cover-and-write reporters, two other groups belong to the city editor's staff. These are:

> *Leg men,* who cover news but do not write it.
> *Rewrite men,* who write news but do not cover it.

The division of duties, of course, depends on the size of the paper. One man alone may handle all the news—perhaps advertising, circulation and management as well—for a country weekly, while scores of reporters are employed by a metropolitan daily with several editions each day and published seven days a week. Every beat man has an understudy, usually a general assignment reporter, who can swing into his rounds when the regular man is off, ill or on vacation. Some papers, because of the five-day week, have trained reporters three deep on all major runs.

THE MIDLAND TIMES
LOCAL NEWS STAFF

CITY EDITOR
Mark Mason

ASSISTANT CITY EDITORS

Day—Harry Baxter Lobster—Kenneth Somers

Suburban—Ralph Dunn

GENERAL ASSIGNMENT REPORTERS

Fred Markham	Edgar Barton	Alice Nestor
Jack Wheeling	Lawrence Lovelace	Ann Kemp
	George Donnelly	

BEAT REPORTERS

Police—Fred Maxwell Schools and
Neil Simpson Churches—Cora King

City Hall—Paul Wilson Suburbs (North)—
Philip Shaw

Courthouse—Michael McCauley Suburbs (East)—
Clyde Schafer

LEG MEN REWRITE MEN

Ray McConnell Leo Burke
Larry Levison Jefferson Harris

SPECIAL ASSIGNMENT REPORTERS

Sports—Edward Clancy Farm—Guy Bransfield
Hugh Dillard

Society—Ruth Ramsey Politics—Howard Robinson

Business and Labor—Frank Fenwick

Drama and Music—Lillian Lowell

Science and Aviation—David Jordan

Organization of the News Staff

In so far as it is practical a reporter is kept on the same type of news and the same story as it develops day by day, but a beat man may be diverted to follow an assignment outside, and all the reporters are subject to switching, sometimes suddenly, to help handle a big story with many angles. The shuffling is in the hands of the city editor and his assistants, who are responsible for the deployment of their reporters so as to cover their circulation areas in the most effective way with the manpower at their disposal.

On a smaller paper one man may make the rounds of city hall, courthouse, police and fire stations this morning, cover a chamber of commerce luncheon at noon, get an interview at the railroad station and pick up a feature story this afternoon—then go to a basketball game tonight for a write-up in tomorrow's paper. He is a combined beat, general and special assignment man.

A big city daily may extend its beats to include hotels, hospitals, law offices, airports, incoming ships, and public offices of varied kinds. These beats blend into more specialized fields, such as news of science, religion, labor, aviation, military affairs, transit and traffic, real estate, travel, radio, television, and so on.

The experts in their own realms often are called editors, especially if they write regular columns or if their copy is departmentalized in the paper. The new reporter is not immediately concerned with the work of these specialists, nearly all of them byliners. However, he may aspire to join their ranks and he can be sure that almost without exception they, like himself, started on general assignments or a beat.

KEEPING TAB ON THE NEWS

"How do they know what is going to happen, so they can have a reporter on hand?" That is a question often in the mind of a reader impressed by the variety and completeness of the news in his paper. In so far as local news is concerned, "they" are the men on the city desk and their reporters.

The beat and special assignment men, of course, constantly check their news sources, uncover and develop stories themselves, and alert the city desk to potential news breaks outside their own zones of activity. General assignment men, too, may trace one story to the next one, especially to follow-up angles and second-day or next-week developments. Stringers in nearby towns and correspondents in other cities also contribute story suggestions.

But the main job of learning when and where news may turn up, so that reporters can be assigned to cover or uncover it, belongs to the city editor and his assistants. Not being omniscient nor omnipresent, they rely on several time-tested methods.

First, they carefully read and clip their own and competing newspapers as fast as these come from the presses, noting the dates, times and places where news may be made. They scan reams of copy teletyped in by the wire services, watching for angles which can be localized. Also passing over their desks are publicity releases or handouts. Many go into the wastebasket. Others give rise to assignments. Tipsters may provide valuable leads. These come from personal callers, by telephone, and in letters to the editor.

Two of the more common devices regulating the flow of news are the clock and the calendar. The time of day when an event occurs influences its news value. For example, an event occurring at 9 a.m. will be covered in the afternoon newspapers. The city desk of an AM paper will concentrate more heavily on an event which occurs at 5 p.m.

The influence of the calendar is constantly reflected in the columns of the daily newspaper. Holidays produce special stories on New Year's Day, Easter, Memorial Day, Independence Day, Labor Day, Thanksgiving and Christmas. Also of news interest are Valentine's Day, St. Patrick's Day, ground-hog day, April Fools' Day, May Day, Mother's Day, Father's Day, Flag Day, Columbus Day and Halloween. Other recurrent dates of news value include the official beginnings of the seasons and Friday the 13th of any month. And still more red-letter days carry significance for civic, religious, racial and patriotic groups in particular localities.

THE PERPETUAL FUTURE FILE

A glance at the calendar naturally will tell an assignment editor that this is Washington's Birthday, but how does he know that it also is the birthday of Midland's only quadruplets? He learns it from his *future file,* an extremely valuable tool for keeping tab on the news.

A future file is a collection of clippings, advance copy, memos and reminders placed in chronological order in folders arranged by years, months and dates. It may be supplemented by a separate future book or desk book. Into it from time to time the city desk men feed data for later use and from it, day by day, remove the pegs for timely stories. Today's folder, for example, will show that:

Mayor Nelson will speak at the Kiwanis Club.
Funeral services will be held for Richard A. Adams.

The Thompson divorce trial will begin.
Bertha Eddy, debutante, will be married.
Senator Manville will return from Washington.
The Artists Club meets today in the Columbia Building.
Two new leopards will arrive at the zoo.
Midland College will play basketball tonight.
School registration figures should be ready.
Police still are working on the Holloway robbery.
Revival services start at the First Baptist Church Sunday.
Fifty years ago today Midland was burned.
Winners of a cherry pie baking contest will be announced.
Next Tuesday there will be a partial eclipse.

Thus, from the future file alone, the city desk is ready at the start of each day to begin arranging assignments. A well-kept file requires endless attention. It needs folders for 365 days of the year. Someone must not only contribute to it constantly but overhaul it annually.

From anniversary books, almanacs and clippings some modern offices prepare permanent sheets or cards, laminating them for use over and over again. They are always returned to the proper folder. Such cards are in two classes—those for fixed dates, such as Washington's Birthday, Independence Day and Christmas, and those for movable dates, such as Easter, the first day of spring, Labor Day and Thanksgiving Day. The dates for filing the latter cards are determined by checking an almanac at the end of the year. The movable and fixed-date cards can easily be distinguished with colored pencil marks.

Some methodical reporters, especially beat men, set up a personal future file or at least keep a desk calendar. Those who do not, find it to their advantage to contribute as often as possible to the file of the city desk.

NEWS SPACE BOOKKEEPING

Type is made of metal—not rubber—and will neither shrink nor stretch. Therefore to fill the news space in a paper each day, and that space only, requires swift and sound judgment by the editors and a good deal of bookkeeping throughout the day.

This starts on the city desk as each reporter receives his instructions. These are typed in brief form on an assignment sheet which serves as a current and permanent record of staff activities. The desk man refers to this sheet and amends it as reporters phone or return to the office.

Tentatively the indicated length of each story is shown in terms of the percentage of a column it seems likely to occupy. As work proceeds, the space may change. A tip turns out to be worthless or a meeting is postponed, and the assignment is stricken off. As unexpected stories develop, new entries are made.

As the first deadline approaches, each departmental editor—city, state and telegraph on the Midland *Times*—prepares a schedule sheet listing the stories he has to offer. These are submitted to conferences with the makeup and managing editors. Some stories are allotted more space, others less. This expanding and trimming to arithmetical precision is repeated before each edition, for space to the editors is like money to a bookkeeper. Every column, like every dollar, must be accounted for. The net result is a dummy of the news sections of the paper produced by the makeup editor.

The suburban editor, with special pages at his disposal, makes out his own assignment sheet and does his own space bookkeeping for those pages.

What concerns the reporter, naturally, is the space given to his own stories. As he gathers material he consults with the desk about how much time and effort he should spend on each one. He may try to "sell" one story, minimize the value of another. The city editor makes the decision and, once it is made, the reporter adheres to it strictly. He is told how much to write. If he underwrites, the city editor will call for more. If he overwrites, either he or somebody else will be compelled to chop his wordage down to space requirements.

THE FUNCTION OF THE COPY DESK

En route from the editorial room typewriters and Teletypes to the composing room Linotypes, all stories stop at the copy desk—a vital processing point in the news assembly line.

The copy desk is shaped like a horseshoe. At the center, or in the *slot*, sits the chief and at the outer edges, or around the *rim*, nis copy-readers. In some shops these men are called copy editors. The task of the copyreader is to edit the day's news, trim it to space requirements, write the headlines, and mark them for type size. He detects and corrects errors in grammar, spelling, punctuation and capitalization. Working with his pencil, he cuts out the deadwood and writes in live wood.

An inexperienced reporter is likely to look upon the rim man for a while as a professional enemy—a word chopper and style butcher bent on destruction. On the contrary, he is a style surgeon, a friendly and constructive critic who helps build the reporter's reputation as a writer and protects him, as well as the paper, from blunders and bungles.

EXAMPLES OF THE
COPYREADER'S MARKS

the ~~one~~ man	strike out
went town	insert
fiften	insert
fo undation	close up
united states	capitalize
Street	small letter
per/cent	separate
it yesterday occurred	transpose
copule	transpose
down. He said that	paragraph
Doctor Smith	abbreviate
forty-seven	use numeral
300 Prof.	spell out
# -30- III	end marks

Symbols Used in Reading Copy

Often it is the wit and ingenuity of this craftsman that rescue a story from stodginess and convert it into clean, clear and concise copy.

Now and then, of course, a *bug man* or a *copy fighter* will land on the rim but he seldom stays long. A bug man devotes himself to the tiniest mistakes. He argues over misplaced commas and alternate spellings, missing a big boner between. A copy fighter changes *that* to *which* and the next *which* to *that*. Under his pencil *quiz* becomes *probe* and vice versa.

So copyreading—like dieting—is a good thing which can be carried too far, but no competent copyreader willfully ruins style to please himself. His function is to aid the writer in telling an accurate and lucid story so it can be grasped quickly by the reader.

The copy desk is the last bastion of defense between the newspaper and the public. While proofreaders correct typographical errors, these final checkers are not concerned with content. The copyreader is the real policeman of the news. Inaccuracies, statements not in good taste, and defamatory matter which bypass him are almost certain to reach the reader in print, sometimes with dire consequences.

The Midland *Times* employs five copyreaders. The number depends on the size of the paper. On the smallest dailies the city editor may perform the functions of both reporter and copyreader. On the largest dailies a dozen or more men may be needed on the copy desk and departments, such as sports, may have their own copyreaders.

A few papers have dispensed with the traditional copy desk and assigned the duties of the copyreader to city and telegraph desk men. However, in every office the reporter's handiwork is corrected, censored, spaced and headlined after it leaves his typewriter and before it goes into print.

A VISIT TO THE MORGUE

Before going afield with reporters, let us look into one more important place inside or near the local room, namely, the *morgue*. It is aptly nicknamed, for in it is stored so-called dead stuff. But the fact is that this material comes to life so often that the troubles of a writer without it would be grievous indeed.

Today's news often flows from yesterday's, and the morgue is the repository where editors and reporters with only human memories swiftly gather many of the facts which go into tomorrow's paper.

The morgue, more properly named, is called the editorial library or reference room. It may consist merely of a few file cabinets in a corner

EXAMPLES OF THE
PROOFREADER'S MARKS

𝛿	take out	⌄⌄ ⌄⌄	quote marks
∧	insert	⌄ ⌄	single q.; apostrophe
stet }	let it stand	⋏	comma
#	more space	⊙	period
⌣	less space	=/	hyphen
⌢	close up	⊢—2—⊣	2-em dash
⌐‾	raise	w.f.	wrong font
⌊_	lower	ital	set in italic
⊏	move left	═══	use small caps
⊐	move right	≡≡≡	use capitals
⊥	push down	/or l.c.	use lower case
×	bad letter	rom.	use roman type
□	quad space	⊔⊓ tr. }	transpose
¶	paragraph	↓1	superior figure
no ¶	no paragraph	⌃2	inferior figure
═	straighten line	b.f.	boldface
𝟗	turn over	·/	use this mark

Symbols Used in Reading Proof

or an expansive and well-organized establishment containing millions of clippings, bound volumes, microfilmed pages, pictures, negatives, matrices and cuts, as well as books, pamphlets and maps, all systematically indexed.

The problems of preservation and compact storage of newspaper files have been partly solved by modern mechanical methods. Experiments with rag paper and miniature editions were followed by microphotography, whereby perishable paper pages are protected against wear and tear and reduced in size. Viewing equipment improves steadily.

However, all newspaper libraries with microfilmed editions also file clippings in envelopes by the thousands. While microfilmed papers can be found by date and scanned rapidly, clippings can be and are filed by topic. When a story must be traced through several issues or the writer wishes to throw out a dragnet for information on one subject, the clips are superior. Furthermore, they can be carried to a desk, be shuffled and extracted or copied handily with pencil or typewriter. To be of use again, of course, the clips must not be lost or destroyed or tossed in a desk drawer but returned to the files immediately after use.

Let us examine a clipping file drawer in the library of the Midland *Times*. Riffling through the letter *A* envelopes we note:

Adams, Richard A.	Arcturus
Aetna Life Insurance Company	armories
Alcohol Control Board	arson
aluminum	artichokes
Ambassador Hotel	Artists Club
American Legion	Ash Wednesday
Anderson, Audrey	asphalt paving
Angora cats	atomic bombs
Annapolis Naval Academy	Auburn Sales Company
A&P Food Stores	auks
Apple Growers Association	Ayres, Dr. William C.
Archer, S. B.	Azwolinsky, C. D.

A glance into the picture files shows the same wide range of names and subjects. There are, for example, a dozen pictures of S. B. Archer, a man prominent in civic enterprises and the holder of several public offices. Archer is shown as a high school graduate, a college football player, at his wedding, taking the oath of office, laying a cornerstone, and so on.

Now walk over to the bookshelves and read a few titles. In orderly array we see such basic reference books as the Bible, encyclopedias, dictionaries, biographies, almanacs, city address and telephone directories, a thesaurus and an atlas in addition to fact books of many kinds.

Test the custodian of this storehouse—the librarian or one of his assistants. Give him even a nebulous clue as to what you would like to read or see and the chances are he'll find it readily. It will be seen at once that he and his treasury of information are valued friends of the reporter.

"LET'S SEE THE CLIPS"

That's the customary remark made over and over again by reporters making a trip to the morgue before leaving the office on an assignment or when about to start writing a story requiring background information. Usually the librarian gives him a check-out slip on which he writes the subject of the file he is taking, his own name and the date. This enables the morgue keeper to get out the material and keep a record showing where it goes.

Reporter George Donnelly, let us say, has among his assignments an interview with *Audrey Anderson,* who is in jail as a hit-and-run driver. Donnelly also is to attend a meeting of the *Artists Club* and afterward check a mortician on the death of *Richard A. Adams.*

The clips show that Audrey Anderson is 37 years old, lives at 925 W. Elm St. Her husband is Earl T. Anderson, a well-to-do manufacturer and sportsman. Three months ago she paid a fine for collecting seven traffic tickets. Her father is president of the Midland Safety Council.

The Artists Club, Donnelly finds, is headed by Spencer E. Franklin. At its last meeting a committee was named to plan a memorial in Island Park. It has 73 members.

His last envelope tells Donnelly that Richard A. Adams was taken to Haven Hospital three weeks ago after suffering serious injuries in an airplane crash. He owned the Adams jewelry store, belonged to the First Methodist Church and was active in the Lions Club. He lived with his wife, the former Sara Hahn, and two children at 1119 Spruce St., in nearby Crestwood.

Within a few minutes Donnelly makes a mental outline of the questions he will ask Mrs. Anderson, the news he will look for at the Artists Club meeting, and the additional information he will need to write the Adams obituary story. He already has a long head start on the day's work.

It is quite possible to write an entire article, especially of the historical or life-sketch variety, from morgue material without ever stirring from the office, and this often is done by a rewrite man who has obtained the main news fact by telephone. A true test of the morgue comes when an important story breaks close to a deadline. More facts and background are needed urgently. A rush call goes to the morgue. What is there and the ability of the newsman to get at it and use it in a hurry spell the difference between a meager, skimpy item and a full-fledged story in the upcoming edition.

SHOP TALK

1. How is the local newsroom staff organized? Discuss the duties of the following: managing editor, city editor, state editor, telegraph editor, news or makeup editor, reporter, copyreader.
2. What are the various kinds of reporters and what are the advantages in classifying their duties in this manner?
3. Outline the progress of a news story from an informant who tipped off the reporter to its final preparation in the composing room.
4. Why must the length of stories be regulated? Discuss the space problem as it relates to assignments and the makeup dummy.
5. Using a half dozen current clippings, show how they would be classified in a newspaper morgue.

CHAPTER 4

Go and Get a Story!

A REPORTER STARTS HIS DAY

"Better plan to get out to the Benson place about 3 o'clock," said As·
sistant City Editor Harry Baxter to Fred Markham, general assignment
reporter for the Midland *Times* who had reported for work at noon.

Coming-in hours for *Times* reporters are staggered from 11 a.m. to 1
p.m., thus allowing time for each to have a brief conference at the city
desk without a waiting line. Since 9 a.m. Baxter, the day desk man, had
been compiling his assignment sheet from overnight memos, newspapers,
his future file, wire service copy, press releases and tips. As he spoke to
Markham he indicated an assignment tabbed MISSING and continued:
"The kid is 12 years old. A neighbor phoned in that the boy didn't come
home last night but the PM's aren't on it yet. Chances are he went to see
his grandmother or has gone west to hunt buffalo, but it may be a live one
if he doesn't show up by the middle of the afternoon. It's good either
way."

"What about the police?" Markham asked.

"The family is holding out on it, according to our tipster. I'm having
Maxwell watch at headquarters."

"All right. Anything else?"

"Go over to the Clarendon first and check up on the ministers' meeting.
ive me a ring from the Rex if anything shows up at the beauty conven-
on for a picture."

Markham jotted down the assignments already entered under his name
on the assignment sheet and picked up several mounted clippings, pieces
of publicity, and other memos marked for him. He helped himself to several sheets of copy paper for note taking, walked back to the morgue and
looked at the clips under the name of R. A. Benson, father of the missing
boy.

A few minutes later he was on his way to the Clarendon Hotel. As he walked he glanced several times at his memos, marshaled the assignments in his mind, and roughly mapped out his afternoon's activities.

PLANNING A PROGRAM

Seldom does a street reporter stumble upon a story and develop it entirely on his own initiative. Nine-tenths of the time he covers specific assignments handed to him by the city desk. Should he by chance pass a burning building he would step to the nearest telephone, notify the office, then proceed on his way unless told to cover the fire. Another reporter probably is on the scene already or will arrive shortly.

Markham, on this particular day, had four assignments. He sorted them with the following mental notes:

Church. Ministers Alliance luncheon at the Clarendon. Must be there by 1:15 p.m.

Beauty. Convention at Rex Hotel. Probably can see program chairman any time.

Store. Written statement about Hart's store moving is ready to pick up. Store is only a block away from the Rex.

Missing. Special mention by Baxter. Check by telephone. Go to the home if promising.

Markham now had arranged his program to save steps. From the Clarendon Hotel he telephoned the Benson home and learned from a maid that the boy was still missing and Mrs. Benson had gone to his uncle's home to ask about him. She would be back about 4 p.m., the maid said. The Bensons were fairly prominent, and a good story, the best of the lot, was now a distinct possibility. Obviously, the thing to do was to clean up the other assignments speedily, go to the home and try to interview Mrs. Benson.

ROUNDING UP THE NEWS

At 1:15 p.m. Markham seated himself with two other reporters at a corner table near the door in the Clarendon dining room, listened to a speech and the reading of a resolution, and jotted down a few notes. He left at 2 p.m.

At Hart's store he learned that moving day was postponed, then went to the Rex to find the cosmeticians in session. Glancing over the program, his eye caught the title of one speech, "The Latest in Lipsticks," scheduled for 5 p.m. Unable to wait, Markham singled out the speaker, interviewed her, obtained a few extracts from the speech manuscript, and at 3 p.m. was free to work on the Benson assignment.

Boarding a bus, Markham rode to the Benson home and there the mother gave him an account of the boy's disappearance. She would notify the police if Johnny did not return by dinnertime, she said. Markham borrowed a picture of the boy and talked to the Boy Scout friend who saw him last. By 5 p.m. Markham had his last assignment completed. Meanwhile, at intervals of an hour to an hour and a half, he had telephoned Baxter, keeping him informed of his whereabouts and progress. On the next call, with his outside work done, he discussed the results of his efforts.

"Do you think the boy has been kidnaped?" Baxter asked him.

"Maybe. Can't tell. His mother says he never ran away before. He started home from a Boy Scout meeting and had a little money, so he might have hiked off. No threatening notes or messages. It's a guess. Better have Maxwell be on the lookout for her to notify the police. Until she does, it's exclusive."

"All right. It's worth a column and a half as it stands. Give the preachers a stickful and the beauty story a half column. Come on in."

Markham's schedule now stood:

Church. Less than 30 per cent of a column.
Beauty. 50 per cent of a column.
Store. No good.
Missing. 1.50 per cent of a column.

On his way back to the office with perhaps an hour to spare before starting to write his copy, Markham revolved the stories in his mind, devising ways of preparing them and projecting them mentally as they might appear in printed form. The church and beauty items gave him little difficulty, as he had written many similar stories before and had only to drop his new facts into set molds.

Most of his thought he directed to the Benson case, visualizing it in various forms. As he left the bus and neared the office he mentally worked out the format of the first two paragraphs of the Benson story.

As a result, Markham had each of his stories rather well thought out when he arrived at the office, and he was prepared to put them on paper with the least possible delay.

AT WORK WITH A BEAT MAN

The *Times* City Hall reporter, Paul Wilson, received his list of assignments shortly after noon. They were:

Hall. Cover the City Hall generally.
Pay. Councilmen vote on firemen's pay raise at 2 p.m.
Build. Get monthly list of building permits.
Water. Health Department to test water samples today.

Wilson, after consulting his own desk drawer future file, told Baxter that a list of new paving contracts might be available today. Baxter added on the assignment sheet:

Pave. Check on new contracts.

Arriving at the municipal building, which he had covered daily for several months, Wilson found himself thoroughly at home. He strolled into the pressroom, hung up his hat, settled down, and read the latest afternoon papers bought at a nearby newsstand.

He found detailed accounts on the paving contracts released early that morning. He checked that assignment off his list. The facts were all there to be picked up and rewritten by the *Times.* As he shuffled through the papers, Joseph Jacobs of the *Herald* and Dale O'Connor of the *Gazette,* two other City Hall reporters, walked in.

In most public buildings frequented by newsmen a pressroom furnishes them a place to write, telephone, read papers and kill time. There they congregate and exchange information. How extensive this pooling of news may be depends upon the city editors. Some insist that their reporters work alone, keeping their news exclusive; others wink at the pool system. In a typical pressroom reporters from different papers cooperate to save footwork on routine stories. In a few they go so far as to trade all news and freeze out the nonconformist or double-crosser, while in others the dog-eat-dog and scoop-your-rival system prevails. A tactful reporter ascertains the viewpoint of his city desk and acts accordingly. Self-preservation, of course, governs his conduct.

Wilson, Jacobs and O'Connor frankly traded the day's mine run of news, but by an unwritten gentlemen's agreement harbored no personal grudges because of occasional scoops earned by special effort or good fortune.

"What's doing?" Wilson asked the pair as they entered. "Anything but the paving contracts?"

"Pretty quiet," Jacobs replied. "The water tests are off until tomorrow, but I hear there may be a row at the Council session. What do you know?"

"Nothing much," said Wilson, jotting down the word "tomorrow" after the water assignment on his list. A few minutes later, after securing the permit figures from the building department, he went to the Council meeting, where a hot dispute ended with approval of the firemen's pay raise.

Between 3:30 and 5 p.m. Wilson toured the building, greeting officials by their first names, chatting with subordinates, looking over license books, reading public records, tapping news sources generally. He gathered several paragraph items and a good yarn about plans for a shake-up at the City Jail.

His schedule at the end of his last telephone talk with Baxter was:

> *Pay.* 1.75 per cent of a column.
> *Build.* Less than 30 per cent of a column.
> *Water.* No good.
> *Pave.* Less than 30 per cent of a column.
> *Jail.* 1.00 per cent of a column.

Like Markham and the other staff members, Wilson started for the office about 5 p.m. to write his copy for the Early edition.

WITH A SPECIAL ASSIGNMENT MAN

We have followed the day's activities of Markham, a typical street reporter, and Wilson, a typical beat man. Let us now go out with David Jordan, who specializes in science and aviation.

Jordan in college had minored in physics and he spent his spare time in a home laboratory-workshop. As a street reporter he had shown an aptitude for handling scientific and technological news.

Because Midland has several airplane plants and is an aviation crossroads, this topic is of special interest to local readers. The aircraft construction operations center around the Municipal Airport, which Jordan covers. Transit, traffic and highway news assignments also come his way. Here is his list for the day:

> *Patent.* See inventor of money-changing device.
> *Museum.* Check Curator Radcliffe re quarry find.
> *Air.* Will Acme Aviation get rocket contract?
> *Bus.* Anything on new bus line to Crestwood?

Jordan followed roughly the same procedure as his fellow workers. Although he enjoys more freedom from city desk discipline, his specializations give him added responsibility as well as latitude. Held accountable for full coverage in his fields, he ranks as a semi-editor, creating some of his own assignments. Strictly speaking, however, like Robinson on politics, Ramsey on society, Lowell on drama, Dillard and Clancy on

THE MIDLAND "TIMES"
SCHEDULE SHEET

Page 1

| Day | Tue. | City Editor | Baxter |
| Date | Oct. 2 | Asst. City Editor | Mason |

Reporter	Slug	Space
Markham	MISSING	1.50
	BEAUTY	.50
Wilson	PAY	1.75
	JAIL	1.00
Jordan	MUSEUM	.50
	AIR	.60
Donnelly	FIRE	1.75
	DOG	.40
Simpson	GANG	1.80
Nestor	STREETS	.75
	GEMS	.60
	GIRLS	.35
McCauley	TRIAL	.75
	DIVORCE	.75
Fenwick	MERGER	1.00

Total _____ 14.00

First Page of Schedule Sheet

sports, Fenwick on business and Bransfield on farming, he is a special assignment reporter.

Baxter had asked the inventor to wait until Jordan came in and Jordan talked to him at once. His "invention" turned out to be just an immature idea and Jordan courteously but quickly dismissed him. He found out the status of the bus line plan by telephone, then walked to the Museum of Natural History and interviewed the curator. He then drove out to the Acme plant and spent the rest of the afternoon touring other plants in search of news. He returned to the office early after scheduling at 4 p.m. His copy was in type at 5:30, but before going home he wrote an overnight article of the informative type for use the next day.

A LEG MAN ON WHEELS

Ray McConnell, one of the leg men on duty, along with George Donnelly, general assignments, held in reserve in the office until 3 p.m. Both then were dispatched with a photographer to the scene of an explosion and a four-alarm fire.

They went in an editorial car equipped with a two-way radio telephone, one of the newer news transmission devices adopted by modern newspapers. The *Times* owns two of these mobile units. Either McConnell or the photographer can handle one alone.

By use of the mobilphone operated on an FM frequency they can communicate almost instantly with the city desk, giving information and receiving instructions. The value of the car-phone combination to newsmen in a hurry is proved daily as they outspeed competitors who must travel afoot, on buses or subways, and who must find and sometimes fight their way to stationary telephones.

Reaching the scene of the fire, both reporters went to work gathering facts. From time to time one of them relayed developments to the desk. The fire spread and McConnell drove Donnelly, with his notes, and the cameraman, with his plates, to the office. McConnell then returned to the fire in the radio car and continued to cover it, phoning in late information to Donnelly until the blaze was under control, when he, too, returned to the office.

LOOK, LISTEN AND LEARN!

We now have traced the outside activities of key men of four kinds on the city desk staff—general assignment, beat, special assignment and leg reporters. Shortly we will look over the shoulders of the writers as they type their stories. And in a later chapter we will watch the work of a re-write man.

We pause here to note some of the principles which guided Markham, Wilson, Jordan, Donnelly and McConnell as they gathered the raw material for their stories. To set forth any brief, all-inclusive formula for covering news would be dogmatic, for each story presents its own equation to be solved according to the circumstances. However, here are several cardinal pointers to remember:

1. *See for yourself.* If possible, go to the scene of an event and witness it firsthand so that you know you are not writing hearsay, guesses and surmises but that what you write is true.

2. *Find the person who knows.* If you must report something that happened out of your presence go directly to the most responsible person concerned and ask him or her for information. Usually a line from the manager is worth a column from the janitor.

3. *Compare all versions.* Tests prove the fallibility of the untrained human eye and ear. The average person is a poor observer—a careless and faulty recorder of what he sees and hears. Get as many versions as you can. Check one against the other. Question inconsistencies. Sift out and verify the facts.

4. *Get both sides.* Much news is sharply controversial. Make every effort to get the pro and con, the affirmative and the negative, the right and the left, the charge of the accuser and the reply of the accused. If only one side is available, say so in your story. Present the other side as soon as you can get it.

5. *Don't give up too easily.* Accept "no" as the final word only if you must. Hunting news can be discouraging business. Patience and stick-to-itiveness will pay off. Keep working on a story until you bring it back alive.

6. *Be tactful and courteous.* Never impose on a busy man's time. Get the facts quickly and leave. Guide a conversation; don't force it. Sometimes you need to be tough but nine times out of ten good manners are better than bullying. Use threats to expose only if the information you want outweighs the loss of your news source.

7. *Make and keep friends.* Dependable informants are your most valued assets, especially if you are on a beat. If possible, give them favorable mention in your stories. Never break a confidence for the sake of a scoop and thereby seal up a source of information.

8. *Get it into print.* This point is the most significant of all. A reporter is not hired to entertain or educate himself. He has an unwritten

contract to bring in news and any effort not pointed to that end is energy squandered. News not printed is wasted.

WORK WITH THE PHOTOGRAPHER

The main task of the news gatherer is to be just that—a gatherer of news to be written and printed—but he often is partly responsible for pictures, especially if his paper uses them extensively.

Without a camera he may obtain prints, posters, charts, maps or graphs for reproduction merely by asking for them. Or he may suggest to the desk that one of these can be found in the library or that a black-and-white sketch to accompany a story can be made by an artist. If the reporter suddenly sees a picture possibility while on duty outside the office he should call for a photographer. And if a cameraman already is with him, the two should work as a team.

The young man with a pencil sometimes takes the attitude that his skill as one of the literati is superior to that of the lensman who merely clicks a shutter. Reader surveys show that pictures consistently outrank printed stories as attention getters and an experienced newsman realizes that a photographer is his equal in skill as well as an ally on an assignment. Either can be and often is the savior of the other in a tight spot.

Because he breaks the ice and does most of the talking the reporter can often arrange a picture for the cameraman. The photographer can pinch-hit for the reporter when the assignment calls him elsewhere. Both reporter and photographer should be careful to see that names, addresses and other data they obtain are identical. Otherwise the story and the picture caption may not agree. Any extra time the reporter may give to securing pictures is well spent, for the graphically illustrated article has instant appeal, earning it preferred play and position.

The coming of ROP, or *run-of-paper,* color in newspapers is an exciting new development in the publishing world and already is spreading glamour from rotogravure sections into advertisements and headlines. As spot news pictures of fires, parades, rocket take-offs, football games and beauty contests go into rainbow hues the camera will become more and more valued as a news conveyer. Eventually a reporter on an assignment with photo possibilities may find that he must help get the picture or his story will land back with the classified ads if it ever sees print at all.

THE REPORTER'S COPY

For the better part of two hours after they returned to the office Markham, Wilson, Jordan and the other writing reporters worked steadily at

SAMPLE PAGE OF
REPORTER'S COPY

```
Wilson ... assigned


PAY - 1


        Midland's 300 firemen were voted salary increases

    ranging from $12 to $16 a month yesterday at a stormy session

    of the City Council.  The raises go into effect Nov. 1.

        Overriding the protests of Mayor Nelson, who called

    the extra $128,000 appropriation required "entirely too large,"

    the Council approved the expenditure by a vote of nine to five.

    At the climax of the debate, Councilman Arthur Forbes, the

    Mayor's floor leader, shouted:

        "Give them a raise!  Sure, give everybody a raise.

    But let's get the money first."

        Supporting the pay boost which he declared was "long

    overdue," Councilman J.R. Fogel said there is enough surplus

    in the general fund for the rest of this year.  He predicted

    that higher realty values would meet the cost thereafter.

                                                    more
```

First Sheet of a Story

their typewriters. The beat men covering the suburbs had come in earlier, typed their stories for special pages, and turned them in to the suburban editor, Ralph Dunn. All followed these copy rules:

Use regulation 8½ × 11-inch copybooks with an original and three duplicates.

Write only one story on each page.

Triple space.

Leave a 4-inch margin at the top of the first sheet, a 1½-inch margin at the top of each succeeding sheet, and a 1-inch margin on the left, right and bottom of all sheets.

Type your last name and one word stating the source of the story (assigned, handout, letter, and so on) in the upper left corner of the first page. Below this type the story title and page number.

Indent each paragraph 10 spaces.

Never divide a word at the end of a line or between pages. Do not split sentences or paragraphs between pages.

If the story requires more than one page, type the word *more* at the lower right corner of each page except the last.

Indicate the end of the story with the double cross symbol #.

Do not strike over letters or words. Do not erase. Mark out with X's or a pencil.

Keep your copy clean. Retype if necessary.

These copy rules vary somewhat on different newspapers, but only in detail. For example, some have adopted carbonless copybooks. Others require more or fewer duplicates. Margins may be slightly wider or narrower; spacing may be double rather than triple; indents may be five rather than 10 spaces; the word *more* may be centered; and *30*, meaning the end of anything in a print shop, may substitute for the # sign.

A Midland *Times* writer keeps one of the duplicates—also called *dupes, flimsies* and *black sheets*. Another goes into an *alibi file* kept at least for several days. The third is used for picture captions.

The original, or top, copy travels to the city desk, where it receives a rough inspection for obvious errors and space appraisal. It then moves to the copy desk for editing and headline writing. Next it goes to the composing room where, after it is set in type, a galley proof or type impression is taken. A proofreader makes final minor and typographical corrections before the story goes through the rest of the mechanical steps en route to the printed page.

While he must learn his own copy rules well and should understand the city and copy desk operations, the reporter, especially on larger papers, is only remotely concerned with the mechanics of publication.

Wilson had difficulty with his jail story and revised it twice before City

Editor Mason finally passed it on. But 8 p.m., the Early edition deadline, found the stories of all the reporters cleared, and thereafter they relaxed and waited for copies of the paper to come up from the presses.

Meanwhile each man reported the disposal of his assignments and wrote memos to the city desk on probable developments for the next day or later.

At 9 p.m. the reporters heard Mason say "Good-night" and, with the exception of two or three who came in late and were held to cover night assignments for later editions, they were through for the day.

SHOP TALK

1. Why does the city desk so closely supervise the hour-by-hour activities of reporters? Do reporters in small towns have more latitude than those in large cities?
2. Compare the field work of general assignment, beat and special assignment reporters; also that of reporters for morning and afternoon papers.
3. If you were a city editor would you ask your reporters to work alone or to pool news with reporters from other papers?
4. Explain how a reporter may mentally prepare for writing his stories before reaching his typewriter.
5. What do you consider the most valuable requisite for good news coverage—energy, stick-to-itiveness or brain work?

CHAPTER 5

Writing the News Clearly

FOUR ACCOUNTS OF A FIRE

The scream of sirens and clang of bells drew a crowd of onlookers one night to the point where several Midland fire-fighting vehicles converged. Among the spectators were Susan Sloan, a third-grader; her mother, Mrs. L. S. Sloan, a housewife; her brother, George, a high school junior; and Jack Wheeling, reporter for the Midland *Times*.

The next day at school Susan's teacher asked her pupils to write about something they had seen. Susan lettered painstakingly:

> I saw a fire. It was a big fire as red as a beet. It burned up a store where I buy candy. I got smoke in my eyes. It made me cough. A whole lot of people were there. Some men put water on the fire and it went out. Then my father took me home and I went to bed.

Mrs. Sloan mentioned the happening in a letter written to a relative:

> We had quite a serious fire last evening in one of our neighborhood stores. We all went over for a while to see it. Several fire engines were called and it was very interesting to watch them. The fire was finally extinguished but it probably will cost the people who own the premises a good deal of money.

George took the fire as the topic for a theme in English composition. He wrote in part:

> It was a fearful sight to behold. Scarlet-tinged tongues of flame, resembling those emitted by satellite rockets, arose to the heavens as the devouring element licked greedily at the doomed structure. The heroic firemen risked their all to quench the devastating conflagration and, at long last, conquered the holocaust to the plaudits of the admiring multitude.

For the *Times* the next morning Wheeling wrote:

> A stubborn two-alarm fire caused by a leaking oil burner partly destroyed the Shop-and-Save Supermarket at 932 Oak St. last night.
>
> Four fire companies brought the blaze under control at 11 p.m. No one was injured. R. M. Gregg, the owner, estimated the damage at $10,000. The market, he said, will be rebuilt at once.

A glance at the four reports shows that each writer used about the same number of words. All obeyed the rules of grammar. And each wrote a sincere description with merit in its own way. Yet they are wholly different types of composition.

A LESSON IN STYLE

In her childish way Susan told a simple story and told it well for her age. Mrs. Sloan displayed the restraint and decorum of an average matron in her correspondence. George lavished the vivid phraseology of an enthusiastic youth just starting to feel the power of words. Wheeling typed with the skill of a trained reporter.

We may characterize each style with one word:

> Susan—*simplicity*.
> Mrs. Sloan—*dignity*.
> George—*color*.
> Wheeling—*clearness*.

Susan demonstrated that simplicity alone may mean immature bareness. If simplicity was the only virtue of style, children's books would be the greatest literature. Dignity is required in most forms of civilized communication, but Mrs. Sloan produced a dull and drab pattern of words. And George overcolored his pattern with a shining mass of embroidery and tinsel, shrouding the facts. Only Wheeling succeeded in clearly conveying to his readers what he saw and learned at the fire.

Simplicity, dignity and color thus are inadequate in themselves. But once in combination, one modifying the other, they add up to clarity or clearness. This is the sole objective in news writing which may be likened to walking on a tightrope. If you step off on either side you'll fall.

To take a muddled mixture of sights and sounds, an obscure idea, or a complex technical operation and by sheer lucidity of presentation compel busy people to stop, read and mentally respond—that is the goal of the writing reporter. He must have something to say but it isn't much good in this hurried and impatient world unless he learns how to say it in crisp, clean-cut words—quickly and unmistakably.

THINK FIRST—THEN WRITE

Look again at the words written by the three members of the Sloan family. Mrs. Sloan, casually including a few superficial sentences about the fire in her letter, wrote with the least mental effort. Trying hard for good grades, Susan and George strained to impress their teachers but they lacked experience. Wheeling started with experience and planned before he wrote.

Good writing is an extension of forceful, ordered thinking. You cannot write a story properly unless you have digested the data you have and know precisely what you are doing as the words travel from your mind to your typewriter.

We have noted how a reporter starts to sort out and analyze facts as he gathers them and how, before reaching the office, he thinks hard, often furiously. With his mind in high gear he visualizes the job ahead as he rides, walks, drinks a cup of coffee, or smokes a cigarette.

Writing looks easy. Almost anyone will admit that he couldn't conduct an orchestra or perform an operation, but rarely do we find a man who doesn't think he could write for the newspapers.

Don't be misled by the fictional phony who chats with a girl friend as he dashes off page after page of flawless copy. A real reporter is more likely to stare at his typewriter or out a window for a while after reaching his desk. He may make several false starts while hammering together an opening sentence. During the ordeal of turning out a balanced and complete story it is not uncommon for a man who has written all his life to X out and pencil in constantly, discarding more of his first pages in a wastebasket than he hands to a copy boy. Only when the last page has gone does he relax physically and mentally.

It is true that a newsman doing a routine piece such as a short obituary or wedding story has merely to drop names and addresses into molds already mentally prepared and used many times before. Or he may need only to pick up lengthy portions of a speech or statement. In such cases he is copying from either a brain blackboard or a mimeograph and he does so easily.

Writing an original story on an unfamiliar topic and from unprocessed raw material is a different matter. The attainment of clearness in style, then, demands sustained intellectual vigor. Only hard writing makes easy reading.

LINES ARE WORTH MONEY

It is an error to say that the average newspaper reader has a 12-to-14-year-old mind, but correct to say that his vocabulary and reading ability is that of a pupil in the seventh or eighth grade. The two statements are not contradictory.

There is nothing wrong with the mind or judgment of readers as a whole. Most of them work with stoves and sewing machines, shovels and hammers, butter and cotton or accounts and files. A reader may be a wizard with wrenches or a wonder with waffle irons—repairing your car or serving you breakfast without mental effort on your part—but he is under no obligation to become an expert with words which he reads in his leisure time. It is *your* obligation to serve him news as satisfactorily as he serves you.

Words are the tools and raw material of the man who writes for a living and it is his task to make them brief, simple and clear to his customers—the readers—while they are eating, clinging to bus straps, or planning to go to the movies.

In her letter to a relative, Mrs. Sloan could afford to use up her paper carelessly. Brevity probably would not have saved her even the price of a postage stamp. But words printed in a newspaper are precious goods displayed in an expensive showcase.

Curt demands to "bite it off," "cut it short" and "boil it down" are drummed so often into a reporter's ears that cultivation of compactness becomes a standing order not to be disobeyed unless he is under explicit orders to fill space. Even so, he may not, like Mrs. Sloan, indulge in such a vague and meaningless expression as "very interesting." He must make every word count in customer appeal.

Brevity, like simplicity, is desirable but not at the expense of clearness. Certainly superfluous details and useless repetition are wasteful and call for condensation. Tight writing is wanted, but too-tight writing can squeeze the life and meaning out of a story.

Space is at a premium, yes, and should be, considering the cost of newsprint. However, what editors seek is not necessarily brevity, but stories which go straight to the target, hitting the reader's mind like a bullet. The reporter needs a rifle—not a shotgun.

CHOOSE THE COMMON WORD

There are millions of words in the English language but 500 of them account for 75 per cent of all that is said in print. Common homespun words such as *face, make, keep, work* and *city* are the sinews of sound style. They are the words in which most people think and with which they talk.

If you can find one of these short to-the-point words always prefer it to one which is long, and complex with syllables. For example:

COMPLEX	COMMON	COMPLEX	COMMON
indisposed	ill	contribute	give
monumental	big	request	ask
terminate	end	endeavor	try
witness	see	summon	call
purchase	buy	category	class
utilize	use	prevaricate	lie
majority	most	incarcerate	jail
reside	live	inaugurate	start
procure	get	facilitate	help
proceed	go	inundate	flood

Short words usually are strong words but it must be repeated that brevity should be a principle—not a rule.

Id, erg, goa and *ohm* are short and good dictionary words as meaning-less to Joe Doakes as the marks on a Chinese laundry ticket. On the other hand, *vulnerable,* as used in a bridge game, and *incompatibility,* as used in a divorce case, are widely familiar. It is not solely the size of a word that should rule it out of print but its obscurity. Common long words are better understood than rare short ones.

The reading public does not want and will not tolerate baby talk. You don't always have to turn *bacteria* and *microbes* into germs, *satellite* into moon and *limousine* into car. People are impatient with technical, foreign and high-hat expressions but they are not ignorant of terms coming into our everyday language.

Nearly every word fills a special function. Its excuse for existing is that it expresses one particular thing better than any other word. It may sub-stitute for a dozen shorter words which would otherwise have to be used. To use it is word economy.

Try to say what you mean and explain if necessary, but you don't need to point out that a cow is an ungulate, ruminant, herbivorous quadruped or a four-footed, plant-eating animal that chews its cud and has split hoofs. Just call it a cow and get on with the story.

It is equally foolish to define a hard word in harder words. *Psycho-analysis* is a hard word which may go over the heads of some readers but it becomes no clearer if you tell them it is a method of psychotherapeutic

A COMPARISON OF
DOLLAR AND DIME WORDS

anent	about		interrogate	question
antagonist	foe		inundate	flood
aperture	hole		peruse	read
beverage	drink		physician	doctor
cognizant	aware		ponder	think
conceal	hide		populace	people
deceased	dead		possess	own
deem	think		purloin	steal
dentifrice	toothpaste		remark	say
depart	leave		remunerate	pay
endeavor	try		require	need
exhibit	show		residence	home
expedite	hasten		sufficient	enough
feasible	possible		transmit	send
imbibe	drink		trepidation	fear
indignation	anger		visage	face
inquire	ask		vouchsafe	assure

Complex v. Common Terms

analysis of the relation of conscious and unconscious psychological processes.

FAULTS IN FANCY PHRASES

For the same reason that he searches for winning words a good writer tries to keep his word groups clear and orderly. Often you can trim a long and loose phrase into a terse word or two which will do the job better. Calling a spade a spade rather than a *long-handled instrument for turning earth in a garden* is the classic example. Here are others:

FOGGY	TERSE
at the present time	now
held a conference	met
at the intersection of	at
put in an appearance	came
in the event that	if
was the recipient of	received
made his escape	escaped
along the line of	like
affixed his signature	signed
with the result that	so that
took action	acted
a sufficient number of	enough
in the immediate vicinity of	near
during the period from	from
with little commotion	quietly

Now note how by chopping out verbal deadwood you can get rid of long and loose phrases which clutter copy and eat up space:

LOOSE	TIGHT
The trouble with the light was that it was not strong enough.	The light was too dim.
All those who are members in good standing were invited.	All members were invited.
The building closed its doors at 5 o'clock in the afternoon.	The building closed at 5 p.m.
The present incumbent served a term of two years.	The incumbent served two years.
His luck may change in the near future.	His luck may change soon.
There are no funds which may be used at this time.	No funds are available.

Superfluous words and foggy phrases should be caught and removed by the writer himself as he examines his copy a second time. Too much patchwork, of course, produces a messy manuscript which should be re-typed if time permits.

STRAIGHTEN OUT YOUR SENTENCES

As we have seen, the choice of words with few syllables and phrases without flimflam tend to make news copy understandable and easy to read. The same logic applies to sentences.

While no rule can be safely set, the average sentence length should be from 10 to 15 words. Some of the most forceful sentences ever recorded contain less than a half dozen words. Consider "Jesus wept," "The die is cast," "Don't give up the ship," and "I will return."

Now try to grasp this one quickly: "Upon the approach of West, in the full glare of the neon lights, Foster vainly attempted to make his escape, but had scarcely started when West made a move toward his pocket and, extracting a revolver partially concealed there, pulled the trigger, firing point-blank at close range, and Foster fell badly wounded." A copy-reader would divide this lumbering sentence into several parts and in a pinch for space would make it read: "West shot Foster."

Note the vigor of short sentence structure, as well as common words, in a brief human interest story wired in by the Larchmont correspondent of the Midland *Times:*

> Five-year-old Jimmy Burke of Midland, here on a holiday, stepped up to a mailbox today with a post card for his father.
>
> Jimmy stood tiptoe and pushed the card firmly through the slot. He couldn't get his arm out. Jimmy yelled.
>
> His mother, Mrs. F. A. Burke, visiting her sister, came running. Bystanders came running. A policeman came. So did an ambulance with a doctor and a pulmotor. The crowd grew. Jimmy yelled some more.
>
> After an hour they called the fire station. The firemen got acetylene torches ready to cut through the box. Then somebody suggested butter. They smeared it on Jimmy's arm. It worked. One tug and the arm was free.
>
> Then the postman, who had been waiting patiently, opened the box and collected Jimmy's card. It said: "Having wonderful time. Wish you were here."

Fewer commas and more periods usually improve news writing. But it must be pointed out that sentence shortening can be abused. A long series of too-short sentences gives a bang-bang effect which can become more irritating and monotonous than the marathon monstrosities.

Alternating long and short sentences seems more reasonable but no mechanical formula can cure basic faults.

A LESSON IN
SENTENCE SIMPLICITY

𝔉rom tɦe 𝔖ermon on tɦe 𝔐ount

No man can serve two masters: for either he will hate the one, and love the other; or else he will hold to the one, and despise the other. Ye cannot serve God and mammon.

Therefore I say unto you, Take no thought for your life, what ye shall eat, or what ye shall drink; nor yet for your body, what ye shall put on. Is not the life more than meat, and the body than raiment?

Behold the fowls of the air: for they sow not, neither do they reap, nor gather into barns; yet your heavenly Father feedeth them. Are ye not much better than they?

Which of you by taking thought can add one cubit unto his stature?

And why take ye thought for raiment? Consider the lilies of the field, how they grow; they toil not, neither do they spin:

And yet I say unto you, That even Solomon in all his glory was not arrayed like one of these.

Gospel of St. Matthew 6:24–29

The key to writing a sound sentence is to make it express one complete thought. Each clause in it should be relevant to that thought. The reader is confused only when prepositional phrases go off on tangents and clutter up the sentence with verbal debris. In the construction of sentences, as in the choice of words and phrases, the aim of the good writer is to use simplicity and brevity with discretion as means to an end—clearness of expression.

CURE YOUR COMPOSITIONITIS

Let us return to the opening of this chapter and look again at the fire reports written by the Sloans. These teach still another lesson meaningful to the young person who has passed through the Susan and George stages and is entering the Mrs. Sloan or Wheeling stage.

A child learning to read and write is full of wonder at his own wit when he thinks he has invented a new comparison like *red as a beet*, the phrase used by Susan. Imitating his elders, he soon discovers and adopts as his own more of the simpler stereotypes such as *fat as a pig, big as a barn, cool as a cucumber, white as a sheet, black as coal, good as gold, cheap as dirt, strong as an ox, weak as a kitten*, and so on.

Later on he proudly reads aloud school essays woven of such worn phrases as *loomed like a sentinel* and *trip the light fantastic*. He still is parading in borrowed plumage which strikes him as something elegant and erudite. Here are a few more favorites:

abysmal ignorance	lacteal fluid
avenging justice	music hath charms
bag and baggage	one fell swoop
beggar description	wrack and ruin
bolt from the blue	ripe old age
green-eyed monster	succulent bivalve
grim reaper	toothsome viands
in durance vile	wee small hours

If a doctor of words should diagnose the case of a youngster showing these style symptoms he might call it *compositionitis*. George Sloan had a bad case of it when he described the fire as a *conflagration* and the *devouring element*. Like mumps and chicken pox, the ailment usually is a sign of growing up.

GET RID OF GOBBLEDYGOOK

Sometimes but not often mumps infects grownups and so does compositionitis. Ordinary folk like Mrs. Sloan who seldom speak in public

and write only an occasional letter or note to the grocer are mostly immune but among somebodies seeking to impress the public with their
literary fluency the "itis" is contagious.

Washington has another name for it—gobbledygook. Its symptoms
show up in such words as *promulgate, facilitate, ameliorate, expedite,
implementation* and *finalize.* It breaks out in Congress when a master of
the purple passage and purveyor of the high-flown phrase rolls into the
Record such Olympian words as *insinuation, innuendo, circumlocution*
and *periphrasis,* or when the spokesman for a new anticrime group an-
nounces that it will:

> secure, analyze, interpret and validate statistical data; determine the
> socioeconomic factors which contribute to antisocial behavior; study the
> efficiency and impartiality of the operation of the municipal government
> correctional institutions and ascertain the agencies working in the com-
> munity, their programs and how best they might be coordinated in an
> effort to combat the incidence of antisocial behavior.

Such a confusing conglomeration causes the reader to ask: "What is
this guy talking about?" A passage from St. Paul is to the point: ". . . except ye utter . . . words easy to be understood, how shall it be known
what is spoken? . . . for ye shall speak into the air."

Unfortunately even news writers never quite escape the temptation
to write *solon* for senator, *lucre* for money, *canine* for dog, *nuptials* for
marriage, *child monitor* for baby sitter, *pachyderm* for elephant, and to
report that *farmers are viewing the cloudless skies with mounting apprehension* when they mean that the farmers are worried about a long dry
spell. Each of these came from news pages:

beautiful and accomplished	fled in scanty clothing
dull and sickening thud	bull in a china closet
eked out an existence	like rats in a trap
explore the ramifications	mystery shrouds the murder
flash in the pan	rests on his laurels
conspicuous by his absence	long arm of the law
burn the midnight oil	sea of upturned faces
beat around the bush	hit the nail on the head

You, too, can find these current clichés sprinkled through the papers.
They are signs of immature or lazy writing. Use of them is justified only
under extreme pressure when a writer must sacrifice skill to speed and
there is no time for careful copyreading. The writer who resorts to them
habitually never quite grows up and cannot hope for recognition.

TENSE CAN BE TRICKY

It is presumed that the rules of grammar are learned in grammar school. Little space can be devoted to them here. However, because of its peculiar application by newspaper writers, tense—the verb form to express time—is worthy of mention.

Listen to a conversation and you will hear the present tense used heavily in such sentences as, "He *says* he *is* going to vote for Jones." Many of the less literate relate past events almost wholly in present tense, thus: "So I *say* he's wrong. Then this other fellow *says*, 'You're crazy,' and I *tell* him off." Although not so colloquial, radio and television newsmen, writing for the ear and often about events in the process of happening, also lean to the present tense.

Newspaper writers, on the contrary, are confined almost entirely to the past and future tenses for a compelling reason. Hours, if not days, elapse between the time of writing and the time of reading. During that interval the facts may and often do change.

It would be absurd as well as ungrammatical for an AM paper to print, "The plane *is* flying to New York last night" and dangerous for a PM paper to print, "The plane *is* flying to New York today." Before the paper reaches a reader, the plane probably has reached New York or may have crashed in Cleveland. Of only one thing could the writer for either paper be certain—"The plane *was* flying to New York" when he wrote the story.

A general rule is that the tense of a verb in the main clause of a sentence determines the tense of the verb in a subordinate clause. There is an exception, however, when the verb in the subordinate clause expresses a permanent fact or continuing action. Then the second verb is in present tense. Examples:

WRONG	RIGHT
the world *was* round	the world *is* round
the date of Christmas *was* Dec. 25	the date of Christmas *is* Dec. 25
cats *were* enemies of rats	cats *are* enemies of rats
platinum *was* a rare metal	platinum *is* a rare metal

Again the rule of grammar is modified when a subordinate clause verb expresses continuing thought or action. It is correct, therefore, to write: "The Governor said he *expects* the bill to pass." Presumably he will continue to think so after publication of the story.

A similar variation applies to *will* and *would*. The rule calls for *would*, thus: "The Governor said he *would* sign the bill now on his desk." It is less awkward to write: "The Governor said he *will* sign the bill now on his desk."

A common newsroom argument centers on the question whether "officers elected last night *were*" or "officers elected last night *are*." They *were* elected last night. That is the truth. But it is conceivable that one died overnight, so *are* is a presumption and may not be the truth when the paper is read.

A few editors and copyreaders tend to follow the sequence of tense rule out the window, but a majority prefer the rule of common sense to the strict rule of grammar. As a reporter, find out by reading your own paper the preferences of the men who edit your copy and conform to them.

SHOP TALK

1. Do you consider writing really hard work? If so, why do you wish to be a reporter?
2. Do you agree that the average newspaper reader has a 12-to-14-year-old mind?
3. Add to the list of complex words and their common substitutes, such as *reside* for *live*.
4. Play a game of comparisons. Have one student speak a descriptive word such as *black*. Others will match it with *pitch, ink* and *ace of spades*.
5. Try the same experiment with *writing instrument, stream of water* and *nice weather*.

CHAPTER 6

The Secrets of Style

CLEARNESS FIRST—THEN COLOR

An aspiring young news writer is likely to be discouraged for a time by the dozens of *don't* signs that dangle about him as he tries to break into print, among them these:

> Don't use weighty words. Beware of foggy phrases. Forgo flowery figures of speech. Do away with marathon sentences. Steer clear of stereotypes. Don't be too technical. Trim it down. Make it shorter, simpler, plainer, clearer.

These stop signals he sees over the desks of the instructor, the city editor and the copyreader. Each of the three seems eager to wield a heavy pencil on his copy.

Are newsmen simpletons or robots—copyists rather than creators? Must they all conform to a set of strict and stultifying rules? Is there no room in modern newspapers for fresh, exciting, colorful prose? Yes, there is plenty of room. Indeed, after the first essential—clearness—is attained, color in style is the most widely sought-after and well-paid-for commodity produced in the editorial room.

Right alongside the *don't* signs are the *do* signs.

> Sharpen it up. Put punch into it. Personalize it. Humanize it. Make it shine, sing and cut. Let them hear it, see it, feel it, cry over it and laugh at it.

Our preceding chapter was devoted to the acquirement of clearness. This one will show how news writers tint their stories with the second major quality in good news writing style—color. Clearness plus color equals copy that clicks.

70

SEARCH FOR SPECIFIC WORDS

Bird, tree and *flower* are three plain words picturing objects anyone can easily see with his mental eye. But how much more easily if you say *blue jay* or *redheaded woodpecker, weeping willow* or *coconut palm, lily of the valley* or *African violet.*

There in a nutshell is one of the secrets of style in any kind of writing. It may be called the art of being specific.

The reader has only a vague impression if you write *structure.* You could mean a *barn,* a *bridge* or a *monument.* It's better if you write *building.* Still you may be referring to a *cottage, mansion* or *hangar.* But if you write *skyscraper* in the first place, the reader grasps your idea at once.

Suppose you wish to describe a *beautiful* woman. Here are a few substitute adjectives:

alluring	enchanting	patrician
attractive	enticing	personable
bewitching	exotic	pert
bonny	fair	piquant
buxom	fascinating	pretty
captivating	fetching	saucy
charming	glamorous	shapely
chic	graceful	sizzling
comely	gracious	stunning
curvaceous	languorous	sultry
dainty	lissome	svelte
demure	lovely	torrid
dreamy	luscious	winsome

The particular woman you are writing about may be *dark-haired, blue-eyed, slim-waisted, jewel-spangled* or *mink-coated.* If so, you can fit your word picture more snugly.

Synonyms for a handsome man are not so plentiful, but you can describe him as *dashing, debonair, jaunty* or *suave.* If you apply such complimentary adjectives, of course, you must not do it sight unseen. A picture may accompany your story with the camera making you a liar.

Abstract words are ambiguous whether they are long or short. One of those most often heard in conversation is *very.* It is perhaps the laziest in the language. News writers seldom use it for it signifies nothing and more specific synonyms are so numerous that they fill a volume entitled "The Very Book."

Some common words have an astonishing number of different meanings. For example, there are more than 100 senses in which the word *run* is used. It is a handy word, provided that when you use it you reject *trot* or *pace* and really are writing about a rush of depositors on a bank or the thing that happens to women's stockings.

Journalism terminology itself illustrates the importance of concreteness in words. The noun *journalist* lacks that quality. It may apply to a book author, a magazine writer, a radio commentator or a newspaper reporter. Choose the one noun you want—author, writer, commentator or reporter.

The word *color* itself as applied to news writing has two meanings. To color a story means to twist or distort the truth. To put color into a story means to brush in bright hues of description and narration along with exposition. In a narrow sense, to write the color story, say of a parade or a prize fight, means to leave straight facts and figures to another reporter and concentrate on scenery, crowd, personalities and side lights.

You must, of course, know the exact meaning of the specific word you choose and what it implies. Can you distinguish between *appointment, date, tryst* and *engagement?* If not, you'd better stay with *meeting* and stay out of trouble.

PERSISTENT PRECISION PAYS

Not with single words only but from the start to the end of his story the news writer pursues his bloodhound hunt for exactitude. Turn now to sentences—general and specific—and note the differences:

Vague: His head was injured by a blunt instrument.
Precise: His skull was fractured by a sledge hammer.

Vague: The chief executive rode down the principal thoroughfare.
Precise: Governor Paulson rode down Main street.

Vague: He spoke in disparaging terms about the radical clement.
Precise: He denounced the Communists.

Vague: She rendered an old-fashioned hymn.
Precise: She sang "Rock of Ages."

Vague: A large number assembled for the meeting.
Precise: Five hundred attended the caucus.

Vague: Officers removed a gun from his clothing.
Precise: Police took a .32 caliber automatic from his hip pocket.

A passion for pinpointing the precise can be carried too far by the use of unfamiliar technical terms. Sometimes stories of everyday automobile accidents abound in words redolent of the hospital. Consider these and the simpler substitutes:

TECHNICAL	NON-TECHNICAL
abrasions	scratches
contusions	bruises
fractures	breaks
lacerations	cuts

Still in the medical field, you would be accurate in writing "ecchymosis of the conjunctiva and the periorbital cuticular tissues" but more intelligible if you wrote "black eye." It is more specific to say "coronary occlusion" but more sensible to say "heart disease."

Presume that you have gathered the facts about a new atomic energy electric plant to be built in your city. You understand and write in terms of nuclear fission, isotopes, thermal units, dynamos and kilowatts. The catch is that you do understand them and others don't.

Your aim is not to get the report *on* paper but to get it *off* the paper and across to the readers. Therefore you must specify in their terms, not yours. You can make the story publishable when you let them see thousands of new homes where families will live in comfort when the plant is built.

APPEAL TO THE SENSES

The impatient reaction of a reader to abstract exposition is: "Don't tell me—show me." He may have no clear conception of five million dollars—the amount of a tax assessment—but he will pause if you portray it as enough cash to buy for every family in Midland a new automobile, a new television set, a new fur coat, and a ton of lollipops. In such visual description emphasize details of color, size, shape, mass and texture.

Pictures came before words. Note here how a reporter injects color into a picture story:

Pink and white cherry blossoms crowned a May queen yesterday in Island Park and—in breath-taking tints against blue sky—formed a backdrop for scores of whirling, sunlit dancers who performed before the royal throne.

The traditional Maypole dance by 200 Center High School girls drew 1,500 spectators to green-turfed Oriental Garden in the center of the park.

Wearing blooms in their hair and as corsages, blonde Barbara Belton, 16, and her court watched their classmates gaily wind the multicolored streamers of the Maypole. . . . .

As he relaxes with his newspaper the reader likes vicariously to hear, smell, taste, feel—and believe—as well as see. With words you can transfer these sensory impressions to him. Teachers of English sometimes call this *empathy*. A better expression is "taking the reader to the scene." He is not at the scene if you write merely that "the chairman was angered." He will be if you write that the chairman shouted, scowled, flushed, bit his lips, waved his arms or banged his gavel on the table so hard the water glasses jumped.

The reader is an onlooker with you if you describe the Christmas gifts awaiting the boy victim of an accident as "a chocolate-brown leather jacket from his father, a red woolen muffler his mother knit, and a black-and-white striped football encircled with a ribbon from his younger sister."

MORE POINTERS ON STYLE

Verbs are triggers to action. They inject life and movement into sentences. With them you can make copy sparkle, glow, sting, alarm, soothe, sing, goad, cut, blister, delight and caress. In "The Bells" Edgar Allan Poe, a master of verbs, shows their range in reaching just one of the senses —hearing. His silver bells tinkle and jingle; golden bells rhyme and chime; brazen bells shriek, scream, roar, jangle and wrangle; iron bells throb, moan and sob.

Adjectives used as qualifiers are useful if they give point to a noun without smothering it. You may picture a factory as immobilized, paralyzed or deactivated, but it is better to call it idle. Colorful adjectives need not be gaudy. Like spice and sugar, they should be sprinkled on sparingly. The writer who pours them on without restraint and neglects his nouns and verbs is a cook serving all cake and no meat.

Generalized adjectives such as *wonderful, lovely, awful* and *terrible,* like other nonspecific words, are overworked in conversation and sapped of their strength. They also are opinionated. News writers let them alone except when quoting somebody.

Alliteration—the commencement of two or more stressed syllables of a word group with the same consonant sound—is a favorite device for putting cadence and rhythm into prose as well as poetry. The newsman uses it, unwittingly perhaps, when he writes "the blaring bands, billowing banners and flying flags" or "bathing beauties and balmy breezes" in his description of a parade.

Alliteration, like lipstick, is lovely if not smeared on too thickly in the wrong places. On a circus poster the newsman expects to find "marvelous mastodonic mammals," "motley-mugged mummers" and "magnificent melodic marches," but if he transfers them into his own copy it will land in the wastebasket.

Still another trick of the writing man is the use of synonyms to avoid the monotonous repetition of names and at the same time to diffuse background material. For example, in his second reference to a man the writer refers to him as "the one-time all-State football star," "a veteran of World War II" or "the serious-minded Sunday School teacher."

Just as the injudicious use of adjectives can bring on a case of *adjectivitis,* so can too many synonyms break out in *synonymitis.* There's nothing wrong with using the plain pronouns *he* or *she* once in a while, and often purely background material is better grouped in one brief paragraph under the lead, enabling the reader to see the word picture and get on with the development of the story.

WATCH FOR NEW WORDS

Fashions in language are changing continually. Living and growing, our vocabularies reflect the ever-shifting scenes of the human drama, and the news writer who confines himself to the terms in yesterday's dictionary is missing part of the performance.

The English language is fluid and changes incessantly. What last year may have been stiffly formal, next year may be loosely informal. Word combinations, slogans and phrases are constantly being added to and becoming part of the language.

New things and situations require new words which arise spontaneously from every field of knowledge and activity. Let us list a few which have become common usage in our own lifetime. War and weapon development, for example, have brought us *jeep, ramjet, superbomb* and *fall-out.* The space age produced *flying saucers* and *guided missiles.* Then, overnight, *Sputnik* orbited into our language.

From medicine came *vitamin, hormone, cortisone, dramamine, neomycin* and *tranquilizer.* Inventors gave us *Dacron, Orlon, aqualung, transistor, mobilphone, helicopter* and *stratocruiser.* From the entertainment world we have *Cinerama, spectacular, colorcast, panelist* and *subliminal projection.* Meanwhile *Veep, Dixiecrat, welfare state, apartheid, Benelux, Comiform, brainwashing* and *cold war* appeared on the political scene. Industry gave us *automation, push-button* efficiency and *streamlined* operations. Newspapers themselves have become one of the *mass media* of communication.

The flow of new words, new meanings for old words and words of bygone times which again have come into vogue is endless. Newspaper-men watch them closely in conversations and in print, ready to introduce them into their own copy as soon as they trickle down from the elite and become the property of the common man.

SLANG MAY PACK A PUNCH

Language is made not only by scientists and scholars but much of it by plain people with literature following after them. For a newsman to be highbrow and aloof from the pungent and picturesque phraseology used daily by the public would be suicidal to his style.

Today's slang may well be and often is tomorrow's usage, especially by Americans who create, understand and enjoy fresh colloquialisms. To the dismay of grammatical purists words like *gimmick, clobber* and *hassle* emerge from underground and force their way into the best circles.

As language lives it also wears out and dies. Expressions once vivid and effective become old and trite, as we have seen in our discussion of compositionitis. Slang, as defined here, does not mean these moth-eaten terms nor such vulgarisms as *swell* and *lousy*. Neither does it include such illiteracies as *you ain't, that there, them fellows, hadn't ought, can't hardly* and *has went*. These are uncouth and unfit, as are provincialisms like *he went that-a-way* or *passel o' brats*.

We must also bar from acceptance the talk of teen-agers who tirelessly invent, adopt and discard jargon meaningless to their elders and often to themselves. The lexicon of this 13-to-19 age group derives largely from the world of entertainment, especially popular music.

For example, in the jazz lingo of the late 50s, a *bopper* would *dig* another talking about a *cool cat* who could *send* him into an *all gone state,* or a *real smoothie* who wished to drive his *doll* in a *hot rod* to see the *flicks* in the local *passion pit*. True, the kids could give you a chuckle with alliterations like "What's your tale, nightingale?" or "See you later, alligator" but teen-ese is mostly puzzling and nonsensical.

Many words of the underworld such as *gat* for gun and *ice* for diamonds fail to reach the surface of common conversation. Even the shop talk of an ordinary occupation, say that of a store clerk, may confound everyone except other clerks in the same line of business.

To be valid in a news write-up slang must conform to exactly the same standard of clearness as other terms. That means it has been accepted by the public.

From the army we accepted *GI, ersatz, blackout* and *snafu;* from aviation, *take-off* and *airlift;* from politics, *boss* and *ward heeler;* from labor, *lockout* and *picket;* from radio, *soap opera* and *disk jockey;* from crime, *holdup* and *con man;* from newspapers, *scoop* and *deadline.*

Even such indispensable words as *bus* and *coed* were slang a few years ago, as were *playboy, bobby-soxer, baby sitter* and *crew haircut.* Each instantly conveys a specific image, doing the job no other words can do as well. They must be and are used if the writer is to be both clear and colorful. Yes, slang is okay and may be needed if your ideas are to be put over to the reader.

THE PERSONAL TOUCH IN STYLE

We come now to a fundamental in sound style—personalization. This subtle but vital virtue is the art of bridging an outside event into the personal life of the reader.

In our definitions of news and analysis of its elements we have seen that the desires of the reader may be summed up by the question: "How does it affect me?" News is news because it affects individual readers personally and is sought, evaluated, selected, edited and printed to that end. How can the writer contribute to personalization?

Advertising copywriters exploit the me-to-you theme without inhibitions. They write directly to you about *your* hair, *your* job, *your* cash, *your* future. Commentators and columnists are free with "I's" and "you's." Editorial writers may take advantage of the personal "we." The reporter, writing in the third person, does not enjoy these liberties.

Unless he is on a special assignment, say reporting his own experiences in a blizzard or during a transit strike, he may seldom write "you" and never "I" except when quoting someone. However, he may and should as often as possible use personal nouns and pronouns. These words, as well as names, touch the intimate life of the reader. And he may and should try to dramatize his stories around knowable people.

"What's the name of the cat?" a city editor asked a young reporter who replied: "I don't think it has one." "Then," snapped the desk man, "give it one! Call it Felix or Flossy or Fuzzy—anything. You can't write about a cat without a name."

A few moments later the city room chief again summoned the writer, who had started the story: "Police last night rescued . . ." Said the editor: "Not that way. You say this cat had no tail? All right, start it: 'This is a tale about a cat without a tail. His name is Fuzzy. . . .' Go on from there."

The editor was creating a human interest yarn out of a routine item. Instinctively he advised the reporter to personalize the cat and to human-

THE PERSONAL TOUCH IN
AN IMMORTAL STORY

The Gospel of St. Luke

And she brought forth her firstborn son, and wrapped him in swaddling clothes, and laid him in a manger; because there was no room for them in the inn.

And there were in the same country shepherds abiding in the field, keeping watch over their flock by night.

And, lo, the angel of the Lord came upon them, and the glory of the Lord shone round about them: and they were sore afraid.

And the angel said unto them, Fear not: for, behold, I bring you good tidings of great joy, which shall be to all people.

For unto you is born this day in the city of David a Saviour, which is Christ the Lord.

And this shall be a sign unto you; Ye shall find the babe wrapped in swaddling clothes, lying in a manger.

And suddenly there was with the angel a multitude of the heavenly host praising God, and saying,

Glory to God in the highest, and on earth peace, good will toward men.

A Humanized Narrative

ize the narrative in a way that would bring a mental response from each reader.

The reporter is both a realist and a romanticist. He tries to make his dry facts come alive and, within the limits of his third-person style, give the reader a feeling that he is a part of the story. While color and humanization must not be allowed to distort essential facts, an active, healthy imagination is a mark of difference between star reporters and newsroom plodders.

It is true that the city editor was not concerned about accuracy in the absolute when he insisted on naming the cat. Certainly the names he suggested did not belong to it. So what? It was only a stray cat. It had no home. No one claimed it. It would not complain about the wrong name nor would it sue for libel if its antics were ridiculed. However, no city editor in his right mind would have suggested offending the policeman who rescued it by hinting that he knowingly played with a cat, ignoring burglars in a nearby store.

As he dips into personalization the reporter must always be aware of its limitations. He may not go beyond the bounds of common-sense accuracy.

Facts which affect human beings rather than merely entertain them are not to be trifled with. If missing, they must be found or omitted—never faked. The reader must know that every story of a serious nature is true. News of this kind must first of all be reliable.

The writer of fiction can make up his characters and move them like puppets as he chooses. The newsman who writes about real people must accept them as they are and confine himself to relating what they do. Accuracy modifies his imagination and controls his style.

ACCURACY AND EDITORIALIZING

To report the news accurately and fairly without prejudice or personal opinion is the No. 1 obligation of the reporter.

Here for the first time we touch the explosive words *objectivity* and *interpretation*. These will be fully dealt with in a later chapter. For the moment we merely warn the new reporter—but warn him sternly—that editorializing is taboo. He is just that—a reporter—not an advocate or a judge. None of his own views may be visible in print.

Later in his career if he becomes a byline specialist or columnist—an expert in a certain field such as politics, finance, science or music—he may be authorized to write his own conclusions but not until then.

Even the new reporter must recognize that he has a boss who has a boss who must keep subscribers, advertisers and owners or stockholders happy. Unless he does, his paper will make no profits and the reporter will have no job.

If his paper has strong policies or if it is engaging in a crusade or an exposé, he may be asked to conform and perhaps participate. But in that case the position he takes will be that of the publisher and may not coincide with his own.

By editorializing is meant the expression of doubt, censure or praise on the part of the writer. While he may and should quote authority, he may not pose as an authority himself.

Let us suppose that firemen were late in arriving at the supermarket fire covered by Reporter Jack Wheeling of the Midland *Times*. Wheeling may not write: "The Fire Department was so slow in answering an alarm at the Shop-and-Save Supermarket last night that it was destroyed." That sounds editorial and it is.

Assume further that R. M. Gregg, the owner, is president of the Midland Merchants Assn., a responsible citizen, and the reporter writes: "R. M. Gregg charged that the loss of his store last night was due to delay by firemen in reaching the scene. Three other witnesses said they turned in alarms 30 minutes before the apparatus arrived." That is factual, not editorial.

Wheeling may remain strictly objective and still write: "Predictions made by Fire Chief Chambers last May when the City Council refused to buy new fire hose apparently came true last night when the Shop-and-Save Supermarket burned to the ground. Leaky fire hose so seriously hampered the firemen, Chief Chambers said, that they never delivered effective streams on the flames."

The reporter's views count for nothing, but what he has to tell counts for much. He writes only what he sees, hears and learns but he does not volunteer approval or censure. He cannot watch from an orchestra seat and at the same time be an actor in the show.

STYLE SHEETS AND BOOKS

Style to a reporter and as used so far in this book is a manner of writing. To a copyreader or proofreader the style of a newspaper is a set of rules aimed to make all of its copy consistent.

The rules in a style sheet or style book cover capitalization, abbreviations, punctuation, numerals and compounds, as well as forms followed in news of religion, markets and sports.

Every newspaper in the United States either has its own style sheet or

REPORTING AS AIDED BY
MECHANICAL INVENTIONS

TELEGRAPH

Created the inverted pyramid structure in news stories.

TELETYPE

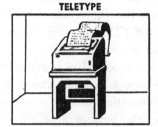

Speeded transmission of copy and saved manpower.

TELEPHONE

Speeded news gathering and broadened coverage.

RADIO-CAR

Made reporters and photographers mobile.

TYPEWRITER

Made handwriting legible and speeded copy production.

TELETYPESETTER

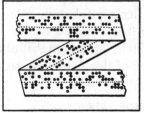

Helped to standardize style books and style sheets.

How Technology Affects Newsmen

book or uses one or more prepared by a wire service or other papers. A wise reporter consults the rules of his paper as he writes and memorizes them as soon as possible. It is irritating to stop writing and find out whether it is *Company, company* or *Co.*, but more so to be constantly corrected by copyreaders or criticized by editors.

Newspaper style rules as well as reporting techniques are affected by mechanical advances such as the telegraph, typewriter and Teletype. In recent years the combination of Teletype and Linotype into the Teletypesetter, or TTS, has revolutionized and gone far toward standardizing style books across the land.

Stories are received over press association circuits on punched paper tape. The tape is fed into the Teletypesetter which operates the Linotype or linecasting machine somewhat like the old player-piano rolls worked on the keys of a piano.

All Teletypesetter circuit tape, of course, must follow the same style rules, and hundreds of newspapers, in order to take advantage of the new laborsaving device and at the same time keep TTS and locally written copy uniform, have altered their style books drastically.

To assist them the Associated Press issued a comprehensive style book which has become the gospel law in many offices—the Bible on the copy desk and in the composing room.

The most radical change came in capitalization. In frontier days metal type had to be carried overland in wagons for long distances. Capital letters, stored in the upper drawer of the hand-set printer, were costlier and heavier than small letters in the lower drawer. Hence papers in the West favored *down* style while those in the East leaned to *up* style. The AP after careful study struck a happy medium.

Because it is a typical newspaper and many such papers have made their own style conform to that of the AP, the Midland *Times* Style Sheet in the back of this book does so, as well as the text of the book itself.

SHOP TALK

1. Suggest and write down at least 25 substitutes for the word *very*.
2. Try the same experiment with *wonderful* and *awful*.
3. Compile and discuss a list of words now in good usage which once were slang.
4. Do you think reporters should be allowed to use the personal word "I"?
5. Define in your own words *objectivity* and *interpretation*. Do you favor more or less of either in your newspaper?

CHAPTER 7

How to Start the Story

THE VITAL FIRST WORDS

"The President was shot in a theatre tonight and perhaps mortally wounded." Thus an Associated Press man in Washington wrote the first report of the assassination of Abraham Lincoln.

His 12 simple words symbolized the discovery of a theretofore unknown form in mass communication—the modern news story lead—and marked the opening of a new era in American journalism.

The printing press long since had been invented and a century earlier newspapers had displaced the town crier in the Colonies. These journals conveyed some intelligence but the nub of the news usually was smothered in the texts of proclamations and partisan essays of that period.

Two events reshaped the structure of news stories into an enduring mold—the invention of the telegraph and the outbreak of the Civil War.

On May 24, 1844, Samuel Morse sent his famous message, "What hath God wrought?" from Washington to Baltimore. Slowly at first, then swiftly, a network of wires spread over the nation.

Ft. Sumter fell on April 16, 1861. As the great conflict raged from Bull Run through Gettysburg to Appomattox, newspapers sent their best reporters to Washington, Richmond and the battlefronts. Never before had so many hungered for and desperately demanded tidings which only the press could provide.

Frequently the telegraph lines broke or were broken down. Driven to despair by interruptions in transmission and delays in battle reports, editors ordered their correspondents to pen the vital facts—the gist or pith of a story—in the opening lines.

The result was revolutionary. In style the dispatches continued to follow the pattern of good prose in any form, but in structure they de-

83

parted from all other kinds of composition. Today's news story is arranged like nothing else in the literary world.

A personal letter may ramble from spring fever to the price of potatoes without a particular plan or purpose. A speech or a sermon usually deals with successive topics, clinched with a closing summary. A narrative, novel or play begins at the beginning, often with a description of the background or a minor scene. It ends when or quickly after the climax is reached.

On the contrary, the standard news story of today—one intended to convey urgent information rather than to entertain the reader—starts with the most important fact or facts. Details follow in order of diminishing importance.

Exactly as his predecessor reported the death of Lincoln on April 14, 1865, so another AP man, on April 12, 1945—80 years later—started a momentous story with six simple words: "President Roosevelt died suddenly this afternoon."

A hundred years from now reporters of the future still will be writing history on the wing in the same forthright, time-tested fashion.

WHY THE FORTHRIGHT LEAD?

The telegraph, as we have seen, strongly influenced the change in news story structure as have all the more modern methods of news transmission, reception and processing for publication.

Newspapers are going to press at all hours of the day and night. There may be time to get into type only the opening paragraph of a story— the bulletin. If it fails to include the salient point it is worthless. In wire news that point might miss hundreds of editions.

The same time-arrangement relation applies to local news. As the clock shows a deadline coming up the city desk cannot wait for each story in every typewriter to be completed. Only the first part may get into print. In it must be the core of the copy.

Stories flood the copy desk as press time nears. They must be assessed quickly, edited rapidly. As fresh ones crowd in, those already written may be trimmed down. This customarily is done by lopping paragraphs off from the bottom up.

The makeup man, also in a hurry, needs to choose swiftly what goes into his available space and what is to be omitted. In the hurly-burly of the composing room he may shorten a story from ten paragraphs to five and then order the tail end jerked to avoid an awkward jump.

None of these processors would ever get his job done right if he had to wade through a welter of words to find the essence of a story. He assumes that it is in the opening sentences and the writer must see to it that this is so.

Now consider the readers. The existence of a newspaper depends on circulation and advertising. To win readers it must display its highly perishable product—news—in as many and as attractive packages as possible. Most readers devote but a scant half hour or so to the daily diary of events. Few have time to peruse a whole paper leisurely. Thousands scan it over breakfast coffee, going to and from work, and in the moments between dinner dishes and the children's bedtime.

Hence every word, headline and picture is prepared and placed with a view to quick comprehension by busy people. Each one must be able to glance from story to story, reading as much or as little of each as he likes but always gathering the gist of it from the first few lines.

After all, news telling in this manner is natural. A man telling an anecdote he heard at work withholds the gag line to the last and his wife, recounting her day's doings, may move chronologically or topically from one thing to the next. But either of them as a bearer of spot news blurts it out: "I got the job." "We won." "John is dead."

THE PYRAMID—UPRIGHT AND INVERTED

We have been careful so far to limit our discussion to reports of pressing interest—news of a single salient happening that cannot wait. It must be told instantly in the briefest possible way. But presidents do not die every day and every lead sentence cannot be a crisp and cryptic message exploded like a nuclear bomb flash into the reader's eyes.

Some stories of a more routine nature—in fact most of them—must incorporate more than one bare name and fact in the lead in order to make it intelligible. Still others call for openers of a wholly different kind, dependent upon the predetermined structure of the article as a whole.

Generally speaking, as we have said, the orthodox news story starts with the climax. Like a good swimmer, the writer does not wade cautiously into shallow water but dives headfirst into the deepest part of the pool. Or, like a bridge player, he tosses out his highest trump first, letting the cards fall in order of decreasing value, saving discards to the last. The end of his story is the part which can be rubbed out with the least regret.

Look at the two pyramids or triangles in the first chart in this chapter, one upright, the other inverted, and you will see the contrast in the frameworks of fiction and the conventional news story.

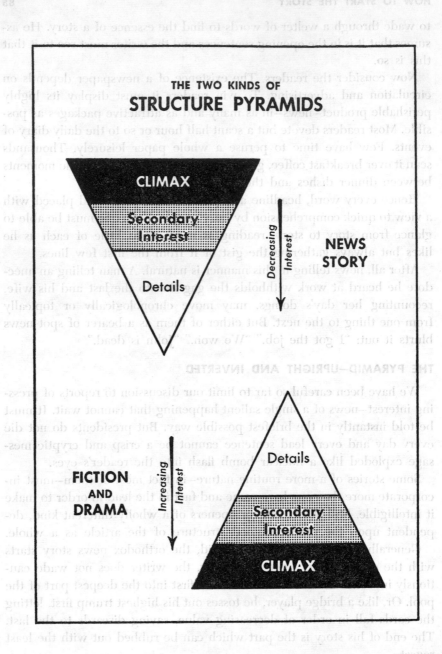

THE TWO KINDS OF
STRUCTURE PYRAMIDS

CLIMAX

Secondary Interest

Details

Decreasing Interest

NEWS STORY

Details

Increasing Interest

FICTION AND DRAMA

Secondary Interest

CLIMAX

Inverted and Upright Construction

Four out of five stories faithfully follow the form of the upside-down triangle but the fifth tips it topsy-turvy. The right-side-up variations seldom are of great consequence and usually but not always are brief and strong in human interest. Many of them start with an attention-getting lead aimed to entice the reader down to a surprise finish.

You will recall the unorthodox opening suggested for the tale about Fuzzy, the cat. The city editor said: "Start it, 'This is a tale about a cat without a tail . . .' Go on from there." Here is another example of a human interest yarn in the same class:

> A nickel doesn't go far any more, so they say. The five-cent cigar and cup of coffee have long since gone the way of the stagecoach and bustles. But wait a minute . . .
>
> A small boy with patched pants and holes in his shoes was almost unnoticed in the jostling crowd bidding on unclaimed articles today at Midland police headquarters. Bicycles were on the block. The auctioneer wheeled up a beauty—new tires, fancy seat, siren, taillight—everything.
>
> The boy, whose name nobody asked, had squeezed to the front. Unable to conceal his admiration, he shouted: "I bid five cents!" Then he backed away sheepishly, trying to hide his shame.
>
> Silence.
>
> Not a voice was lifted. No more bids. And the kid got the bike by spending his entire fortune—one worn nickel.

Here is a shorter one with a suspended interest arrangement:

> Peace reigns again in the Fair Oaks section of Crestwood.
>
> Judge J. B. McKinley in Municipal Court yesterday settled a dispute between two families of neighbors—the Frank Martins and the C. A. Johnsons living next door to each other in the 1400 block on Birch St.
>
> He persuaded the Martins to keep their children out of the Johnson garden. At the same time the Johnsons promised to get rid of the new plants they had set out—poison ivy.

These are examples of good storytelling as against fast storytelling. There is little news of significance in the bike and ivy incidents and the narrative-anecdote form is appropriate and effective. Primarily the newspaper has important facts to present, but secondarily it has human interest material with the personal touch which enables the writer to tip over the triangle.

We will deal with novel news leads, human interest and suspended interest more fully in later chapters. For the present let us keep in mind that these are exceptions to routine and return to the problem of starting a serious story.

DIGGING OUT THE LEAD

You have reached the nub of news reporting when you first try mentally to locate, mold and then maneuver into position the main point you decide should start page one of your copy.

Afield on an assignment a reporter gropes constantly for a fact or feature, or a combination, that will be suitable for a lead. After he has the data he faces the task of converting it into a brisk beginning. Sometimes he hits upon it at once. More often he evolves it after intense thought. He ponders, chooses, revises, discards and tightens until finally the pieces fall into place and he can visualize his initial sentences in print.

Here, for example, are certain facts which Reporter Lawrence Lovelace of the *Times* has assembled, preliminary to grouping into a well-organized story:

> A meeting was held this noon at the Chamber of Commerce at which a number of civic improvements were discussed.
>
> President R. E. Johnson presided.
>
> Mayor Nelson was the principal speaker. He talked about the future of Midland as a music center with its two schools, the Academy of Fine Arts and the Midland College of Music. "The city has decided," he said, "to build a new opera house if the businessmen will subscribe $300,000 to pay for half of it." He stressed the demand of Midland people for good music.
>
> The opera house will cost $600,000.
>
> Members of the Chamber responded readily.
>
> President Johnson assured the Mayor the organization would cooperate and $96,000 was pledged when cards were passed around.
>
> Nelson pointed out that his administration is sponsoring an important street paving and park program. Island Park is the best in the state, he said.
>
> The new opera house will be located at the southeast corner of Main and 10th Sts.
>
> The opera house will be large enough for 3,000 people.
>
> At the close of the meeting, President Johnson announced plans for next Saturday night's social. All members are invited to bring their wives, he said. Tickets are $2.50 each.

Through this jumble of data Lovelace searches to find the facts of most concern to the citizens of Midland. By elimination he singles out the following:

1. Meeting of Chamber of Commerce today.
2. Mayor Nelson spoke on civic improvements.
3. Midland people are music lovers.
4. Midland will erect a new opera house.

5. The city will pay $300,000 and businessmen $300,000.
6. The building will be at the southeast corner of Main and 10th Sts.
7. Its capacity will be 3,000 persons.
8. Chamber of Commerce social Saturday night.
9. Tickets to the social are $2.50 each.

The lead already shouts for attention. It is No. 4 and this is how Lovelace started it:

Plans for a new $600,000 opera house, to be erected at the southeast corner of Main and 10th Sts., were announced yesterday by Mayor Nelson, speaking at a luncheon of the Midland Chamber of Commerce.

When a projected story offers two or three possible approaches—all good—a reporter sometimes seeks the counsel of his superior before deciding on the angle to bring to the fore, but his own judgment ordinarily is accepted by the city desk.

ANOTHER LEAD EXPERIMENT

No magic wand for detecting the story lead is available to the apprentice. If there were no puzzling problem of selection there would be little sport and less work in discovering and arranging news for publication. Consider this raw material gathered by an energetic investigator on the trail of a story:

Two automobiles pile up in a ditch on the Lincoln Highway, two miles west of Midland.
Both machines are partly wrecked.
Mr. and Mrs. E. R. Stevens occupied the first car, and Albert Nixon the second. All live in Midland.
As Nixon sped by the Stevens car a small stone flew up from one of his tires and struck Stevens in the face.
Stevens swerved and the two machines collided. Mr. and Mrs. Stevens suffered injuries and are in St. Mary's Hospital.

Now observe Edgar Barton, Midland *Times* reporter, as he shuffles the cards and plans his opening play. Briefly he has these facts:

1. Two automobiles were wrecked on Lincoln Highway. (A possible lead.)
2. Mr. and Mrs. Stevens of Midland were injured. (Another possible lead.)
3. Mr. and Mrs. Stevens are in St. Mary's Hospital with broken arms. (A better lead.)
4. A pebble struck Stevens in the face, causing him to lose control of his car. (This is *the* lead.)

Accordingly, Barton shapes the introduction in the following words:

> A tiny pebble, flung from the tire of a speeding automobile, sent two
> persons to the hospital today when the driver of a second car, struck by
> the stone, lost control of his machine.

When no outstanding fact is apparent, the reporter must weigh the
parts of his story and select his lead arbitrarily. Usually, however, his news
sense ferrets it out at once and his problem becomes that of guiding it into
forceful English.

INTRODUCING THE FIVE W'S

A copy boy at the Midland *Times*, Paul Parker, wore a worried look
as he came in from the first tryout assignment given to him by Day City
Editor Baxter. He fumbled through a handful of notes, typed and threw
into the wastebasket several pieces of copy, and from time to time glanced
nervously at the clock. Leo Burke, a rewrite man, noted Paul's distress.
He stepped over to the beginner's desk and asked: "Having trouble?"

"If I could just get started . . ." replied Parker, hesitatingly.

Burke picked up the notes and quickly underlined several of them.
"Here," he said, "is the story. Now go ahead and shoot the works in your
first paragraph."

Shoot the works, spill the beans, all at once. What Burke meant was for
Parker to write a summary or digest lead. Had he elaborated on this
advice he probably would have added: "Answer the *W's*—*Who? What?
When? Where?* and *Why?*" Once more his suggestion would have been
sound, for the formula is successfully applied by reporters everywhere.

The *What?* in the traditional five *W's* may refer either to an occurrence
or an object, so sometimes an *H* for *How?* is added. In this case *What?*
refers to a happening itself and *How?* to how it happened.

The straightaway summary lead is the simplest, safest and most widely
used of all the openers. In pure form it attempts to answer the *W's*, thus:

> Governor Paulson (*Who*) announced today (*When*) that he will ask the
> legislature for a $60,000 appropriation (*What*) to build a new dome on
> the State Administration Building (*Why*) in Midland (*Where*).

> Three persons (*Who*) were killed and nine injured last night (*When*)
> an S&M freight train crashed into a speeding Overland Line bus (*What*)
> at the Bay Route crossing three miles southwest of the city (*Where*). A
> faulty signal caused the crash (*Why*).

> Roberta Small, 13 years old, of Green Forest, and Harry Sanford, 12, of
> Meadville (*Who*), were chosen as the healthiest girl and boy in the Timber

AN EXAMPLE OF
THE FIVE-W FORMULA

THE FACTS

WHO? . . . William Dix, attorney,
381 Cedar St.

HAT? . . . was fatally injured.

HEN? . . . today.

HERE? . . . at Main and 17th Sts.

HY? . . . . his automobile struck a bus.

THE LEAD

William Dix, an attorney, of 381 Cedar
St., was fatally injured today when his
automobile crashed into a bus at Main
and 17th Sts.

How to Compose a Summary Lead

County schools (*What*) as a result of examinations (*Why*) concluded here (*Where*) today (*When*).

Mrs. Myron Bloom (*Who*) had five stitches (*What*) in her hand (*Where*) today (*When*) because her 3-year-old son put a pair of scissors in his back pocket for protection (*Why*).

How? replaces *Why?* when the method instead of the reason for the action seems of greater interest, as in this example:

Midland's champion golfer, Dr. E. S. Bryant (*Who*), sinking a 14-foot putt on the last hole (*How*), defeated Richard Marks of Southfield (*What*), in the finals of the Tri-City Tournament at Larchmont (*Where*) this afternoon (*When*).

Again the summary lead may answer both the *Why?* and *How?* thus:

Mrs. John Bascomb (*Who*) won first prize (*What*) here (*Where*) today (*When*) for her description of "My Most Useful Household Gadget" in a newspaper contest (*How*). She described her husband (*Why*).

IDENTIFICATION IS NECESSARY

Three of the *W's*—*Who? Where?* and *What?*—serve to identify persons, places and things or events. These identifications must be made at once either in the lead paragraph or quickly thereafter.

Persons are identified most simply by name and address. Age, occupation, title—former or current, relationship, reputation, achievement and connection with the news are given if pertinent to the story. In death, accident and crime stories and those about children age almost invariably is included, but not in other accounts such as those of a wedding or business deal. Title or position is important to attribution, that is, when a statement needs to be attributed to an authority. Relationship, reputation or achievement may be cited to explain why a person is newsworthy.

Adequate personal identification not only shows the reader immediately who's who in a story but is a vital safeguard against trouble, if not defamation, caused by name similarity.

Places are usually identified by street address or, if distant, with relation to better-known geographical names or identification with previous news events. Thus Oakton is placed in Clay County, 32 miles south of Junction City, the better-known place, while Liberty Island is described as the site of the Statue of Liberty.

Things are identified by citing the quality which gives them prominence, thus: "the Star of Hope, a famous diamond." Events are identified

so as to refresh the reader's memory about something that happened before. An example: "Screen Star Betty Breathtaker, who vowed after her
third divorce she was through with love forever, was married . . ."

Sometimes words, as in the names of organizations, need identification
beyond their names. In writing of the Soroptimist Club, as an illustration,
it is best to say that it is a group of women business executives. Half your
readers may not know what you mean if you write *nom de plume*. Either
explain it or choose the simpler term, *pen name*.

A problem for the reporter or rewrite man is how to get into the fore
part of his story just enough identification to introduce his cast and set
the scenery without unduly delaying the stage action.

If only one or two persons are involved they sometimes can be identified in the first sentence, but it usually is best to work more extensive
identifying data into the second paragraph or summarize it in 1–2–3
order. In any event it should not be fed in bit by bit throughout the
story at places where it is irrelevant to the exposition, action or narration.

PUTTING YOUR BEST W FORWARD

In a conventional summary lead the five *W's* adjust themselves in the
order indicated, like this:

> William Kennedy, a painter (*Who*), died (*What*) at his home, 54
> Oak St. (*Where*), early today (*When*) from injuries caused by a fall
> from a ladder three weeks ago (*Why*).

Clear, accurate and easy to write, this normal arrangement of the
W's nevertheless calls for quick realignment when one of the group
carries more punch than the others. A writer may succeed in devising a
fine five-point lead—technically speaking—and yet fumble the main
idea, the news itself. The important question should be answered first—
simply and emphatically—and this can be done by intelligent evaluation
of the *W's* before the reporter starts to write.

Note the arrangement of the *W's* in these specimens:

1. *The Name—Who?*

President Wrightman announced today that he will attend the Centralia State Fair at Capital City during a 10-day precampaign tour starting
next Monday. He will speak at the Coliseum the night of Oct. 17.

A former heavyweight boxing contender, *Charles (Bruiser) Norris,*
ruefully admitted in court yesterday that his 100-pound wife, suing for
separation, routed him from home with a hairbrush.

2. The Thing—What?

A pair of tortoise-shell glasses, dropped in the doorway, today furnished the police with a single clue to the murder of Edward Godfrey, wealthy coal dealer, in his office at 417 Douglas Ave., two days ago.

A black powder bomb, tossed into a basement window, wrecked the plant of the Sno-Wite Cleaning and Dyeing Co., 521 Bates St., at 1 a.m. today. Windows were shattered three blocks away. No one was injured.

3. The Time—When?

With one minute left to play, Midland College defeated St. Anthony's University by a score of 13–7 in the opening game of the Centralia Conference Football League yesterday afternoon.

Yesterday, for the first time in 28 years, the mercury rose to 100 degrees, causing seven prostrations from the heat.

4. The Place—Where?

Atop a flagpole 600 feet above Grand Ave., a daring steeple jack today untangled the Columbia Building flag which had been knotted by the wind, while 1,500 spectators blocked traffic to watch the performance.

Trapped a thousand feet below the ground, three miners were entombed in the shaft of the Pittston Coal Co. mine this morning after the explosion of a pocket of coal gas.

5. The Cause—Why?

Humiliated when her mother scolded her in the presence of her boy friend, Alma Parsons, 16, screamed and jumped from the third-story window of the Parsons home at 16 Hayes Ave. this morning. She died an hour later at St. Mary's Hospital.

Failure of a switchman to set a red signal caused a derailment of a Mid-Continent passenger train at Plymouth Junction, 14 miles south of Midland, today, resulting in minor injuries to 12 passengers.

6. The Circumstances—How?

Masquerading as a meter reader, a holdup man was admitted to the home of Dr. and Mrs. Lewis H. Holloway, 1221 Adams Ave., today and ransacked the house, taking jewelry valued at $3,000.

A teakettle boiling over and extinguishing a gas flame in her stove caused the death yesterday of Mrs. Walter Wentworth, 638 Maple St.

RHETORICAL DEVICES IN LEADS

Although usually unaware of it, the practiced news writer takes advantage of several grammatical tricks in order to add force or dramatic effect to a summary lead. Some of the most common variations are:

1. *Participial Phrase*

Digging his way through a stone wall with a soup spoon . . .

Returning from their adventure in Antarctica, 12 members . . .

2. *Prepositional Phrase*

In an effort to set a new altitude record, two fliers . . .

With a roar heard for five miles around, a bomb . . .

3. *Noun Clause*

How a police dog saved the life of its master was revealed . . .

That the Senate will adjourn at midnight seemed assured . . .

4. *Infinitive Phrase*

To win back his wife's affection, Frank Burroughs stole . . .

To talk 145 hours without a stop was the feat accomplished by . . .

5. *Absolute Construction*

Alone and unarmed, Albert Wilson, a tailor, thwarted three bandits who . . .

Exhausted after winging its way across three states, a carrier pigeon . . .

Probably not one newsman in five can explain offhand the difference between an infinitive and a participle, but he makes use of these parts of speech every day as he writes. Certainly he never deliberately decides to fashion, say, an adverbial clause. He knows when a lead is good or faulty by its *feel*, by the way it reads.

You, as an apprentice, also can acquire the ability to feel the tightness and rightness of a lead sentence without consulting a grammar. But you must do it by writing and rewriting and writing again. Once you have drilled sufficiently to compose summary leads with ease you are well on the way toward skill and speed in writing long and difficult news stories.

DON'T OVERLOAD THE WASHLINE

Any useful device used over and over again—a clothesline, for example—sometimes is loaded to the breaking point. You can put into a summary lead such a long row of detailed W's that the line sags into the mud.

One of the most important reforms in news writing of recent times—a reform long overdue and all to the good—came about largely as a result of summary lead abuse. Writers tended to hang among their shirt-and-skirt facts too many sock-and-handkerchief items dangled from clothes-pin commas and semicolons. Some leads tried to take into the trial of an antitrust suit everything from the secretary's elopement with the book-keeper down to the installment due on a payroll tax. The effect was ridiculous.

The tabloids and the radio hit pay dirt by rediscovering the secret of the AP man who wrote the Lincoln dispatch—simple, streamlined sentences with little if any internal punctuation. The movement spread into newspapers everywhere, and the length of the average lead shrank from 40 to 50 words to 20 to 30.

However, you can still find in print such exhaustive—and exhausting —first sentences as this:

> United States Congressmen James Simpson, Charles S. Duncan and H. H. Wilkinson spoke last night at the 10th Infantry Armory, Center St. and Broadway, before a crowd of 3,000 persons who jammed the hall to capacity in behalf of pending federal legislation designed to extend the St. Lawrence and Lakes-to-Gulf Seaway and thereby help solve the farm surplus problem and stimulate prosperity in the Midwest.

More than 60 words! If you read them aloud you run out of breath. Let's reduce the size of this overstuffed monstrosity by trimming off the fat:

> Three congressmen, speaking from the same platform here last night, urged immediate extension of the inland seaway system by the federal government.

You can avoid overcrowding by the simple expedient of counting words and lines. When you reach the fourth line on your typewriter—stop, look and see if you can find a place for a period. If not, back up and start again. It is a rare lead that is improved by writing beyond 30 words.

Periods are beautiful things when they end a statement that says something, but that something should, if possible, bring the essence of the story to a quick focus. Here is an orthodox but somewhat cumbersome and unimaginative summary lead:

> Described as a member of an international ring, Lester Spiegel, 31-year-old native of Austria, was taken into custody by customs officials here yesterday on a charge of trying to smuggle into the country $100,000 worth of diamonds hidden in the heels of his shoes.

A better writer started the same story this way:

> A man whose heels were too high walked into trouble yesterday at the customhouse.

Note again the fore parts of two more stories written from the same set of facts:

POOR

More than a score of drivers for the Midland Taxicab Co. attacked John Williams, 30, of 1905 Seward St., and E. B. Lasson, 43, of 317 Bay Rd., at Peters and Elm Sts., at 11 a.m. today at the climax of a series of street fights marking the third day of the taxicab strike which has kept police busy with clashes between strikebreakers and pickets . . . . .

BETTER

Violence flared in the taxicab strike today when bands of pickets forced strikebreakers from their cabs and fought with the drivers.

The battling reached a climax when 20 Midland Taxicab Co. drivers attacked the operators of two Green cabs at Peters and Elm Sts.

The Green cabmen, John Williams and . . . . .

The better versions of the stories we have cited, of course, leave the details of the *W's* to the second and later paragraphs, which sustain the lead and link into the body of the article. But before we study structure we will, in the next chapter, delve deeper into variations of the all-important lead.

SHOP TALK

1. Draw on the blackboard and discuss the upright and inverted pyramid diagrams to show the contrast between the structure of a news story and that of a play or fiction narrative.
2. Read a "short, short story" and show how it would be rearranged in news form.
3. Analyze several five-W leads to see if the answer to the most interesting W has been given the place of honor in the sentence.
4. Find and criticize several overloaded summary lead sentences.
5. Show how you would improve these leads.

CHAPTER **8**

Novelty in News Leads

CATCHING THE READER'S EYE

" 'Damn!' said the Duchess, as she lit her cigar." The Eton schoolboy who thus started a story, said Edith Wharton, would have achieved literary immortality had the rest of the tale lived up to its opening. As Robert Louis Stevenson put it, he had produced a "peg" on which a reader could "hang his imagination."

The news writer with a feature-type story on his hands often tries to achieve the same effect—to grasp the attention of his readers with a pungent and provocative lead. Unlike the Eton lad, however, he must make the rest of the story back up the beginning.

A newspaper may be compared to a restaurant menu. It would be unappetizing if it offered only meat and potatoes served on the same plate and never a cocktail, soup, salad or dessert. The five W's furnish an old and time-tested recipe for chefs in the news kitchen. There is no substitute for facts—the solid food on the newspaper bill of fare—but there is plenty of room, too, for taste-tempting appetizers which please the palate of the customer and prompt him to read more.

A summary lead need not always consist of a name (*Who*), and action (*What*), a time (*When*), a place (*Where*) and a reason (*Why*). It often can be improved by variation. Nor need the news writer confine himself to any such rigid recipe. For stories motivated by oddity, emotions and suspense rather than prominence or consequence he should without hesitation bypass the W's and mix a cocktail opener.

Let us see how some of the more popular ones are compounded and sample several as served by experienced writers.

THE W'S IN NEW FORMS

The weather—news of almost universal interest—can well be used to show the flexibility to be found within the framework of the summary lead. In weather reports at times, especially if human life is lost or imperiled, the consequence element is so overwhelmingly strong that the W's are not to be tampered with. Fatalities compel the writer to forgo fancy phrases and remain conventional, as in this example:

> Three persons were killed and at least 20 injured as a 100-mile-an-hour tornado struck near Booneville last night and whipped with savage fury across southeastern Centralia.

Now assume that the consequence element is less impelling, the weather is merely seasonal—hot or cold—and observe how versatile writers handle their leads:

COLDER

> Button up your overcoat and hit that coal pile again! Much colder weather for today was predicted last night by Weatherman Robert M. Bennett.

> Freezing temperatures today should drive off the springlike atmosphere which has fooled the buds and birds this week, according to the charts of R. M. Bennett, head of the Weather Bureau.

> Pour in the antifreeze, stoke up the furnace, shake out the moth balls— the first freeze of the season is forecast for the suburbs tonight.

> Old Man Winter sneaked out from behind an ill wind today and tossed big damp snowflakes over Midland in a chilly reminder that it's the first day of Novemberrr!

HOTTER

> Midland will swelter again today in the grip of a week-long heat wave which now is threatening gardens and crops throughout the state.

> A bubbling thermometer boiled up to 96 degrees yesterday, baking the city and driving thousands to beaches, parks and rural resorts to cool off.

> Today's sun, shooting the thermometer up to a June 10 record of 103 at 1 p.m., claimed the first heat prostration victim of the year.

> A merciless sun beat down on the parched prairies of the Midwest states yesterday with no prospect of relief for the drought-stricken areas in sight.

Swinging a first sentence around a holiday motif is another way to lighten a summary weather lead:

> There was wading instead of parading yesterday as a chill, drenching rain transformed Midland's traditional Easter Parade into an endurance

test for those hardy souls who wanted to show off the latest thing in umbrellas.

Pack up your picnic baskets, folks, for the weatherman has blinked his eyes, scowled at the sky and pulled a great big handful of fine weather out of the bag for the Memorial Day weekend.

If Santa Claus fails to arrive today, you'll know the old boy was so befuddled by the weather that he went back to the North Pole to wait for winter.

A LIST OF LEAD VARIETIES

Any attempt to ticket types or classes of news leads is necessarily academic and arbitrary, for originality is what makes them most attractive. They are as diverse as the men and women who invent them.

An effort is made here to sort out, classify and label a few of these storytelling devices so that some, at least, will stick in the mind of the beginner until they become habitually used tools. However, don't expect to find authors or professors in agreement on a standard list or to hear their labels spoken in a newspaper office. You probably won't.

It would be accidental if a city editor told you to write a "picture lead" or a "quotation lead"—two of the lead names used in this text. He is more likely to say: "How did it look down there, Joe? Kick it off with a little more color," or "Bring that quote up to the top." If he still doesn't like your product he may merely toss it to a rewrite man with the order: "We're leading page one with this piece. Steam it up."

Picture and quotation nevertheless are legitimate classifications in which we will try to pocket several types of openers. We will tab and define them as follows:

Punch—A brief, arresting epigram.
Picture—A colorful word sketch.
Contrast—Two opposite extremes.
Question—A pertinent query.
Background—The setting or surrounding circumstances.
Quotation—A succinct remark or statement.

In order to give us a catchall category, we will add one more to the list—the freak lead—and define it as a unique opener of any kind—an oddity.

PITCHING A PUNCH LEAD

Phineas T. Barnum once said: "The American public likes to be fooled." And as that great showman proved, it also likes to be surprised and

EIGHT TYPES OF
NEWS LEADS

1. SUMMARY

Twenty-eight passengers and a crew of four were killed last night when a four-motored CH-3 Centralia Airliner crashed and burned in a soggy cornfield 24 miles south of Midland.

2. PUNCH

A mouse put out all the lights in Crestwood last night—and a baby mouse at that. It crawled into the switchboard at the Crestwood Power Co. plant.

3. PICTURE

Smeared with mud, wet and chilled, 12-year-old Robert Forbes today told police about a 300-mile ride on the spare tire of an overland moving van.

4. CONTRAST

Members of Phi Beta Kappa can recall the seven turns in the River Styx and know the number of curls in an acanthus leaf. But they can't remember where they lost their PBK keys.

5. QUESTION

Have you paid your income tax yet? No?

Then you'd better hurry, for tomorrow will be too late to avoid a penalty. But all returns postmarked before midnight tonight will be under the wire, Peter F. Winston, internal revenue collector, promised today.

6. BACKGROUND . .

Dimly lit recesses in historic old St. John's Church hallowed by the pious worship of a half dozen generations echoed yesterday with angry cries of "Sit down!" climaxed by a threat to call the police.

7. QUOTATION

"I've lost my train—it's headed your way!" the engineer shouted into a telephone after his streamliner started rumbling backward down a seven-mile hill with no one in the cab.

8. FREAK

By law abide
Put trash inside.

Oscar B. Antrim, street department superintendent, poised his pencil today over this couplet being painted on the city's waste cans. Scratch—scratch—scratch—scratch—scratch. One word, *trash*, remained. "That's enough," he remarked wryly.

A Directory of Openers

shocked. Startle the reader in the first line and you may be sure he will go on to the next. It can be done with a so-called punch or cartridge lead which sends a single, isolated declaration straight to the bull's-eye —without reservation or explanation. Typical samples follow:

There's no place like home—for accidents—the Midland Safety Council reported yesterday.

Johnny Jessup gulped as he ate his seventh pie.
"I—I guess that'll do for a while," he said, as his friends crowded up to congratulate the new champion pie-eater of Timber County.

Found: John Doe, in person, by Municipal Judge O. R. Lane. He was brought into court today for failing to shovel snow from his sidewalks.

Cold weather cramps Cupid's activities. More girls between 14 and 24 years of age living in warm climates get married than girls of the same age in colder cities, a survey by Midland College students revealed today.

The housewife of today can prepare a meal in one-fifth the time it took her mother 25 years ago.

When you sit down to dinner tonight, there will be 50 more people in Midland than when you had your breakfast.

Here's more proof that you can't win.
Although more than half of them are accused of committing murder for profit, the prison bank accounts of seven men and one woman in death cells at the State Prison average only $4.46 each.

Friday the 13th is over but the casualty list still is growing.
Possibly the jinx's most extensive victory was the attack on the marriage license bureau where applications dropped to zero.

It should be remembered that the sentences immediately following the short opener must sustain the initial declaration and not wander off to other matters once the reader has been induced to scan the story. Clever tricks to get attention—in direct opposition to the news content of stories—are not countenanced by the copy desk.

SKETCHING A PICTURE LEAD

A vivid word picture of the chief actor in a news situation brings prompt reader response and provides an easy approach through the visual. Allow the reader to see a man as you saw him, to view a scene as it unrolled before your eyes, and you make him an intent witness to the performance as pictured in print. Women especially react to the realistic challenge of faces, behavior and costume in leads like the following:

Miss Mary Louise Vaughan, black-eyed, 21, and svelte-looking as a fashion advertisement, will cast her first vote next Tuesday—for herself.

Winsome Wanda Worthington, a modest blonde miss from Center High School, is the champion figure skater of the state. This Midland knew. But last night in Memorial Stadium she captivated a capacity crowd and gave them living proof of her graceful ability.

A bullet-punctured volume of drawings made in 1872 by a Sioux Indian chief while a prisoner at Ft. Monroe has been acquired by the Midland Museum of Natural History.

His eyes half closed and his face an impassive mask of indifference, Harris S. Pell slumped in his chair yesterday as Prosecutor Arthur M. Selby described him as a "heartless killer."

It happened quickly. Incredibly quickly. One instant there are four young people, vibrantly alive, and then there is the shriek of rubber on asphalt, a thunderous crash, metal ripped apart, torn bodies and death.

A 35-year-old woman who lay shivering with a fractured leg for 73 hours in the snow-coated wreckage of an airplane said today she had only pine needles and two mints to eat during her ordeal.

A pretty girl of 19, a willowy, green-eyed redhead, was thrown into a plain old jail cell last night. Who did this? Why, no one else but a big, beautiful, blue-eyed blonde, also 19.

THAT FIRST—THEN THIS!

A circus giant shaking hands with a midget draws from the crowd more "Oh's" and "Ah's" than either of them alone because visual contrast accentuates their sizes, a fact which a news-minded cameraman is quick to recognize when he takes a picture. Similarly, incongruous extremes— old age and youth, poverty and wealth, comedy and tragedy, luck and misfortune—make word pairs which dovetail nicely into a balanced opening sentence. To be effective, the contrast must be sharp and swiftly stated. Examples follow:

Frank Jergen, 56, last week won a safety award for 12 years of driving without an accident. Today his truck ran over and killed a 7-year-old girl.

A week ago Tony Borelli, street cleaner, was just the son of a poor Italian immigrant. Today he was found to be a descendant of a Florentine family of noble blood and the claimant of a fortune.

Ferocious jungle beasts held no terrors for Rudolph Raymond, explorer and big-game hunter. But a playful pup sent him to the hospital today with a chewed leg.

Fifty years ago last night three brothers, Daniel, Walter and Joseph Perry, set out from home to seek their fortunes after agreeing to meet again in exactly half a century. The three, now old men, kept their appointment.

A wedding was to have been held in Bethany Baptist Church yesterday for a couple who had been sweethearts since they were 6. Instead, there will be a funeral for the bride-to-be in the same church tomorrow.

Last week John Wilcox, 25, was the hero of Ferndale. Today he is in jail. His bravery in saving a drowning boy led to his exposure as a fugitive from a Georgia chain gang.

Seven months ago when the L. G. Thorne family moved to Midland they left their collie, Spot, with neighbors in Boston. Today they heard a barking at the front door and in walked Spot.

ASK-AND-ANSWER OPENERS

A question steered into the opening sentence has obvious advantages in arousing interest, but many writers shy away from it on the ground that an interrogation—often unanswered—fails to convey definite information with quick incisiveness. They argue that the reader should be told, not mystified, and that an abrupt query smacks of the witness stand. Such a practice is a rhetorical rather than a natural procedure. For this reason a question lead seldom is advisable except when the problem itself is the crux of the story. Note the following samples:

Will the college professor of tomorrow give way to color television?
Will the campus laboratory of the future be a projection room where talking pictures will do the lecturing?
These are the questions . . . . .

Has a husband the right to slap a wife who bids a small slam without a single face card?
That was the brow-knitting problem confronting Judge Bertrand E. Corrigan in Domestic Relations Court yesterday. He decided in the negative.

What's in a name?
A woman here says she's been embarrassed all her life because her parents gave her a name that belongs to a man—"Bobby."
Hereafter it will be "Billie."

Should men wear wedding rings?

This question was asked of students in marriage classes at Midland College. The girls said yes. . . . .

BACKGROUND IN THE BEGINNING

Frequently the setting of a news incident overshadows the men and women who participate in it—in fact it becomes more interesting than the action itself, which may be negligible. Such a story suggests the use of a background lead. Exhibitions, parades, crowds, festive days lend themselves to picturesque treatment on a larger scale than other stories concerned primarily with the description of a man or woman. Observe how incorporation of colorful atmosphere gives these stories a lively start:

> The National Capital's famous Japanese cherry trees burst into full bloom today and 250,000 men, women and children, nearly half of them out-of-town visitors, trooped to the Tidal Basin to feast their eyes upon the scene of beauty.

> Green bunting fluttered in the breeze and songs of Ireland filled the air as 2,000 sons of old Erin paraded up Main street this afternoon in honor of their patron saint.

> Out of gas, minus a parachute flare and at the mercy of Lady Luck, a steel-nerved pilot made a forced landing in a swirling snowstorm near the Municipal Airport last night without so much as scratching his wings.

> Flashing a dazzling greenish light over half of Clay County, a meteor burned a pathway from the heavens to the earth last night and plunged into Lake Limpid near Oakton.

EYE-CATCHING QUALITY IN QUOTES

Sometimes a succinct remark, a flashing epigram, stands out so boldly from a discourse, an interview or a statement that it deserves to be moved forward into the front rank of the lead.

No amount of writing around the point could improve upon such memorable utterances as:

> "I have just begun to fight."
> "A nation cannot exist half slave and half free."
> "Speak softly and carry a big stick."
> "Never have so few given so much for so many."

Warning should again be issued to the reporter to be sure that the lead quotation, wrenched from its position, is thoroughly buttressed and explained in the body of the story. Like a lawyer introducing testimony, the writer must link it with the case at issue. Generally speaking, a direct quotation is most serviceable when it compresses a point of view into a telling phrase that lends itself to headlines, as in the following instances:

"I could have any one of you murdered for $300," Police Chief Thomas Green told 200 members of the Kiwanis Club at the Hotel Harper yesterday. "Prices of gunmen have come down," he added.

"The Ten Commandments have been outmoded."
With this bold statement the Rev. Lucius Simons startled an audience of clergymen and church workers during a discussion of "Modern Ideals" at the annual meeting yesterday of the 3rd District Missions Society.

"We will now have closing exercises given by the student body." Thus spoke Miss Zell Rogers, principal and teacher of the Fairfield School, 10 miles southwest of Midland. Little 8-year-old Ida Mae Weidman, "the student body," arose and gave two readings while County Superintendent Sloan Baker listened approvingly.

"So I wasn't too late . . ." With these words on his lips, Patrolman Kenneth Stanton, whose heroism saved 7-year-old Grace Barker from death in the Midland Shore Line train wreck Sunday, died early today at Mercy Hospital. They had just told him she would recover.

FREAKS IN THE LEAD FAMILY

Inventive stylists in words produce many uniquely fashioned lead paragraphs that cannot be classified except as freaks. Some of them require unusual typographical effects to enhance their appeal. Struggling to avoid the conventional, writers bid for attention with odd and unique lead constructions such as:

Penelope Creighton to . . .

Arthur S. Trent . . .

For a broken heart . . . $50,000

Her lawyer didn't write it in exactly those words, but that was the substance of a bill sent by the former musical comedy star yesterday to her erstwhile fiancé, heir to the Trent mining millions.

Marie Madison: Please cut short your elopement honeymoon. Your mother is dying.

Out again, in again, gone again—Branigan.
. . . New version of popular old song.
Leaving a zigzag trail which baffled pursuers, Tom Branigan, convicted safebreaker, escaped the third time this morning from the Timber County Penal Farm.

Ho, hum!

Don't get excited, folks. Keep your seats. This is just another rumor that spooks are up to funny business in the old Horseshoe Bend granite quarry. Yes, sir, no foolin' this time. Three Boy Scouts saw 'em last night.

Those redskins out Wyoming way can relax now. A couple of young "Indian fighters" from New York have been pulled off their trail.

Wanted in Clay City: A railroad engine whistle that can be heard 1,000 feet away, but not an inch farther.

Alliterations sometimes help give a lift to a lead, thus:

Good fortune, in the guise of everything from layettes to lollipops, and even an electric refrigerator, engulfed the lately destitute parents of the New Year triplets yesterday.

Rhyme is another device now and then employed for an unusual effect, thus:

Andrew Erskine claimed his wink was just a blink, but it threatened to put him in the clink today.

Dialect may be employed provided it causes no offense to a reader, like this:

Biggest hoss stampede in years had folks running for cover out Bayview Park way yesterday. Durn critters busted out of a corral at the Bar-Q Riding Academy and galloped all over the bridle paths before a posse got 'em.

Tricks with type are rare, but occasionally a lead sentence can be turned upside down or some other novel effect achieved, as in these examples:

A c-c-cold f-f-front nudged Midland's winter heat wave today and dropped the temperature to a low of 38—a plunge of 26 degrees since early last night.

The Midland Rubber Products Co. gave away to 200 employes yesterday fake dollar bills that s-t-r-e-t-c-h l-i-k-e t-h-i-s.

$ammy $mather$, who i$ ju$t $even, wa$ digging in the $and ye$terday at the Lake Luce beach and what do you think he found? Ye$, $ir, $$$$$$$$$$—ten of them—all $ilver dollar$.

CHOOSE YOUR OWN LEAD

Specimens of unconventional leads in this chapter do not by any means cover all possible combinations, nor are they recommended too enthusiastically. Desire for novelty may defeat all the aims of good reporting as a factual medium. To insist that a given story shall take a set type of lead would be to carry the attempt at classification to absurd lengths.

As an experiment let us attempt to apply all the listed forms to a single situation—a session at a murder trial. Some of the following combinations are exaggerated in order to prove the contention that news may flow along many channels to the reader, but observe the wide range of choices open to the writer:

1. *Summary (Who)*

Gloria Lamar, 22-year-old night club entertainer, on trial for the murder of Chester Sands, stockbroker, took the witness stand in her own defense before Judge Henry Dayton and a jury in Circuit Court today.

2. *Summary (What)*

Telling her own story of the Chester Sands slaying of which she is accused, Gloria Lamar, cabaret dancer, today tried to convince a Circuit Court jury of her innocence.

3. *Summary (Where)*

Before a jury of 2 women and 10 men in Circuit Court today, Gloria Lamar, dancer at the Frolics Inn, sobbed out her version of the fatal gunplay leading to the death of her sweetheart, Chester Sands, on July 17. She is charged with his murder.

4. *Summary (When)*

At the climax of her drama-packed trial for the slaying of Chester Sands, Gloria Lamar suddenly was placed in the witness box by her attorney, Lloyd Perkins, at 2 p.m. in Circuit Court today.

5. *Summary (Why)*

In a last-minute effort to slash through a web of evidence woven by the state, Gloria Lamar, a witness at her trial for murder, today denied she fired the bullet that killed Chester Sands in his Polk Ave. apartment last July.

6. *Punch*

Darkness . . . a shot . . . a glare of light . . . and Chester Sands lay dead.

That is all Gloria Lamar remembers about the three-minute tragedy that placed her in the shadow of the electric chair as an accused murderess.

7. *Picture*

Dabbing her eyes with a lace handkerchief as she wept out her story in a strained voice, Gloria Lamar, cabaret dancer, described the shooting of her fiancé to a jury in Circuit Court this afternoon.

LEAD EVOLUTION

THE FACTS

Drillers struck oil . . . in a well five miles southeast of Midland
. . . well is a wildcat . . . they summoned owners and lessees . . . then
shot the well . . . petroleum went over the derrick . . . at 3 o'clock
. . . spectators were soaked . . . but they demonstrated pleasure.

ROUGHHEWN

A gusher came in . . . sending oil over the rigging . . . of a wildcat well . . . five miles southeast of Midland . . . at 3 o'clock yesterday afternoon . . . financially interested onlookers danced happily
as they were soaked.

POLISHED

A giant column of oil rose over the rigging of a wildcat well
five miles from Midland at 3 p.m. yesterday while delighted investors danced in the sudden shower of riches.

COMPLETED

A gleaming geyser of oil spouted skyward over the rig of a
wildcat well five miles from Midland at 3 p.m. yesterday while
lucky investors danced in delirium under the rain of riches.

How the Reporter Molds a Lead

8. *Contrast*

Blithe, gay and popular, 22-year-old Gloria Lamar a few weeks ago bowed her thanks to the hand clapping of admirers at the Frolics Inn. But today her audience sat tensely silent as she sobbed out her story of the Chester Sands shooting at her trial for murder.

9. *Question*

Who snapped off the lights ten seconds before Chester Sands was fatally shot?

A jury in the court of Judge Henry Dayton pondered that question late today after Gloria Lamar, charged with the shooting, testified that someone pressed the switch to hide his identity as the killer.

10. *Quotation*

"I didn't shoot him. I loved him. We were going to be married."

With her face half covered by a lacy handkerchief, Gloria Lamar ended a tearful hour of testimony with these words yesterday at her trial for the slaying of Chester Sands, wealthy stock dealer.

11. *Background*

While 200 spectators leaned forward to catch her half-whispered words, golden-haired Gloria Lamar, testifying in her own defense, told a dramatic story of the Chester Sands shooting in Circuit Court today.

12. *Freak*

Glamorous Gloria Lamar played to possibly her last audience today and she played for her life.

Her performance featured the final scene of "The Chester Sands Murder Case," as staged this week in the courtroom of Judge Henry Dayton.

After taking a mental inventory, a trained writer by a process of elimination will discard the lead which does not suit his story and proceed to evolve a plan of development which best pilots the narrative to the mind of the reader.

Despite the dissimilarities among the leads demonstrated, each one clings to the fundamental W's as a basis. Camouflaged, rearranged, the answers to the five summarizing questions in each case are given to the reader before the main body of the story is reached.

No attempt will be made in this chapter to discuss leads for the rebel in the news story family that turns over the inverted triangle and whose behavior upsets the accepted rules of news writing. This rebel is the suspended interest narrative in which disclosure of the surprising feature is purposely withheld until the last paragraph. We will meet it in a later chapter.

SHOP TALK

1. Why are not all stories written with summary leads? Is a newspaper more attractive if the leads vary?
2. Suggest several stories for which each variety of lead outlined in this chapter would be suitable. Can you specify and illustrate any other varieties?
3. Discuss the advantages and shortcomings of picture, question and quotation leads.
4. Choose an ordinary summary lead story and show how the opening paragraph could have been written in several different ways.
5. Why is it necessary for the premise in the lead to be borne out in the body of the story?

CHAPTER 9

The Story Structure

AFTER THE LEAD, WHAT?

With the first facts of his story selected and put into attention-getting words, the news writer may well pause and survey his handiwork with satisfaction.

The most exacting part of the job has been done and finishing it is more a matter of coordination than of creation. It consists of arranging and then writing the remainder of the information at hand in logical and orderly sequence. There are well-worn blueprints to guide him.

In the process of gathering data and taking notes and again of digging out and perfecting a lead the reporter weighs and discards subordinate facts and alternate word patterns. These are likely to become usable as he types the body of his story.

We have compared a reporter to a painter and a chef and later we will liken him to other artisans, for he is one of the fraternity of craftsmen who create in their minds and work with their hands. We now will symbolize him as a sculptor molding a human figure and then as a builder of pyramids.

Either a statue or a pyramid should be formed so that the final product is symmetrical and complete with no essential feature distorted or omitted. If, in the role of a word sculptor, you have fashioned your lead or head of a figure like that of a dainty maiden or a wistful child, you certainly do not plan to spoil it with the torso of a gaunt warrior or a weighty wrestler.

Looking downward from the top, let us next examine the neck of a news statue—the portion of a story connecting the opening statement to the main bulk of copy which follows.

THE LEAD-TO-BODY LINK

The neck, or bridge, segment of a story may be only a few words or a fat paragraph or two. While not always required, it usually serves one of these purposes:

1. To fill in identifications too detailed for the lead.
2. To bring in one or more secondary but significant facts.
3. To attribute the lead statement to authority.
4. To explain one of the W's, usually *Why*.
5. To recapitulate what has gone before.

To illustrate the first point, here is a stripped-down summary lead opener:

> Two Midland High School students were seriously injured today when their speeding sports roadster struck a trailer truck on Highway 77 three miles south of the city.

Further identifications are called for immediately, before the story proceeds:

> George Marks, 17, of 229 E. Hemlock St., suffered a brain concussion and Jay Larkin, 16, of 435 Harding Ave., internal injuries. The truck driver, L. R. Stewart, of Clay City, was unhurt.

Note again how identifications are withheld from the lead but are inserted before the narration starts:

> An unscheduled water excursion by two young Huckleberry Finns ended happily at 2:30 a.m. today when a police launch rescued them from a raft in the Timber River.
>
> The boys, Edward Kemple, 13, of 1731 Hester St., and John Cunningham, 14, of 1602 Maple St., built the raft from logs and old planks. . . . .

The identification link may be extended into a longer list if several persons are killed, injured, invited, honored, elected, arrested or otherwise involved. If lengthy, the list may be set apart under its own headline, thus clearing the way for the writer to reach the body of his story at once.

In the following story the writer properly leads his report, aimed at a big bloc of his readers—the taxpayers—with a résumé of what happened. Going on, he inserts a point of significance to a minority—the teachers:

> In the face of a warning that new taxes must be levied, the City Council voted 8–7 yesterday to boost the pay of 350 teachers in the Midland schools.

The pay raises of $400 a year go into effect Jan. 1.

Mayor Nelson, who opposed the $240,000 appropriation bill, told the Council it will call for money the city does not have. . . . .

Now a punch lead in a lighter vein but requiring attribution to justify its flat assertion:

Curiosity kills few cats but they get into a lot more trouble than dogs.

So says Kenneth King, head of the Midland Humane Society, in his annual report of animal rescues made during the year ended Dec. 31.

"The reason is," King said, "that dogs don't climb trees."

In another example the writer finds that his opening sentence will be unwieldy if he crams into it the full answer to the *Why* or *How*. So he sandwiches in a brief explanation as his second sentence:

For the first time since the series started ten years ago the Blue Sox captured the Intercity pennant today by trouncing Junction City 3–2 before 3,912 fans at Midland Field.

Lifting a homer over the left field stands, Frank Tripp scored the winning run in the last of the ninth.

Already champions of the Valley League, the Sox. . . . .

While it is necessary in a local speech story to say where and before whom the talk was made as a part of the setting, a writer can bring in an awkward prop so that it will serve as a link from lead to body, thus:

On behalf of Midland's children from "6 to 60," Park Commissioner L. B. Turner formally accepted the gift of $25,000 yesterday for a new monkey house at the Island Park zoo.

Speaking to the donors—members of the Midland Zoological Society— at the Ambassador Hotel, Turner said:

"We're all kids while watching the antics of monkeys. . . . .

Still another purpose of a connector is to recapitulate swiftly an earlier chapter in a serial—to bring the reader up-to-date on what has gone before. In this form it is known as the *tie-in* or *tieback*, a segment of a follow-up story to be discussed later.

It should be repeated that not all stories need a special link to merge the start with the main portion of the manuscript. The in-between matter should be used only as a handy device and not as a requirement.

THE PYRAMID IN NEW SHAPES

We switch our symbolism now from statues to pyramids in order better to visualize the structure of the more common types of news stories.

The upside-down pyramid, or triangle, represents the makeup of a standard news story more adequately than any other figure yet devised.

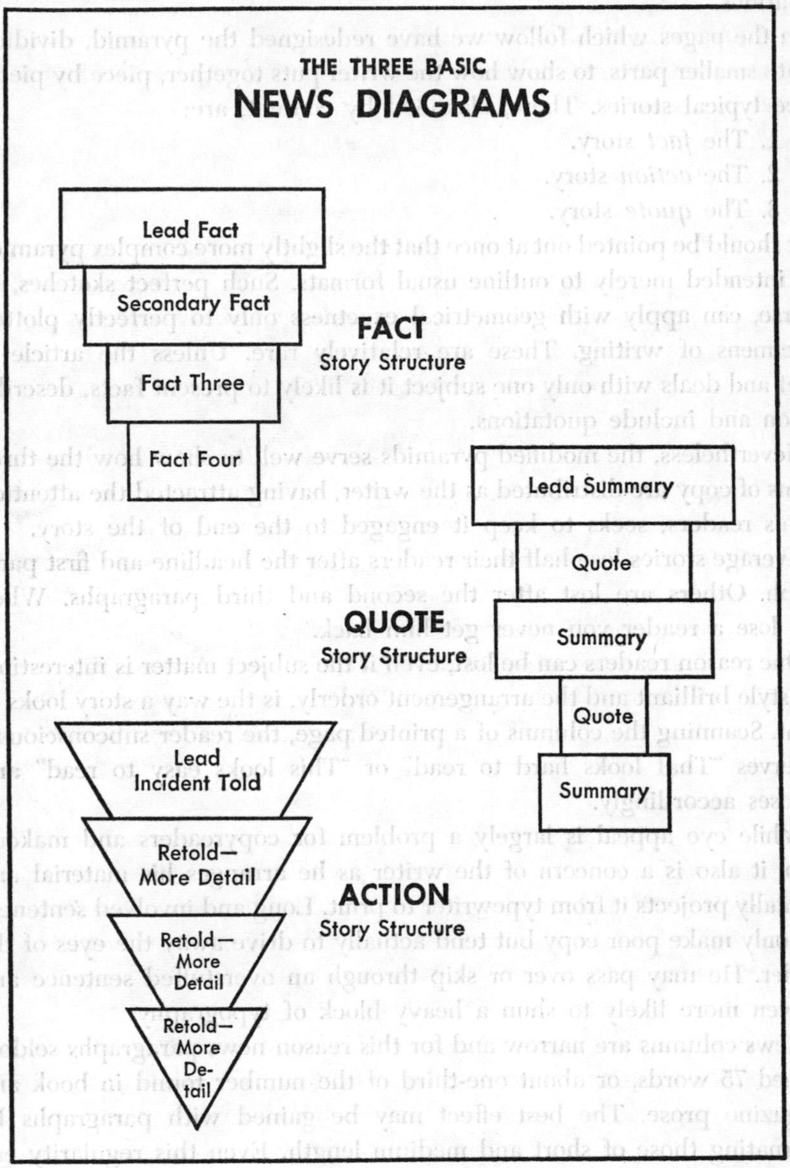

THE THREE BASIC
NEWS DIAGRAMS

Lead Fact

Secondary Fact

FACT
Story Structure

Fact Three

Fact Four

Lead Summary

Quote

QUOTE
Story Structure

Summary

Quote

Lead
Incident Told

Summary

Retold—
More Detail

ACTION
Story Structure

Retold—
More
Detail

Retold—
More
De-
tail

Charts for Three Types of Stories

However, its lines are too straight and its shape too regular to depict variations.

In the pages which follow we have redesigned the pyramid, dividing it into smaller parts, to show how the writer puts together, piece by piece, three typical stories. These, classified by content, are:

1. The *fact* story.
2. The *action* story.
3. The *quote* story.

It should be pointed out at once that the slightly more complex pyramids are intended merely to outline usual formats. Such perfect sketches, of course, can apply with geometrical exactness only to perfectly plotted specimens of writing. These are relatively rare. Unless the article is brief and deals with only one subject it is likely to present facts, describe action and include quotations.

Nevertheless, the modified pyramids serve well to show how the three forms of copy are distributed as the writer, having attracted the attention of his readers, seeks to keep it engaged to the end of the story.

Average stories lose half their readers after the headline and first paragraph. Others are lost after the second and third paragraphs. When you lose a reader you never get him back.

One reason readers can be lost, even if the subject matter is interesting, the style brilliant and the arrangement orderly, is the way a story looks in print. Scanning the columns of a printed page, the reader subconsciously observes "That looks hard to read" or "This looks easy to read" and chooses accordingly.

While eye appeal is largely a problem for copyreaders and makeup men, it also is a concern of the writer as he arranges his material and mentally projects it from typewriter to print. Long and involved sentences not only make poor copy but tend actually to drive away the eyes of the reader. He may pass over or skip through an overstuffed sentence and is even more likely to shun a heavy block of typography.

News columns are narrow and for this reason news paragraphs seldom exceed 75 words, or about one-third of the number found in book and magazine prose. The best effect may be gained with paragraphs by alternating those of short and medium length. Even this regularity can well be broken up by dialogue, tables and summaries, giving graphic variety to conventional makeup.

Each paragraph, if possible, should complete a single thought so that it can be stricken out, revised or replaced without disturbing those above and below.

STRUCTURE OF THE
FACT STORY

LEAD FACT

William O. Kellogg, manager of the Dalton Feed Co., was re-elected to his second term as president of the Timber County Fair Assn. by the board of directors at its 14th annual meeting in the Rex Hotel last night.

FACT TWO

The other officers for next year will be Robert McArthur and F. E. Jonas, vice presidents; Mrs. Martin L. Corning, re-elected secretary; and Horton P. Leroy, treasurer. Frederic S. Sorenson will head the board of directors, with Adam Bernays and B. F. Hinchman as members.

FACT THREE

The total attendance at the fair this year was 167,402, according to a report submitted by Mrs. Corning. This exceeded the attendance of the previous year by 16,291. Receipts were $141,291, of which $10,879 was paid out in prizes.

FACT FOUR

The Timber County racing meet, held in conjunction with the fair, had its most successful season with an attendance of 41,478 during the ten days from Sept. 14 to 24. Its receipts were $72,977, the secretary, F. A. Farwell, reported.

FACT FIVE

Plans for the fair next year call for the addition of a new fruit division to be in charge of Charles Daniels, secretary of the Timber Valley Fruit Growers Assn. An aviation meet with daily stunt flying and races also is to be arranged.

FACT SIX

All the exhibition buildings at the fairground will be renovated and repainted during the summer. A new building will be constructed to house the fruit exhibits.

Application of the Fact Diagram

FITTING THE FACTS TOGETHER

Plain exposition setting forth one fact or a series of related facts and figures conforms closely to the inverted pyramid design. The component parts—fact one, fact two, fact three, and so on—may be likened to rectangles of diminishing length laid brickwise in the order of their importance. Fit the diagram mentally to the following event:

Fact 1

A total of $60,240 was pledged to the Midland Community Chest in the two weeks' subscription drive staged by ten teams of businessmen, Mark E. Warner, chairman of the finance committee, announced today.

Fact 2

A team of five merchants, headed by S. J. Simpson, manager of the Sure-Fit Shoe Co., won first honors with $10,219 signed up in pledges. The physicians' team, with Dr. Lawrence Hill as captain, ran a close second with $9,178.

Fact 3

The subscriptions surpassed those of last year by more than $12,500 and those of the previous year by $14,000, Warner said.

Fact 4

Four Midland organizations engaged in welfare and relief work will share the money equally. They are the Red Cross, the Salvation Army, the Associated Charities, and the United Council for Social Betterment. The latter two groups include many smaller organizations.

There is nothing difficult about charting a fact story such as this one. The key to proper arrangement consists solely in judging the relative value of the data at hand and in grouping it in the order of importance. The composition breaks logically at every paragraph and can easily be cut or lengthened as space requirements dictate.

DIVIDING THE ACTION STORY

Much more difficult to arrange is a narrative of action involving not merely simple facts but also dramatic incidents, descriptions of persons, perhaps testimony of witnesses, as well as explanatory data.

In writing an action story the cub reporter is often tempted to regard his opening as finished when he has fashioned the lead. He proceeds forthwith into a chronological narrative without giving sufficient attention to the elaboration of important information, background and explanation. If the story is to be effective, its units must closely interlock, sometimes at the expense of rapid progress.

STRUCTURE OF THE
ACTION STORY

**LEAD
INCIDENT
TOLD**

Gov. John Paulson was shot to death on the steps of the
State Capitol Building today by Francis Holt, a state employe,
recently dismissed, who is believed to have been crazed by
the loss of his position.

**RETOLD
MORE
DETAIL**

In company with Sen. Glover Young, the Governor had just
stepped from his car when Holt, gun in hand, accosted him.
"You're starving my family," Holt shouted, "and I'll make
you pay for it!"
He fired three shots in quick succession. One bullet pene-
trated the Governor's left temple. He sank to the walk at the
foot of the stairs. Ten minutes later he died without regaining
consciousness. The killer was arrested.

**RETOLD
MORE
DETAIL**

Ordinarily Governor Paulson would have had a bodyguard
with him, but this morning, in his haste to be present at the
opening of a session of the Senate, he drove alone with Senator Young. En route to the capitol, Young said he had mentioned the possibility of trouble because of the recent slashes
in departmental pay rolls . . . .

**RETOLD
MORE
DETAIL**

The Governor had held office two terms. Last April he was
elected by a plurality of 343,000 votes, the largest ever given
a Democratic chief executive in this state. He was inaugurated
March 10. . . . .

OBITUARY

Born in New Jersey, May 4, 1898, John Paulson spent his
boyhood in the East, coming here with his parents, Mr. and
Mrs. Peter Paulson, at the age of 14. He attended school .....

The foregoing specimen follows the tell-retell-retell-again pattern with
precision. The reporter, usually, has additional material which
structure.

Application of the Action Diagram

The question arises: How, then, can a reporter manufacture a coherent narrative and at the same time keep the high lights prominently in the foreground? The answer is that he achieves this by telling the complete story briefly in the lead, then again more fully, and finally with still greater detail. This threefold structure may be diagramed as a series of overlapping triangles. Apply the diagram to the following narrative:

Lead—Incident Told

Leaping from a large sedan which had trailed their victim eight blocks, two men held up Joseph Rickler, cigar store proprietor, in front of his store at 452 Garfield Ave. today, and robbed him of $2,000.

Retold—More Detail

Wearing black masks, the pair leveled guns at Rickler as he stepped into the store with a satchel of currency. One grabbed the satchel, while the other growled: "Keep quiet for ten minutes or we'll be back." They returned to the car and fled.

Two bus drivers who witnessed the holdup thought it was a joke or that a movie was being staged. Then, realizing what had occurred, they flagged a passing car and gave chase, but were outdistanced.

Retold—More Detail

Rickler said he was on his way from the Victory Trust Co. at Broadway and Spruce St. to his cigar store with $1,500 in $10 bills, $250 in $5 bills and $250 in $1 bills. It is his custom, he told police, to have a supply of money on hand to cash pay checks for bus drivers, as his store is adjacent to the Midland Bus Terminal.

"As I neared my store, I noticed the car following me, and hurried to the door," Rickler said. "As I did, the two men jumped out and barred my way. Each had a snub-nosed pistol pointed at my head.

"I was too frightened to shout and I think they would have murdered me if I had resisted. It was all over before I knew what was happening."

The bus drivers, M. C. Bruner and John Tanner, chased the robbers north on Garfield Ave. to 9th St. Police found the sedan abandoned later at 2nd and Walnut Sts.

The foregoing specimen follows the tell-retell-retell-again pattern with precision. The reporter, however, usually has additional material which he must include somewhere along the course followed by the story, but he will find the arrangement here outlined to be workable as a basic structure.

CHOOSING AND MESHING QUOTES

Speeches, statements and letters—and to some extent interviews—may be described from the structural point of view as quote stories. All

STRUCTURE OF THE
QUOTE STORY

LEAD SUMMARY

A million-dollar model housing program for Midland was advocated by Mrs. Frank W. Thalberg, head of the Front Street Settlement House, yesterday noon. Speaking at a luncheon of the Midland Real Estate Board at the Ambassador Hotel, Mrs. Thalberg declared:

QUOTE

"To completely eliminate the firetrap dwellings in the Front street area a long-range building plan requiring at least $1,000,000 would be necessary. A start in that direction should be made without delay. Other cities are going ahead with model housing construction and Midland must not lag."

SUMMARY

The ideal housing unit would consist of three- to five-story apartments, renting for $10 to $12 a room, Mrs. Thalberg said. Each building would be complete with stores and recreational facilities. Families with children would be welcomed as tenants.

QUOTE

"Over a period of 30 years these projects would pay for themselves and become self-sustaining," the speaker continued. "They would have to be financed first by private corporations or a governmental agency."

SUMMARY

The death toll in fires in wooden dwellings in Midland last year was fourteen, Mrs. Thalberg reminded her listeners. Six of the victims were children. All these deaths, she contended, were preventable.

QUOTE

"The Fire Department has done excellent work in the enforcement of the housing laws, but only a permanent construction program will solve the problem," she added.

SUMMARY

The speaker at the next meeting of the Real Estate Board on Jan. 3 will be Harold P. Frink, president of the Frink Realty Corp.

Application of the Quote Diagram

are based on recorded information delivered either in written form or orally and transcribed by the reporter in the form of notes.

A favored structure built for quotable data—diagramed as alternating large and small rectangles of diminishing size—may be classified as the summary-quote-summary-quote arrangement. The chart consists of direct quotations interspersed with and bound together by indirect quotations, paraphrased passages and condensation. A sample follows:

Lead—Summary

Midland is the state's best city in which to rear children, Dr. J. M. McClure, superintendent of schools, declared yesterday before 700 members of the South Side Parent-Teacher Assn. at the Hotel Harper.

Quote

"Our schools rank as high or higher than those of any other community, while our recreational and library facilities are unexcelled," Dr. McClure asserted.

Summary

To maintain its leadership, however, the building program of the public school system must not be curtailed, he said. He urged approval of the proposed $1,500,000 school bond issue at the general election in November.

Quote

"We have two or three old wooden buildings that must be replaced," he explained. "Although they are safe now, in a few years they will approach the danger stage."

Summary

The Superintendent described as especially urgent the construction of a new high school in the Island Park neighborhood. A half million dollars will go for this structure if the bond issue is approved.

Here once more is a comparatively simple method of procedure easily imitated by the beginner who finds himself with several thousand words of direct quotation on his desk and wonders what to do with them. After selecting a lead, his best plan is to underline the most pungent and pertinent statements, lift them out, and arrange and condense them in order to make a strong, cogent structure which hangs together logically and invites rapid reading.

COMBINATION OF THE DIAGRAMS

The fact, action and quote stories, although differing in subject matter, are structurally the same in that each builds information from top to bottom with progressive orderliness, thus:

Fact Story: lead fact; fact one; fact two; fact three.
Action Story: lead narrative; narrative retold; narrative retold.
Quote Story: lead statement; summary-quote; summary-quote.

Frequently a story will contain all three elements: facts, action, quotes. In this event the structural problem becomes more complex, but essentially the same arrangement can be followed with the three kinds of data interwoven, as follows:

Lead

While a thousand shouting men and women fought to get inside, W. C. Lawson, Independent candidate for mayor, charged the city administration with a "million-dollar sellout" to the traction companies at Central Auditorium last night.

Lead-to-Body Sentence

His fiery attack climaxed the whirlwind mayoral campaign which ends at the polls Tuesday.

Action—Narrative Told

Police reserves, summoned to handle the crowd storming the doors of the auditorium, formed a cordon from Main to 7th Sts. at 7 p.m. after 2,500 had already jammed into the building. Despite their efforts, one woman was hurt in the melee. Loud-speakers, hurriedly installed, finally quieted the street disturbance.

Fact—Facts One and Two

Lawson based his "sellout" charge on a report from the Citizens Transit Commission estimating at two million dollars the value of the municipal bus lines signed over to the United Traction companies for one million under the new franchise.

Within 20 years, the report stated, the lines will be worth five million dollars if the city continues its present rate of population growth.

Quote-Summary-Quote

Waving aloft a copy of the report, the Independent candidate assailed the franchise in caustic language.

"They robbed you, and you, and you of a million dollars," he declared. "You are the victims in this monstrous deal and 20 years from now you and your children will still be paying the bill. . . . ."

Presuming that two or three columns of the story have been ordered, the reporter at this point would start his series all over again. Next he would retell the action narrative, explaining how the crowd gathered and what occurred in detail, with identification of the injured woman. Next he might return to the report and cite facts three and four, finally reverting once again to the summary-quote form to recount more of Lawson's speech.

In this fashion the writer has arranged his story with a downward technique, in effect combining three kinds of articles in one. Each section can be diagramed individually.

One of the cardinal principles of an expository writer is to group related ideas together. The news writer can obey this principle in only a limited way. He is compelled to give the main news in his lead. If his story is run-of-the-mine he cannot be certain how much of it will be printed or where it will be cropped. However, if he is writing a major story with ample space assured to him he may and should follow the grouping principle, his groups, rather than single points, coming in the order of diminishing importance.

TRANSITIONS AND CONNECTIVES

As we have built the news story pyramids section by section and brick by brick, it has been necessary to mortar them together with in-between words and phrases. These are called *transitions* or *connectives*.

If we portray a complete story as a train, rather than a statue or pyramid, the component parts are an engine—the lead; various kinds of cars—the facts, incidents and quotes; a caboose—the end. In this analogy the transitions are coupling pins.

Coupling pins are common to all forms of communication, especially the oral media. They are vital to continuity in speeches or radio and television scripts. While not so necessary to newspaper composition, a minimum number are indispensable to carry the reader from thought to thought without jerks and bumps.

A transition implies action. Each one indicates a movement. Here are a few specimens and what they do:

Time

earlier, previously, formerly, now, a new development, nowadays, at the same time, meanwhile, simultaneously, coincident with, while, all this time, next, thereupon, since then, later on, thereafter, on the heels of, soon after, finally.

Cite

as, like, thus, therefore, to show, for example, also, likewise, thereby, as a result of.

Contrast

but, yet, unless, nevertheless, despite, in spite of, otherwise, in contrast to.

Refer

about, as to, regarding, in reference to, in connection with, with relation to.

Localize

locally, nearby, here at home, in this area, closer to home, not far away.

Relate

namely, along with, not only, whereas.

A tendency of the copy desk is to delete transitional words or phrases in order to condense. However, a careful copyreader will not pencil them out blindly, sacrificing in clearness what he gains in space. If the writer has omitted needed transitions, the copyreader should supply them.

One of the dangers in choosing a coupling pin is that it may be editorial. The writer must be wary of any which can be interpreted as giving his own opinion. Among these are *indeed, above all, for this purpose, having this in mind, accordingly, undoubtedly, naturally, maybe, probably, in fact, obviously, clearly, of course.*

So long as he does not editorialize, the writer has a right to use any legitimate literary device to add elasticity to the body of his production and to help make it a logical, progressive development of thought, conducive to easy reading.

THE END OF THE STORY

Unlike any other kind of composition, the standard news story, built like an inverted pyramid, tapers to an end. This, of course, is not true of the suspended interest story in which the point rests in the final telltale word or words without which it would be ridiculous. Stories with this arrangement will be taken up in a later chapter.

However, there is no dodging the fact that the end of a standard inverted pyramid article is the least interesting phase of it. All such stories stand in peril of the falling ax and few readers get to the end anyway. Just the same, a sufficient percentage of concluding lines do remain and are reached by the reader to warrant the writer's giving his final words a bit of extra attention.

A quotation extending over several paragraphs should not come at the end of a story nor should a concluding paragraph answer a question in the preceding one. Certainly the writer needs to finish the point he is making even if he has to trim out an earlier paragraph. Sometimes he can return with a twist to the main theme of the story. Or, better, he may wind up with a tomorrow angle: "The trial will be resumed at 10 a.m. tomorrow."

If his ending is clever enough, the copy and makeup editors may keep it. If it is lost, no tragedy will occur. If it rides through into print, the story will seem more complete and satisfying to the faithful reader who has stayed with it to the last word.

SHOP TALK

1. Compare the structure of a news story to a statue, a train and a pyramid. Can you think of other structural comparisons?
2. What is meant by the lead-to-body sentence? Why is it sometimes necessary? Give examples.
3. Draw on the blackboard diagrams of the fact story, the quote story, the action story. Analyze examples of each clipped from current newspapers and show how the segments conform to the diagrams.
4. Study and discuss the diagrams. What are the advantages of these arrangements?
5. How does the reporter achieve smoothness in the body of his story? Find and underline the connectives in a half dozen news articles.

CHAPTER **10**

News of the Neighborhood

PLAIN PEOPLE IN PRINT

Across the pages of the press march the mighty men and wondrous women who make modern history. The famous and the infamous—their deeds and misdeeds—seem to be the sole principals in the passing parade while common folk sit forever on the side lines and watch. Don't you believe it!

You may never see or hear your name on the radio or television, in a magazine or book, but there is hardly a person alive who doesn't find his or her own name from time to time in a hometown newspaper. No other medium of mass communication reaches so often into the lives of plain John and Jane Does.

In purses and wallets, enclosed with letters, and reposing in scrapbooks, dresser drawers, attic trunks and basement boxes are newspaper clippings by the millions—all eagerly read, reread again and again, then carefully saved by ordinary citizens who never ran for office, won a medal, jumped off a bridge or shot a spouse.

Inspect these clippings and you will find that most of them identify people, their relatives, friends, associates or acquaintances, while the remainder deal with the doings of groups in which they participate. The bulk of these diminutive stories can be classified like this:

1. Births.
2. School, church, club and other organizational activities.
3. Social events.
4. Engagements, showers, marriages, honeymoons and wedding anniversaries.
5. Trips, visits and family gatherings.
6. Illnesses and recoveries.
7. Deaths.
8. Funeral services and burials.

AN AVERAGE HUMAN
LIFE IN THE NEWS

BIRTH

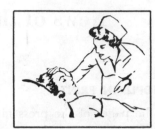

ILLNESS

ENGAGEMENT

DEATH

MARRIAGE

FUNERAL

Incidents Which Make Copy

The Simpsons announce the arrival of their third child; the Girl Scouts start their cooky-selling campaign Monday; the PTA meets at Bryant School tomorrow night; Mrs. Green is entertaining her sister from Dallas; the Wicks family is off on a tour of Canada; Bobby Wilson sees the year's first robin; the Hawthornes invite friends to a housewarming; the Carsons' son in service is promoted to sergeant; the Snyders' daughter, away at college, is pledged to a sorority; the Whites have sold their Colonial house to the Lees—all these morsels of information concern the people involved more intimately than national or global affairs.

Even those living elsewhere are interested if they have an attachment to a place. If George Layton, a Baltimore banker, spent his boyhood in Midland he will likely subscribe to the Midland *Times* and remark as he explores it: "Well, well, Joe Wright's daughter, Edna, *did* marry the Gleason boy after all." "I see that the old Higgins place is going to be turned into a golf course." "Old Doc Simms finally has retired. He's going to California." And certainly Layton's wife will scissor out this one:

> Friends of George Layton learn that he has been made a vice president of the Security State Bank in Baltimore. Layton, a native of this city, started work as a messenger for the Midland National Bank. Mrs. Layton is the former Emily Erskine. Her mother, Mrs. R. L. Erskine, lives at 714 Cedar St.

Few newspapermen ever chronicle world-shaking events. Far more write items of lesser moment, such as the one about the Laytons. And no matter to what heights he may aspire or climb, a reporter must begin by learning to handle little stories about little people.

In this chapter we will study some of these items which the cub is likely to be called upon to collect and write during his first weeks on the job, especially if he is employed by a small paper or is on the suburban section of a big one. Items about social events, as well as engagement and wedding stories, will be taken up further in the chapter on writing by and for women.

THE SWING TO THE SUBURBS

At one time in America the population could be divided into simple groups—people living on farms, in small towns and in large cities. Newspapers also fell into three classes—rural or country weeklies published in villages, six-day-a-week papers in medium-sized towns and metropolitan dailies, complete with Sunday editions, in the cities.

At the turn of the century a suburb consisted of a few scattered houses, usually somewhat dingy, on the fringes of a community. They were the last stops on the route of the carrier boy, the first for the RFD mailman. Newspapers paid scant attention to these sparsely settled areas. Their inhabitants were too few.

In the late 20's a mass shift in habitations started to take place. This movement turned out to be the most remarkable since the migration to the West after the Civil War.

Prosperity had lifted the standard of living and uncounted families, once needy, moved up into the middle-income brackets. Meanwhile, the World War I marriage boom boosted the birth rate. Schools were jammed, recreational facilities overtaxed. As congestion increased and breathing space shrank, the lure of fresh air and green grass began to beckon city dwellers to the countryside. Popular-priced automobiles and hard-surface highways took them there. First in a trickle, then in an onrushing torrent, millions moved into satellite towns.

As row upon row of bright homes blossomed in subdivisions, new shopping centers, each with a supermarket at its hub, mushroomed up at the crossroads to serve them. Lacking a local newspaper, merchants in some places advertised in throwaways.

Then, just as the pioneer printer-editors trailed the wagons westward, the newspapers followed their readers into the city environs and sliced into the fresh circulation and advertising pies.

A new journalistic era opened up. Special columns of suburban news were followed by whole pages and sections. These hometown newspapers within a newspaper, printed separately and inserted in the main issues, brought about split-run editions and zone coverage by expanded staffs of editorial workers.

Thus the cycle made a full turn. Thousands of reporters and desk men on big papers found themselves, like their counterparts in the rural regions, handling neighborhood news about the doings of Mr. and Mrs. Average Citizen. The suburban sections scratched the surface of the downtown throngs and found each individual tied up with his own affairs in the locality where he lived.

In one respect, of course, the larger papers had never abandoned the personality pieces. Their society, sports, business and entertainment sections—especially the columns covering show business and night life—always have been replete with brevities about individuals in the public eye—athletes, social registerites, business barons, stage, screen, television and radio celebrities. Items in these columns giving the low-down on the higher-ups sometimes are uncomplimentary.

The stories from the suburbs, reflecting the lives of the rank and file, are almost always complimentary and sympathetic, seldom scandalous or sensational. Papers want to build good will and they do it constructively by emphasizing achievement. As depicted by newspapers, the neighborhoods, for the most part, are wholesome with thoughts of physical, spiritual and educational betterment uppermost.

Sometimes, to the chagrin of the suburban staff, a story of wide interest, especially one of crime, is removed from the neighborhood section and pre-empted for the main section.

PICKING UP PERSONALS

As we have pointed out, the briefest and least pretentious of all news stories—tiny swirls in the broad river of current events—are personal or local items, also called *brevities*.

Many come in the mail or are taken over the telephone from school, church and social groups. Others are picked up by reporters making the rounds of rail and bus stations, hotels, hospitals, barber and beauty shops, real estate offices, dairies, gas stations, markets, stores and other places where people gather, talk and exchange information.

The job is not so easy as it appears at long range. Collecting 15 or 20 personals that possess real reader interest requires time, unwillingness to be bored by routine, patience and care—above all, care with names.

There's magic in a person's name. In this little package is wrapped his background, reputation, pride and prestige. Consider how flattering it is to receive a monogrammed gift or to have a child named for you. Many a building, institution or charitable enterprise came into being because a man wanted his name to be remembered.

It is axiomatic that "names make news" and, whether it appears in the Smalltown *Sun* or a suburban section of the Bigtown *Blade*, the name's the thing to watch. The *Sun* reports:

> Fred Swanson has harvested 100 acres of wheat on his farm two miles east of town on the Belt highway. Fred is the first farmer in this vicinity to cut his crop. He says it averages 20 bushels to the acre. He will start threshing next week.

A good item, this, which may be matched by one in the *Blade*:

> Home from a six weeks' tour of Europe, Kenneth P. Goodrich, head of the Goodrich Importing Co., wine distributors, today reported that shipments to his company of wine from abroad will be doubled next year. Italian wines, he said, are gaining favor in this country. Mr. and Mrs. Goodrich, who live at 1753 Park Pl., visited London, Paris and Rome.

In gathering the data for such items the reporter makes sure his names are correct to the last letter. To print *Curtis Vandeveer* when the right designation is *Vanderveer Custis* alienates that reader and disgusts his friends. It is evident that the reporter guessed badly or was so careless he could not decipher his own notes.

Names that can make both news and trouble include John and Johan, Herbert and Hubert, Ann, Anne and Annette, the Mc's and Mac's, the Kellys and Kelleys, the Johnsons, Johnstons and Johnstones, the Cohens, Cohns and Cohans.

Personal items, swung around one or more names, may consist merely of single paragraphs with no individual headlines. Sometimes they are scattered as space fillers but more often are grouped under such label headings as *People You Know* or geographically, thus: *Avon Activities, Taunton Topics, Riverdale Review.* Or the groupings may be occupational, as: *Real Estate News and Notes, Men of the Pulpit, Students at College, Our Men in Uniform* or *Serving Uncle Sam.* Birth notices may come under *The Stork Reports* or *Welcome Newcomers,* engagements and marriages under *Wedding Belles,* deaths and funerals under *To These Farewell.*

Such arrangements have the variety-show appeal of brevity in each act. The names, sometimes in boldface type, provide change in eye appeal as the reader scans the column.

WRITING THE BREVITY RIGHT

Although it is a comparative pygmy in size, a personal item should conform in style and structure to the same standard as the bannered and bylined story which wins the giant headlines on page one. It is, in essence, a summary lead which answers the *W's,* thus:

> A gold-embossed Bible, symbolic of his 20 years of service, was presented (*What*) to the Rev. Thomas Rawlins (*Who*) last evening (*When*) at a box supper on the lawn of Bethany Baptist Church (*Where*). The Rev. Mr. Rawlins is retiring as pastor of the church next Sunday (*Why*).

A personal item need not be stiffly formal but, like any other good news writing, should aim at presenting specific facts concisely. Here are two versions of the same item, one loosely written, the other lucid:

> POOR
>
> When it comes to the piscatorial art, local talent is as good as any, it seems. Bert Roberts, our w.-k. rod-and-reel expert, tried his hand with the big ones on a trip to Florida recently. The one that didn't get away

was a whopping sailfish. Bert wrote his partner, Hank Jordan, all about it. Hank is another ardent member of the Ike Walton clan.

BETTER

A 74-pound sailfish was caught by Albert Roberts, local insurance man, last week on a vacation trip to Surfside, Fla., according to a post card received by his partner, Henry Jordan. The catch won Roberts the first prize of $100 in the Surfside Fishing Festival tournament.

Guesswork and opinion have no place in the personal item, particularly if susceptible of causing offense. This one, as sent in by a rural correspondent, would put the paper into potential trouble:

Hal Mason tells us he found several of his fine sheep dead this morning and he thinks a timber wolf got them or maybe one of Ed Jackson's dogs. Ed has some mean hounds and we haven't seen a wolf hereabouts for a long time. Ed better watch those dogs.

An editor stripped the item of its unwarranted innuendo and pointed up the news interest like this:

A timber wolf, surviving the packs which roamed this region years ago, may still be at large in Boone County today. Hal Mason reports that a marauding animal killed seven blooded sheep last night at his farm seven miles north of Booneville. Mason believes that a wolf or a vicious dog was the raider.

It's better to be content with a prosaic list of names and merely mention the flowers or refreshments than to inject an uncomplimentary comment. Their husbands may have chuckled over this item, but you may be sure the writer won no favor with the ladies:

The Southern Society met Monday at the home of Mrs. James T. Kirk, 1432 W. 15th Ave., in East Crestwood. No prizes were given because the members could not agree on how to keep score. It is hoped that this situation will soon be corrected.

Lack of caution in writing of trips and visits also can cause embarrassment. Find out if a man was accompanied by his wife or vice versa and include both in an item if you can. But never associate the name of a man and that of a woman not his wife within the same item like this:

Clifford Berger and Mary Norman returned Sunday after spending three days in Meadville attending the State Teachers Convention and visiting friends.

In an effort to be patronizing or do a favor, a reporter may incorporate an editorial *puff* within a personal item. For example:

Genial Floyd Humphrey, owner of the Quick-Fix Appliance Shop at 752 Hampton Rd., has started a novel repair service for his numerous patrons. He says any radio or TV set bought from him hereafter will be kept in perfect working condition without charge for six months.

This item needs to be killed, for it cannot be trimmed of its salesmanship. Why should a paper give away its advertising space any more than Floyd Humphrey should give away radios or television sets?

However, wider community interest warrants the use of an item like this:

Thirty-two of the 50 new split-level and ranch type homes in the Parkside section of Hillview have been sold, according to R. F. Kirkland, the builder. A model home is open at 716 Oriole Ave.

THE PERSONAL ITEM EXPANDS

Personal items are the pocket change of the press—the pennies and nickels of the news columns—but if each one a reporter gets and writes is well handled they add up to more folding money in his pay envelope.

An alert newsman will not be content with a mere name or two and a bare statement. With persistence and resourcefulness he tries to uncover enlightening details to give the item sparkle and punch. Nor will he always cast it into a timeworn mold, starting inevitably with a name.

Two reporters, one easily satisfied with lazy monotony and the other beating the bush for hidden facts, might produce the following contrasting items:

SCANTY

Alderman Francis C. David, an alumnus of Midland College, paid a week-end visit to the J. H. Uhls. Alderman David lives in Chicago.

IMPROVED

Alderman Francis C. David of Chicago, who was a star fullback for Midland College in 1937, spent the week-end at the home of Mr. and Mrs. J. H. Uhl. Alderman David, recently reelected to a third term in the Chicago City Council, was a classmate of Uhl at Midland where David's 67-yard field goal against Ridge Normal still is recalled.

SCANTY

Burton Post, of Cedar Township, a Booneville visitor today, has leased part of his place to an oil company. He hopes to strike it rich.

IMPROVED

Thirteen landowners in Cedar Township now have signed leases with the Capital Oil Co., according to Burton Post, who reports that 40 of his

160 acres are under lease. Post, here today on business, said an offset to Marigold No. 1, a 500-barrel well, will be drilled on his property at once. It should be brought in next summer.

Merely because a reporter starts to jot down the data for a personal is no reason he should limit the item to a single paragraph if some unexpected news feature thrusts itself into the picture.

Buried in almost every column of brevities are clues to one or two first-class stories. Meeting a plane, perhaps, a reporter finds Prof. Anton Forsythe, who has just returned home after a vacation trip to Europe, so he might write:

Prof. and Mrs. Anton Forsythe, after a six weeks' European tour, arrived home today. While abroad they visited England, Germany, France, Italy and Austria. Professor Forsythe will resume his teaching duties at Fairmount Teachers College next week.

Suppose, however, that the reporter knows the professor to be an instructor in modern European history and therefore qualified to speak on international relations. Certainly the reporter would grasp the chance to expand a brevity into an interview. After asking a few questions he probably could produce a story starting like this:

Good faith and morality are needed for nations to get away from a "treadmill existence" of blocs and alliances, declared Prof. Anton Forsythe, head of the modern European history department at Fairmount Teachers College upon his return today from a six weeks' tour of Europe.

Praising the efforts of the United Nations, Professor Forsythe said signs of unrest. . . . .

Seldom indeed does a cub scoop an old-timer, but he often scoops himself by passing up a chance to develop an important story that belongs to him for the asking. If he does not see the implications in a commonplace item, how can he ever hope to produce lead stories for the front page?

Successful in his role of finding distinctive detail for his items, then making the commonplace more newsworthy, a wide-awake reporter is bound to win attention. He is on his way up when the city editor remarks to him: "That was a fine bunch of personals you turned in yesterday. I liked the Forsythe piece. Guess I'll try you on something different next week."

ACCOUNTS OF ILLNESS

A tip that "So-and-So is sick" ordinarily gives rise to an illness story, and with this meager announcement a reporter seeks out reliable informants for further details. His informants may be business associates, members of the family, the attending physician, nurses or supervisors at the hospital.

The most trustworthy informant is a physician, but sometimes he is reluctant to release news about a patient's condition, holding such information as confidential. When the physician does not submit to an interview, the reporter must turn elsewhere but in that event he should be extremely careful of what he writes, especially if he uses medical terms. Here are two typical illness items:

Striken with apoplexy, Frederick R. Gibbons, owner of the Star Drug Co., 1342 Main St., was near death last night at his home, 472 E. 17th St. Physicians held out slight hope for his recovery. The druggist collapsed in his store yesterday afternoon. He is 73 years old.

A slight improvement in the condition of Mrs. Clayton Mercer, wife of the manager of the Hale Printing Co., was reported today at the Oakton Nursing Home where she was confined after an operation.

Accounts of illness usually are brief, although further detail may be added if warranted by the prominence of the person. An example:

Circuit Court Judge John R. Roper, unconscious and gravely ill after a heart attack, made a slight gain today in his battle for life.

Haven Hospital authorities reported tonight that his condition remained the same as this morning, when a bulletin said: "Judge Roper is still in a coma but his general condition is somewhat improved."

The 62-year-old jurist was stricken last Saturday while on an upstate hunting trip. He is under the care of his personal physician, Dr. Edgar S. Bryant.

Should the nature of a person's illness be reported? This is a question to be answered according to the circumstances of the case. Societies raising money to fight certain diseases want them mentioned. However, physicians regard it as unethical to identify the ailment unless the patient or family approves. They may be willing to do so if he suffers from a heart condition or pneumonia, but unwilling if it is cancer. They may consent to a report that he "underwent surgery" provided "for gallstones" is not added. To be on the safe side the reporter should omit the specific diagnosis unless he is sure that it will give no one offense.

BIRTH ANNOUNCEMENTS

The arrival of babies furnishes newsy paragraphs for papers in communities of any size. In the big city press the reports are limited to families of prominence and usually consist of an announcement by parents, their identification, the sex of the child, and perhaps the place of its birth and the name given to it. Here are typical examples:

> Mr. and Mrs. Calvin Richards, of 434 E. 64th St., announce the birth of their first child, a daughter, Cecilia, on Thursday at St. Mark's Hospital. Mrs. Richards is the former Barbara Burns of Los Angeles.

> A son, James Michael, was born on April 25 to Mr. and Mrs. Lawrence Taylor, of 1618 N.W. Belmont Blvd. The child is their third. Mrs. Taylor is the former Alice Winston, daughter of Mr. and Mrs. Gerald Winston, of 175 Fulton St.

> Twin daughters were born yesterday to Mr. and Mrs. Ralph Hunter, of 1422 Farwell Ave., in Holy Name Hospital. Mrs. Hunter is the former Sheila Young of Boston. The children will be named Sharon and Shirley.

Writing for a suburban section or a small town paper, a reporter may add one or two details of more neighborly interest. One of these is the weight of the baby; another, for whom it was named. An example:

> Mr. and Mrs. Vernon Baird are the parents of a son born early today at Mercy Hospital. The baby weighed eight pounds at birth. He has been named Philip after Mrs. Baird's father, State Senator Philip Kenyon. Senator and Mrs. Kenyon live in Hillview.

A birth item may be stretched a little further by including the names and ages of other children in the family.

Don't try to be facetious about a birth, resorting to such bromidic expressions as *proud parents, Old Doc Stork, bouncing baby, bundle of joy, little stranger, blessed event, new arrival to bless their home.* A typical sample of "baby talk":

> Jim Pearson was handing out the "smokes" at his law office over Melton's Store this morning. Congratulations, Jim. Yep, it's a boy, and a fine bouncing youngster at that. We hope he grows up to be a distinguished lawyer like his dad.

But even greater sins are committed in writing the birth announcement. One of these is to state that a child has been born to one parent, without mentioning the other. Libel suits have arisen over mistakes in the dates of marriages. It is wiser to omit the telltale date altogether if printing it would add a lively topic for village gossip.

A birth item, like any other personal, may be worth more than a paragraph, if it was, say, the first one after the stroke of midnight on New Year's Day or if it occurred in a taxicab or any other unusual place. If the baby is one of quadruplets, or even triplets, the reporter is on his own. He notifies the desk, calls for a photographer, goes after all the angles and aims for page one.

Following up a birth announcement, another personal item sometimes may be written about a christening in which the names of the child, its parents, the sponsors and clergyman appear.

DATA FOR A DEATH STORY

Probably no reportorial procedure is more standardized than covering a death story. The task nevertheless presents difficulties for the reason that specific personal data must be obtained to make the account adequate.

Since funeral homes, hospitals and morgues constitute dependable sources for news about deaths, many city editors have arranged a special beat—sometimes called the *gloomy run*—which is usually assigned to a newcomer in the office who keeps in daily touch with these centers. Failing to obtain complete information from them, as often happens, the news getter goes directly to a member of the family—preferably a man, who is more easily approached under trying circumstances. Questioning that is straightforward, specific, sympathetic but not maudlin will generally elicit all the needed facts.

Some papers provide printed forms with spaces for data on the death proper, the obituary and funeral to be filled out in detail, thus assuring complete accuracy. If the reporter obtains information covering 10 points, he may be fairly certain that he has sufficient material for an article. Here are the points and the facts as filled in:

1. *Name:* Samuel R. Seaman.
2. *Address:* 2223 Pierce Ave.
3. *Age:* 52.
4. *Occupation and affiliations:* Owner of Seaman Garage, president of Rotary Club, member of First Baptist Church.
5. *Cause of death:* Pneumonia.
6. *Duration of last illness:* Two weeks.
7. *Place of death:* St. Mary's Hospital.
8. *Members of family who survive, with addresses:* Wife, Ada, 2223 Pierce Ave.; one son, George, 20, student at University of Centralia; two daughters, Alice, 15, Eunice, 17, both at home.
9. *Place and time of funeral:* First Baptist Church, 2 p.m. tomorrow.
10. *Place of burial:* Highland Cemetery.

It is now a simple matter to knit the various threads into a firm fabric. In fact, the story almost writes itself:

THE MIDLAND TIMES
OBITUARY REPORT

Full name__ _Clarence Robert Cox_ _____ Age _64_ ____

Residence__ _376 McKinley Ave._ _____

Place of death __ _Home_ _____

Time __ _6 p.m. Monday_ _____ Cause _Apoplexy_ _____

Duration of illness ___ _Sudden stroke_ _____

Wife__ _Martha Ellen Cox_ ____ Address _Home_ _____

Father__ _Robert L. Cox_ _____ Address _Jackson, Miss._

Mother__ _Not living_ _____ Address _____

Children__ _Harold, 16_ _____ Address _Home_ _____

__ _Stella, 18_ _____ Address _Home_ _____

_____ Address _____

Time of funeral __ _2 p.m. Thursday_ _____

Place____ _St. John's Church_ _____

Clergyman __ _Rev. Preston Banks_ _____

Pallbearers __ _Neighbors_ _____

_____

Out-of-town mourners __ _None_ _____

Burial place__ _Highland Cemetery_ _____

Birth date___ _April 7, 1897_ ___ Place ___ _Jackson, Miss._

Marriage date__ _June 3, 1923_ __ Place _Midland_ ____

Occupation____ _Hardware salesman_ _____

Education____ _Midland College, B.A., '20._ _____

Church and Lodges__ _St. John's, _ Elk _____

_____

Miscellany __ _Secretary Hardware Dealers assn._ ____

_____ _for 10 years_ _____

Form for Death and Funeral Data

> Samuel R. Seaman, owner of the Seaman Garage and president of the
> Rotary Club, died today at St. Mary's Hospital after a two weeks' illness
> of pneumonia. He was 52 years old and lived at 2223 Pierce Ave.
>
> Seaman is survived by his wife, Ada; one son, George, 20, a student
> at the University of Centralia; and two daughters, Alice, 15, and Eunice,
> 17, both living at home.
>
> Funeral services will be held at the First Baptist Church, of which he
> was a member, at 2 p.m. tomorrow. Burial will be in Highland Cemetery.

If the wife or other family members were at the bedside when death
occurred, this may be mentioned.

A person dies *of* an ailment, not *from* it. Note also that a man is survived by his wife, not his widow. A married woman is survived not by
her widower but by her husband. It works both ways. However, after the
funeral services of a husband the wife becomes a widow and is referred
to as "widow of Samuel R. Seaman" rather than "widow of the late
Samuel R. Seaman."

The family may request that flowers be omitted. Such announcements
win no favor from local florists who advertise. It is best to find out if your
own paper has a rule on the matter and act accordingly.

Again, as with the birth story, an unstereotyped answer to any of the
questions may set the story apart as unique and therefore of more than
routine importance. If the individual had reached the century mark, for
example, a special method of treatment may be adopted. And if the
death is that of a distinguished person, the story calls for an elaboration
of each of the points, with emphasis on the circumstances and effects.
The story now combines action, fact and quotes, but in outline still follows the 10 points.

From one to three days may elapse between a death and a funeral. In
the interval, especially if the death report has been printed previously, a
second-day lead or an advance may say that funeral services are being
planned or completed for So-and-So or that services will be held at such-
and-such time and place.

ACCOUNTS OF FUNERAL SERVICES

Like the death story, the account of a funeral answers certain fixed
questions with more or less detail. In addition to the usual five W's, these
include:

1. What clergyman officiated?
2. What was the nature of the ceremony?

3. What out-of-town visitors were present?
4. Who were the pallbearers?
5. Where was the burial?

Having secured such data, either by attending the services or from interviews with the undertaker, clergyman or relatives, the reporter brings them together into a pattern like this:

> Funeral services for Samuel R. Seaman, president of the Midland Rotary Club and proprietor of the Seaman Garage, who died Friday, took place today in the First Baptist Church.
>
> The Rev. Edward R. Johnson, pastor of the church, conducted the rites, assisted by the Rev. John Carston. A quartet from the Men's Bible Class provided the music. Burial was in Highland Cemetery.
>
> Pallbearers were members of the Rotary Club, which Seaman headed for the four years preceding his death. His wife, Ada, and three children, Alice, Eunice and George, attended. George came from Capital City where he is a student at the University of Centralia.

If the funeral is that of a news personality, other angles are developed, such as quotes from the sermon, eulogies from friends, descriptions of the scene and ceremony, possibly the behavior of mourners and spectators.

Stories of deaths and funerals have pitfalls for inexperienced reporters who often stray into stilted language and bad taste in their eagerness to be sympathetic or vivid. No substitute exists for the dignified and simple word *died*. Don't shy away from reality and try to masquerade the facts by using such expressions as *passed into the Great Beyond, went to his reward* or *was called to his eternal home.*

A body is a body and not a *corpse, the remains* or *the deceased,* and it rests in a coffin, not a *casket.* It is not always *decked* with *floral offerings* from *sympathetic friends.* The body is sent, not *shipped,* and buried, not *interred.* Such literary affectations stamp stories as grotesque, sometimes grimly humorous. Compare these accounts:

POOR

> Scores of sympathetic friends paid tribute today as their old neighbor, Mrs. Thomas Caxton, was laid to rest after a long and useful life in this community. She was known to be a gracious personality and there were many who mourned her passing.
>
> The First Methodist Church, which she faithfully attended, overflowed with floral offerings, and the casket of the deceased was banked with white lilies, her favorite flower.
>
> Mrs. Caxton slipped peacefully away last Tuesday after a paralytic

stroke. The remains were interred in Mount Olivet Cemetery beside the
body of her husband, who departed into the Great Beyond several years
ago.

Both were valued and respected members of the community.

BETTER

Funeral services for Mrs. Thomas Caxton, a resident of Midland for
30 years, were held yesterday at the First Methodist Church, of which she
was a member. Burial was in Mount Olivet Cemetery.

Mrs. Caxton was prominent in the work of the Midland Flower Guild
and for years served on the board of visitors of Mercy Hospital. She made
many gifts to charity, notably for playgrounds.

Mrs. Caxton died Tuesday at the age of 69, following a paralytic stroke.
She is survived by a son, Louis, local hardware dealer, and a daughter,
Mrs. Cyril W. Fuller, of San Diego, Calif. Her husband died three years
ago.

The Rev. George M. Crandall conducted the services. Pallbearers were
Walter F. Dunn, J. L. Hamilton, Matthew S. Little, Samuel Palmer, Robert
Casey and Alfred P. Branner, all neighbors of Mrs. Caxton.

Stories of funerals should be natural and straightforward but also
tactful in their terminology. The reporter must not permit his feelings to
sway him unduly. As in any other reportorial task, he must requisition his
facts from the most reliable sources and write them dispassionately with
a sense of their importance and value as news.

PREPARING THE OBITUARY

Distinct from the death story proper—but ordinarily merged with or
added to it—is the obituary or biographical sketch, known in shop
parlance as an *obit*. Once the prominence of the subject has been established, the obit may offer a few sentences about a person's occupation and
affiliations or it may become a lengthy review of his entire career.

Knowing full well that they will be printed sometime, metropolitan
newspapers keep obituaries of notables on file in their morgues ready for
emergencies. Announcement of serious illness will prompt an editor to
set the obit in type, ready for instant publication beneath a brief bulletin
announcing the death. From time to time obits in type are brought up-
to-date.

The first step in shaping an obituary, after the facts of death have been
ascertained, is an examination of material in the office morgue. If the
sketch is not already prepared for print, clippings and reference books
are available from which it may be drafted. Otherwise, comments and
background material must be solicited from relatives, friends and associates.

Preliminary to writing, the reporter must decide the approximate length of his sketch and then summarize or expand to fit the measure. The story runs chronologically like this:

> Born Nov. 3, 1877, Mrs. Bentley emigrated to America with her parents at the age of 5. The family came to Midland from New England in 1888. On Dec. 9, 1899, soon after he was mustered out of the 28th Regiment, with which he served through the Spanish-American War, she married Richard Bentley. As far back as old-timers can remember, Bentley led the Fourth of July parades until his death in 1944.
>
> The Bentleys watched Midland grow from a small trading post to its present size. They were among the early residents who saw the first industries built here and lived through the fire of 1914. Their home was demolished.
>
> Recalling the fire, Mrs. Bentley often told her neighbors how the homeless citizens spent two days and nights camping out on the riverbank until relief provisions arrived.
>
> Mrs. Bentley organized the First Presbyterian Church Sunday School and taught classes until her health began failing a few years ago. Her husband was a deacon in the church for 39 years.

An obituary need not be dull and stodgy simply because the topic of death is a depressing one. The writer is dealing with life, not death, and should therefore humanize his material. Historical references, characteristic anecdotes and long-forgotten but enlivening episodes in a career enhance the readability of an obituary.

It is said that a man is dead a long time and that yesterday's newspaper is as dead as he is. This is not true. An obituary, like other personal stories, is clipped, saved, read and mailed, sometimes halfway around the world. It's well worthwhile to do the last story right.

SHOP TALK

1. From your observation, is the personal item outmoded or is it gaining in favor? Are city dwellers justified in scoffing at brevities as small town stuff?
2. Should the suburban sections of a newspaper stress culture and minimize crime or present them in the same ratio as elsewhere in the paper?
3. Discuss the importance of illness, death and funeral reports in the news. Is too much or too little space devoted to stories in these categories?
4. Do you agree with the injunction, "Concerning the dead, nothing but good," or should a newspaper let "the evil that men do" live after them in the obituary?
5. Are small town newspapers justified in employing such phrases as *bereaved friends, loved ones, sympathetic neighbors* to soften the tragedy of a death and funeral?

CHAPTER 11

Accidents, Fires and Suicides

CONWAY LOSES A STORY

If a single trained news gatherer had been available in the local room of the *Times* on the afternoon of the Midland Shore Line train wreck, Robert Conway, a copy boy anxious to be a reporter, would never have been hurried out with a photographer to cover it. He telephoned to the *Times* office 45 minutes before the first deadline—excited, dazed and somewhat unnerved by what he had seen. City Editor Mason answered.

"Pretty bad wreck!" gasped young Conway. "Lots of cars smashed. Lots of people hurt."

"Anybody killed?" abruptly asked his superior.

"Why, sure. They were pulling passengers out of the wreckage."

"How many?"

"Four or five, I think, maybe six."

"Know who they were?"

"I couldn't get their names. There was too much excitement, but I heard someone say a big railroad official in a private car was killed."

"That so? Did you get the official's name?"

"I heard that his name was McBride, the traffic manager of the road, but nobody seemed to be very sure," answered Conway, hesitatingly.

"What caused the wreck?"

"Well, they don't know, but I think the engineer got his signals mixed. He seemed all upset. Everybody was too busy and excited to tell me. I couldn't find out."

"Well, what in blazes *did* you find out?"

"Oh, almost everything else! It's awful! Tracks torn up—coaches burning—ambulances rushing up—people screaming. I think I can write a swell descriptive piece with lots of color."

What City Editor Mason said next is unprintable. Of course he had already dispatched other reporters to the scene of the wreck, but the *Times* went to press with meager bulletins in its Early edition.

Conway thought he had enough stuff for a story. In reality he had collected only hearsay, rumors and emotionalized impressions. He needed much more experience.

NAILING DOWN THE FACTS

Day in and day out in every edition newspapers are reporting sudden and violent occurrences caused by the forces of nature and human weakness or error interrupting the normal course of living. These range from minor mishaps to disasters of history-making magnitude.

They include traffic accidents, train wrecks, plane crashes, ship and boat sinkings, fires, explosions, drownings, tornadoes, hurricanes, floods and such combinations as a fire following an explosion or a flood following a storm. In this chapter we will see how several of the most frequent of these unfortunate events reach the printed page.

The Conway episode points up the all-important role of the reporter who assembles the original data on which the account is based. A professional assigned to such a story goes directly after facts and all the facts—plain, cold, solid, unshakable facts.

He seldom is on the spot when an unexpected event occurs, or starts to occur. The first report may come from a tipster but usually is received at police or fire headquarters. A beat man relays it to the city desk. He may accompany police or fire squads himself but never does so, leaving his own news source uncovered, without instructions from the office.

At the scene a reporter may find himself in a thicket of hubbub and hysteria. He walks straight through this barrier. He has no time for gossip or guesswork conversation and even less for personal thrills or excitement. He keeps his head and attends to the business at hand.

If a crowd has collected, he doesn't tarry on the fringes. Using his credentials if necessary, he pushes through to the working policemen, firemen, ambulance doctors or rescue squads, finding those in charge as quickly as possible. From them—or fellow newspapermen already there —he accumulates the main facts and thereafter, if time permits, seeks out supplemental details.

From first to last you will find him pinning down authorities, talking to witnesses, listening to those in a position to know. As swiftly and thoroughly as he can he collects and gets down on paper the points which answer the inevitable news questions *Who, What, Where, When, Why* and—especially for a story of this kind—the *Who*.

LOOK FOR LOSS OF LIFE

As Mason spoke to Conway, he asked three questions in rapid-fire order:

"Anybody killed?"

"How many?"

"Know who they were?"

The most urgent task of a news fact-finder covering an event involving dangerous or destructive action is to obtain accurate answers to these questions as fast and fully as he can. In any account of an accident all other considerations take second place to the number and identities of the dead.

Why is this so? Nothing except birth is as commonplace as death. Every day dozens of people expire of diverse ailments and their passing is recognized, if at all, only in the obituary column. The explanation goes back to the basic elements of news itself. Eventual demise by disease or old age is inevitable; sudden and unexpected or multiple deaths by violence are rare, surprising, shocking, and therefore more newsworthy.

Next in news precedence to lives lost are lives imperiled. As soon as he tallies the dead the reporter finds out the number, then the identities of persons injured, with descriptions of their injuries, of those missing, if any, and of the unhurt survivors.

An identity may spring into a strong position if one of those on the list is well-known, thus bringing to bear the prominence element. But even comparatively unknown victims need to be identified, at least by name, age and address.

Who was killed, by *What, Where, When* and *Why?* With the five *W*'s in hand—the *Who* in full—the reporter is ready to search for answers to secondary questions such as:

What caused the incident?

Who learned of it first and reported it?

What did witnesses observe?

What is the property loss?

Is there insurance?

Was anything or anybody at fault?

Are arrests likely?

Is a lawsuit for damages probable?

Will an investigation ensue?

What the witnesses observed may have been an escape, a rescue or an act of heroism. If so it will crowd closely into the account or may even overshadow the other elements, turning the story into a real-life drama.

Deadlines, of course, determine the completeness of an accident story. Time may limit the first reports to essentials without names or with an incomplete casualty list.

And if the occurrence ranks as a calamity or catastrophe, its ramifications may expand the single story into a multiangled production or separate it into sectional units and extend it into a day-after-day serial.

INTEGRATING THE IDENTIFICATIONS

If only one or two persons figure in an accident they may be named in the lead or second paragraph of a story, but if the reporter has an extended casualty list—a series of names, addresses and ages—how shall he push it to the front without hopelessly clogging the action? Obviously he must not subordinate the *What, Why* and *How* altogether to the *Who*. The reader wants to know what happened as well as who was killed or injured.

To meet this difficulty, a special casualty structure often is employed. Occasionally, if the list is extremely long, the summary is lifted from the story and boxed in an adjacent column. More often it is skeletonized within the story, conforming to the accompanying diagram.

When this structure is used, the lead should run no longer than one or two paragraphs. It should answer the five *W's* in summary form, linked to a brief résumé of secondary facts and a swift sketch of the action. The casualty list is then inserted. Thereafter follows a telling and re-telling of the story with detailed information as to the cause, investigation, rescue work, eyewitness testimony, and so on, in order of news value.

The casualty structure not only is widely favored for death and injury stories, but is recommended in any write-up in which a number of names and addresses must be compiled quickly. Prisoners seized in a police raid, defendants in a trial, honor students receiving awards, officials attending a convention, beneficiaries of a will, may be listed in the same fashion. Additions and corrections are readily made without disturbing the lead as originally written.

As a test of its effectiveness, apply the diagram to the following story:

> Two workmen were killed and three seriously injured today in the collapse of a tenement building which they were wrecking at 605 W. 13th Ave. A weakened crossbeam snapped, hurling a mass of masonry and wood into the group at work on the first floor.
> The dead are:
> Vincent Losher, 43, 3760 Pine St.
> David Delancy, 31, 492 W. 14th St.

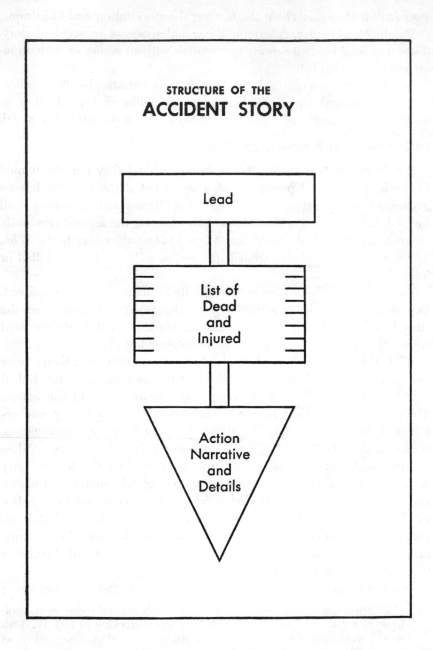

STRUCTURE OF THE
ACCIDENT STORY

Lead

List of
Dead
and
Injured

Action
Narrative
and
Details

The Casualty List Diagram

The injured are:

Antonio Fascelti, 21, Fairfield, right leg broken.

Patrick O'Connor, 37, 2954 Weston St., back sprained, internal injuries.

Joseph Lenwood, 50, 173 Oak St., bruised and cut.

The building, a 5-story, 20-family dwelling, was being demolished by the Wicks Wrecking Co., 1002 Main St., with A. J. Sampson, superintendent, in charge.

The three upper floors had been razed.

"Look out below!" Aaron Beckstein, one of three workmen at the top of the structure, called out as he noticed the crossbeam tottering. But his warning was too late. . . . .

ACCIDENT STORY LEADS

If anyone has been killed or seriously injured in an accident, the law of life-and-limb-first is invoked upon the reporter both on the assignment and at his typewriter. His lead almost automatically incorporates what happened to a man, woman, child or group of persons, thus:

Darting in front of a speeding automobile after a football, Harold Sherwin, 14 years old, was knocked down and cut about the face and arms at Bates and 12th Sts. at noon today. The boy is the son of Mr. and Mrs. H. L. Sherwin, 1614 Taft Ave.

Three hundred rail commuters were saved from a cold plunge into the Timber River yesterday when an infallible mechanical safety device clicked after a fallible engineer had missed a signal.

Two passengers and a pilot narrowly escaped death when a small cabin plane nosed over while making a forced landing on a meadow near the Skyport landing field today.

Scores of theatergoers scrambled to safety as a sewer explosion blasted a half dozen manholes from the pavement in the neighborhood of Clark and 16th Sts. last night.

A mother of five children raced through billows of smoke yesterday to rescue her 1-year-old daughter when flames swept the living room of their home at 1704 E. 12th St. in Highland.

Deaths and injuries can be withheld for the space of a few words in order to describe the action which led to them—but no longer. Examples:

A passenger train smashed an automobile on a private road crossing here this afternoon, killing a mother and daughter and injuring three other members of a family.

A Midland car, skidding on a rain-splattered curve, collided with an oil truck on Main St. today, causing the death of Sidney Skelton, of 1702 Elm St., and injuring his wife.

There is no hard and fast rule that a person must figure in the lead, for in certain types of accident stories the human application is minor or missing altogether. In that case the writer singles out for his lead the next best point, usually the cause or property damage:

A lighted match, tossed by a careless cigar smoker into a pile of oiled waste, today started a fire which damaged the Triangle Motor Co. garage at 2719 Grove Ave.

Flooding basements over a four-block area, a broken water main caused damage estimated at $100,000 in midtown Midland yesterday. The pipe burst under the pavement at Main and 3rd Sts.

A sea gull swerving into a propeller of an Over-Ocean airliner sent the plane and its 60 passengers back to its take-off base here this afternoon.

Left unbraked and out of gear, a five-ton truck careened downhill for two blocks on Grant Ave. last night before crashing into a dirt enbankment. The driver recovered his machine undamaged.

A FIRE AND AN EXPLOSION

A reporter at the scene of a fire or an explosion pursues the same scientific fact-gathering method as when covering any other violent occurrence. And whether his story is long or short this is about how the formula works out:

Basic Facts

Casualties	Two firemen injured
Time	This afternoon
Place	Davis Clothing Co.
Damage	$75,000
Insurance	$50,000

The Story

Two firemen, Gail Brayman, Engine Company No. 9, and Thomas Burroughs, Engine Company No. 14, were critically injured this afternoon while fighting a fire which destroyed the building occupied by the Davis Clothing Co. at 1117 Seward St. Brayman may die.

The firemen were struck by falling timbers when a rear wall of the structure collapsed. Brayman's skull was fractured and Burroughs suffered a broken leg and internal injuries. Both were taken to Haven Hospital.

Defective wiring in the basement started the blaze, according to Fire

Chief Ralph Chambers. The flames spread rapidly through the upper floors of the three-story building, but all the occupants, most of them clothing workers, escaped.

W. E. Davis, owner of the establishment, estimated the damage at $75,000. The building was insured for $50,000.

At times when there are no deaths, injuries or material damage, an unusual circumstance may give the story a lift. Oddity and sex come to the fore in this one reporting a minor explosion:

Basic Facts

Casualties	None
Time	Today
Place	Bettye's Beauty Shoppe in the Rex Hotel
Cause	Nail polish remover exploded
Damage	$100

The Story

A gallon bottle of nail polish remover exploded in Bettye's Beauty Shoppe in the Rex Hotel today and sent three women scurrying outdoors with their hair in pin curlers.

The blast occurred when a hairdresser, Pierre Valtin, 32, dropped the bottle in the rear of the shop. He was unhurt. Acrid fumes spread as he put out the fire with an extinguisher.

Three women were in booths having their hair shampooed and set and two others were waiting their turn. All rushed to the street, some leaving their purses behind as the smoke billowed in.

"It sounded like a little atom bomb," declared Mrs. Oliver Lake, one of the patrons. "But we really were more scared than hurt."

Miss Bettye Banks, manager, estimated the damage at about $100. She said that the shop will be open tomorrow and that each of the three customers in the booths will be given new hairdos on the house.

MOTOR VEHICLE MISHAPS

Every community has its daily quota of traffic accidents. They are so numerous that only the most spectacular make the main sections of metropolitan papers, but every paper, large or small, reports them regularly and the job frequently falls on the shoulders of the newest reporters.

A routine form at police headquarters or the sheriff's office may give a reporter all the data necessary for a short write-up, but if the smashup is a major one he may be sent directly to the scene.

Study the reporter as he works. He ignores curbstone or roadside onlookers, shoulders through the crowd and gets to or near the authorities

APPLICATION OF THE
ACCIDENT DIAGRAM

LEAD

Three persons were killed and four injured when a crosstown bus crashed into a United Transportation Co. moving van at Green and 14th Sts. last night. All the victims were occupants of the bus, which was demolished.

LIST OF DEAD AND INJURED

The dead:

Mrs. Leslie Hillman, 63, 712 Fillmore Ave.
Helen Hillman, 14, granddaughter of Mrs. Hillman.
Heinrich Schultz, 42, 517 Spruce St., driver of bus.

The injured:

Miss Clarice Thompson, 23, 461 Walnut St., a stenographer, skull fractured.
Milton Marks, 19, 65 Wentworth Pl., high school student, internal injuries.
Mrs. Harold H. Morton, 37, Meadville, arm broken, internal injuries.
Arthur Strickman, 41, Hotel Harper, salesman, lacerations.

ACTION NARRATIVE AND DETAILS

Speeding north on Green street, the bus struck the heavily loaded van squarely in the center, hurling it into a high-tension wire pole. Vivid flashes of blue lightning were given off by the live wires, hampering the work of extricating the passengers from the bus.

At Mercy Hospital, an hour after the smashup, physicians said the condition of Miss Thompson was critical. The others injured were expected to recover.

Edward McGrady, driver of the van, told police investigators the bus swerved toward him as the bus turned right into Green street from 14th street. He applied the brakes too late to avoid the collision

With a terrific crash, heard for several blocks, the motor coach . . . . .

How Casualties Can Be Compiled

who, like himself, are bent on gathering facts. Satisfied that he has them, he requisitions the nearest telephone or returns to the office with the following facts in his possession:

1. Identities of the dead and injured, if any.
2. Exact location.
3. Description of the vehicle or property.
4. Cause and circumstances of the accident.
5. Extent of the damage.

At his typewriter, if writing his own story, the newsman analyzes his information and designs a lead. As always, he gives first attention to the loss of life and limb, but if he can, varies somewhat the routine formula: So-and-So was killed when the such-and-such car in which he was riding crashed into this-or-that object at such-and-such place yesterday or today.

Note how this writer stresses the human life factor and at the same time dramatizes the action, inserts the casualty list, then moves on to retell the incident in more detail:

> Death came roaring out of the blackness last night for a Midland couple as they tried to help two women fatally injured in a head-on smashup five minutes before.
>
> As the couple looked up into the headlights of what they thought was a mercy car, they were killed when the speeding vehicle plowed through the wreckage. The three-car pile-up occurred at 10:30 last night on the Lincoln highway near Bay road.
>
> The dead:
>
> Donald Cole, 42, of 604 Clinton St., Midland.
>
> Elizabeth Cole, 37, his wife.
>
> Mrs. Peter Lewis, 54, of Junction City.
>
> Miss Susan Norcross, 48, of St. Louis.
>
> The Coles and Mrs. Lewis died instantly and Miss Norcross an hour later in Mercy Hospital. In the same hospital with internal injuries are Daniel Woods, 24, of Clay City, and Nathan Carter, 18, of 715 Laurel St., Midland. Carter's condition is critical.
>
> The first crash occurred when Woods, passing a truck, lost control of his car, swerved into oncoming traffic, sideswiped and almost demolished a four-door sedan driven by Mrs. Lewis. She was returning from a movie with Miss Norcross, a house guest. Both women were crushed as their car overturned. The Woods car halted in a ditch. Seeing the accident, Cole pulled up alongside the overturned car and tried to lift it as Mrs. Cole struggled to pull Miss Norcoss free. Two other cars and Motorcycle Officer Clyde Rawlings pulled up at the side.
>
> "Get off the road!" Rawlings shouted as the headlights of Carter's sports car approached, traveling too fast to stop. The Coles ignored the

warning too long. A split second later Carter's machine ground into the already battered Lewis machine, crushing them both under its wheels.

"I had no time to set up a warning signal," said Rawlings. "All I could do was shout before it was all over."

The writer now has covered all his main points and the story is complete as it stands. With further space at his disposal he would have elaborated on the identifications, quoted other witnesses, and perhaps retold the incident, giving further details.

Be careful in auto accident reports about fixing responsibility. It is safe to say and easy to prove that two vehicles collided. It is not so safe to say that one crashed into the other. Never write that a driver ignored a signal, drove on the wrong side of the street or recklessly, unless you want to be a witness in court.

THE TREATMENT OF SUICIDES

A suicide story is akin to but not identical with that of a natural death or an accident. It is touched upon here because it is usually covered like an accident and often is assigned to cubs early in their careers.

As in the case of any accident, the reporter needs to identify the victim fully and, as in the natural death story, name the survivors and note funeral arrangements. Such data come from the police, coroner, physician, family or friends. The nub of the story frequently lies in the motive or method rather than the name.

Three typical leads, stressing name, motive and method respectively, follow:

Name

Judge Frank Quinn, who recently was appointed to the Circuit Court bench by Governor Boland, died today in a plunge from his sixth-floor apartment in the Clarendon Hotel. He was 57.

Motive

Shamed because she was scolded for staying out late with boys, 16-year-old Gladys Hilder shot and killed herself this afternoon with a revolver she took from her father's wall safe.

Method

Leaping a hundred feet from a tower of Highgate Bridge, Jason Lightner, an unemployed laborer, ended his life this morning in view of 50 spectators who mistook him for a repairman or painter.

Name and method are shoved down to make way for motive in this story, which is laden with the sex news element:

A high school track star, one hand clutching a newspaper clipping of a poem of unrequited love and a girl's picture, was found dead in his automobile today.

Alan Walters, 18, a senior at Central High School, was shot through the heart. A .22 caliber rifle lay in the seat of the car, parked in a "lovers' lane" near Lake Luce.

Sheriff John E. Fisher said that Walters apparently shot himself.

The girl in the picture, June Meeker, 16, told Fisher she left Walters Sunday afternoon after a talk in which they agreed to break off an engagement of three months. She said she had given a ring back to him.

Walters, an only son, lived with his parents, Mr. and Mrs. Henry Walters, at 1415 Forest Ave. Funeral services will be at the First Methodist Church at 2:30 p.m. Wednesday.

HANDLING SUICIDES WITH CARE

While a suicide story is a cousin to stories of accidents, it likewise is related to those of crime. Unless culpability is clear there is no stigma attached to the victims of an accident but the deliberate taking of life, including one's own, is generally looked upon as an act against the interests of society.

Unfortunately suicides are numerous. Definitely they are news and newspapers do not hush them up, especially if they concern prominent persons, spectacular or unusual circumstances. A newspaper may minimize, even omit, those with no impelling news element, but if a public official kills himself or a woman stands teetering on a window ledge for an hour while hundreds watch below, prominence in the one case and suspense in the other puts them on page one.

However, exceptional precautions are taken against inaccuracy or poor taste. Look back at the examples and note how carefully the writers protected themselves against both.

Judge Quinn, said the writer, died in a *plunge.* Or he might have said the body of the judge was found on the sidewalk beneath the window of his sixth-floor apartment. But since nobody witnessed the incident, the story does *not* say he *fell* accidentally or *jumped* intentionally. *Plunged,* in fact, is the only safe verb and it is found frequently in suicide stories.

In the track star story the writer at no point said on his own authority that Walters died by his own hand. He protected the sheriff with the word *apparently.* Nor did the writer pretend to read retroactively the mind of the dead youth. Adroitly but forcefully he pointed up the lost-love motive with noneditorial evidence.

Other hazards lurk in suicide stories. One of these is the danger of using the power of suggestion to encourage others who are consider-

ing suicide to go through with it. This can be avoided to some extent
by generalizing rather than specifying the method used. To state that a
person died of poison is quite different from disclosing that he drank a
brand of weed-killer easily bought at a garden supply store. In fact, if
he thinks any detail may assist another to take his own life the writer
if he can keeps it out of his story altogether.

SHOP TALK

1. Which of the following three facts about an explosion would you choose for
   emphasis: (a) one laborer killed; (b) entire business district shaken; (c)
   $25,000 damage? Explain your choice.
2. Does the average newspaper place too much emphasis on human life in
   in catastrophe stories?
3. At what official sources in your city would news of the following events
   originate: (a) a fire; (b) an automobile accident; (c) a drowning; (d) a
   train wreck; (e) a suicide?
4. Should motor vehicle mishaps be given more or less space in newspapers?
5. Do you think the publication of suicide stories encourages or discourages
   readers contemplating suicide? Discuss the treatment of suicide news. Should
   it be handled in the same way as other news?

CHAPTER **12**

Forecasts and Follow-Ups

HOW THE NEWS UNWINDS

Lying on your doorstep or under a pile of coins at the corner stationery store, a daily newspaper is an inert object. However, as it comes rolling from the presses it can be pictured as swiftly spun fabric unwinding edition after edition, day in and day out.

Carry the comparison a bit further and visualize each page as part of a colorful carpet woven yard by yard from the threads of a flying loom. Every issue offers a new design. Here and there a bright pattern appears, then suddenly vanishes, only to reappear. Strands slip in, spread, interlace with other strands, then gradually fade away.

The spots and patterns are news topics and serials—an endless web of words which forms a moving record of the past, a portrayal of the present and a chronicle of the future.

An unexpected news event such as an accident or suicide, of course, cannot be anticipated. Its life history therefore begins at its occurrence. But an expected event like a meeting or an anniversary can be foreseen and written about before it takes place. All events may be reported as or immediately after they occur, and again and again if there are new developments.

A single happening may be forecast once or several times. The topic may survive but a day, it may live a week or two, or it may extend its stay for years, breaking out at intervals and flashing brightly on the news carpet after months in oblivion.

In workshop parlance, the chronological phases of a news serial are known as an *advance,* a *spot story,* and a *follow-up.* These may be defined as follows:

> *Advance*—a story foretelling an event expected to occur at a definite time in the future.

Spot story—a report of a fresh occurrence, usually unexpected, and demanding immediate publication.

Follow-up—the second or subsequent chapter of a news serial.

The advance story answers the question, "What is *going to* happen?"; the spot story, "What actually *did* happen?"; the follow-up story, "What happened *thereafter?*" Trained newsmen have tools and tricks of technique for each kind of story. We have studied spot news. Let us now inspect the forecast and follow-up.

THE COMMUNITY BULLETIN BOARD

One of the important functions of the press, indicated by such flags as *Herald, Sentinel* and *Beacon,* is to provide the public with information about coming events.

No other medium can match the newspaper in the delivery of this service. Radio and television announcements are too few and fleeting to place and pin down for practical use the specific information about upcoming affairs needed by people wishing to participate in them, while magazines are too limited and far behind the parade to be of value. The newspaper alone serves as the bulletin board of the community.

Literally scores of notices setting forth the time and place of events ahead—gatherings of every variety—appear in print daily. Some are scattered and others are grouped on departmentalized pages or in special columns. The simplest are paragraphs such as these:

New officers of the Washington School Parent-Teacher Assn. will be installed at 8 o'clock tonight in the auditorium of the school at Harrison Ave. and 14th St.

Mrs. Earl Chapman, president of the Greenview Garden Club, will be hostess to the board of directors tomorrow at 10:30 a.m. in her home at 1712 Jackson Ave. A luncheon will be served after the business session.

The Beverly Park Legion Auxiliary will conduct a thrift sale from 10 a.m. to 4 p.m. Tuesday in the Clarendon Hotel arcade. Members are asked to contribute articles of clothing.

City Councilman J. R. Fogel will speak at the annual dinner of the United Taxpayers Assn. at 7 p.m. Friday in Community Hall. His topic is "Our New City Charter."

Little effort is expended by reporters in gathering such items as these. If a paper makes a practice of publishing them they are usually mailed, brought or phoned in by officers or publicity chairmen. The chore of the writer is to see that the item is brief but complete and accurate, especially the names.

As it comes in, the announcement may be full of fluff and puffs like this one:

> Come one, come all! Every member is invited to attend and bring her husband to the monthly meeting of the Ladies Literary Society at the Melrose Library next Thursday. An interesting program has been arranged. One of our members will show slides and tell of her thrilling trip to Europe this summer. Delicious refreshments will be served during the social hour and a good time is promised to everyone by the chairman, Mrs. Tobin.

The news writer would check the time of the meeting and the first name of Mrs. Tobin, then condense the announcement into a form like this:

> The Ladies Literary Society will hold its monthly meeting at 8 p.m. Thursday in the Melrose Library at Birch and 17th Sts. Mrs. R. M. Tobin is in charge. Husbands are invited.

THE VANGUARD OF THE NEWS

An upcoming event of community-wide interest is worth more space than one of concern only to a neighborhood group and it is developed accordingly. An example:

> Formal dedication of Paulson Park in Hillview will take place on the nights of June 17 and 18 with the presentation of "Midsummer Night's Dream" by the students of Hillview High School.
>
> The performances will be given in the band shell at the eastern end of the park, which was named in honor of the late Governor Paulson.
>
> The cast will number 120, including a ballet of 20 high school girls and the 25-piece high school orchestra. The presentation is sponsored by the Hillview Civic Assn. It will be directed by Miss Leone Smith, teacher of drama at the high school.

From the city desk future file come reminders of events observed by large segments of the population. These automatically call for advance coverage and a reporter may be assigned to round up the plans and write a comprehensive story. It need not be a mere recitation of prosaic facts. It can be an imaginative and colorful preview as is this one in the Midland *Times:*

> The echo of marching feet, the crashing volley of rifle salutes and flag-and-flower-decorated graves in all Midland cemeteries will signalize the city's Memorial Day observance tomorrow.
>
> Fair skies and balmy temperatures are promised by the weather forecaster for today and through the weekend.
>
> Led by the American Legion band, more than 5,000 American Legionnaires and Veterans of Foreign Wars, their auxiliaries, and members of

school, labor, fraternal and civic organizations will march in the annual Main street parade starting at 10 a.m. It will proceed from 1st to 14th avenues.

The marchers will pass in review before Mayor Nelson, retired Brig. Gen. Frank Logan, honorary marshal, and other officials at a banner-draped stand in front of City Hall.

A colorful feature will be floats showing "Washington at Valley Forge," "Lincoln at Gettysburg" and "The Flag at Iwo Jima." Behind these will come simulated atomic artillery and models of the latest military missiles. Squadrons of jet fighters will fly overhead.

As a prelude to the parade, veterans of the Spanish-American War will meet for services in Mount Olivet Cemetery. A rifle and color salute will be given over the markers on soldiers' graves.

After noon Midland is expected to be an almost deserted city as citizens take to highways and lake resorts to celebrate what has come to be regarded as the formal beginning of the outdoor season.

By projecting himself ahead the composer of the foregoing story not only gave his readers a satisfying foretaste of the day's doings, but won an advantage for the *Times*, a morning paper, over its afternoon competitors. While the PM's will beat the *Times* into print *after* the events occur, the *Times* has described them well *before* they occur.

DON'T TRY TO PROPHESY

"Taxes and high water are always sure to happen" has become a popular saying which is handicapped by the lack of demonstrable truth. Little is quite certain in this world and no reporter should plume himself as a soothsayer or an oracle.

Of course, there is no question at all about the arrival of Memorial Day. Common sense dictates that there is no danger in flat fore-statements about any birthday, holiday, anniversary, eclipse or change in the seasons. The almanac says Memorial Day arrives on May 30 and nothing can change it. The traditional observance of the day in Midland also is fixed by repetition year after year and, therefore, safe to write about. In fact the only uncertain factor is the weather outlook which is attributed to an authority, the forecaster.

However, many other types of advance stories need to be handled conservatively and with care, especially when alternatives are involved. Contrast the approaches—one wildly speculative, one cautious—in this pair of stories:

DANGEROUS

Somebody may be killed at the Fulton Fuel Co. mine today when 500 union miners walk out on a strike for a living wage scale of $12 a day.

Twenty deputy sheriffs, to be on guard when the men lay down their shovels, will shoot down the first man who dares to touch any of the company's property. Sheriff John E. Fisher, it was learned, means to tolerate no violence.

The miners, who are exasperated by the company's refusal to meet their demands, will go on a showdown strike. . . . .

SAFE

Five hundred miners will walk out of the Fulton Fuel Co. mine at 5 p.m. today, if the plans announced last night by A. C. Harte, union president, are carried out. The union is demanding a $12-a-day wage scale.

"We have talked long enough and now we are going to act," Harte declared. "We are ready for a showdown strike."

Prepared for trouble, the mineowners yesterday asked Sheriff John E. Fisher to assign 20 deputies to guard their property. . . . .

The dangerous story assumes that the miners will strike and the deputies will shoot, putting the newspaper in the role of a fortuneteller. The safe story makes no such assumptions. It is accurate regardless of the turn of events during the day.

FAIR HEADSTARTS AND GUN-JUMPING

Newspapers go to press at set hours of the day and night and news happenings are not necessarily timed for their convenience. Still they must stay as nearly abreast of the news parade as possible.

We have seen how a morning paper, the *Times*, exploited the Memorial Day plans in an advance story. An afternoon paper, going to press in the morning, at noon or in midafternoon, is confronted with the same problem in handling evening and nighttime events and, if it can, covers them in advance stories.

The advance writer often can overcome the handicap with such expressions as *were to be* and *was planned*. Examples:

Two former inmates of State Prison *were to be* arraigned in County Court today as the bandits who lugged a safe down two flights of stairs and were forced to flee without it.

A requiem mass *was to be offered* today at St. John's Church for Edward R. Cleveland, 62, who died at his home here yesterday.

A mass meeting to protest the proposed ban on daytime parking in the downtown area *was planned* for today by members of the Main Street Merchants Assn.

Use of the past tense, *were*, rather than the present tense, *are*, is forced upon the newspaper writer in these passages because the situation may change after the paper is printed. However, he may sometimes avoid awkwardness with phrases such as *is scheduled for* and *is expected.*

The present tense verb *faces* also is handy in a lead like this:

> The City Council *faces* a showdown vote today on a resolution providing for an immediate extension of the municipal water system to Hillview and Crestwood . . .

Assume that a public official is to make a newsworthy speech tonight. A reporter or rewrite man is asked to write an advance for the Early edition. He has a copy of the speech and may have permission to quote it with the proviso "as prepared for delivery last night."

While it is entirely proper thus to get off to a fair start in the way described, it is improper and dangerous to jump the gun on a clear release time or date. Had the speech manuscript been tabbed "For Release at 9 p.m." or "Release on Delivery" it would have been taboo until then. The usual release time for afternoon papers is 6:30 a.m. and for morning papers, 6:30 p.m.

Publicity pieces and time material often are unmarked or marked "Release on Receipt," in which case they may be used at once. More valuable and confidential statements carry exact release times.

Whatever the time specified for first publication, it is respected by reporters. Reputable newspapers keep faith with those who extend to them the courtesy of advance information.

WHAT HAPPENS NEXT?

A spot news story—even one widely heralded in advance—may die with a single printing. On the contrary, if strong with prominence and suspense, it may call for one or many follow-ups.

When he arrives at the office to begin the day's work the reporter is almost certain to find several clippings marked *watch* or *folo* by the city desk man. Few assignment sheets fail to instruct staff men to *folo strike, folo shooting, folo divorce, folo tournament.* Ordinarily one reporter handles the same story as long as it produces live copy. Thus he becomes familiar with its background, is able to recognize fresh developments instantly, and is prepared for quick recapitulation. Beat men, thoroughly conversant with their own territory, receive a larger proportion of *folo* assignments than their comrades on the street.

We have seen that the first element of news is timeliness. The public and the city editor want to know "What's the latest?" and "What happens next?" Consequently a follow-up story always begins with something distinctly new, a requirement that adds to the reporter's worries and taxes his resourcefulness.

"But it's all been written before," the cub protests in vain. It is up to him, if possible, to uncover a fresh angle, a new twist. Why is dynamite permitted within the city limits? Why did that dynamite let go and blow a house to splinters? What will be done about it? Answers to such queries as these may start him off on another line of productive inquiry.

Some serials develop automatically. Illness terminates in recovery or death, death in a funeral and a will. Romances culminate in engagements, engagements in weddings, weddings in honeymoons. Candidacies melt into nominations leading into campaigns followed by elections and inaugurations. A crime story, for example, often spins itself out in this fashion:

May 25. A robber shoots a storekeeper and escapes; police hunt starts.
May 26. The storekeeper dies.
May 28. Police capture suspected killer.
June 3. Suspect indicted and arraigned.
June 17. Trial starts with jury selection.
July 18. Testimony presented.
July 19. Jury retires.
July 20. Verdict delivered.
July 30. Defendant sentenced.
Aug. 10. Notice of appeal filed.
Aug. 31. Sentence upheld.
Sept. 3. Prisoner starts prison term.

If there is a lapse of time between chapters, the investigating reporter may refresh his memory of events by reference to the morgue. Careful reading of clippings on what has gone before will save him time and effort.

FOLLOW-UP AND SECOND-DAY STORIES

The terms *follow-up* and *second-day* both refer to articles written after the original event has occurred and been reported in print. They overlap and are used loosely and interchangeably in newsrooms. However, in this text it is necessary to define them explicitly for study and practice purposes.

> *Follow-up assignment.* An order given to a reporter to find out what, if any, new developments have occurred in connection with news previously printed. He may or may not obtain fresh facts.

Follow-up story. A spot news story consisting mainly of new facts with only short references to the original or previously printed stories on the same topic.

Second-day story. A story consisting mainly of facts previously printed, rewritten, but containing no report of new developments beyond those which can be assumed by the writer.

Second-day lead. The fore part of a second-day story.

The true follow-up story, as dealt with in this chapter, is spot news covered by a reporter and written by him unless he is a leg man. The second-day story is essentially work for a rewrite man and therefore is withheld for detailed discussion in Chapter 20, "Give It to a Rewrite Man."

There are, of course, gradations between follow-up and second-day stories. However, we will distinguish them arbitrarily by stating that while both are written in fresh words, the bulk of the information in a follow-up story is *new* and in the second-day story, *old*.

The opener of either a follow-up or a second-day story is called a *new lead* since it always consists of new words if not of new facts. Here are two examples of new leads with new facts:

> Seven-year-old Mary Douglas was buried today, while police searched for clues to the tall stranger who gave her a pickaback ride and left her dead or dying in a lonely wood.
>
> The girl's body was found yesterday. . . . .

> A 3-year-old boy got all the candy he could eat today for being brave while emergency crews dug him from a narrow abandoned well where he was trapped for an hour.
>
> Dickie Stevens stumbled into the temporarily unguarded hole last night. . . . .

The true follow-up story in a serial may forecast a new development and thus qualify also as an advance. Here we have new leads for combined follow-up and advance stories:

> A conference of four county health officers is scheduled to be held in Midland tomorrow as an aftermath to outbreaks of diphtheria this week in a dozen southern Centralia communities.

> A full inspection of the Midland County Jail where a riot raged for two-and-a-half hours last night was promised today by Sheriff John E. Fisher.

TYING IN THE BACKGROUND

Let us now observe the chronological developments of a news serial. The Midland *Herald*, an afternoon paper, prints an original story on Monday beginning thus:

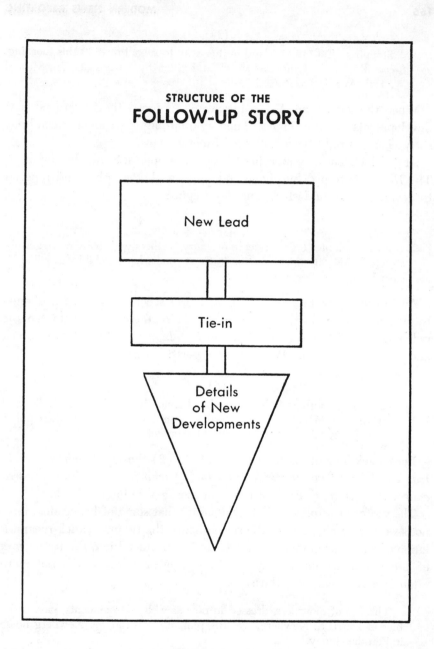

The Follow-up Diagram

(1)

Stepping off a safety island on her way to school at 8:30 this morning, 8-year-old Gracie Lane was struck and killed by a truck at 17th St. and W. 13th Ave. in Crestwood.

When the *Times,* an AM paper, went to press, there were no new developments, so the *Times,* Tuesday morning, carried a second-day story changed only by a notice of funeral plans.

At 8 o'clock Tuesday morning there is an important new development. The *Herald* is tipped by phone and sends a photographer and reporter to cover. The *Herald* story Tuesday begins:

(2)

For 20 minutes today, a score of angry mothers with baby carriages obstructed traffic at an intersection in Crestwood where a child was killed by a truck yesterday.

Again the *Times* must be satisfied with a second-day story freshened by an advance angle that a committee of mothers will try to see the police chief at noon Wednesday. The *Herald* once more gets the break and in its late editions Wednesday reports:

(3)

Crusading mothers, who formed a human barricade at 17th St. and W. 13th Ave. in Crestwood yesterday, won a victory today when police promised to install new traffic lights at the corner.

Look back now at (2) and (3). Note in (2) the words *where a child was killed by a truck yesterday* and in (3) *who formed a human barricade . . . yesterday.* Each of these phrases is a tie-in or tieback.

The writer of a follow-up story assumes that some of his readers have not seen earlier chapters of the serial; hence the tie-in, a quick recapitulation of what has gone before. A tie-in is introduced into the framework of late developments. It may consist merely of a few words but more often is a full sentence, thus:

Throngs of mourners, dressed in rags as well as frock coats, passed the bier of Harris S. Newberg, wealthy philanthropist, at the Newberg home in Ferndale today.

After a brief illness Newberg, who gave a fortune to charities, died following an operation Thursday.

In a secluded wing of the 14-room Georgian mansion, Mrs. Newberg remained in bed, prostrated by grief, while the body lay in state. Fifty were in line at 8 a.m. when . . . . .

An expanded synopsis is needed to recapitulate more complex action, as in this example:

> With the recovery of three bodies from the ruins of the Rockford Chair Co. factory late today, the number of dead in *Friday's tornado* was increased to nine. A hundred men were tearing away the debris trying to find four unaccounted-for workers.
>
> *The chair factory was demolished by a 90-mile-an-hour wind which swept the lower part of the state. All but 15 of the 300 workmen inside escaped when creaking timbers warned them of the impending crash.*
>
> The bodies of the following were recovered today:
>
> John S. Hawkins. . . . .

Many stories require even more background information than can be crowded into a paragraph or two. In stories of business, politics and other complex topics, it often becomes necessary for the reporter to awaken the memories of his readers with more detailed explanatory material. This is usually summarized in a tie-in near the top of the story and elaborated upon at the end.

DIAGRAMING THE FOLLOW-UP STORY

With the two essentials, a new lead and a tie-in, as the main features, it is now possible to diagram the typical follow-up story with a design like that shown in an accompanying chart.

This diagram, of course, is applicable only to the average story, its parts varying with the length and importance of the tie-in data. But you can diagram any follow-up narrative to carry out the general arrangement. Try it on this one:

> A furnace tended by an unskilled hand was blamed today for the deaths of four students in the coal gas catastrophe in Haven Hall at Midland College yesterday.
>
> They were killed when deadly carbon monoxide fumes from a disconnected pipe crept through the 16-room dormitory while they slept.
>
> President Ralph Cummings asked the grief-stricken undergraduates today to "carry on" their activities in order not to heighten the effect of the accident. He said that "the whole college sympathizes with the parents of those who died."
>
> A statement issued by Coroner R. E. Williams said: "The position of the shaker arm and of the check draft lever indicated that the furnace had been fixed the night before by someone who was not entirely familiar with it."
>
> While funeral plans were under consideration, it had not been decided yet whether the bodies would be sent by their families for burial at their homes. One suggestion was that all four of the victims be buried here, with a fitting monument to rise later over their graves.

APPLICATION OF THE
FOLLOW-UP DIAGRAM

**NEW
LEAD**

Miss Daphne Sloane, 23-year-old Clay City school teacher, accepted her crown and scepter as "Queen of the Blossoms" last night at the annual carnival of the Timber Valley Fruit Growers Assn. in Central Auditorium

TIE-IN

Miss Sloane, a golden blonde, won her honors over 150 competitors in a countywide popularity contest sponsored by the association two weeks ago. She received 762 votes.

The crowning of the new "queen," climaxing the two-day festivities of the association's annual convention, was witnessed by 2,500 spectators. Mayor Nelson presented Miss Sloane with a crown of blossoms and a silver scepter.

Her attendants were the Misses Carol Hunt, of Southfield, and Lucy Hempstead, of Midland, runners-up in the contest.

Later Miss Sloane, with William O. Kellogg, president of the group, as her escort, led the grand march in a ball following the blossom ceremonies.

**DETAILS
OF NEW
DEVELOP-
MENTS**

Others in the promenade included Mayor and Mrs. Nelson, Senator and Mrs. Theodore Lee, Judge and Mrs. Henry Dayton, Daniel Perkins, county commissioner, and Mrs. Perkins, Sloan Baker, county superintendent of schools, and Mrs. Baker, and Postmaster and Mrs. Harold M. Skipworth.

At a business session in the afternoon, the association re-elected Kellogg for his third term as president. Other officers re-elected were Charles Daniels, secretary, and Louis Harrison, treasurer. The association voted to hold its convention next year in Southfield.

Three Parts of the Follow-up Story

Diagraming mentally helps the beginner in difficulty with the fol-low-up story because of the tie-in complications. His greatest blunder is an attempt to include too much material in the tie-in and thus clog the story. A synopsis of the barest facts, stripped of nonessentials and wordi-ness, will serve to bring the chronicle up-to-date. Do this in a few swift sentences, then hurry back to the new material. A long, heavy tie-in slows up the account and annoys the reader in his search for fresh bread instead of stale crusts.

The reporter's second blunder, also bad, is to forget the tie-in alto-gether. To repeat: Merely because *you* know what has happened pre-viously you are not warranted in assuming that the reader is similarly well informed. Perhaps he has not seen a paper for several days or has entirely overlooked the earlier account.

In each instance the fault may be remedied by careful planning. Think out your story divisions and fact grouping before you begin to write. Weigh the tie-in material judiciously, estimate the amount of background necessary, then piece the material together, giving special display to the latest tidings.

SHOP TALK

1. Discuss the day-by-day and month-by-month development of news subjects, tracing the life histories of several topics of current interest.
2. How does the community newspaper render service as a bulletin board for information about events to come? Cite several examples.
3. What is cumulative interest in the news? Analyze the psychology behind the demand of readers for follow-up stories.
4. Define and discuss the terms *follow-up* and *second-day*.
5. What is a new lead in a follow-up story? A tie-in? Find several examples in newspapers. Underscore and discuss them.

CHAPTER 13

From Platform to Press

AN X QUANTITY IN THE NEWS

Sifting out and preparing for print utterances made from public rostrums is a public duty as well as a perplexing problem for reporters and editors on newspapers of every size.

Talks, speeches, addresses and debates are a normal and necessary outlet for expression in a democracy. Freedom of assembly and speech are fundamental to freedom of the press. From Colonial public squares and town halls to modern microphones and loud-speakers the journals and gazettes of America have fulfilled their obligation to report every spoken point of view on matters of public concern.

The problem lies in selection and space. Lectures, after-dinner discourses, sermons, radio and television talks produce such an overwhelming and inexhaustible supply of material that they are an X quantity of the news pages.

Crossroad hamlets have their farmers' granges, assemblies at schoolhouse and church. Small and medium-sized cities and the suburban neighborhoods of larger ones have their political rallies, town, union, lodge and society meetings, luncheon and lecture clubs, lyceums, Chautauquas and revival meetings. Metropolitan centers have their conferences, conventions and forums of nationwide import, as well as countless lesser gatherings. And legislative chambers from village board and city council rooms to the halls of state legislatures and Congress resound with the discourses, discussions and disputes of lawmakers.

Thousands of speeches and millions of words pour from many mouths every day and only the fittest can survive to be seen in print. These fill columns of space.

Before the advent of radio and television the press alone provided a sounding board to broadcast public utterances beyond the range of the human voice. The air wave carriers have failed to reduce speech coverage in print. Instead they have expanded it.

It is the task of the editor, by applying the eight-element yardstick, to choose newsworthy speeches for assignments. It is the task of the reporter to cover them honestly and write them compactly, pointing up the news and putting aside propaganda, platitudes and piffle.

THE SPEECH STORY ASSIGNMENT

The coverage of a speech can be a pleasure or a plague to the reporter and sometimes it is a mixture of both.

There is nothing difficult about sauntering into an auditorium with a pass or badge, being escorted to a comfortable up-front press table, chatting with fellow-newsmen awhile, then languidly looking at a mimeographed manuscript of a speaker who never varies the text, pocketing the paper, and returning to the office with plenty of time to ponder and type the story.

But it can be difficult indeed to arrive late, to be regarded perhaps as an unwanted spy, to elbow into a crowded corner, to try to take notes on the back of a man standing in front of you—if you dare to take any at all—and wonder if another reporter caught the climactic comment you failed to hear.

It can be just as frustrating at a convention or conference to find two noteworthy speeches being made at the same hour in different rooms and have to pick up one or the other secondhand, or to discover that you must leave in the middle of an extemporaneous speech in order to meet a deadline.

Maybe you will lunch leisurely on the house and on working time. Or, again, you may need to skip or gulp your dinner in order to cover a night speech on overtime when you have tickets to the theater. You must, of course, take the good with the bad and make the best of the situation as you meet it.

If possible, it is wise before leaving the city room to visit the morgue, riffle through the clippings on the speaker or speakers and the sponsoring group, clip and pocket an advance story or two if available in the current papers.

Upon arrival, time permitting, the newsman should supplement his library data on the speech setting. Who are at the speakers' table? What are their names and positions? What is the size of the audience? And at what point during the program should he plan to telephone the office or leave the meeting?

These preliminary precautions and labors pay off as departure time approaches and when the city desk calls for copy or corrections just before a deadline.

Assuming that he is not hurried, a reporter sometimes can improve a story by a short interview after the conclusion of the talk, using an idea implanted by the speaker but not fully treated. He also may obtain additional facts, statistics and quotations for use in building up opinions on a certain phase of the discussion.

SPEECH COPIES IN ADVANCE

To obtain his background facts a trained reporter tries first to find the group secretary, publicity man or head of the program committee. If none is on hand, he should consult the chairman or the speaker himself.

He may obtain not only factual data but something far more important —a verbatim copy of the speech, prepared in advance, or abstracts of pertinent passages. These are provided by news-wise publicity people and practiced lecturers. It is inexcusable to ignore them.

Frequently an advance copy of a speech is sent to newspapers with the date and time of release specified. As pointed out in the previous chapter, newspapers seldom incur a charge of unfairness by violating release restrictions.

If the text or any part of it is used in print before a speech is made, the writer says so. He may report that the speech is scheduled and prepared for delivery and that arrangements have been made for a crowd of, say, 3,500—not that the speaker will address an audience of 3,500. He may become ill and send regrets, while rain may reduce the crowd to a handful, making the story false and ridiculous.

Even more serious trouble can ensue if a controversial speech is quoted without a reporter either on hand or listening to it by television or radio to be certain that the text is followed.

If the speech is an important one and the speaker interpolates a newsworthy comment off the cuff or if he is interrupted or engages in a caustic exchange with a heckler, the paper failing to check may find itself scooped on the extracurricular development.

Still another danger lurks in blindly accepting and printing portions of a prepared-in-advance version of a controversial speech. At the last moment—even after he has started—a speaker may omit passages appearing in print as though they had been spoken.

There are on record successful suits for libel against defendant newspapers which printed parts of speeches which would have been privileged. However, the questionable material was deleted and never delivered. As there was accordingly no privilege, the plaintiffs won judgment and the newspapers paid.

Even though the words dropped out are not potentially libelous, their use astonishes a reader who heard the speech and knows that they were not spoken. In such a case the newspaper loses face and its reputation for accurate reporting.

SHOULD YOU STUDY SHORTHAND?

Without a carbon copy or mimeo of a speech, or excerpts from it, in hand a reporter must take notes. The city editor who told a cub, "Don't bother with notes because if the guy says anything worth printing you'll remember it," gave poor advice.

Unless you possess a phenomenal memory, exact words and phrases, sharp sentences and precise paragraphs—quotes to dress up your story— will escape you before you reach a telephone or a typewriter. Few faults lose friends faster than loose paraphrasing and sloppy quotations of what you thought you heard instead of what actually was spoken.

A beginner tends to take too many notes, rather than too few, and rightly so. A veteran may be able to write a column from the back of an envelope but the new man needs more. Otherwise he may find himself sorely handicapped by a scarcity of material. Better too much than not enough.

Is a knowledge of shorthand desirable? Editors and reporters themselves disagree. There is no question, however, that shorthand of some kind, conventional or homemade, is necessary. The average speaking speed is 150 to 160 words a minute; the average writing speed, 30 to 40. No pencil or pen can spell out a script as fast as it is spoken, much less keep up with a machine-gun orator or a dogfight debate. The question therefore is not whether short-cut notetaking is needed but what system should be employed.

All literate people—a student taking notes during a classroom lecture, a doctor writing a prescription or a housewife jotting down a grocery list—use abbreviations. Most of us write *U.S.* for United States, *Co.* for company, *Feb.* for February, and so on. A majority of American reporters merely extend this method, producing notes like this one:

> M opnt sys elct me & sv Md mny. Lts lk at rec. Wre $100,000 in dt. On rd to bnkpsy.
> If I wn wl rse tchrs py & bal budg 2. Cn b dun & wl b dun b4 n yr.

Some experienced reporters write out significant quotes almost in full, even though while writing they may miss the speaker's next remarks:

> My oppont says "Elect me & save money." Let's look at the record. We're $100,000 in debt.
> If I win I will raise tchers pay and balance budget too. It can b done & will b done b-4 next yr.

Such handwritten notes are made more legible and are easier to follow if important passages are underscored or upright marks are placed at the margin to emphasize quotable high lights.

To learn a more complicated system such as Pitman, Gregg or Speed-writing, like learning to use a typewriter, requires time and training. Is it worth the effort for a newsman?

The antis say no. Shorthand makes a stenographer out of a reporter. It is a nuisance and a drawback rather than an asset. It robs the reporter of perspective, deflecting him from watching the face and gestures of the speaker and the reactions of the audience. Finally it results in long and labored transcription of too many pothooks when writing speed counts.

On the other hand, the pros point out that not just a word or phrase here and there needs to be quoted verbatim but frequently a lengthy passage, replete with statistical or technical data which cannot possibly be reproduced from squiggles and memory. A speaker goes on inexorably and there is no salvaging what you miss because you can't get it down fast enough. As for taking too many notes, there is no more compulsion to take them in shorthand than in crudely abbreviated longhand.

The argument that shorthand is a valued tool when taking question-and-answer notes at a trial or a prepared statement read by telephone adds strength to the pro position.

Surveys indicate that the shorthand advocates are gaining ground. A few years ago self-respecting reporters took notes mostly on tradi-tional copy paper. Now more and more carry stenographers' notebooks.

The secret of using any short-cut system, of course, is to make it auto-matic—a tool, not a master. Think before and as you write. Anticipate if possible when an apt or pertinent quote is coming, or try to detect it instantly. Catch it. Get it down. Then stop writing. Thus your notes will be neither too scant nor too lengthy as you convert them rapidly into compact copy.

Few reporters keep their notes after a story has been written. Some preserve them for a day or two to see if there is any kickback, but thereafter they simply clutter up the drawers of a desk.

In recent years a newcomer has entered the note-taking picture—the portable tape recorder. It is more useful in interviewing than in speech covering and therefore will be discussed in the next chapter.

EXTRACTING NEWS FROM A SPEECH

Several important considerations test the value of any public address. Who is the speaker? Every word uttered by the President of the United States is news, whereas the ramblings of a schoolboy orator count for nothing.

Second, what is the speaker's authority for his statements? A physicist commenting on nuclear energy, a senator discussing government policies, an opera star talking about voice culture, a clergyman about the shortcomings of the church, a business executive about trade rivalry create news that people want to read. But if they attempt to speak on subjects with which they are not conversant, the result is a mere jumble of inconclusive conjectures. Test the worth of a speaker's remarks by his qualifications for making them.

Again, are the statements offered by the speaker timely? If an influenza epidemic is raging, what a noted doctor has to say about the flu might make page one, but what he thinks about the bubonic plague at this particular time would sink into obscurity. The wise newsman extracts from any address such comments as apply to situations and events immediately before the public eye.

Does the speech strike fire? A single ironical jibe, one caustic comment, may furnish just the spark to ignite the tinder of the lead. Look for it but be careful not to give an unfair estimate of the main purpose of the talk.

Finally, have the speaker's opinions been printed in previous reports? Be sure your lead material, at least, is not old stuff. Perhaps the Congressman has delivered the same whirlwind speech in your city time and again. At the outset the reporter should be familiar with earlier statements made by the same stem-winder on an identical topic in the same community.

Now and then a speaker will hurl a bombshell of tremendous lead significance and then repent his outspokenness. Before using the phrase as an opener the reporter should reflect upon the problem of sustaining it with quotations or explanations strong enough at least to give excuse for publication.

The surest criterion for judging the value of a speech story is the reporter's own reaction to it. What impresses, intrigues, startles or amuses you will probably impress, intrigue, startle or amuse the readers of your story. What falls on your ears as flat and innocuous will probably affect readers in the same way. Watching the audience also helps gauge the effectiveness of the discourse.

The question of policy, which cannot altogether be disregarded in reporting a speech, will be discussed fully in another chapter. It is sufficient here to say that the reporter, fortified by diligent daily reading of his own paper, should know the views of its publisher. Within reason therefore he will select and play up passages from an address that uphold the position held by the paper he serves.

TYPES OF SPEECH LEADS

Fortunate is the reporter who finds a man so gifted in the art of public address that he keeps the audience attentive by delivery of pithy epigrams and razor-edged opinions. These characteristic phrases lend themselves to quotation and are injected into the lead with telling effect. Some speakers originate epithets that instantly hit the target. Other men do not have the faculty for making burlike statements that cling to the listener's memory. Their minds are more plodding, their convictions conventional.

Capture the striking point—that is the only universal rule applicable to all speech story leads. The lead is not likely to be the fact that somebody made a speech, but something striking that he said. Although the name of the speaker, his subject and the circumstances of the meeting must be mentioned, they rarely make strong openers. Do not write:

> Judge George H. Mather gave a talk on "Archaic Laws" today at a meeting of the Midland Bar Assn.

> "Archaic Laws" was the subject of an address by Judge George H. Mather before the Midland Bar Assn. today.

> Members of the Midland Bar Assn. heard a speech on "Archaic Laws" by Judge George H. Mather today.

The lead should be *what Judge Mather said* about archaic laws:

> You can be fined $5 for driving a mule faster than 10 miles an hour past a cemetery, under an old city ordinance still on the statute books, Judge George H. Mather told members of the Midland Bar Assn. today.

Three types of leads are available to writers who undertake to digest and summarize a speech. The first and most widely used is an indirect quotation stressing a striking point; the second, a forceful direct quotation; the third, a blending of the high lights into a keynote statement that indicates the main conclusions reached by the speaker. The three types are illustrated in the following examples:

Indirect Quotation

One-third of Midland's public schools were described as firetraps by Frank S. Robins, secretary of the South Side Parent-Teacher Assn., at a meeting of the Board of Education today.

A slightly messy home is likely to be a happy home. That is what Prof. J. Lloyd King of the University of Centralia told a meeting of the Midland Woman's Club last night.

Direct Quotation

"There are more slot machines than church pews in Timber County," the Rev. John Carston told his congregation last night at the First Baptist Church.

"We have hit bottom in the business slump and are on our way out," Louis R. Stebbins, manager of the United Products Co., asserted at a luncheon meeting of the Midland Merchants Assn. today.

Keynote

Federal control of all truck size and weight regulations was urged by H. C. Hopkins, New York highway expert, in an address today at a luncheon of the Traffic Club.

Drastic revision of Centralia's divorce laws which he said now benefit only the wealthy was recommended by Senator Simon Latour yesterday. He spoke before the Midland Welfare Council at the Hotel Harper.

Pertinent direct quotations sometimes are placed in a box accompanying the story to give a better typographical effect.

WATCHING FOR THE UNEXPECTED

Even if he has in advance a complete copy of an address or excerpts from it a reporter should if possible be in the audience when it is delivered. The speaker may discard or wander from his manuscript and coin epigrams which make the prepared speech sound tame and commonplace. An interpolation may figuratively bring down the house. The speaker may be heckled. The chairman may steal the show.

The reporter must be prepared to readjust himself to any sudden shift in the program. If an unexpected development outweighs the speech itself in news value, let him discard everything else and give that feature full play in the story.

Speech Quotations in Box Form

This one might never have seen print had not the reporter seized upon and exploited the surprise incident:

> A bewildered bat all but broke up a meeting of the Midland Woman's Club yesterday during a speech entitled "How to Overcome Your Fears" by Dr. C. A. Brooks.
>
> Just as the psychiatrist was describing the fear of harmless creatures as "silly," the bat flew in an open window. Several women ducked screaming as the bat darted to and fro.
>
> "That little fellow isn't going to hurt anybody," said Dr. Brooks. With a broom he calmly chased it back out the window, then resumed his talk.

SPEECH STORY STRUCTURE

We previously have likened a newspaper story to a railroad train. The analogy fits the standard report of a speech. As it is made up, the engine represents the lead; the tender, the background or setting; the baggage and passenger or freight cars, the body of quotes and summaries of quotes; and the observation car, or caboose, the conclusion.

The comparison may be carried further. Just as the length of a train is determined by the number of baggage, passenger or freight cars, so may the reporter control the length of his article. Lead, setting and one quote or summary, coupled together, make a complete unit. He may add as many additional passages as necessary to fulfill desk and space requirements.

The arrangement of the speech write-up follows the quote diagram. This diagram is used for any story composed largely of quotable material. For practice, apply it to the following:

Lead—Summary

Critics of the "activity" or "learn-by-doing" program in the Midland public school system were challenged today to prove their charges that pupils are not learning the fundamentals of the three R's.

Setting

The challenge was made by Dr. J. M. McClure, superintendent of schools, before 300 members of Midland's Parent-Teacher Associations at their monthly luncheon in the Rex Hotel.

Quote

"There is an organized drive afoot to uproot the modern approach to education in our schools," Dr. McClure declared.

Summary

The avowed purpose of these attacks, in the opinion of the superintendent, is to turn back the clock and get rid of the program entirely.

STRUCTURE OF THE
SPEECH STORY

**LEAD
SUMMARY**

Midland College stands at the crossroads where it must either march forward to a place of leadership or turn aside into the pathway of obscurity, President Ralph Cummings declared last night.

Addressing 400 members of the Midland Merchants Assn. at the Commercial Club, Dr. Cummings urged them to subscribe to the $400,000 endowment fund needed for a new Administration Building.

QUOTE

"I appeal to you, not alone as men interested in the educational advancement of the community, but as practical businessmen," said Dr. Cummings. "You cannot afford to see Midland College slip backward."

SUMMARY

Stressing the growing enrollment at the college—an increase of 15 per cent in the last three years—the speaker warned that unless its building facilities are expanded, matriculations next year must be limited.

QUOTE

"Every inch of the five buildings now on the campus is in use and we are even using the gymnasium for classes," he continued.

SUMMARY

Students are compelled to sit on stairways in the old library at some hours because of the shortage of space in the reading rooms, according to Dr. Cummings.

QUOTE

"Midland College is your institution," the President went on. "Pioneer Midlanders founded it and have carried it on through the years. We must not fail in this time of crisis."

SUMMARY

Dr. Cummings was introduced by Henry Sturtevant, president of the association . . . . .

The Speech Diagram

Quote

Dr. McClure continued: "It is significant that these attacks are being led by groups that are not primarily concerned with the schools and their problems. It is clear from the nature of the criticisms that they are based on lack of understanding of the new concepts of pedagogy."

Summary

Praising the work of John Dewey, pioneer proponent of "progressive schooling" in the United States, Dr. McClure asserted:

Quote

"Our children can read, write, spell, do arithmetic and use grammar—which is more important than learning a lot of meaningless rules."

Summary

In criticizing "drill or rote" teaching, the school superintendent argued that under former methods "a child might win a medal in American history and still not have learned the meaning of American democracy."

Despite the comparative ease with which such a story may be handled, it requires a certain degree of craftsmanship which may be translated into plain willingness to work. The lazy way to write such a story is to pounce upon the first lead that presents itself and attach to it a mass of quotations, important and trivial, in haphazard order. The result is a slipshod, disorganized conglomeration, heavy and hard to digest.

Select your quotations carefully. It may facilitate your work to underline with a pencil the possible leads and best quotations, if you have not already done so. Then study the material critically and classify it in an orderly fashion.

HELPFUL WORDS AND PHRASES

Active verbs contribute much to the movement in speech quotations. In a speech story *said* is a simple, sound word but it can quickly become overworked and flavorless. In fact it is the custom of some writers to use it with the first of a series of quotes, then move on to *declared, asserted* and so on, and finally, on the theory the reader will not realize he is getting a warmed-over word, start again with *said.* The aim is not to use *said* or any of the substitutes twice in succession.

The best word is probably different for every quotation. Whatever it is, it always is the exact word. Here are just a few of the handiest variants which can stand duty for *said,* when appropriate.

added	demanded	pleaded
admonished	disclosed	proposed
agreed	emphasized	remarked
announced	entreated	repeated
answered	exclaimed	reported
argued	held	replied
asked	insisted	retorted
charged	interjected	shouted
commented	laughed	snapped
contended	maintained	stated
continued	observed	urged

If you want to hang a statement exclusively on a speaker, dissociating yourself and your newspaper from it, avoid expressions which imply that what is being quoted, directly or indirectly, is a fact. To write that "the Senator has a record of broken promises, his opponent *pointed out*" is to concur in the accusation. Similar danger expressions include *admitted, affirmed, conceded, explained* and *cited the fact that.*

Other substitutes for *said* may be uncomplimentary and therefore are used only with discretion, if at all. Among these are *barked, begged, bellowed, cried, drawled, insinuated, grumbled, mumbled, muttered, ranted, roared, shrieked, spouted* and *stammered.*

Use of direct quotations in a speech story can be overdone. Too many quotations tend to make the text as monotonous as none at all. The best arrangement is a happy medium with quotations and paraphrasing interspersed.

After trimming out irrelevancies the reporter arranges his best quotations by topics, linking them together with such coupling-pin phrases as the following:

> Insisting that this theory is "wrong in principle," he declared . . .
> Turning to the question of taxation, he argued in favor of . . .
> Cheers greeted his attack on . . .
> As proof of this assertion, he cited . . .
> Detailing the plan, he listed three improvements . . .
> Meanwhile, he explained . . .
> Lashing out at the foes of his proposal . . .
> Holding aloft a copy of the pamphlet, he urged . . .
> He concluded with a eulogy to . . .

Avoid repetition of phraseology in both direct and indirect quotations. The moment a reader reaches a series of words or ideas previously expressed his tendency is to leave the rest of the story unread. Variety and freshness must linger to the end.

CATCHING QUOTES IN DEBATES

Every experienced reporter appreciates the value of specific quotations in an account of a conference, debate or meeting where arguments develop. Although he makes no effort to take down in full all the conversation, he does endeavor to capture and weave into his story the liveliest and most pertinent samples.

Debate quotations in print serve to break the solidity of paraphrasing and give the reader's eyes a pleasant coast between uphill climbs through monotonous country. Frequently they will add an edge to a seemingly dull story.

George Moore of the *Gazette* and Jack Wheeling of the *Times* each covered a session of the Midland Apartment Janitors Union. Compare these extracts from their stories:

Gazette

President O'Rourke, insisting that the present wage scale of $15 a day is insufficient, pointed out that during the last few years wages for similar kinds of work have gone up steadily. This argument was answered by the secretary, who declared that since the janitors have been relieved of coal handling, their labors are less strenuous.

The controversy between the officials became so personal that at one point a physical clash seemed likely. Other members were forced to hold Carswell after O'Rourke replied to his charge that the president was a "white-collar dictator" by calling him a "traitor to the labor cause."

There was much noise and confusion as the strike vote was taken. . . . .

Times

O'Rourke and Carswell divided sharply on the wage issue and nearly came to blows. The president contended that $15 a day is too little when carpenters and plumbers get $20 to $25. Carswell held that, as the janitors recently won on the coal handling question, their demand for $17.50 is excessive.

"You know we can't get away with it," asserted Carswell. "You'll put us all out of work."

"Have you sold out to the landlords?" O'Rourke asked him.

The secretary in reply, described O'Rourke as a "white-collar dictator" unaware of real working conditions.

"That's a lie!" the union president shouted. "You are a traitor to the labor cause."

O'Rourke advanced belligerently across the room. Other members, however, kept the two officials apart.

Tense excitement prevailed during the strike balloting. . . . .

The *Times* account not only is specific and noneditorial but is more attractive to the eye in print. The *Gazette* story is generalized and looks logy with lumps of solid type.

SHOP TALK

1. Do you believe radio and television have lessened the usefulness of the printing press in broadcasting public addresses? Compare the merits of each.
2. If he has an advance copy of a speech, why should a reporter be in the audience? What other information does he need?
3. Should a prospective reporter study shorthand? Cite circumstances where it might be an advantage; a disadvantage.
4. Discuss the readability of direct and indirect quotations in a speech report.
5. See how many substitutes for the word *said* you can add to those listed in this chapter. Race your neighbor in a five-minute synonym test.

CHAPTER 14

Interviews and Press Conferences

THE IMPORT OF INTERVIEWS

Face-to-face and phone-to-phone conversations between reporters and persons from whom they seek information provide the basis for perhaps two-thirds of all news in print and are incidental to most of the other one-third.

From the start to the end of his career the reporter is an asker of questions, a listener to and recorder of the replies. Like Diogenes with his lamp searching for an honest man the reporter searches ceaselessly for people in possession of opinions and facts which he desires.

In his quest for news the reporter successively plays the role of prying detective, successful salesman, probing psychiatrist, wily diplomat, confidential friend, examining attorney and questioning quiz-master.

Some beat men, among them airport and ship reporters, devote themselves almost exclusively to interviews with incoming or departing travelers. Others, making their daily rounds or stationed in pressrooms, also collect much of their copy from conversations and conferences. On-the-street reporters seldom cover a wedding, funeral, fire, wreck, business deal, crime or convention without interviewing somebody and they constantly are sent to see and talk to specific news makers.

As discussed in this chapter, interviews are those specialized stories secured from noteworthy persons whose names, activities and opinions win public attention. Interviews of this variety, like speeches, produce a wealth of reading raw material for newspapers of every size.

There is never abatement of curiosity about statesmen, athletic champions, society leaders, millionaires and their heirs, gang chieftains, leading scientists, inventors and explorers, and stars of the entertainment world. Not only these but anyone who has done, said, or seen anything out of the ordinary—even the Smiths who hold a winning sweepstakes ticket—are subjects of the interviewer's typewriter.

Movies, the radio, television, magazines and phonograph records—all help to make us familiar with the physical appearance, voice, mannerisms, life histories and views of prominent folk to the point that privacy is almost an unknown quantity in America.

Despite the development of the competing communicators, the newspaper is the prime purveyor of day-to-day as well as background data about newsy people and the interview story continues to hold, if not increase, its popularity in the press.

PLANNING AN INTERVIEW

"Go and see Mr. Big from Boston and find out what he has to say about business conditions" or "Meet Miss Beauty from Birmingham and ask her why she's changed from a blonde to a brunette"—these are assignments familiar in every local room. The city editor's assignment sheet sometimes carries a half dozen citations like these:

> See Morley of the Motor Club about his traffic plan. He's back from tour today.
> Coroner Williams ought to have a folo on the Krossroads Kafé shooting last night.
> Jet plane tests at Municipal Airport at 3 p.m. today. Interview the pilot.
> What do Midland parents think about the row over discrimination in high school sororities?
> See Museum Curator Radcliffe about the pottery dug up in rock quarry.

Occasionally the reporter is directed to secure a specific statement or try for a special slant, especially if policy is involved. But more often the desk assignment merely suggests one or two timely topics and the writer gets what booty he is able to appropriate in the course of the interview.

As in the case of a speech assignment, an interview order ordinarily offers the reporter a chance to get ready for it in advance. To be forearmed for the interview not only is an advantage but often spells the difference between haphazard seining and skilled casting. You may be a veteran fisherman but you cannot predict how many fish a particular trout fly will catch. Why? Because you will never know enough about fish. Just so with people. It's best to have several kinds of lures in your kit.

If you have time, go to the morgue, look at the clips and find out what

TYPICAL KINDS OF
INTERVIEW ASSIGNMENTS

Hollywood Actress Sylvia Steel arrives at Union Station. Will she marry her director?

What's the damage? Any evidence of arson? Ask the chief.

Call Postmaster Skipworth. Ask him why the snow isn't shoveled off the post office sidewalk.

See Professor Laird, astronomer at Midland College, re sighting of satellite last night.

Inquiry Jobs for Reporters

you can about your man in advance, especially about the topic or topics on which he can speak with authority.

Plan to localize if possible, linking up the interviewee with something familiar to your readers. Note if the person to be questioned has anything in common with the community or its citizens. Also plan to make the interview timely. If the town is in a hubbub about the need for stronger levees to keep back high water, don't quiz a consulting engineer about municipal government; extract his views on flood control.

It may even be helpful to write out some of your questions. While you are not likely to read them off, they at least should be in the front of your mind. If you have none your interview may quickly collapse.

Perhaps you have no chance to prepare for the interview. In that event you must "feel" your way through the conversation and trust to ingenuity and luck to guide you into the right pathway. An answer to one query may furnish a capital lead and chart the way for the rest of the interview.

Again, the conversation may drift into unrelated topics—startlingly bizarre—with disastrous consequences to the story the reporter expected. If so, excellent! The reporter then abandons his previous line of inquiry and pursues the unsought story which is more interesting than the one he had originally planned.

THE ART OF ASKING QUESTIONS

The approach in an interview depends entirely upon the character of the person you are seeing and the circumstances under which it is being conducted. Certainly you cannot talk to a hysterical mother whose son has just killed his best friend as you would to a publicity-wise actress at ease and awaiting you in her hotel suite.

Generally speaking the more distinguished or well-publicized person, used to appearing in the public eye, is the easiest to approach. Those less experienced may need to be flattered, cajoled and, in rare cases, bluffed. Some are silent as statues; others garrulous as loud-speakers.

Under ordinary circumstances make the approach direct. Explain that you represent a newspaper and if you want quotes on a particular subject state briefly what it is. Ten to one your man will respond in the same frank way. Certainly he will try to do so if he is accustomed to being interviewed.

To help establish a friendly atmosphere and put a man at ease, it may be well at the start to mention something in which *he* is personally interested—his new grandchild or latest golf score—and then lead him into the more provocative topic in which *you* are interested. Don't let pleasantries or anecdotes last too long or lead to nothing.

Be natural. Neither arrogance nor humility is likely to impress favorably the person from whom you expect information. Remember that an interviewer represents a responsible newspaper which deserves his loyalty and is not a beggar asking for alms. You need not be too humble in seeking a statement; on the other hand, do not throw your weight around. The temptation to turn on the heat, to put the squeeze on is to be resisted at all times. Above all, don't antagonize a person by argument. Courtesy, firmness and an intelligent curiosity are assets to the skillful interrogator.

Keep your attention on the interviewee. A meeting of eyes is conversational art anywhere. Look as though you are interested in every word he speaks. Nothing repels like an appearance of boredom. However, do not exclaim over the tremendous news value of something he has just told you or he may begin to hedge and qualify.

Finally, judge what you are hearing by the same scale of standards applied to other news. The interview will be played up or down in proportion to immediacy, proximity, oddity and the other news elements.

NOTE-TAKING AND TAPE-TALK

Note-taking is a practical problem for reporters on any assignment. When covering a speech, perhaps, notes may be made unobtrusively or during a press conference openly. But during an interview, especially with a person unaccustomed to talking with reporters, it often must be done warily, if at all.

The sight of pencil and paper may be a red flag that will stiffen a man and make him shut up like a clam; or, less frequently, it can be a green flag that starts a marathon of chatter. In either case the newsman loses control and his subject takes over the interview.

You are commissioned to get interesting quotes and if you can jot them down as you hear them, good! But don't poise a pencil until you are sure you will not alarm the quarry and make the news hunt hopeless.

If you must get along without notes, fix the conversation in your mind, get the key words on paper as soon as you can, and make the best of it. Better a few quotes than none at all.

In the preceding chapter we discussed the pros and cons of learning shorthand. In recent years another kind of note-taking has been introduced, largely by radio and television newsmen—mechanical recording.

At one time making old-fashioned cylindrical Gramophone records was a laborious process calling for cumbersome equipment. Then came reproduction of sounds on disks, wire and tape machines, some operated with miniature batteries and even tinier transistors. Modern recorders are compact, lightweight and as portable as a camera. They can capture any sound with the flick of a switch.

The broadcast media, of course, have made the widest use of recorders, especially radio, which is entirely oral, but newspapers are finding them usable in limited ways.

Recorders are used by some metropolitan papers for receiving phoned-in stories dictated by leg men and, on occasion, when a verbatim text is wanted, for press conferences and interviews.

A recorder has obvious advantages and handicaps as compared to note-taking. Working with a pencil, you must stop and write, now and then interrupt and ask for something to be repeated. Sometimes what didn't appear worth putting down at the beginning becomes essential toward the end. That may call for backtracking.

The disadvantages which make a recorder impractical except for specialized work are that the equipment is expensive, it frightens a shy person even more than a pencil, and it involves time-consuming effort transcribing to a typewriter.

Nevertheless, reporters of the future may find recorders increasingly useful as a supplementary tool as they become easier to carry and control.

GUIDING THE CONVERSATION

Let us now accompany a reporter on a typical interview assignment—in this case Ann Kemp of the Midland *Times* who was told to "See Morley of the Motor Club about his traffic plan." She would have preferred the sorority assignment. She drives a car but cares little about solving traffic problems. But she must visit Morley and write an informative article within a few hours. She telephoned him for an appointment.

In the library she learned that (1) Melvin Morley is an expert engineer; (2) he recently was employed by the Midland Motor Club to study the city's street congestion problem; (3) he left a month ago on a tour of Eastern cities; (4) his recommendations will carry weight with city officials. Thus she discovered what previously had been written about Morley and ensured herself against embarrassment from poverty of information when she confronted him.

In a way conducting an interview is like playing a game of tennis. The reporter first gets the ball over the net, then keeps it in play, trying with each stroke, however, to plant it so that it comes back with a bounce.

Once the interview is under way the reporter's task is to direct its course intelligently and with unwavering purpose. This can usually be done by introducing a remark here, a question there, without recourse to extended cross-examination.

An interview conversation might proceed like this:

KEMP: Mr. Morley, my name is Ann Kemp, of the Midland *Times*. Hope I'm not intruding.

MORLEY: Not at all. I was expecting you. Will you sit down?

KEMP: I'd like to take a few minutes of your time, if I may, to get some data about your tour and your views on the traffic problem. Councilman Forbes, I think, suggested that we see you.

MORLEY: Yes, my report will go to his committee. All right, what do you have in mind?

KEMP: First, I'd like to check a couple of things about you personally. Your home is in Capital City, you are a traffic engineer and have been retained by the Midland Motor Club to study conditions here?

MORLEY: All correct.

KEMP: And in the East you visited Boston, Pittsburgh and New York?

MORLEY: Also Cleveland on my way back—to study parking plans there.

KEMP: Well, if you could help me find a parking place near the *Times* office on Main street . . .

MORLEY: There's just one answer to that, Miss Kemp—parking meters. They'll need to be installed from 1st street south to the river. That will be one of my recommendations.

KEMP: Nickel or dime meters?

MORLEY: One cent for ten minutes, a nickel for an hour.

Miss Kemp learns the estimated number and cost of the meters. She now has a fair story with meters as the lead, but she pursues her inquiries:

KEMP: Do you think parking meters will solve the downtown problem?

MORLEY: Not entirely. They will help. But the Main street bottleneck can never be broken without a new bridge to South Midland. That is our main objective.

Miss Kemp has heard nothing about a new bridge. There was nothing about it in the library. She follows up:

KEMP: You mean instead of the ferry line?

MORLEY: Yes, either a bridge or a tunnel is essential.

KEMP: But I understand city funds are very low. How can it be paid for?

MORLEY: With a bond issue and a 10-cent toll. It would pay for itself in 25 years.

Miss Kemp pins down details about the proposed bridge. She now has a first-class lead. She ascertains and lists the minor points in Morley's report, then is ready to close the interview:

KEMP: Well, that gives me a story and I'm grateful for your courtesy. You will remain here, now?

MORLEY: Yes, until the report is acted upon. I will discuss it before the Motor Club Thursday evening.

KEMP: Where will that be?

MORLEY: At the Clarendon Hotel—7:30 p.m.

KEMP: Maybe I'll be there. I'm interested in that bridge now.

MORLEY: Thanks. Goodby.

KEMP: Goodby.

Guiding a conversation is not always as simple as in this dialogue between Morley and Miss Kemp. The interviewee may be a chronic grouch with an aversion to newspapers or a talkative promoter with a flair for publicity. He may even be a swindler seeking to palm off misleading information for his own profit. The reporter must study his man and topics, charting his course accordingly.

THE INTERVIEW STORY LEAD

There is no standard form for the interview lead corresponding to that for a birth, a death or an accident story. As in writing the speech lead, use whatever strikes you as most newsworthy, remembering, however, that you must be able to sustain the lead as you go deeper into the story, thus:

> Construction of a new million-dollar toll bridge across the Timber River will be proposed to the City Council by Melvin Morley, traffic expert of the Midland Motor Club.
> Morley announced yesterday that he also will urge the installation of parking meters on Main street.
> "A bridge to South Midland would break the bottleneck. . . . ."

Novelty leads of every variety appear on interview stories. The opener may be a straight statement of fact, a provocative observation, a humorous quip, a startling disclosure, a rapid description or personality sketch. A few samples:

> A record-breaking corn crop for southern Centralia, outstripping the banner yield of last year, was predicted today by State Secretary of Agriculture John Carr.

> "Home in a big city is little more than a filling station by day and a parking lot by night," Rev. George M. Crandall declared upon his return from a church conference in New York yesterday.

"Fiddlesticks! I never drank or smoked in my life." That's what Mrs. Ogden Blake thinks about people who credit ripe old age to nips and puffs, and she ought to know. She was 100 years old yesterday.

" 'Sno snow at all," said Weatherman Robert M. Bennett today when asked about those "snowflakes" citizens have been seeing recently out Highland way. "They're dandelion seeds."

A desperate winning fight against fire in a heavily laden oil tanker was described today by Capt. John Parsons, skipper of the Atlantic Line freighter City of Norfolk.

Hazel-eyed and blonde-haired Elaine Eubanks, 18-year-old winner of the "Miss Midland" beauty crown, would rather be a good cook than a Hollywood actress.

"Even Leonardo da Vinci would have a tough time peddling the Mona Lisa nowadays without a press agent," in the opinion of H. Robert Molloy, Chicago art collector.

INTERVIEW STORY STRUCTURE

In the majority of interview stories statements made by the man interviewed overshadow his personality and the circumstances prompting the remarks. In the main the structure resembles that of the conventional speech or statement story in that it uses the quote-summary-quote-summary arrangement. An example:

An ancient tribe of Indians roaming in the Timber River valley long before the advent of white men probably left the pottery pieces dug up from the Midland Gravel Co. quarry.

"These are at least 300 years old—probably 400," declared Dr. C. A. Radcliffe, curator of the Midland Museum of Natural History yesterday, after inspecting the relics.

John Merrick, a truck loader, picked up the pottery pieces after a blast in the quarry east of the city Tuesday night. He brought them to the museum.

"There have been other evidences of this tribe found before in the Midland area," said Dr. Radcliffe. "We don't know too much about them yet, but the arrowheads and tomahawks plowed up last year, as well as this pottery, have not been identified with the comparatively modern Plains Indians."

Dr. Radcliffe noted that the fragments found by Merrick bear crude red and yellowish designs and apparently were used as water vessels.

"We are going to make further searches in the quarry as blasting continues," he said. Meanwhile the pottery will be sent to the University of Centralia for inspection by experts in the department of archaeology.

What Dr. Radcliffe had to say in the foregoing interview carried its own news value. Whether he wore horn-rimmed spectacles and gesticulated as he spoke are matters of no moment to the story. However, if the reporter had interviewed Mrs. Astor Lorillard, a vivacious matron recently returned from explorations in South Africa, he would have included more about the personality of the interviewee at the expense of what she said. *What* a man says may be less important than *how* he says it. Rest assured that what a charming woman is wearing when interviewed will catch the fancy of feminine readers, many of whom are quite indifferent to what the charming woman has to say.

PRESS CONFERENCE PROBLEMS

The conversation of a single reporter with one other person is a comparatively simple form of interviewing. It is quite different from a press conference in which several—even scores—of newsmen participate in a free-for-all question-and-answer session.

This may be a more or less informal gathering of two or three beat men invited into the office of a public official or a carefully planned, elaborately produced and expertly stage-managed affair with all the paraphernalia of radio and television newsmen on the scene.

Old-time newspapermen who recall when it was necessary to tolerate only the flash bulbs of photographers from their own papers are prone to condemn the intrusion of microphones, newsreel cameras, bright lights, technicians, cables and wires into what was once their own monopoly. They say that pen-and-pencil men have become wallflowers or, worse, unpaid actors and actresses.

There is some merit in these complaints but they are futile. Electronic journalism is here to stay and no amount of sniping will destroy it.

Modern newspapers and newspapermen have learned to live side by side with the newer media. They cannot logically—and few do—advocate any restriction of the free gathering and reporting of news. Further, it has been clearly established that radio and television not only stimulate the circulation of newspapers but create interviews, conferences and panel discussions which the papers exploit in print.

The recording devices make it impossible for an interviewee to take refuge in the claim that he has been misquoted. They also tend to discourage *off-the-record* and *for-background-only* statements.

These, however, remain a problem in many interviews and press conferences. If a reporter agrees to an off-the-record basis he must then hold the disclosure in confidence. His only alternative is to protest or leave in order to remain free to seek the story elsewhere.

For-background-only means: "You may print this but don't quote me." This may be well warranted if the interviewee's name cannot be disclosed for reasons of public policy or personal vulnerability. In such cases the reporter again is honor-bound not to hint, imply or suggest his identity.

As in any other story, the reporter must keep and respect confidences born in an interview or press conference. If he breaks faith he may have trouble at the next one.

COLLECTIVE INTERVIEWS

Symposiums obtained through interviews are printed when a consensus is desired on some current happening or controversy after the manner of an "inquiring photographer" column made up of thumbnail quotes and the snapshots of persons questioned.

The reporter's assignment may be: "Find out what a dozen motorists think about the new traffic lights" or "Interview members of the City Council about the antiboxing ordinance." His problem now is to combine several statements into a general story dealing with a single topic. The following example illustrates the form:

> Sentiment among members of the City Council is sharply divided on the Johnson antiboxing ordinance recommended to the Council by its judiciary committee Thursday.
>
> Although most of them admit the need for more stringent regulation of professional bouts, some councilmen believe it would be too drastic to kill the sport entirely.
>
> "A better plan would be the establishment of a city boxing commission," said E. K. Wallace of the 4th Ward. "If that failed after a tryout, I would be willing to vote for the Johnson ordinance."
>
> Similar doubts as to the advisability of putting a ban on all kinds of boxing were expressed by Councilmen J. R. Fogel, Charles Harrison and Otto R. Vincent, although they all favored stiffer regulation.
>
> Others approved the ordinance as it is drafted.
>
> "We have experimented long enough—it's time to end the whole business," declared L. M. O'Brien of the 3rd Ward. . . . .

Another way is to prepare a general lead, then compile the interviews as follows:

> . . . Among the statements of others advocating the plan were:
> Miss Margaret Herrin, secretary of the Bryant School Parent-Teacher

AN ARRANGEMENT OF
MASS INTERVIEWS

QUESTION

DO YOU FAVOR THE PROPOSED LAW REQUIRING DOGS TO BE LEASHED IN MIDLAND?

J. B. BRINK, grocer, 1365 Forest Ave.—I certainly do. And they ought to be kept out of stores, too. I say tie them up or leave them at home.

MAURICE T. WINSLOW, lawyer, Midland Trust Building.—A dog has as much right to freedom as a man and this is a free country. I'm opposed.

MRS. VINCENT LAKE, housewife, 2010 3rd Ave. — All dogs should be leashed for the protection of our children. My little girl has been bitten twice.

GEORGE WILSON, student, Haven Hall.—It's a favor to a dog to leash him and keep him away from traffic hazards.

LUKE LOGAN, retired, 3040 Polk Ave. —Dogs do more damage to my garden than weeds. They ruined my tomatoes this year. Don't let them run loose.

KATHERINE SMITH, stenographer, 517 Maple St. — I have a little spaniel named Toots. He runs in the park every evening. He wouldn't hurt a fly. It would be a sin to leash him.

TOMMY TUFTS, grammar school pupil, 916 Grand Ave.—My dog Pal carries in the *Times* every morning. How can he do that if we put a rope on him?

LAWRENCE W. HOPKINS, insurance man, 1302 Cedar St.—I'm for the bill and I propose another to keep them out of the city entirely. Dogs belong on the farm.

R. F. THOR, athletic coach, 853 Center St.—I think every boy should have a dog. Dogs do more to protect children than to hurt them. Keep them free.

ALBERT WADE, bricklayer, 2014 Hayes Ave.—I'm against the bill. Why condemn all dogs because a few are vicious?

A Cross Section of Opinion

Assn.—Paintings of battle scenes and other symbols of carnage have no place in school classrooms. They should be removed.

J. R. Hart, principal of the Washington School—It is hardly necessary to drill accounts of past barbaric necessities into the minds of school children, although I do not object to truly patriotic pictures.

Henry M. Lutz, judge of the Juvenile Court—Why foster the war spirit any more than necessary?

Those against the proposal were equally emphatic. They included:

R. T. Owen, commander of the American Legion—It would be an insult and a desecration to remove from the schoolrooms pictures portraying the heroism of our forefathers.

Mrs. Benjamin Bronson, president of the Timber County Flag Assn.— The sacrifices made by the nation's patriots should be constantly kept before the eyes of our school children. I am opposed to the plan.

In the second type of mass interview it will be observed that the statements are printed without quotation marks, each paragraph beginning with a person's name, followed by a dash and what he said. The grouping of interviews illustrated in the first example is done more loosely. That arrangement is best when only three or four persons are quoted.

SHOP TALK

1. Discuss the importance of the interview in all kinds of news gathering. What percentage of beat stories is obtained through interviews?
2. How should a reporter prepare for an interview? Where would you look for advance information about a senator, an actress, an explorer?
3. How would you open an interview with a man in prison, a child, a public official?
4. Prepare a list of 20 celebrities. Select those whose statements would transcend in news value sketches of their personalities, and vice versa.
5. Do you believe that mass interviews, such as those gathered by an "inquiring photographer" in public places, are circulation builders?

CHAPTER 15
Libel Will Make You Liable

THE RESPONSIBILITIES OF REPORTING

For the eager young beginner who looks forward to newspaper work as full of fun and frivolity and without risks and responsibilities this chapter and the next may be none too pleasant reading.

Covering and writing news for print is no job for carefree and capricious children with slight concern for the rights of others as set forth in the conventions of society and the canons of the law. It is a task for mature men and women of serious purpose who are willing to shoulder the stern obligations that fall upon those permitted to publicize the acts and lives of other people.

While enjoying the freedom of fair comment and the privileges of public service, the reporter moves and works in a thicket of thorny thou-shalt-nots and is in constant danger of demotion or dismissal, if not legal punishment, should he overstep the hedge of restraints around him.

In this chapter we shall deal with the laws of libel and in the next with associated laws, written and unwritten, which limit the reporter for the purpose of ensuring and keeping the good will of the community.

Accuracy and objectivity go a long way toward protecting a reporter from prosecution but not far enough. His own sense of fair play is a safer shield for, despite devious and sometimes doubtful applications of the law, its purpose is to guard human rights.

As you write, apply your words to yourself and members of your own family. If they would injure your own feelings, then think twice. Be sure that the injuries you inflict upon one or a few persons are necessary for the good of the many.

If by nature you are inclined to push people around, choose some other work. Stay out of journalism. While newspapers need men and women with courage rather than cowardice, they do not want novices with more nerve than discretion.

The remedy for both ailments—rash disregard of others and gun-shyness to the point of timidity—is careful study, observation, vigilance and experience. Veterans sometimes say: "You've never learned until you're burned." That is not so. You can learn and never be burned.

In this volume we cannot set forth all there is to know about news and the law. There are excellent books on the subject and full courses of study well worth the attention and time of students. Here, however, we can only outline the broad principles of the law as it affects the handiwork of the reporter.

LIBERTY IS NOT LICENSE

The first amendment to the Constitution of the United States says that "Congress shall make no law . . . abridging the freedom of speech, or of the press . . ." That guarantee is contained in each of the constitutions of the states. The Supreme Court has called it the master matrix of all liberties.

With the adoption of this history-making proviso we had come a long way from the time when the king was a god and the crown could do no wrong. But we also left behind us an era when the king's subjects were serfs with no privacy and no rights as individuals.

Balanced against the first amendment is the fifth, which states that "No person . . . shall be deprived of life, liberty or property, without due process of law . . ."

The first amendment concerns a need of society—the right of the public to know—while the fifth protects the right of each person to be protected against abuse by others. An interpretation by the Supreme Court puts it this way:

> All men have a right to print and publish whatever they deem proper *unless by doing so they infringe upon the rights of another.* For any injury they may commit against the public or individual they may be punished. . . . The freedom of speech and the press *does not permit the publication of libels, blasphemous or other indecent articles or other publication injurious to morals or private reputations.*

To illustrate, any man has freedom to say "Pfui!" about the act of a mayor—even one of the President—but he has no license to yell "Fire!" in a crowded theater when there is no fire. If he does that he can be punished.

Freedom of speech and the press as applied to a newspaper means

FREEDOM OF THE PRESS

The United States
CONSTITUTION

Congress shall make no law respecting an establishment of religion, or prohibiting the free exercise thereof; or abridging the freedom of speech, or of the press; or the right of the people peaceably to assemble, and to petition the government for a redress of grievances.

The United States
SUPREME COURT

It is recognized that punishment for the abuse of the liberty accorded to the press is essential to the protection of the public, and that the common-law rules that subject the libeler to responsibility for the public offense, as well as for private injury, are not abolished by the protection extended in our Constitutions.

that it can print anything it pleases but thereafter can be held liable for it.

In this country there is no censorship prior to publication except in wartime. In other words, a reporter may write and his paper may circulate damaging falsehoods or personal attacks, injurious to the rights of the public and of an individual, but at the same time they obligate themselves if necessary to justify their actions in a court of law.

Writers as well as publishers are liable in libel lawsuits. To bring this home to the reporter, the first link in the chain of publication, it means that if he violates the law under the guise of gathering and writing news he must be prepared to defend his words before a judge and jury.

THE LAW OF THE PRESS

The legal field embraced by laws limiting the communications media is wide and complex. It covers libel of two kinds—civil and criminal— slander, contempt of court, invasion of privacy, violations of the copyright and postal laws and the orders of quasi-judicial bodies like the Federal Communications Commission and the Federal Trade Commission.

Civil libel, which is governed by state laws, is the main concern of the reporter, but we will pause here before going into it further to define and distinguish from one another the other legal limitations.

Although comparatively rare, there are criminal libels punishable by fine, imprisonment, or both. These include the publication of material which is obscene, blasphemous or seditious. It also includes material which advocates the overthrow of the government by force or tends to incite a riot.

Civil libel cases, far more numerous, are those based on articles which unjustly defame character or hurt business. Damages can be collected as well as fees for filing pleadings and cost of counsel.

Libel is written or printed defamation. Slander is defamation by word of mouth. Is defamation in radio and television news libel or slander? This question has not yet been fully answered in all states but the trend is toward libel because most news programs are written out and read from script. Libel laws are more severe than those of slander because of the permanent form and wider dissemination of written defamation.

A newspaper may be in contempt of court if an editorial or the reporting of a case delays or interferes with the administration of justice. A publication may not with immunity intimidate a party to a suit, prejudice the jury, impute unfairness to a judge, discredit attorneys, or in any way prevent a fair hearing. Contempt proceedings normally concern pending cases rather than those which have been completed.

State laws on the right of privacy vary but in general they exempt legitimate newspaper news. It is clearly established that a name or picture of a living person may not be used in advertising or for trade purposes without consent. Such identifications in entertainment presentations, not strictly news, are in a twilight zone.

However, persons involved in timely public proceedings or actions lose their right to be let alone. They are subject to publicity even if it is unwanted. A court has held, for example, that a newspaper may publish the picture of a murdered child's body even though the parents suffer embarrassment and mental anguish. This is a news situation.

No law forbids the publication of pornographic material, but the postal laws do halt its distribution through the mails. The Post Office also bans the mailing of information about lotteries but not newspapers reporting newsworthy events in which a lottery is incidental.

Lottery information likewise is barred from radio and television by the FCC, which regulates the broadcasting industries. The FTC concerns itself with advertising but not news. It can and does from time to time order advertisers to "cease and desist" from certain practices.

We will describe and discuss the copyright laws in the next chapter since they, as well as ethics which are outside the law, bear upon the work of news writers.

WHAT IS LIBEL?

As we have stated, civil libel in its simplest sense is anything published which unjustly defames character or hurts business.

Defined more fully in legal language it is any false and malicious representation which tends to hurt the reputation of a person, to expose him to hatred, ridicule, contempt or obloquy or to injure him in his occupation; or which damages a firm financially. As we have seen, a libel can be communicated by print, camera or microphone.

There are two types of libel. Libel *per se* is libel on its face. Libel *per quod* is not apparent on its face but is made so by the surrounding circumstances.

A story can defame a man and yet on its face make no reference to him as an individual. It is not necessary to name him to libel him if he can be identified by those who know him. And it is not necessary for all readers to be able to do so as long as there are some who do.

The same principle applies to so-called group libel. A group or class of people can be defamed. If the words reflect on every member of a restricted group, each one may have a cause for action. However, if the words contain no reflection on a particular individual—an ascertainable person—the courts have held that none may sue. A case in point was one depicting taxicab drivers in a city as ill mannered and dishonest. An action was dismissed on the ground that *all* drivers were not so labeled.

There are some state laws which ban libel against religious or racial groups, forbidding newspapers to attribute depravity, criminality, unchastity or lack of virtue to classes of citizens of particular races, colors or creeds.

A story may contain words or phrases of uncertain or two meanings. For example, *deficit in funds* may indicate a routine bookkeeping operation or a misappropriation. *Changed his testimony* could imply either forgetfulness or perjury. The test is the effect or impression naturally produced in the minds of average persons among whom an article circulates.

The word *malice* needs to be understood. Malice can be *actual* or *legal*. There's a difference. Actual malice—the deliberate intent to injure because of ill will or hatred—need not be proved. It is sufficient to show legal malice in the article itself to recover damages, regardless of the intent of the writer or publisher.

A damaging statement made by a newspaper on its own authority must be genuinely true. If A says B is a thief and C publishes a statement that A said B was a thief, in a certain sense this would be the truth. A did say it. But in court it is incumbent upon C—the newspaper—to prove that B actually *is* a thief, not merely that A called him one. Therefore, you are not necessarily immune if you reprint a libelous remark made in a speech or interview nor does the fact that the story was supplied by a wire service or syndicate relieve a newspaper of responsibility.

Can the dead be defamed? It has long been held that after death one is not a "person" and that the right to bring a libel suit vanishes when a person libeled ceases to live. However, it is also well established that if blackening the memory of a dead person reflects directly upon his living relatives or descendants it gives them the right to sue.

BE CAREFUL WITH CRIME NEWS

There are so many possible ways in which a newspaper story may prove libelous that they cannot be detailed at length. One of the commonest is unjustly or falsely to accuse a person of committing a crime. Legal precedent affirms that anyone suspected of or charged with a crime is innocent until proved guilty. The danger of libel is greatest if the offense has an aura of social disgrace, such as arson, bigamy, blackmail, forgery, keeping a house of ill fame, criminal extortion or an unnatural sex act.

Much news falls into the crime category, and the shades of legal innocence and guilt are difficult to define.

In a homicide case a man wanted for questioning about a death is not automatically a suspected murderer. A man arrested on a homicide charge is not necessarily a killer. A man arraigned as a killer is not necessarily an accused murderer. A man who confesses to a murder is not necessarily a criminal. And a man convicted of murder is not necessarily a murderer.

The best safety-first rule is never personally to presume that anyone is guilty of any kind of offense no matter how overwhelming the evidence. A statement of wrongdoing must come from a privileged source, and you should so credit it. We will discuss privilege in a moment.

Most libel suits are based upon words libelous per se, that is, on their face. Here are a few of them:

abductor	deadbeat	grafter
abortionist	degenerate	impostor
adulterer	deserter	kidnaper
bigamist	drunkard	libertine
blackmailer	embezzler	loan shark
burglar	extortionist	racketeer
cardsharp	felon	shoplifter
conspirator	fixer	seducer
counterfeiter	forger	smuggler
criminal	fraud	swindler
crook	gambler	thief

You may not impute that a person is a Communist and the terms *pink* and *fellow traveler* are dubious. Neither may you wrongfully impeach a man's loyalty by implying that he is an agent or propagandist for a foreign government.

Beware of any expression commonly accepted as imputing a crime to anyone. Here are a few more dangerous expressions: *criminal operation, easy money, false pretenses, guilty conscience, lucrative racket, notorious neighborhood, phony procedure, public nuisance, unsavory record.*

It is emphasized again that the insertion of such spurious attributions as *it is said, it is alleged, understood to be* or *neighbors say* are sham defenses which offer little if any protection from a libel suit. And even if you

EIGHT EXAMPLES OF
LIBELOUS WORDS

DRUNKARD

QUACK

FIREBUG

SCAB

GAMBLER

SHOPLIFTER

HYPOCRITE

TRAITOR

Causes of Suits against Newspapers

attribute a libelous statement to someone you must be sure that he is an authority speaking in line of duty and in his official capacity.

REPUTATIONS AND LIVELIHOODS

Whether or not punishable as a crime, it is libelous to attribute to a person any act of moral turpitude or misbehavior that damages reputation, exposes physical handicaps or hurts him in his occupation or business. You may not with impunity steal a man's good name.

Reputations are fragile, especially those of women. To libel a woman you need not describe her specifically as a *courtesan, mistress, street-walker* or *prostitute.* Merely implying want of chastity can rush a reporter into libel of the worst variety. For example, to hint that a woman is pregnant, although unwed, is libel on its face. To give the dates of wedding and childbirth, indicating conception before marriage, or to mention an overnight trip of a woman with a man not her husband is just as dangerous.

Imputation that a person is insane, feeble-minded or to any degree mentally defective is damaging, as it is to reveal that he has an ailment looked upon by the community as communicable or loathsome. If you reveal that he is suffering from smallpox or leprosy, it may cause him to be shunned by society. Syphilis and gonorrhea are no longer unprintable words but they may not be attributed to an individual since they usually are contracted in ways widely regarded as censurable.

People in public positions are protected by law against untruthful charges of wrongdoing. Although you may annoy or irk him with unpleasant language about his official actions you will be in trouble if, outside the pale of fair comment, you accuse a legislator of grafting or a city treasurer of embezzlement or dishonesty.

Professional people and others whose ability to earn a living hinges upon good reputation are especially vulnerable to criticism. You may not with impunity call a doctor a quack, butcher or charlatan, a lawyer a shyster or ambulance chaser, a clergyman a hypocrite or a scientist a pseudo-scientist.

Even in the sports world a livelihood, if not a good name, is valuable. A sports writer can be sued if he says a boxer appeared *cowardly* or that an umpire is *partly blind.*

It is not necessarily actionable to say that a salesman is a poor plumber but it is libelous to say that he is a poor salesman, making him appear unfit in the vocation whereby he earns a living.

Finally you need to exercise the utmost discretion in writing news that may jeopardize business standings or transactions. Banks, insurance companies and other financial institutions in some states are protected by special libel laws. The words *bankrupt* and *destitute* have both been causes of successful suits against newspapers.

Food distributors can be ruined if it is indicated that their products are spoiled or are handled by diseased persons or under unsanitary conditions. In fact any business concern can sue for damages if news reflects harmfully on its dealings with customers or clients. The only safe rule is never to identify a concern with a derogatory implication or rumor without a complete checkup and full justification for doing so.

Various kinds of damages may be claimed in libel suits. These are *general,* awarded for loss of reputation; *special,* for the loss of a job or sale; and *punitive* or *exemplary,* to punish a libeler. Actual damages may be either special or special and general together while *compensatory* damages are all those not punitive.

THE PROTECTION OF PRIVILEGE

There are so many don'ts and can'ts in any discussion of libel that a beginner is likely to wonder how anyone or anything can be described in print other than as a paragon of virtue.

Yet it is obvious to anyone who reads that newspapers are replete with news of wickedness and wrongdoing—chronicles of crime from delinquency to murder, exposures of rascality in public office, intimate information about immorality and infidelity, reports of fraud and folly which blast reputations to bits, and accounts of crookedness and cheating in business.

True, every day reporters *do* write and newspapers *do* publish statements which hurt and humiliate hundreds of human beings—stories of dishonesty, depravity and disgrace. How come?

To answer we must return to our starting point—freedom of the press as guaranteed by the Constitution. Inherent in that freedom is the privilege of publishing news entailing the fulfillment of a social, judicial or political duty and the right of fair comment on the doings of people in the public eye. We shall discuss privilege first.

It is the right of society to know how governing bodies operate and the right of the press to print fair and true reports of most official proceedings.

Privilege is of two kinds—*absolute,* or unconditional, and *qualified,* or conditional. If a publication is absolutely privileged there can be no remedy in a civil action. Absolute privilege is accorded by the Constitution to members of Congress in their speeches or debates in either House

While there is no application directly to newspapers, great latitude is permitted in reporting official proceedings of all legislative bodies as well as judicial proceedings, even though libels may be in them, if the publication is in good faith and in the public interest. However, some sessions can be closed and reporters excluded and certain documents can be sealed or kept secret.

Generally speaking, however, conditional privilege protection extends from Congress down to and through statements, proclamations and records of all subordinate officials, city and town councils, and other groups deriving their authority from the executive, legislative and judicial branches of the federal, state and local governments.

The sanctuary of privilege also usually reaches from actual courtroom testimony and statements by attorneys in court to the official statements of all county prosecutors, coroners and heads of other law-enforcement agencies. In most cases it is safe to print their statements about investigations in progress or completed by them, but only when they speak in their official capacities and not privately. Mere investigations by policemen or the statements of complaining witnesses fail to fall within the scope of the law.

While details differ in various state laws, the reporter may feel fairly certain that he is on firm ground when he bases his story on official actions and documents.

THE RIGHT OF FAIR COMMENT

In the case of qualified privilege a publication possesses a right which others do not enjoy, but in the case of fair comment any person possesses it—as long as his facts are true—under the guarantee of free speech.

The right to criticize and condemn persons, groups and institutions in the public arena is of the utmost importance to reporters and even more so to editorial writers and critics. The rule applies to officeholders, candidates for office, official agencies, universities, hospitals and asylums.

It applies with equal force to speeches, art works, books, athletic performances, and to stage, film, television and radio presentations. It is presumed that the speaker, artist, athlete or entertainer invites criticism, good or bad, when he asks the public to view his efforts.

The comment may be harsh or sarcastic to the extreme. In the classic Cherry Sisters case of 1901 the Iowa Supreme Court held the following criticism to be fair comment without malice: "Effie is an old jade of 50 summers, Jessie a frisky filly of 40, and Addie, the flower of the family, a capering monstrosity of 35 . . . Effie is spavined, Addie is stringhalt, and Jessie, the only one who showed her stockings, has legs and calves as classic in their outlines as the curves of a broom handle."

The right of fair comment applies in particular to editorials and to special reporters, such as art, music and book critics. Privilege, granted on the theory that the public is entitled to know the manner in which laws are enacted and administered, more closely concerns police, court, political and public affairs reporters.

The right of fair comment does not extend from the substance of the action into the personal character or private life of the person whose work is criticized. For example, a book reviewer may call a book immoral but not its author. A drama critic may call a performance second-rate but goes out of bounds if he passes on a backstage report that an actress was upset by a spat with her husband.

WATCH NAMES AND ADDRESSES

Let us return now to the workaday problems of an average reporter faced with the dangers of defamation. Nine times out of ten he gets into trouble as a result of haste and carelessness rather than ignorance of the law.

Editors and copyreaders usually eliminate references openly libelous but have no way of checking back on sources. The reporter must be right. His haste or gullibility counts for little before a judge and jury. His intentions are immaterial. His words speak for themselves. The product, not the thought or lack of thought behind it, is what does count in the courtroom.

Mistakes in printing are bad enough when an article is complimentary but when it carries sharp criticism in any form the names should be checked and double-checked. Errors in a surname or initial have caused many a suit for libel.

This story lead, based on information secured at police headquarters, found its way into print:

> Jacob Rankin, an insurance man, 40, was brought back to Midland from Clay City yesterday to face a charge of larceny. According to Detective John Larson, who trailed Rankin to Clay City, the man absconded with $700.

In this case the man arrested was Jacob R. Rankin. Jacob L. Rankin of Midland sued and recovered damages for libel. The police memorandum contained the name Jacob R. Rankin but the reporter slipped up on the middle initial and steered his paper into trouble.

The need for extreme care and accuracy in the matter of identification

lays a heavy burden on reporters, especially in large cities where there
are many persons of the same name. The commonest names, such as
Smith, Jones and *Johnson,* are the most dangerous. One life insurance
company carries policies on more than 18,000 *John Smiths.* Look in any
metropolitan telephone directory and you will see the same name listed
many times.

Accuracy in addresses is equally important. Like names, they should
be checked in every story and in those containing potential libel double-
checked. If you are not sure that a man lives at 134 Banks St. then write:
"He gave his address as 134 Banks St."

SAY IT WITH SAFETY

When it becomes necessary to write stories damaging to reputations or
business, be certain the derogatory references are supported by documents, data or other evidence to prove privilege. Note the danger lurking
in the first statements and the precautions taken in the second:

Dangerous. Judge Corrigan, the police say, probably will give the
wife-beater a long term in jail.

Safe. The suspect, charged with assault, will be tried before Judge
Corrigan. The penalty on conviction is 30 days to 6 months in jail.

Dangerous. The alleged house of ill fame was raided last night. Among
the inmates were Laura Jones, 23, and Julia Easton, 19, who police said are
known prostitutes.

Safe. Police raided the house last night, arresting two women who gave
their names as Laura Jones, 23, and Julia Easton, 19. They were booked
on charges of disorderly conduct.

Dangerous. The concern appears to be in bad shape financially as indicated by the 20-point slump of its stock on the market.

Safe. Stock of the concern sold at 142, a drop of 20 points since
yesterday. A week ago the quotation was 187.

Dangerous. He has an insane son.

Safe. The court record showed that he has a son in the psychopathic
ward of the State Hospital.

Dangerous. He is said to have murdered his former wife seven years ago.

Safe. Seven years ago he was convicted of manslaughter in the slaying
of his former wife.

Dangerous. Boland's expenses were outrageous. This was shown by
Senator Kenyon, who gave to the House figures showing he spent the
huge sum of $145,000.

Safe. Senator Kenyon told the House that Boland's expenses were
$145,000. This sum, he asserted, was "outrageous."

When you have news containing the slightest hint of libel do this: First verify it beyond the shadow of a doubt, checking one informant against another. Then either discard the item altogether or take it to the city editor, explaining fully the circumstances and the facts as gathered. Keep constantly in mind that an ounce of prevention is worth a pound of cure. Defamatory words in print cannot be erased. When in doubt, don't write them!

IT PAYS TO TAKE PRECAUTIONS

The following stories further illustrate how an incident may be treated in two ways. The first is loaded with libel; the second is free of objectionable reference:

LIBELOUS

Sweeping into the joint after a telephone tip, the police last night raided the notorious saloon and gambling house operated by Lee Saunders, an ex-convict, at 1242 Willow St.

Four men and two women were captured. All of them had been drinking or gambling. Saunders, who the police say was too drunk to tell a plausible story, tried to explain that what was going on was "just an innocent game, not for money."

Those participating in the orgy included two prominent West Side businessmen and their wives, Mr. and Mrs. R. E. Curry, 1719 Clark St., and Mr. and Mrs. W. B. Douglass, 932 Monroe Ave. The prize catch, according to police, was Terry Lawrence, an automobile thief.

The police predicted that Lawrence and Saunders will go to the pen, although the businessmen and their wives are likely to get off with easy fines.

NOT LIBELOUS

Swooping into the place after a telephone tip, the police last night raided a house at 1242 Willow St., owned by Lee Saunders, and arrested four men and two women. They were booked as patrons of a gambling resort.

A dice game was in progress when the police entered. Saunders said it was "just an innocent game, not for money." Several partly filled liquor bottles and a roulette wheel were found on the table.

Those arrested gave their names as Mr. and Mrs. R. E. Curry, 1719 Clark St., Mr. and Mrs. W. B. Douglass, 932 Monroe Ave., and Terry Lawrence. Lawrence, the police said, is wanted for questioning in connection with auto thefts.

The six persons will be arraigned today before Judge J. B. McKinley of the Municipal Court.

Here again, two contrasting versions show how trouble-freighted news should and should not be written:

"Dr." W. Edward Shelton, 1943 Saxon St., was arrested for murder today following the disclosure that he has performed numerous illegal operations, one of them resulting in the death of a young woman.

The murdered girl was Miss Stella Lee of Ferndale. She was a patient of the alleged quack M.D. last February. She died in "Dr." Shelton's apartment hospital under mysterious circumstances which caused suspicion at the time. The arrest of Shelton today confirmed the suspicion.

Mrs. Neil Hawkins, a nurse and accomplice of the doctor, also was arrested. She is said to have confessed her part in several illegal operations.

Dr. W. Edward Shelton, 1943 Saxon St., was placed under arrest today by order of County Attorney Howard Ford on a warrant charging him with the slaying of Miss Stella Lee last February.

Miss Lee died in Dr. Shelton's apartment hospital. According to charges filed by the county attorney, she had undergone an illegal operation. Several other cases of Dr. Shelton's are under investigation, Ford said.

A woman who identified herself as Mrs. Neil Hawkins, a nurse, also was taken into custody. She was questioned by the county attorney in connection with the operations.

AN APOLOGY MAY HELP

As we have seen, the chief defense against libel is proof that a statement is true, is privileged or fair comment, and is published with good motives for justifiable ends. Another defense is the prompt publication of a retraction.

Many states have statutes softening damage claims when a correction tends to prove lack of malice or intent to injure. These "honest mistake" laws free a newspaper of liability for exemplary damages when a libel is committed as a result of an innocent error and an adequate retraction is published.

Some papers maintain a *Beg Your Pardon* column for the specific purpose of making apologies such as these:

> In an account of police raids on gambling houses yesterday the *Gazette* inadvertently gave one address as 2151 Peters St. instead of 2115 Peters St. The first address is that of F. M. Roberts who was in no way connected with the raids. We regret the error.

> In its issue of May 7 the *Times* stated that Dr. Carl D. Watson, 1926 Forest Ave., was one of the physicians arrested by County Attorney Howard Ford for practicing without a license. This statement was erroneous and was caused by a confusion of names. Dr. Watson is in no way involved in Ford's investigation. The *Times* regrets the error.

The headline on the story of the marriage of Miss Beatrice Rogers that appeared in yesterday's editions of the *Herald* incorrectly identified her bridegroom as Lucas C. Logan, who was best man. She was married to Darrell D. Denton, as the story made clear.

Various courts have held that the retraction of a libel must, to be fully effective, be frank, unequivocal and unmixed with any attempted justification. It should contain no ambiguous words. And it should be published as soon as the newspaper learns of the libel and be given the same prominence and display.

A retraction, no matter how ungrudgingly given or speedily printed, does not provide complete redress or a legal escape for the offending newspaper. Often, however, it softens the ire of the aggrieved person and causes him to refrain from action or to withdraw the complaint. After all, most people of sense realize that vindication is not accomplished by the mere entry of a judgment as effectively as is a polite and public admission of error with an apology.

If a retraction fails and a lawsuit is begun, the matter is out of the hands of the newsmen and in the hands of the lawyers. Some papers employ detectives whose business it is to investigate the reputations of plaintiffs who may withdraw rather than face evidence of bad character. Frequently settlements for nominal sums can be made out of court.

But from the reporter's point of view a serious kickback on his story, or even a mild protest, forces him, if in the wrong, to eat humble pie and reflects on his reputation as a fair and accurate newsman. Far better for him to exercise proper precaution before the story reaches print than to repent afterward when the damage has been done. Truth, privilege and fairness—these are the preventives of libel, the nightmare of the newsrooms.

SHOP TALK

1. Define libel. How does it differ from slander? Point out a half dozen ways a person or business firm might be libeled. Differentiate between civil and criminal libel.
2. Examine the libel law of your state. Do you know any specific cases in which it has been applied?
3. Explain the difference between privileged and unprivileged news. Do you consider the limitations on press freedom too stringent or too liberal?
4. Add to the libelous words and phrases listed in this chapter. Explain why each one is dangerous.
5. What precautions should a reporter take to avoid libel? How do the city editor and copyreaders help guard against danger?

CHAPTER **16**

The Taboos of the Trade

THE PRESS GOVERNS ITSELF

This chapter is not entitled "The Ethics of Journalism" because that expression seldom, if ever, is heard in a newsroom. If you speak to a hard-bitten reporter or desk man about his "ethics" he is likely to give you a look of pity or mock bewilderment and a reply like this: "Where do you think you are? In Sunday School?"

A few minutes later the same newsman will instinctively invoke one of the many taboos imposed by newspapers and their employes upon themselves for the sake of decency and justice or in the interest of safety-first and self-preservation. Like any other craft, the newspaper business maintains within itself a code of conduct created out of experience and generally conformed to as a matter of caution if not conscience.

We have discussed the laws of libel, which are imposed upon the press by outsiders. In this chapter we shall look at the inside censorship as applied by newspapers to their own columns to ensure fair play and good taste. We also will examine restrictions on free advertising and the appropriation of news from other papers.

While there are statutes forbidding the publication of outright obscenity, profanity, blasphemy and, in a few states, libels against minority groups, these are rarely used. And there are no laws against reporting rumors, ridiculing race or religion, spreading superstition, spoiling the appetites or disturbing the sleep of readers. These offenses are outlawed only by an unwritten code.

The severity of this code and the strictness with which it is enforced vary with the type of publication and the readers it appeals to. Some papers are sternly conservative; others are informal and racy. A majority are moderately in between.

The moral persuasions of the local populace exert a form of indirect censorship on the press. People in smaller, closer-knit communities incline to be less tolerant than those in larger, looser cosmopolitan centers. Liquor drinking, for example, is looked upon quite differently in various localities.

And public sentiment changes with the times. In the Victorian era an editor was assailed for calling a limb a leg and mentioning such things as petticoats. Not too long ago the sight of a cigarette-smoking woman shocked almost everybody. One was arrested on Fifth avenue in New York. Today the sight is commonplace.

Newspapers and the movies are less outspoken than plays and books, which may go much further toward blasphemy, profanity and gruesomeness. The novel-reading and playgoing public is made up of relatively small adult groups, whereas newspapers and movies are produced for general consumption at all age levels. However, both newspapers and films enjoy more leeway than radio and television. Newspapers can be kept out of homes where there are squeamish people or children and motion-picture theaters can hang up a sign "For Adults Only." Radio and television can offend a living-room audience before the dials can be twisted.

These observations are generalities and to all generalities, of course, there are exceptions. But all the mass media are governed in some degree by self-imposed standards of propriety.

WHEN SUPPRESSION IS WARRANTED

Suppression as a word applied to news is anathema to newsmen—and no wonder. As a group they hate the hushing up of information. They are dedicated to the principle of revealing it. That, in fact, is the sole objective of their occupation.

Yet when a reporter goes to his typewriter he seldom, if ever, writes all he knows about an ugly story situation. Even if he has space to spare and privilege aplenty he withholds from his copy offensive facts and phraseology. When he writes them they are ruthlessly deleted by editors and copyreaders. And all conform to the over-all taboos of higher executives.

A publisher has a right, within legal limits, to decide what will go into his paper. And along with the right to publish goes the right to reject.

The law of privacy has been upheld in the courts but rarely except as it concerns paid advertising. Time and again the bench has stamped approval on publicity given to a person connected with unsavory news even if he is innocent and wants to stay anonymous. His protection must come from the press itself.

Unquestionably newspapers in pursuit of circulation do at times over-step the bounds to gain readers for keyhole stories. However, the Canons of Journalism which are widely accepted across the land say flatly: "A newspaper should not invade private rights or feelings without sure warrant of public right as distinguished from public curiosity."

There are violators of this code, of course, but most reporters and editors adhere to it. They often refuse, for example, to hound the parents, wife, husband or children in cases where a black sheep relative is accused of a heinous crime.

Some newspapers have a rule that the names of women and girls subjected to rape or attempted rape are withheld even though the identification is legally permissible. Many more suppress the names of juvenile first offenders and some go so far as to omit those of adults arrested for the first time for misdemeanors.

Again, a person's place of employment may be omitted if his home address, age and occupation are adequate for identification. Newspapers also are loath to publicize unnecessarily a hotel or place of business in any kind of damaging story.

While thus frequently shielding guiltless individuals and business firms editors are less likely to ignore or soft-pedal news on the ground that it will hurt local business generally or will give the town a bad name.

Newspapers are in the forefront of any move to boost the community—to picture it as a good place in which to live and trade, but when pressed to stifle or muffle news of civic corruption or reports of frauds and swindles few fail in their obligation to print the truth without fear or favor.

DON'T DERIDE RACE OR COLOR

America is a land of many racial and color groups and the home of peoples with diverse national origins. And the average American is more sensitive about these than any other phase of his personal life, except his religion. They are not to be treated with aspersion in print. On the contrary, more and more newspapers are at every opportunity printing news and pictures of achievement and advances which reflect credit on individuals in minority groups.

No laws, written or unwritten, totally ban the association of wrongdoing with ethnic identification. Censorship of this nature would suppress the Bible and the works of Shakespeare. But there certainly is merit in criticizing the designation of race and color in derogatory news unless it clearly is vital to description, say that of an unidentified fugitive and dangerous criminal.

No reporter in his right mind would write *nigger* for Negro, *greaser* for Mexican, *spick* for Spaniard or *dago* for Italian. Those terms are obviously derisive and vulgar. It is the good-intentioned reference that he must watch.

Fiction authors and playwrights often use dialect to flavor their character sketches but newsmen must be extremely careful with it.

A reporter, perhaps, may write a lead like this for a St. Patrick's Day parade story: "Faith and begorra but 'twas a fine mornin'—the luck of the Irish—as the Kellys, McOlsens, O'Cohens and other true and adopted sons of the old sod stepped up Main street in honor of their patron saint." If the story is manifestly friendly, there is little risk of ridicule. But generally speaking, the "ach's" and "ja's" of the Germans, the "velly's" and "tickees" of the Chinese, the "dese" and "dems" of the Brooklynite, and the "suh's" and "you-all's" of the Southerner are unwelcome in writing about real people.

It is the practice of most newspapers to put the statements of an uneducated person into good grammar. There is no need to make him speak like a college professor but fairness forbids making him sound illiterate. No reporter would think of quoting word for word the verbal errors of an important citizen or visiting dignitary. He would correct them or the copy desk would *brush up* his story. Everyone quoted is entitled to the same courtesy.

RESPECT FOR RELIGIOUS BELIEFS

This is a nation of many faiths, all protected by a freedom—the right to worship according to conscience—as fundamental to democracy as freedom of the press. Freedom of religion implies freedom from unfairness in the press as well as from interference by the state.

It is an ironclad rule in the newspaper code that religion must be respected, and therefore the libel laws against blasphemous or sacrilegious writing are virtually dormant.

The name of the Deity is not to be used except with care. This rule applies not only to the Deity of the Christian faith but with the same force to divinity in any contemporary doctrine no matter how rare or odd it may be.

From time to time in covering church news a reporter will be tempted to quote a clergyman's statements attacking a creed other than his own.

These, as well as appeals to prejudice by leaders of narrow religious orders, should be ignored unless they leave the realm of pure theology and enter that of public welfare. In any case disputed points of creed and worship, if used, need to be fully justified and qualified.

Never deride religious ceremonials, such as baptism, marriage or burial, or make a minister the subject of amusement. In your writing respect every religious practice as you respect your own.

Aside from moral principles there is another reason why publishers do not knowingly offend a religious or racial group. Minorities, especially in large cities, are organized and quick to make themselves heard if antagonized. No newspaper wants to be picketed, besieged with angry phone calls or swamped with protesting letters accusing it of bias.

By the same token no reporter wishes to have his story the target of such counteroffensives and it behooves him therefore to delete the danger from his copy before he submits it for publication.

WHAT ARE PROFANITY AND OBSCENITY?

While newspapers almost without exception rule out blasphemy in which the name of the Deity is used in a coarse expression, the limits on rough language and spicy expression vary considerably from city to city and paper to paper.

Many newspapers in the larger cities permit not only "hell" and "damn" but still stronger words if used by a newsworthy person under extraordinary circumstances. The editors of these papers reason that it fools nobody to quote Sherman as saying "War is h——" or Farragut as ordering "D—— the torpedoes." They argue that novels and dramas should have no monopoly on virile language understood by everyone over the age of 5. Some of these papers spelled out the epithet "S.O.B." when a President applied it to a columnist.

A majority of newspapers in smaller communities bar anything that smacks of profanity on the ground that it offends community morals and brings complaints, particularly from churchmen and parents. The editors of these papers reason that people with little moral stamina, as well as children, are exposed involuntarily to newspapers whereas there is deliberate selectivity among persons who attend plays and read novels.

Worse than profanity in print are synthetic substitutes such as *Gad* for God, *Hades* for hell and *darn* for damn. These substitutes are grotesque and ridiculous.

The larger papers in general are also more liberal than the smaller ones in permitting candid writing about sex and crime, although there are wide variations. For example, some papers taboo the word *rape* despite the amount of news produced by this crime. They prefer such terms as *assault, attack* and *statutory crime.*

Here again the reasoning seems sound in both directions. Certainly it may be embarrassing for a father to be called upon to explain the word *rape* to a young daughter who finds it in the paper he has brought home. And the irate father may write a complaint to the editor. On the other hand, is it not absurd to say a man "dragged her up the stairs, beat her with a club and then assaulted her"?

Each newspaper draws its own line between propriety and profanity, decency and obscenity, vigor and vulgarity, but there always *is* a line. Grossness is not tolerated anywhere. The newspaper audience is not a table of tipsy celebrators in a saloon or a theater full of sophisticates. It must be considered as a family in a living room. However, the reporter seeks to determine and conform to the limitations in his own office.

GOOD TASTE IS GOOD SENSE

There are several miscellaneous subjects in the "Danger—Handle With Care!" class, among them medical advice and descriptions of bodily processes and other things disagreeable to the senses of touch, taste and smell. There are plenty of unpleasant things in life, but good manners exclude many of them from newspapers.

Medical advancement is a proper function of the press and the dissemination of facts about public health serves as a stimulous to that end. But doctoring, as distinguished from reporting legitimate health news, should be restricted to medical columns, and these do not diagnose or prescribe for particular patients.

People are prone to believe stories of new medical devices and cures and to try to treat themselves. While few modern folk believe that rabies can be cured with a madstone, or in liquor as an antidote for snakebite, there are plenty who are ready to try "cures" for baldness, deafness and blindness, remedies for alcoholism, devices and treatments to develop busts or increase height.

We have mentioned earlier that libel lurks in stories of illness and that reputations of doctors are fragile. Do not blame anyone for causing the illness of another and never ascribe a malignant disease to a person unless you are absolutely sure of the diagnosis. Never hint at lack of proper professional care either by doctors or in hospitals without good reason and airtight privilege. A story like this is loaded with trouble:

> After eating what his wife called tainted meat at Hicks' Restaurant, Ruben Lippman, 712 Cross St., was rushed to Mercy Hospital this afternoon. Dr. William C. Ayers told him the ptomaine poisoning was only

SUBJECTS TO
HANDLE WITH CARE

**GHOSTS AND
HAUNTED HOUSES**

**MOON'S EFFECT
ON HUMANS**

**INTERPLANETARY
INVASIONS**

**"MIRACULOUS"
CURES**

EPIDEMICS

RIOTS

Supernatural and Scare Stuff

acute indigestion although Mrs. Lippman said he had never been sick a day in his life.

Talk about the internal functions of the body belongs in the doctor's office or clinic and not in a news story. Although an advertiser selling a remedy may go as far in this direction as his lawyer and the newspapers will allow, the reporter is under no compulsion to describe symptoms or ailments in detail and should not do so.

In any group of readers there are bound to be people who not only are squeamish about bodily functions but who can be repulsed by disagreeable things such as stories about reptiles and insects and nauseated by descriptions of unpleasant odors and tastes.

Some newspapers, for example, invariably use *stench* rather than *stink* and prefer *trash, debris* or *waste* to *garbage*. Other words to watch are *decay, disgorge, gut, scab, spit, vomit* and *worm*.

Unless your paper demands it, it's better to tone down gruesomeness in crime and accident stories, too. Don't picture victims as having their stomachs shot open and intestines spilled out or their legs and arms blown off. Go easy on screams, moans, sounds of physical pain and death rattles.

Your newspaper is a guest in the homes of its readers. Take care that it is mannered like one.

SUPERNATURAL STUFF AND SUPERSTITION

Whereas the newspaper code calls for the utmost sincerity and seriousness in writing about religion and medicine, it calls for exactly the opposite—disbelief or levity—in writing about clearly unscientific phenomena.

Promoters, cranks, unbalanced inventors and pseudo-scientists of every kind and cult clamor for publicity. Superstitions and beliefs in the supernatural are commonplace. Newspapers do not ignore these matters but give them tongue-in-cheek treatment if there is a chance that they may be taken seriously with harmful results.

The arrival of April 1, Friday the 13th and October 31 inevitably brings into print stories of April Fool jokes, so-called unlucky incidents, make-believe ghosts and goblins, but they are all in fun and the readers know it. In the same vein are the yarns written about haunted houses, sea serpents, and those who forecast weather by the behavior of groundhogs and katydids.

The fact is that much space in the press is allocated to folklore. Local legends, widely preserved, are recorded again and again in the newspapers on special dates and days. But they are never treated as the solemn truth.

Every newsman needs to be a skeptic and to demonstrate his skepticism with a chuckle or two when writing of charms and amulets, divining rods, the secrets of ancient alchemists, the moon's influence on humans, crops or fishing, the intelligence of trained fleas, seeds that grow after 1,000 years, horned toads found alive after years in a rock or stone—all myths, claptrap and fairy tales designed for airy entertainment rather than sober acceptance.

Not so innocuous are stories about unsound claims and unscientific processes which may lead gullible folk astray. Among these dangerous subjects are reports of vampires, end-of-the-world predictions and the creation of life.

Knowing what scientific stories not to print is as important as knowing what to print. News dealing with obvious supernatural stuff and superstition requires either light treatment or elimination. Such news, apparently sound but suspect, requires investigation and verification. No such material can be safely accepted offhand and presented seriously as news. During the past 150 years, with such things as satellites and space missiles becoming realities, the public has become inclined to take "miracles" for granted and to accept stories of scientific wonders as accurate and reliable. It is up to the newspapers to distinguish fact from fiction.

RUMOR CAN BE RUINOUS

The first rule in the newsroom code of honor calls for elimination of harmful hearsay. It is imperative that the reporter recognize rumor and gossip and equally imperative that the newspaper not become a party to spreading them.

If you ask a dozen people to describe the same scene individually you will discover how guesswork grows into gossip. Pass an innocent remark from ear to ear around a room and you will understand how rumors grow. Two men standing still in a crowded bus become five men fighting over a seat. A man and a woman on an innocent overnight business trip become illicit lovers in a sex escapade. Water becomes whisky, pencils become pistols and postmen become policemen.

The reporter often finds it difficult to run down and get rid of rumor, for he seldom is an eyewitness to what he writes about. His sources of information may be twice or thrice removed from the eyewitness whose own accuracy is none too certain.

A DOZEN

UNWRITTEN TABOOS

DON'T

Print rumor or hearsay, even to deny it.

Use terms such as "dago" or "greaser."

Present unscientific phenomena as factual.

Print repellent stories or photographs of reptiles.

Copy verbatim the style in a rival paper.

DO

Check and verify gossip before writing it.

Correct the grammar of uneducated as well as
educated persons.

Use the name of the Deity only with reverence.

Treat lightly stories about anything supernatural.

Judge handouts by their news value.

Get news facts fast even if you must take them
from a competitor.

From the Code of the *Times*

Check and *verify* are the only effective procedures against ignorance and error. Evidence is the sole criterion of the reliable reporter as he sifts fact from fiction and weighs the motives of malice or justice behind the statements of his informants. As a final test the reporter should ask himself: How would this affect me if I were the person involved? Do I know this to be the truth? Is it fair and just for me to report this information for print?

Gossip about marital trouble, impending divorce and infidelity and false reports about missing persons, a birth, marriage or death, are sometimes deliberately passed to newsmen by malicious persons or practical jokers. These can lead to a family breakup or even suicide and murder. And as previously pointed out, business, too, can be ruined by a rumor, for example, that cases of a contagious disease have been found in a food-processing plant.

In the rumor class, unless so designated by an authorized medical or health officer, is the word *epidemic*. This is a *scare* term. Beware of it.

Paradoxically, the denial of a rumor in print can be merely another way of spreading it, for credulous people believe the old maxims that "where there is smoke there is fire" and "there must be a grain of truth in it somewhere." To mention a rumor is like telling a friend: "They say you stole the money but I don't believe you are a thief." Don't quote a danger-laden rumor even for the sake of spiking it. A wastebasket is the proper place for rumor and that is where it goes in a well-run newsroom.

PUBLICITY AND FREE ADVERTISING

We move now to other types of taboos controlling the relations of reporters and their newspapers to both their supporters and competitors, namely, the exclusion of free advertising from news columns and the ban on stealing style from a rival newspaper.

One of the recognized shibboleths of the newspaper craft is that opinion goes into the editorial columns, advertising goes into the advertising columns, and news—news alone—goes into the news columns. As a principle this rule is sound and is to be obeyed by the beginning reporter unless he has specific instructions to overstep it.

In the face of this rule—that advertising shall not be combined with news, which must be divorced from exploitation by money-seeking persons and firms—comes the problem of publicity men and how to handle them in an era devoted to warfare against sales resistance.

Certainly there is no justification for the arrogant flaunting of out-and-out advertising blurbs in the guise of honest-to-goodness news. Decades ago the better papers abandoned the practice of issuing puffs, suitably headlined and in approved news form, to assist an advertiser whose patronage they were cultivating. On the other hand, papers do not arbitrarily discard news copy merely because it tends to promote the popularity of some person, firm or product even though it may be prepared by a paid publicity agent employed to secure favorable space for his clients.

Any number of promotional stories may be tabulated in newspapers every day. For example:

> Three hundred pounds of birthday cake plus 40 gallons of ice cream and 150 children equal a glorious party.
>
> And this is not a fairy-tale recipe either. The combination was tried out yesterday afternoon on the top floor of the Midland Department Store and proved a huge success. There are unlimited possibilities to the recipe.
>
> Max Crews mixed the batter and frosted the big birthday cake to celebrate the 11th anniversary of the store's residence in the present building. He made it in 10 rich layers and decorated it with a fancy frosting.
>
> Then he went out into the highways and byways and collected the boys and girls. . . . .

An occasional beginner regards all information offered by a publicity agent or public relations man as buncombe and feels that reputable reporters should scorn it, choosing rather to obtain their own stories unaided. Daily contact with press releases soon modifies his point of view. PR men, he finds, are a present help in time of trouble and as liasons between the newspaper and business firms, corporations, universities, theaters and churches. From them he receives many timely tips as well as foundation facts and official reports. He obtains pictures from them for the asking.

Safe rules for a reporter to follow are these: (1) Write what is actually news regardless of its source or its advertising value. (2) Do not extend special favors in print to any firm unless the story has demonstrable reader interest. (3) Check all statements carefully, particularly when in doubt as to their authorship and reliability. (4) Digest and rewrite publicity copy in your own words so that all the papers will not offer identical wording. (5) In writing the lead consider the rights of the reader first, not the interest of the promoter.

BORROWING FROM OTHER PAPERS

In the unwritten newspaper code there is a series of do's and don'ts which regulate the relations between rival publications. These go unnoticed by the reading public but so well are they followed that a case of literary theft by a newspaper seldom reaches the courts.

Newspapers do appropriate news material from each other, and rightly so. It is common practice for afternoon papers to lift data from stories in morning newspapers, and vice versa—without credit. Radio and television newscasters take news from the papers, and vice versa. A major scoop lasts little longer than the time it takes a newspaper to reach a competitor's office or the microphones of a studio.

News facts, like ideas, are not copyrightable because it is unquestionably to the public interest for them to be circulated as fully and rapidly as possible through every medium of communication.

But a news article has two elements—the information contained therein and the manner and sequence of presentation. The former, after it has been disseminated, is public property; the latter is private property and therefore can be, and sometimes is, copyrighted and must not be pirated. In other words, you may appropriate the facts or news elements already published or broadcast but not the style or literary color and flavor of stories lifted from papers other than your own.

A loophole in the copyright laws permits the use of excerpts or quotations, but seldom does a newspaper copy and credit a local competitor. Wire services do not credit each other but do sometimes credit a newspaper in order to give its clients the benefit of a spot news scoop in another city. However, the excerpt privilege applies less to news stories than to quotations from books, songs and plays. Here the question of piracy depends on the extent and character of use. A test frequently applied is whether the extracts used are likely to injure the sale of the original work. Critics and book reviewers are permitted to use direct quotations because these are usually brief and help rather than hurt sales.

As reporters and rewrite men work at their typewriters they often have before them clippings from competing publications which they use for reference. Sometimes a single clip is the sole source of information. The task then is to pick up the gist of the story without picking up all the words—to clothe the skeleton in fresh raiment.

Of course no newspaper worthy of the name is printed wholly or continually from purloined raw material. The element of immediacy in news compels it to cover its own sources and pay for its own wire services. However, it must not and does not ignore primary news even though such news comes from a competitor. It simply reprocesses and prints it as soon as possible.

SHOP TALK

1. Try a game of spread-the-rumor. Whisper an innocent remark around the classroom and see how it comes out.
2. Specify conditions under which race and color may properly be mentioned in a news story. As an editor would you use *Negro* or *colored* or neither?
3. Do you think it is proper to use dialect in humorous news stories?
4. Do you think newspapers generally are too sensational in printing scientific and medical news?
5. Is it morally right for newspapers to steal news from competitors so long as they do not purloin literary quality?

CHAPTER 17

Composing the Composite Story

THE SINGLE STORY SPREADS OUT

As he advances along the pathway of experience a young reporter discovers that a news event does not always produce itself in standard form neatly wrapped into a small individual package and labeled for his own convenience. At times it arrives in scattered pieces which need to be sorted out, rearranged and tied into a bigger bundle.

The simple *one-incident story* such as the account of a death, a speech or an interview deals with an isolated occurrence. Having learned to handle such stories, the apprentice will now be introduced to the multi-angled or *composite story* in which two or more divergent aspects of a news topic are drawn together in the interest of coherence and economy of space.

We hasten to say that the terms *one-incident* and *composite,* while accurate and clear for the purpose of analysis, are too formal for shop talk. Newsroom equivalents for reporting a composite story are "Cover all the angles," "Round it up" and "Wrap it together."

To a limited degree the composite story resembles an accident story containing a casualty list or series of eyewitness interviews. In another way it suggests the follow-up which also calls for the consolidation of component parts. It differs from both in that a name or brief quote in the one and the tie-in or background in the other are not true angles. An angle we shall define as a major unit of spot news in a composite story.

Often several members of the staff work on covering a composite story but usually only one reporter or rewrite man writes it up as a single article. In a later chapter we shall demonstrate the *sectional story* wherein each of several reporters covers an angle and writes it as one of a group of separate stories on a topic of paramount news value.

CITY ROOM PROCEDURE

Let us assume that Assistant City Editor Harry Baxter finds from death notices and hospital reports that five Midlanders have died from influenza within 24 hours, indicating that the malady is widespread. Assigned to interview the city health commissioner, Reporter Paul Wilson is told that 50 cases of flu have been reported. Other reporters learn that a school has been closed, a rooming house is quarantined, and state health officials have called a conference on precautionary measures.

On another day a half dozen fires break out in one section of Midland. Oil-soaked rags started four of them and Reporter Fred Maxwell phones that police are searching for a firebug. Meanwhile, a fire truck en route to one of the blazes skids on the icy pavement, injuring a pedestrian. One of the fires destroys Treaty House, a historic landmark.

Each chain of facts, although covered separately and reaching Baxter's desk by devious routes, will be handled as a unified composition. To publish a series of separate items would result in duplication of material and wasted space. It would inconvenience and confuse the reader.

The real news is not deaths and fires but epidemic and arson. In other words, interest centers not in the occurrences separately but in their correlation. The city editor's orders will run:

> "Put the FLU stuff together for a column."
> "Everything on the fires, a column and a half. Slug it ARSON. Let it run to two if they arrest anybody."

All available data, including the angles covered by other reporters, will travel to one writer to be made into a composite story.

Many newsrooms have standing titles or slugs for composite story subjects which repeat themselves frequently in print. All automobile accidents may be assembled under SPEED, political news under POL, agricultural news under FARM, holiday news under HOL, educational news under SCHOOLS. Composite story slugs like STRIKE, CONVENTION, WEATHER, TOURNEY may be used for several days in a row, dropped, then picked up again when needed.

COVERING COMPOSITE STORIES

A multiangled news situation may arise unexpectedly, upsetting the assignment sheet, or it may be anticipated and split up for coverage before the reporting staff is on duty. A typical story of the unexpected variety develops like this:

Rains pour steadily in Midland and the surrounding region for two days with a heavy fall of 1.3 inches last night. Tributaries of the Timber River are high and the stream itself, skirting the south side of town, is out of its banks and rising. Reporter Fred Markham is assigned to the story, to be slugged FLOOD.

When he visits the river district Markham finds a dozen blocks inundated and 50 families driven from their homes. He learns that a tramp asleep on the river bank was drowned while trying to swim to safety and that a score of auto tourists barely escaped from a trailer camp swept away by the flood. One approach to the Pierce Avenue Bridge is under water.

Reporter Larry Levison, meanwhile, discovers that 75 refugees are housed in uptown church basements and police stations. The Red Cross and Salvation Army are caring for them. He also learns that Main street merchants have started a drive for $10,000 to aid the stricken families.

Fred Maxwell at headquarters phones to Jefferson Harris, rewrite man, reports on police activities, including the announcement that heavy patrol lines will be established around the flooded district tonight and that the body of the tramp has been recovered and identified. The weather bureau informs another rewrite man, Leo Burke, that tomorrow will bring clear skies and cessation of the rain. Dispatches from an upstream point say the river still is rising, that the crest of the flood will reach Midland at noon tomorrow.

Returning to the office, Markham receives the information gathered by Levison, Maxwell, Harris and Burke orally and in typed memorandums. He also finds on his desk dispatches from other towns, clips from the PM papers and miscellaneous data. He outlines the facts, finds out what space is allotted and proceeds to blend his assorted material into a unified story.

Here is how another composite story—this one of the fact variety based on a fixed event—might be rounded up:

Tomorrow is Christmas Day and every man, woman and child in Midland is affected in some way by the year's most absorbing and emotional festival. Baxter assigns the HOL story to Alice Nestor. She learns by telephone from spokesmen for the Merchants Association and department stores that gift sales this year will top a million dollars—a record. Postmaster Skipworth tells her that 50 extra carriers will deliver all packages by nightfall. Weatherman Bennett promises more snow to make it a white Christmas. She then goes to Central Square to cover a ceremony at Midland's official tree with Mayor Nelson playing the part of Santa Claus.

Reporter Edgar Barton finds out that 300 underprivileged youngsters will be fed turkey and trimmings by the Kiwanis Club and that the Community Chest will distribute 500 baskets to the needy. At the Midland Orphanage every child will get a toy from the Fire Department repair shop.

Reporter Clyde Schafer phones in to Burke that 5-year-old Jamie York, in St. Mary's Hospital with both legs broken in a sled mishap last week, will have a special tree trimmed by kids in his neighborhood plus a new sled.

The Midland Motor Club sends over to David Jordan an estimate that 12 persons will die in Centralia traffic accidents over the weekend, together with a warning of icy roads and a plea for sober driving. Jordan also checks the airport and the rail and bus terminals. He finds that travel is up 15 per cent over last year.

Miss Nestor comes in early to do the Christmas story. After shuffling through the material she writes an over-all lead featuring the spirit and spending. The snowfall comes next, then churches, and so on, to the extent of her space.

LEADS FOR COMPOSITE STORIES

Three types of leads are available to the writer of a composite story. He may (1) reduce the important angles to a comprehensive paragraph, (2) single out and play up the salient feature or (3) combine the two methods.

A general or comprehensive lead, most common of the three, may well be used when the various angles are of about equal value, as in this instance:

> From a dozen pulpits yesterday, Midland clergymen denounced the movement launched by the Timber County Racing Assn. to permit pari mutuel betting under a bill pending before the State Legislature.
> The concerted church antigambling campaign came to a climax . . . . .

A comprehensive lead arrangement is almost indispensable when the interrelation of the units is the outstanding news factor, as here:

> Federal and city officers raided three stores, two hotels and a restaurant last night in an all-out drive to smash the Midland headquarters of an interstate dope ring.
> Striking swiftly between 10 and 11 p.m., the raiders arrested . . . . .

Out of a scattered range of facts may emerge one clear-cut peak high enough to crowd the others from the sky line. The writer now bends his lead into one emphatic statement, thus:

> Five hundred cans of milk en route to the Galena Creamery were dumped into the road early today by embattled dairymen who mobbed the drivers of seven milk trucks and forced them to surrender their loads.
>
> The milk dumping marked the first violence in the Boone County "dairy strike." It came as a climax to these developments: . . . . .

The third type of lead—a combination of a general statement and a specific angle—is useful when one feature is significant but not important enough to warrant subordination of associated facts. An example:

> With the campaign ending in a swirl of angry words over the budget issue, both Republican and Democratic leaders last night predicted overwhelming victories in today's mayoral election.
>
> Speaking from the same platform at Central Auditorium, the major party candidates charged each other . . . . .

In building the combination lead the writer must be careful not to overload it with explanations. The advantage, in fact the sole purpose of the composite framework is to foreshorten a long stretch of separate but related facts. The lead, in particular, should be pithy, compact and stripped of everything but the frontage of the story to follow.

LINKING THE ANGLES

In the chapter on story structure we touched upon the value of coupling-pin words and phrases to smooth transitions from one fact, quote or action detail to the next in a one-incident story. These pins are needed to weld together the more widely separated angles of a composite story:

> *Another development* in the investigation . . .
> *At the same time* word came from the capital that . . .
> *Earlier in the day,* Center High won its opener with . . .
> *Coincident with* the arrival of Governor Boland, a delegation from . . .
> *Piecing the clues together,* the sheriff concluded that . . .
> *On the heels of* this disclosure came a report that . . .
> *As a climax* to the celebration, 2,000 school children marched . . .

While such connectives are necessary they should not be allowed to eat up too much space or to clog the movement of the story. Those like *in addition to* or *also significant* serve only to tell the reader that you are going into the next angle. Otherwise they are useless. More valuable are those like *from several points upstate* or *as an aftermath to* specifying place or time or containing other factual information.

At best the writer's connectives are hardly more than literary tools and no number of them can knit together a haphazard tangle of news threads. Essentially preparation of a readable composite story is a problem of organization and arrangement.

In a one-incident story the writer merely arranges a group of facts bearing on a central happening; in a composite story he arranges a series of groups, each the equivalent of a one-incident story. Instead of making up a train of a dozen cars he assembles several trains, all piloted by one locomotive—his lead.

USE OF THE ACTION DIAGRAM

Turning again to the inverted pyramid symbols, we find that all those studied thus far can contribute to the makeup of the multiangled story. By its nature the composite structure is more complicated than the simpler triangle variations but it is merely a combination of them.

Usually it conforms to the action or fact diagram, as we shall illustrate. Often it is a mixture of action and facts with a sprinkling of quotes. The follow-up diagram with a swift summary of all angles in the tie-in block and especially the casualty list or 1–2–3 arrangement after the lead also are adaptable to composite structure.

Let us look first at a shortened version of the Markham flood story to illustrate application of an elaborated action diagram:

Lead Incidents

Swirling out of its banks at a score of places in south Midland, the rain-swollen Timber River went on a rampage yesterday, drowning one man and driving at least 50 families from their homes.

Summary of Other Incidents

Police threw patrol lines around the flooded area as the raging waters continued to rise. The crest is expected at noon today. Meanwhile, welfare agencies were caring for refugees and a relief fund campaign got under way.

Details of First Incident

Widespread rains for the last two days plus a heavy fall of 1.3 inches which drenched the Midland region brought the Timber River to flood stage Tuesday night. Between midnight and 7 a.m. it rose five feet . . . . .

Details of Second Incident

The yellow floodwaters tore out the riverbank just south of the city limits and cut a channel through the Pierce avenue small home area. Fifty families were evacuated . . . . .

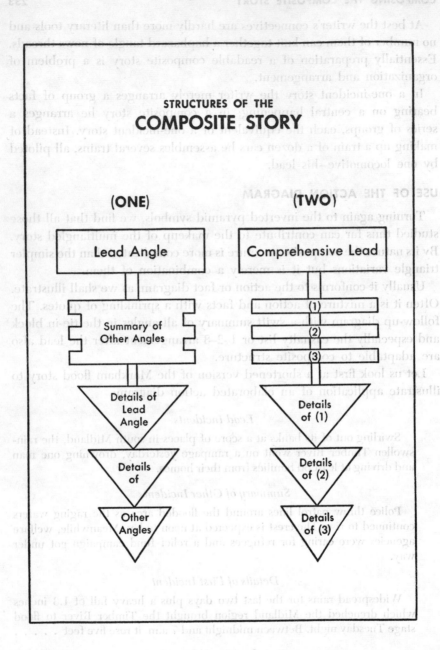

STRUCTURES OF THE
COMPOSITE STORY

(ONE)	(TWO)
Lead Angle	Comprehensive Lead
	(1)
Summary of Other Angles	(2)
	(3)
Details of Lead Angle	Details of (1)
Details of	Details of (2)
Other Angles	Details of (3)

Composite Story Diagrams

Details of Third Incident

The drowned man, a vagrant, trapped as he slept near the Pierce Avenue Bridge, was identified by police as Timothy Weeks, 42, of Booneville. His body was recovered . . . . .

It will be noted that although Markham had considerable leeway in arrangement he chose to write a mixed comprehensive lead. He followed it with a swift summary of other angles and then wrote the details of each angle in order of news value—a logical pattern of development.

THE FACT STRUCTURE EXTENDED

The composite story of Christmas as it came into the hands of Miss Nestor consisted chiefly of facts rather than action and her organization problem was primarily one of fact distribution. Like Markham, she laid out an outline and conformed to it, as follows:

Lead Facts

Jingle-belled Donder and Blitzen will slip Santa's sleigh into Midland on a white carpet tonight but his bag, bulging with a million dollars in gifts, may give him trouble in the chimneys.

Summary of Other Facts

The spirit of the jolly saint spread over the city yesterday in every direction. While businessmen agreed it will be a bountiful holiday, plans were completed to see that the needy are not forgotten. In churches, hospitals and hundreds of homes the joyous scenes of the season will be reenacted tonight and tomorrow.

Details of First Fact

For the first time in 12 years Midland will have a white Christmas with fresh flakes due to cover the two-inch blanket of snow already on the ground . . . . .

Details of Second Fact

Last-minute shoppers gave Midland stores the busiest pre-Christmas Day on record as sales soared past the million mark. This estimate, made by the Merchants Assn., was confirmed by department store spokesmen . . . . .

Details of Third Fact

Turkey and all the trimmings will be on the Christmas menus for 300 underprivileged youngsters invited to dinner by the Kiwanis Club. Five hundred loaded baskets will go to . . . . .

Details of Fourth Fact

Meanwhile, a word of warning to drivers came from the Midland Motor Club. The snow and ice are just dandy for sleds and sleighs, but

APPLICATION OF
COMPOSITE DIAGRAM ONE

LEAD ANGLE

With its rudder broken and lifeboats smashed by giant waves, the yacht Rameses II, carrying ten persons, last night was reported sinking in Lake Luce. Coast Guard and police cutters were speeding to her aid.

SUMMARY OF OTHER ANGLES

From two other points on the lake, swept by a violent storm at dusk yesterday, came word of rescues. Four persons were picked up after the launch Gaybird sank off Burns Landing. Two others swam ashore from a sailboat which overturned nearby Scores of smaller craft were damaged.

DETAILS OF LEAD ANGLE

The Rameses II, owned by Dr. C. R. Lang of Midland, a 75-foot Diesel-motored yacht, left Midland on a pleasure excursion at 3 p.m. Aboard were the owner, his wife, a party of friends and three crewmen. The first distress call came from the yacht at 10:20 p.m. .....

DETAILS OF SECOND ANGLE

A dory carrying Arden S. Simms, owner of the Gaybird and two fishermen friends, drifted for several hours after the launch went down two miles from shore. The men were picked up by the tugboat Marie, exhausted but otherwise unharmed .....

DETAILS OF THIRD ANGLE

A series of violent squalls struck in the Burns Landing area, 18 miles north of Midland. Except for the sailboat, from which two young men swam ashore, all boats reached the harbor.....

Lead-Summary Arrangement

dangerous for automobiles, said a club bulletin which estimated that 12 deaths . . . . .

THE 1–2–3 ARRANGEMENT

Welding the day's developments into a 1–2–3 summary attached to the lead—in the same way that the dead and injured are listed in an account of an accident—frequently solves the problem of composite technique, especially when the parts have about equal news value. The 1–2–3 arrangement pockets the main facts quickly and effectively, but the device should not be overworked. Note this example:

Lead Angle

A heavy windstorm cut an erratic path across southern Timber County today, leaving in its wake one injured person, damaged crops and buildings, and broken telephone lines.

Summary of Other Angles

Midland escaped the storm which struck near Twin Forks, hit with greatest force three miles south of Fairfield and traveled eastward as far as Green Forest. Early this afternoon the state police reported that:

1. Lawrence Bremer, 44, a farmer, was hurt by a plank blown from a shed he was building.

2. Several hundred acres of wheat, ready to harvest, were ruined, at an estimated loss of $50,000.

3. Roads were made impassable in the Fairfield district because of the rain following the windstorm.

4. Telephone lines were down from Green Forest to Midland.

Details of Lead Angle

Scores of farmers and their families took refuge in cellars at the height of the storm about 11 a.m., but Bremer, who lives near Fairfield on the Frank Meltzer farm, remained at work on the roof of the shed, thinking it would last but a few minutes.

Ripped up by the gale, a two-by-six board struck him on the forehead, cutting a severe gash. He was brought to Haven Hospital for treatment. He is expected to recover.

Details of Second Angle

County Agent George Duval, after a survey of the wheat fields, made the $50,000 damage estimate. Much of the crop, he said, would have been harvested in a week or 10 days. Heavy with grain, the wheat in some fields was beaten into the ground.

Duval was forced to turn back on Highway 14 because of washed-out culverts and water hubcap deep in several places. Side roads in that neighborhood cannot be used by automobiles for several days, he said.

APPLICATION OF
COMPOSITE DIAGRAM TWO

**COMPREHEN-
SIVE LEAD**

Swift activity by local law enforcement agencies today followed the escape of seven prisoners from the Timber County Jail last night after a gun battle with Sheriff John E. Fisher and several deputies.

POINTS

Today's developments were:

(1)

1. José Torrez, convicted bank robber and the jail-break leader, was wounded and recaptured by a posse in Woodland Park two miles south of the city.

(2)

2. Rewards of $500 each for the capture of the six men still at large were offered by the County Board of Supervisors.

(3)

3. Resignation of Sheriff Fisher for "gross neglect of duty" was demanded in a resolution adopted by the executive committee of Post 17, American Legion.

**DETAILS OF
(1)**

A second shooting affray preceded the capture of Torrez as the posse, led by Deputy Sheriff Edwin Barth, closed in about his hiding place, which was located by farmers in the neighborhood . . . . .

**DETAILS OF
(2)**

The rewards for the return of each of the fugitives "dead or alive" were approved at a special meeting of the county board this morning . . . . .

**DETAILS OF
(3)**

The Legion resolution, bitterly assailing the sheriff for his purported failure to post sufficient guards in the jail, was passed following a luncheon meeting debate . . . . .

1–2–3 Arrangement

Details of Third Angle

Emergency crews from the Midland Telephone Co. were dispatched to repair the Green Forest lines which were torn from the poles. Officials of the company said the lines would be open by nightfall.

Many such stories as this one have been prepared by news writers and in all of them the writers faced and solved the same problem—organization.

There is only one sure way to proceed. That is to analyze, segregate and skeletonize all the material before attempting to write. If necessary, jot down the high points on a piece of paper, then weigh them carefully. Finally, arrange the points in their proper sequence and calculate the space merited by each. With the framework of the story fixed the job of building loses much of its complexity.

SHOP TALK

1. Define a composite story. Choose a dozen stories at random from a current newspaper and show which are one-incident and which composite.
2. Why do editors merge the angles of a news topic into a single story instead of offering separate items? Cite examples of multiangled news topics.
3. How does the local staff coordinate in gathering material for a story with several angles?
4. Discuss these types of composite story leads: comprehensive, single angle, combination. Cite illustrations.
5. Chart on the blackboard the diagrams for composite stories. Test them with sample stories.

CHAPTER 18

The Human Touch in News

THE CASE OF THE LOST SHOE

Millions of people ride daily on the subways of New York and never get their names into the newspapers they read—or try to read—in the jam-packed cars during rush hours.

At the start there was nothing unusual about the ride of 19-year-old Joan Wilson, a typist, who boarded a train bound for her job. But the next day she found herself in every newspaper in town—all because she lost a shoe! "Subway Crowd Makes Her a Cinderella" said one headline. The story went like this:

> Joan Wilson knows how Mickey Mouse must feel when he gets caught in a cement mixer, and if anybody thinks that is funny—well, it all depends on who is being churned up.
>
> Miss Wilson, who is 19, blonde and blue-eyed, left her home at 1176 E. Jackson Ave. about 8 a.m. and started for her job as a typist on the other side of the Bronx. She squeezed aboard a southbound Lexington Express, intending to change to a northbound local at 125th St.
>
> "Let 'em off first!" shouted a platform guard at 125th. Joan, who is 5 feet 1 and weighs 98 pounds, was shoved out, then hurled back in by the stampede of boarding passengers. The doors shut. Her right shoe was missing.
>
> At 86th street she called, "Out, please!" but was wedged in deep. At Grand Central the general eruption ejected her. Her nylons were ripped. Her hat hung on one ear. And she hopped on one foot.
>
> "What happened to you?" a cop asked. Joan told her tearful story. The policeman found a shoemaker who loaned her a pair of shoes—a mite too big. Police sent out a wanted notice for one right pump, gray, size 5½–AA.
>
> Joan called her boss and, she said, "He thought it was a good joke," smiling a little herself.
>
> Undaunted, Miss Wilson will be in there fighting again tomorrow morning.

The police notation was the clue that tipped off the city desks and started the reporters and photographers. Stories and pictures went on front pages. Wire services carried them near and far. Editorial writers followed up with comments on the subway situation.

As the policeman asked, "What happened?" Miss Wilson's excursion into print can hardly be accounted for under any definition of news which insists that it must be of social significance. Her adventure was of little moment to anyone but herself. Yet it was awarded places of honor in the press. Millions in and out of the city—in fact anyone who ever rode in a subway—read about and sympathized with her.

Why did the incident strike such a strong emotional chord in the minds of so many? The answer can be called *human interest*—the human touch in news—sometimes shortened in shop venacular to *H-I*.

WHAT IS HUMAN INTEREST?

We have previously recognized in news an elusive but potent quality with a powerful pull on the inner senses of men and women. It is found in the elements of oddity, suspense and emotions. It manifests itself in writing style as personal appeal.

Human interest is as difficult to define as human nature. In fact it is a reflection of human traits, a revelation of human instincts in action.

It is axiomatic that the most fascinating things to the average human being are other human beings and how they behave. All of us are moved to laughter, anger, pride, pity, envy and sympathy through direct personal experience but more often through imaginary participation in the experiences of others. Nor is emotional experience, real or by proxy, limited to impressionable young girls and sentimental old ladies. Even the so-called hardheaded businessman, absorbed in matter-of-fact affairs, possesses a battery of emotional outlets instantly sparked by the human touch. What normal person does not find satisfaction in watching the behavior of others under a play of circumstances with which he is intimately familiar?

All of this sounds somewhat academic, and it is. So let us go back to the newsroom for more shop expressions to throw light on *H-I stuff*.

Loosely and in an extremely broad sense there are two kinds of news, namely, *straight* and *feature*. Straight news is intended primarily to inform. Feature news seeks rather to stir emotions, to stimulate, divert and entertain.

Human interest copy inclines toward the feature classification. However, the term *feature* is so diversely used that it is not a specific synonym.

Newsmen refer to any significant point in a story, a lead or an angle, as the feature of the story. Feature articles include expositions of the Sunday magazine type, ranging from "Why Gloria Glamour Lost Her Fifth Husband" to the "Man-Eating Tigers of India." Cartoons, comics, puzzles, short stories and various commentary columns also are referred to as features.

Nevertheless, a news story strong in human interest is often designated by editors and reporters as a feature or a feature story.

No sharp line of division runs between straight and human interest or feature news any more than there is a clear cleavage of colors in a rainbow. One hue shades into another within many individual write-ups. Indeed some editors contend, with logic, that human interest is merely an offshoot of straight news and that the root must be embedded in it.

"Do you have a peg to hang it on?" is a common question from the city desk man. He means: "Is there something new that warrants our printing this?" The news peg may be weak—as in the case of the lost shoe—but it is always present in a true news story, which must have the immediacy element.

The key to unlock emotional reaction is a word picture of another person or persons in a situation known to the reader from personal or vicarious experience.

For example, we all have found stray dimes, if not diamonds, and understand the thrill of sudden wealth. We all have had the hiccups and can sympathize with the plight of another who hiccups for ten days. We all know bullies and brutes and cheer when they are brought to justice. The lives of all of us have been touched by romance and everybody loves a lover.

Of all human beings, next to lovers, children evoke the greatest sympathy, humor and pride. A baby crying in a basket on the steps of a foundling home and a tear-stained 4-year-old eating ice cream in a police station interest everyone. And our own junior's name in print when he carries a spear in a class play is about the most sensational news in the paper.

Human interest extends beyond human beings and into the animal kingdom. Living creatures of every species from bees to elephants excite and amuse us, in particular those which most nearly duplicate our own instincts and intelligence. A monkey in the zoo enthralls onlookers hour after hour. A monkey loose in a lingerie shop lands on page one. Next on the news scale are domesticated animals and birds, such as dogs, cats, horses, parakeets and canaries.

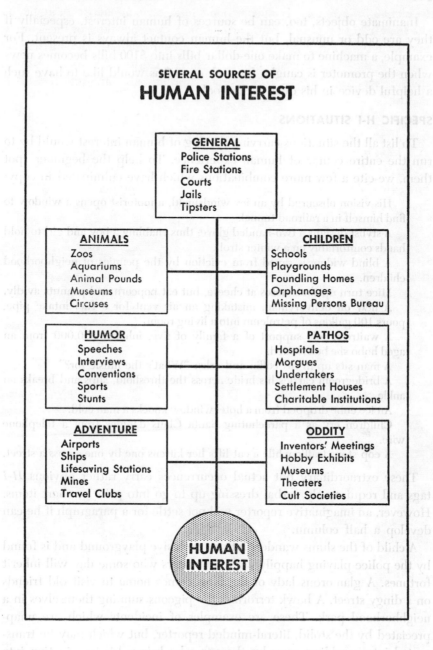

SEVERAL SOURCES OF

HUMAN INTEREST

GENERAL
Police Stations
Fire Stations
Courts
Jails
Tipsters

ANIMALS
Zoos
Aquariums
Animal Pounds
Museums
Circuses

CHILDREN
Schools
Playgrounds
Foundling Homes
Orphanages
Missing Persons Bureau

HUMOR
Speeches
Interviews
Conventions
Sports
Stunts

PATHOS
Hospitals
Morgues
Undertakers
Settlement Houses
Charitable Institutions

ADVENTURE
Airports
Ships
Lifesaving Stations
Mines
Travel Clubs

ODDITY
Inventors' Meetings
Hobby Exhibits
Museums
Theaters
Cult Societies

HUMAN INTEREST

Where H-I Copy Originates

Inanimate objects, too, can be sources of human interest, especially if they are odd or unusual, but the human contact always is present. For example, a machine to make one-dollar bills into $100 bills becomes news when the promoter is caught, for each one of us would like to have such a helpful device in his own pocketbook.

SPECIFIC H-I SITUATIONS

To list all the situations carrying the flag of human interest would be to run the entire course of human experience. To help the beginner spot them, we cite a few more combinations which have culminated in copy:

> His vision obscured by an icy windshield, a motorist opens a window to find himself in a railroad tunnel.
>
> A stylist designs a two-handed glove, thus enabling a boy and girl to hold hands comfortably on a winter stroll.
>
> A blind widow is saved from eviction by the pennies of neighborhood children.
>
> Mice turn up their noses at cheese, but eat popcorn and peanuts avidly.
>
> A new oil deliveryman, mistaking an air vent for a fuel intake pipe, pours 100 gallons of petroleum into a living room.
>
> A waitress, sole support of a family of five, inherits $50,000 from an aged hobo she befriended.
>
> A man sits up in his coffin and asks: "What's the music for?"
>
> A bridegroom carries his bride across the threshold, slips and breaks an ankle.
>
> An ice cube dropped from a hotel window knocks a man cold.
>
> Children cry as a parachuting Santa Claus dangles from a telephone wire.
>
> A cop stops traffic while a cat lifts her kittens one by one across a street.

These extraordinary but actual occurrences carry rather obvious *H-I* tags and require only verbal dressing up to go into print as short items. However, an imaginative reporter will not settle for a paragraph if he can develop a half column.

A child of the slums wanders into an exclusive playground and is found by the police playing happily with youngsters who some day will inherit fortunes. A glamorous lady of the films comes home to visit old friends on a dingy street. A hawk terrorizes the pigeons sunning themselves in a neighborhood park. These are examples of incidents which are unappreciated by the stolid, literal-minded reporter, but which may be transmuted into sparkling copy by the one who brings his imagination into play.

The unimaginative writer who contents himself with recording "The

TYPICAL TOPICS OF
HUMAN INTEREST

Starving mother. . .deserts baby. . .kind policeman

Alley cat. . . . . .up a tree. . . . . .brave fireman

Destitute family. . father killed . . generous neighbors

Pigeon flock. . .attacked by owl. . .crack marksman

Small child. . . .runs away. . . .thoughtful stranger

Country visitor. . . . .meets slicker. . . .buys bridge

Childhood lovers . surprise meeting . happy wedding

Amateur gamblers. . .bet on game. . .loser barefoot

Bored society. . . . .treasure hunt. . . . .stern judge

Boy asleep. . . .imperiled by fire. . . .faithful dog

Ill explorer. . . . .needs antitoxin. . . . .daring flyer

Formulas for Human Interest Stories

police arrested last night . . ." when he might be producing a real-life comedy or tragedy is doomed to remain on a level of mediocrity.

"DOC" HICKOCK COMES HOME

From Mercy Hospital one spring day Reporter Clyde Schafer tipped the *Times* city desk that Dr. Hickock of Booneville would be discharged the following afternoon. Assistant City Editor Harry Baxter had already been in touch with his Booneville correspondent but he took no chances. He sent one of his stars, Ann Kemp, to Booneville.

Nobody in Midland ever heard of Dr. Hickock. But in the hands of a keen-witted reporter the situation made news that tugged at the heart-strings of all who read the *Times* next day:

> They brought 69-year-old Dr. Jonathan Hickock home today—and home was waiting for him. He stared at it from his wheel chair. A tear trickled from his eye when they told him the house was his. Finally, he said:
>
> "I—I—Well, Martha, I just can't believe it, that's all."
>
> "Doc" Hickock's friends and neighbors built the house—a gleaming white four-room cottage—in exactly six weeks. It is valued at $12,000, but to Hickock and his 67-year-old wife it will be more than a place to spend their declining years. It symbolizes a lifetime of kindly community service.
>
> For 45 years "Doc" Hickock has been Booneville's only physician. He brought into the world the babies who are now the leading men and women in that town of 2,500 people. His buggy and then his secondhand car were tokens of skill and sympathy to nearly every home in this area.
>
> One day last March the Wilkses' house next to the Hickock place caught fire. "Doc" helped to get out Mrs. Wilks, a widow, and her two children. Both children were burned. As he treated them in the yard, sparks ignited his own home. The Wilkses' house was saved; the Hickocks' was destroyed.
>
> Afterward it was found that "Doc" himself was hurt while saving Mrs. Wilks—a serious leg injury. He has been in Mercy Hospital since. The hospital bill took most of his savings.
>
> The new-house movement began at a Town Hall meeting when George Lorie, local lumberman, offered to supply the materials. A builder, two carpenters and a plumber volunteered their services. They worked evenings and Sundays.
>
> Other townsfolk pitched in to help, haul and hammer, put on paint and wallpaper, plant grass and flowers. Mrs. Hickock, staying with neighbors, knew all about it but they didn't tell "Doc" until yesterday.
>
> An old-fashioned housewarming took place at the new Hickock home last night. Nearly a hundred of those who helped erect the cottage came to see the "Doc" and tell him the sign over the door means what it says: "Welcome home, Doc. Good luck!"

THE APPEAL OF CHILDREN

Without exception grownups are interested in youngsters for one of two basic reasons—recollections of their own childhood experiences or because there are children currently in their lives.

An item like this one brings a nostalgic smile from each adult reader who recalls his first earned penny:

> Three small businessmen bucked the big show today and emerged as winners of the economic struggle.
>
> Frank Strother, 8, assisted by his brothers Sam, 7, and Freddie, 5, opened a lemonade stand on an orange crate at the entrance to the Colossal Carnival grounds.
>
> They pegged their product at four cents a glass. The standard carnival price is ten cents.
>
> The carnival reestablished its lemonade monopoly by buying out Strother & Bros. for three free tickets to the rides.

Stand among the baby carriages in front of a supermarket or eavesdrop on a smoking compartment forum and, even if you are not a father or mother, you will learn something about parental pride. And you certainly will compare this baby with your own if you have one:

> Six weeks ago a baby girl was born to Mr. and Mrs. Paul Porter of 604 Hemlock St. She hasn't a name yet—but she already is walking.
>
> Mrs. Porter's physician, Dr. Lewis Holloway, didn't believe it at first. But yesterday he cautioned the mother not to let the energetic baby walk too much.
>
> "I was giving her a bath a few days ago," related Mrs. Porter. "I turned her over to wash her back. She raised herself and took several steps."
>
> Dr. Holloway told a reporter he had seen the baby lift her knees and take four or five steps with one hand on her mother's arm.
>
> Porter, the father, a floorwalker, seemed not a bit surprised. He observed, "I guess she gets it from me," adding, "Next month I'll bet she'll be talking."

This harmless but amusing anecdote was worth space in the paper even though the police withheld identifications. The parents probably enjoyed it as much as all others who read it:

> Police at the Midtown Station yesterday quizzed a chap who knew all the answers but it didn't help them one bit. He was just 3 years old and had been picked up on Main street lost in the Christmas shopping crowds.
>
> "What's your father's name?" they asked him.
>
> The kid replied brightly: "Daddy."
>
> "What does your mother call your daddy?"
>
> "She calls him Honey."
>
> "Well, what's your name?"

The youngster knew the answer every time. "My name," he chirped cheerfully, "is Sonnyboy."

The cops gave it up and bought the boy an ice cream cone. A few minutes later Mother showed up and took Sonnyboy home to Honey.

ANECDOTES ABOUT ANIMALS

You don't need to go to the zoo to see the instinctive human interest in animal life. You'll find it fast enough near your own home. Next door lives Smith, whose dog totes meat from the market in his mouth. Across the street lives Brown, whose goldfish—he says—come up to be fed when he whistles. Around the corner lives Mrs. Jones, whose cat has been taught to chase sticks.

Maybe the animal story is worth just a paragraph or so and perhaps a telegraph toll. Consider these:

> A droopy, sad-eyed, floppy-eared basset hound owned by Jenny Winkler, 7, of 363 Pine St., was named yesterday as "The Most Tired and Run-Down" dog of the year. He won out over 20 other entries in a contest sponsored by the Kiwanis Club. The winner's name? Bouncer.

> How many cats are enough? After a week of speeches, the Clay City Council has come up with the answer:
> Three cats are enough—according to an ordinance passed today. To have more you'll have to get a permit.
> Now, about kittens: If you have three cats, you can keep as many kittens as arrive—until they're six months old. Then they become cats—illegal cats.

Birds, like animals, are candidates for publicity, especially if they do something just a bit extraordinary. For example:

> Once peace and quiet reigned in the 700 block on Fillmore avenue. Last evening everything was changed—all because two blue jays are nesting in front of No. 716.
> For a few days the jays behaved like decent law-abiding citizens. They scolded the squirrels and jabbered at the cats but otherwise minded their manners.
> Then two baby blue jays arrived in the nest. The fledglings tried their wings last evening. Virtually everybody in the block was out watching.
> One little jay—a strong one—fluttered up to higher branches. The second, a weakling, fell on the lawn. Mary Denhart, 10, picked him up and stroked his feathers.
> Swi-s-s-sh! A gray-blue-black streak flashed down. An adult bird banged at Mary's head. She screamed and handed the baby bird to William Ward, 14. He made the mistake of accepting it. Swi-s-s-sh! The other parent bird dive-bombed downward. Result—a gash on William's forehead. He dropped the fledgling and ran for home.

While William and Mary were being patched with band-aids, a brave grownup, Stephen Sparks, finally picked up the baby bird to restore it to a limb. Swi-s-s-sh! Sparks, with a clawed arm, went to the drugstore for iodine.

About that time a police patrol car pulled up to find the onlookers clustered in doorways. They pointed to the little jay on the lawn, but as Sgt. R. M. Thomas started for it they yelled, "Look out!" Thomas peered upward, then retreated to his telephone.

Thirty minutes later an agent of the ASPCA arrived. He put a cardboard carton over his head and carried the baby bird to the tree while the two parent jays struck screeching at the box. After a rest the baby fluttered up toward the nest and once more peace and quiet reigned on Fillmore avenue.

From time to time an animal story laden with conflict or suspense springs out of nowhere into a serial sensation. A zoo lion on the loose, a dog marooned by a flood, wild geese frozen on an ice floe are examples of human interest plus suspense—another attention-pulling combination.

Mix an animal story with other human interest elements—children, for example—and your story steps up in news value. Mix it with such powerful elements as prominence and conflict and you may produce a masterpiece.

HUMOR AND PATHOS

Among the most welcome stories reaching the city desk—and the most difficult to find and write—are those with the human touch of comedy or tragedy.

Humor is the rarest commodity on the news market, for it seldom can be printed without the risk of ridicule. However, if part of a public record or written with good will, a funny occurrence can be relished by both the readers and the participants. An example:

Five-year-old Dennis Moran watched with wide eyes last night as a stealthy hand reached for his sister's throat while she lay asleep.

Appearing in a class play at Center High School auditorium, the sister, Daisy, 16, supposedly was drugged.

The hand came closer. Dennis squirmed. The hand descended. Dennis couldn't stand it any longer. He ran up the stage stairs. He was over the footlights in a flash.

"Hey, sis, wake up!" he shouted. Then he shook Daisy by the shoulder.

Dennis brought down the house—and the curtain, too—but he didn't see the rest of the play. Daisy borrowed a dime for candy and persuaded him to go home with his mother.

Little less difficult to handle is tragedy, told with restraint and understanding. Stories like the following erase the lines between poverty and wealth, between metropolis and hamlet, and penetrate deeply into the sympathies of readers:

> Little Harry Sutter telephoned Santa Claus today. He wanted a lot of things but he will never receive them, for he is dead.
>
> Harry was 3½—almost 4, his mother used to say. When Mrs. Wilbur Sutter went marketing this morning she left him alone in the house at 432 Adams Ave.
>
> It was Harry's big opportunity. He wanted to phone Santa about a red sled he hoped to get. The kitchen phone was purposely placed high on the wall so he could not reach it. Such a silly idea, with him the best climber in the house.
>
> So Harry dragged over a chair, piled several books on it and pushed it up to the telephone. Then he climbed up and took down the receiver. The cord looped itself under his chin, but Harry was too busy to notice.
>
> Then his foot slipped—and the busy line to Kriss Kringle became a hangman's trap. The chair shot out from under him. The tangled noose tightened around his neck.
>
> When Mrs. Sutter came home she found Harry, his chubby face blue, hanging limp from the phone. Fifteen minutes later an ambulance surgeon examined the motionless form and shook his head.
>
> Harry had asked for Santa Claus and death had taken the call.

Reader pity responds to stories of loneliness, helplessness and the anxieties of unfortunate folk but their effectiveness depends upon the skill of the reporter.

SENTIMENT V. SENTIMENTALITY

The greatest shortcoming of the beginner in his handling of human interest copy is a propensity to exaggerate—to spread sticky sentiment too thickly upon the bread. Eager for dramatic effect, he rifles his vocabulary of ornate, high-pitched words and phrases, feeling that once outside the restriction of sober facts and figures he may indulge in vivid writing and give his fancy free rein.

It should be remembered that humor, when forced, becomes buffoonery, pathos a burlesque, and melodrama a farce.

Fashion the human interest story in simple, sincere, unaffected style, using even more restraint than in the straight news story. If a child cried, do not say "The tot sobbed as though her little heart would break." Do not write "The little fellow embraced the forlorn animal with touching affection" or "The poor old fellow begged piteously for assistance" when you mean the boy hugged his pup or the old man asked for help.

Contrast the literary gait and methods employed by three different reporters in the following stories. Which version is the best?

Version I

John Sabo, who became 21 yesterday, gave a birthday dinner last night to celebrate his majority. He had seven guests and the toast of the evening was this:

"Eat, drink and be merry, for tomorrow we die."

Many other guests at many other parties may have jokingly drunk the same toast, but it was no joke at John's party. For his birthday anniversary was his last. Today at noon John will die in the electric chair, and soon his guests will follow him in death.

Young Sabo is awaiting execution in State Prison for the holdup slaying of William Janson, Midland grocer, in July. As a last request Sabo asked the warden for permission to give the birthday dinner to the other condemned men with the $23.03 he had in the prison treasury. His request was granted.

Around the bare pine table in the death row exercise room they gathered. There were tin dishes with rounded edges, and knives and forks of stiff cardboard. Armed guards stood a few yards away and looked on. For a full half hour the seven guests and their host dined, drank and smoked. Then they smilingly shook hands and returned to their cells.

"Never had a better time in my life," Sabo told one of the guards. He sent the warden a note thanking him for his kindness.

Version II

Considerable comment was evoked here last night by an unusual affair at State Prison, participated in by several condemned prisoners. It was learned that the prisoners were allowed to eat together in the exercise room adjacent to their cells.

One of the group, John Sabo, who is scheduled to pay the death penalty for a capital crime today, requested and received permission from the warden to spend what little money he had for what might have been called a farewell party. Sabo was 21 years old yesterday, so the occasion was somewhat unique.

Because of the strict regulations, the men were closely watched so that there would be no opportunity for them to start trouble. They were permitted, however, to have smoking tobacco and were given 30 minutes in which to eat.

Despite the peculiar circumstances under which the banquet was put on, the guards said the men ate heartily as though they enjoyed it.

The Sabo execution will take place at noon today. It will be the fifth in the prison this year.

Version III

Staring the grim reaper in the face, standing as it were on the very brink of eternity, eight men with nerves of steel staged in State Prison last night one of the most amazing dramas in the history of American penal institutions.

Iron bars surrounded them and guards with deadly weapons stood nearby to cheat the electric chair of its victims should one of them make a false move. But did they falter? Not these men. They laughed and joked and made sport of the fate in store for them.

The grim comedy was a party put on by John Sabo to celebrate his 21st birthday anniversary. Sabo, who is hardly more than a boy, will pay society's price at high noon today for the taking of a human life. Other young men at 21 are just looking forward to life with all the exuberance and courage of youth. For him—disgrace, death and a prison grave.

All that was forgotten last night as John and his seven guests celebrated. It was their last fling and they made the most of it. For 30 precious minutes they made merry; and then, one by one, they parted, never to meet again. Back to their cells they went; the locks clicked; and out went the lights. Thus, without a tear and without a sigh, ended John Sabo's birthday party.

Comment upon the three stories is scarcely necessary. The first is vivid and convincing; the second dull and lifeless; the third spoiled by sentimentalizing. Of the three, the last is the worst.

FAKING AND "FEATURIZING"

Every alert reporter is a practical psychologist. He delves into the rich veins of human behavior, chooses, imprisons in words and passes on to his readers the situations and incidents that agitate the emotions of men and women everywhere.

In producing human interest copy a reporter often is tempted to draw heavily upon an active imagination to supply details that have little basis in fact, but which he considers desirable to add punch to his story.

Fictionized dialogue—harmless interludes—often appear in papers, but the faking of important news is not countenanced anywhere. An old copyreader once remarked that the best source of human interest copy is "the old hokum bucket," which was his way of saying that the highly artificial, melodramatic formula of rags and riches, love and duty, city wickedness and country innocence still finds expression in newspapers engaged in entertaining their readers with stock situations masqueraded as realities.

Human interest has a legitimate contribution to make to journalism. When it becomes adulterated and mislabeled, its worthlessness is apparent, and the paper suffers a loss of reputation as a reliable medium of news.

A word of advice to the amateur writer should be inserted at this stage of the discussion. No reporter can handle human interest or feature narratives competently until he knows how to produce a compact, coherent straight news story, well fortified with names, quotes, particulars, trustworthy data.

Unfortunately, many a local room novice enters upon his work with an ambition to specialize in feature stuff. He has a conviction that literature is the only calling worthy of his devotion and that novels, plays, poetry are his proper fields rather than newspaper reporting, a writing trade that helps pay expenses until the great moment arrives. He much prefers dabbling with atmospheric stuff, leaving the hard plugging to the more stodgy old-timers who prefer facts to frills.

Such beginners are likely to become pests to city editors. Although quick to recognize literary talent, experienced newsmen know that feature technique is acquired only after long and diligent practice on the simpler patterns of routine news. Let the apprentice, therefore, avoid the temptation to "featurize" every assignment. Instead let him begin by cautiously weaving threads of human interest into straight news accounts, then watching to see what happens to his copy after it reaches the editor's desk.

SHOP TALK

1. Distinguish between straight and human interest news. What are the characteristics of each?
2. As an editor with two stories, one about the lost shoe and the other about a tax bill passed by Congress, which would you choose for favored position?
3. Tabulate a half dozen typical topics of human interest stories, citing examples of each.
4. Outline several three-point human interest news situations in addition to those listed in this chapter.
5. Is a reporter, writing human interest copy, ever justified in faking? If so, with what kind of material and to what extent?

CHAPTER **19**

Suspended Interest Stories

AN ADVENTURE WITH AN INDIAN

Idly scanning the police blotter Fred Maxwell of the *Times* took a second puzzled look at this notation:

> Geoghan, F. C., 32, 317 Laurel St., D.C. Fighting statue. Cor. Main & 14th. 2 a.m. Arr. Off.: Horton.

Maxwell stepped over to a classified phone directory and thoughtfully ran down the yellow page list of cigar and tobacco stores. His finger stopped at the Circle Smoke Shop, 1401 Main St. He dialed the *Times* office and asked for the morgue.

"Les," he said to Lester Wheaton, an assistant librarian, "do you remember a Sunday piece we carried a year or two ago about wooden Indians?"

"Hold a minute, I'll look it up," replied Wheaton. A few moments later: "Yeah, I have it. A cigar store, Circle Smoke Shop on Main street, found one in an attic and painted it up. Story says it's the only one in town. There's a picture. Want any more?"

"No, that's it. Give the stuff to Baxter, will you? And switch me over to the desk."

Maxwell found Patrolman Horton and interviewed him, walked over to the Circle Shop and talked to the proprietor. He again called Baxter, who turned him over to Leo Burke, a rewrite man. Burke wrote as follows:

> Accustomed as he is to queer goings on after midnight, Patrolman Joseph Horton lifted a surprised eyebrow at 2 a.m. yesterday as he watched a man in evening clothes walk up to a stranger standing in front of the Circle Smoke Shop, 1401 Main St., and smack him on the jaw.

As Horton told it, the man in the tuxedo, Frank Geoghan, of 317 Laurel St., shouted:

"Listen here, fellow. I suppose you think the White Sox are going to win the pennant. Well, I say they won't!"

The other remained discreetly silent.

"Well, say something. Do you think that bunch of rookies and old men can lick the Yankees?"

No answer. Whack! Geoghan unlimbered a right to the jaw and followed it with a left hook to the midriff, but his opponent could take it. He didn't try to strike back.

"Dumb cluck," muttered Geoghan as the policeman led him away under arrest for disorderly conduct. But still the "dumb cluck" made no reply. He just stood there.

It's an old custom with wooden Indians.

The net product of Maxwell's memory and enterprise, Wheaton's clipping file and Burke's writing skill was a sparkling *suspended interest* story.

A DOWSER DID IT

To illustrate again the suspended interest structure as contrasted to the standard inverted pyramid format let us look at another story as written each way:

INVERTED PYRAMID

A dowsing rod wielded by Henry Hilton, owner of a filling station on Hampton road, caused a water shortage in Ferndale today.

Needing an extra supply of water for car washing, Hilton located it with a peach tree fork, dug a hole and punched through a six-inch main. Service to 70 homes served by the main was shut off while repairs were made.

Hilton agreed to pay for the damage and to get the water he requires from the Ferndale Water Department.

SUSPENDED INTEREST

Henry Hilton, who runs a filling station on Hampton road in Ferndale had—and still has—faith in the water-finding powers of a dowser.

His grandfather, according to Hilton, used a peach tree fork to locate wells, so, needing extra water for car washing, he cut a Y-shaped stick for himself. This morning he tried it out. It worked fine.

"I squeezed just a little and it pointed straight down," said Hilton. "So I got a well digger and we went to work."

They hit a gusher. In rushed the water—clear, pure water—with a big swoosh. And it kept right on coming.

Two hours later 70 homes at the edge of Ferndale got their service back after the repair of a hole the digger had punched through a six-inch water main.

HUMAN AND SUSPENDED INTEREST

The wooden Indian and dowser stories bring us to a full-dress discussion of what may be called the black sheep of the news family—human interest content and suspended interest structure.

In the early stages of this course we glimpsed these strangers several times but confined them rather closely in a closet on the theory that it is better to study the habits of white sheep first since there are more of them.

Human interest or the emotional *content* in news, as contrasted to prominence and consequence, was discussed in the preceding chapter. In this one we take up suspended interest or dramatic *structure* in news writing.

To prevent our nomenclature from becoming too tangled we resort again to the loose term *feature*. A story with human interest content often is built up with suspended interest structure and the combination results in one type of feature story as against the straight news story.

Because of the contradictory nature of this new creature it can easily bewilder the beginner who is trying to learn and follow standard procedures. It shatters the ordinary conception of news as something necessarily important, defies the "spill the works" arrangement, abandons the five W's and jumps fences into the pastures of the comedy gag, the short story, the novel and the drama.

"Get the big stuff, the important facts," the city editor tells a cub. Then, to the beginner's astonishment, his "big" story is shoved aside to make room for a yarn about Petunia, a skunk, and Tillie, a turtle, who won prizes at a pet show.

A reporter's ears ring with orders to "tell the whole story in your lead" and "dig out the buried high light and put it up front." But no sooner has he acquired that skill than along comes an unbranded feature story revealing in the last line that the nitroglycerin turned out to be water. Ho hum! There are no rules after all, the beginner decides, and in this quandary he finds himself lost in the fields with his sheep scattered and nothing to guide him. What to do?

The solution, of course, lies in distinguishing between various types of newspaper stories. To the experienced reporter there is as much difference between straight recitation and feature stuff as between prose and poetry. He recognizes the earmarks of each type and classifies them readily. This ability to separate the black sheep from the white the beginner acquires by experience.

THE DRAMATIC FORMULA

Before you start writing a story you must make up your mind how you are going to arrange it. There is no swapping horses in the middle of the stream. Your decision is based on the content of the raw material you have in hand.

Ask yourself: "Do I have one or more urgent news facts which need to be reported at once?" "Should the reader be able to catch the main point or gist of this story by glancing at the headline or lead?" If so, you have no choice. You are compelled to use one of the inverted pyramid structures—fact, quote or action.

On the other hand, if the story is replete with human interest and appeals primarily to the emotions, especially the sense of humor, you need to question yourself again: "Does the appeal lie in the characters and the sequence of incidents?" "Is there within the material one fact or occurrence which will surprise the reader if withheld to the end?" If the answer to the first question is "Yes," adopt the narrative plan. If it is "Yes" to the second question, follow the dramatic plan.

Several stories in the preceding chapter illustrate the narrative structure, one of them the blue jay tale which, after the opening, recited the events chronologically, thus: Peace reigns—jays behave—babies arrive—Mary picks one up and first parent strikes—William takes it and second parent strikes—Sparks picks it up and parent strikes again—police call agent who restores bird—peace reigns again.

The wooden Indian feature typifies the dramatic arrangement: Patrolman on beat—sees Geoghan smack a man—Geoghan asks man question and other remains silent—Geoghan hits man and calls him "cluck" —policeman takes him away—the "man" was a wooden Indian! This is the dramatic plan.

There is suspense, of course, in either the narrative or the dramatic order. The reader of a narrative wonders as he proceeds, "What is going to happen next?" while the reader of a drama wonders, "How is all this going to come out in the end?"

The designations *narrative* and *dramatic* as applied to news stories suggest parallels with other taletelling forms. A bedtime story may be in either form. Many novels are narratives while most short stories and all mystery or detective stories—the "Whodunits"—are strictly dramatic productions with the payoff in the final chapter or lines. And the stage play, of course, is pure drama with suspense building up to the curtain at the end of each act and the climax in the last.

AN EXAMPLE OF THE
NARRATIVE PLAN

ONCE UPON A TIME . . .

Dr. William C. Ayers sat smoking last evening in front of his vacation cottage near the Lake Luce beach. He noticed the saw grass move alongside the road. "A dog," he mused.

AND THEN . . .

Presently Mrs. Ayers came into the yard and sat down. She said: "I wonder what's moving in that ditch."

Doctor Ayers read his newspaper awhile. His wife was knitting. Then they heard a splash.

NEXT . . .

Mrs. Ayers peered closely and said it looked an awful lot like a baby. Doctor Ayers said oh no he didn't imagine it was a baby. Mrs. Ayers then walked out to the ditch. And sure enough it was a baby, with its head stuck in the mud. She emptied the mud out of the baby's mouth. Meanwhile, Doctor Ayers called the beach house.

SO . . .

The baby turned out to be Barbara Ann Boling, 20 months old, the daughter of Mr. and Mrs. Charles Boling. They had been swimming and left Barbara Ann with her sister, Betty, 4. Betty had tugged her to the ditch to play.

After a 30-minute search, the frantic parents found Betty, but the baby was gone. They alarmed the beach authorities.

. . . HAPPILY EVER AFTER

As for Barbara Ann, once her head was pulled out of the mud and her mouth emptied, she seemed all right. Betty, too, was okay. She didn't cry a bit until her mother made her put back in the ditch a tadpole she had in her pocket.

Leisurely Storytelling

The average newsman does not conceive himself to be an Ibsen or a Shaw but he instinctively applies the dramatic formula to a suspended interest story. In entirety it consists of five points:

1. Introduction and characterization.
2. Rising action.
3. Crisis.
4. Falling action.
5. Denouement.

This formula can be more briefly summarized as (1) opening, (2) suspense, and (3) climax. It can be charted as a short horizontal line, followed by a line rising to a peak and completed with a line dropping sharply from the peak to an end.

LEADING INTO SUSPENSE

With the five-W arrangement temporarily sidetracked, let us consider the lead for a dramatic formula story—the introduction or prologue for the news playlet.

The simplest opening is a variation of "Once upon a time . . . ," "Now gather close, children . . . ," "Pull up a chair . . . ," and "I'm going to tell you how . . ." Examples:

> Shiver my timbers, lads, and splice the main brace, for this is a story of as bold a buccaneer as ever set sail on Lake Luce to seek pirate gold at the age of 6.
> The treasure hunter, Tommy Touhy . . . . .

> This is a story about a cat and a squirrel in Paulson Park—a cat named Carrie and a squirrel—oh, well, he didn't have a name so let's call him Squinky.
> Carrie was just prowlin' around when Squinky . . . . .

Note that the writers of these openers set the stage and introduced the characters quickly so that they could hasten onward without delay. A news storyteller writing for people in a hurry cannot dawdle through two pages of description or a minor dialogue between the maid and the butler or he will lose his audience.

Remember the man who wanted to jump over a hill. He ran a mile to work up momentum, then had to sit down and rest. He gave it up and your readers will too. So if you use a *once upon a time* lead, hint at least that something more exciting is coming. Try teasers like these:

> Has anybody seen a black and yellow puppy about as long as a little boy's arm who wags his tail up and down like "Yes, sir"—not back and forth like "No, ma'am"?

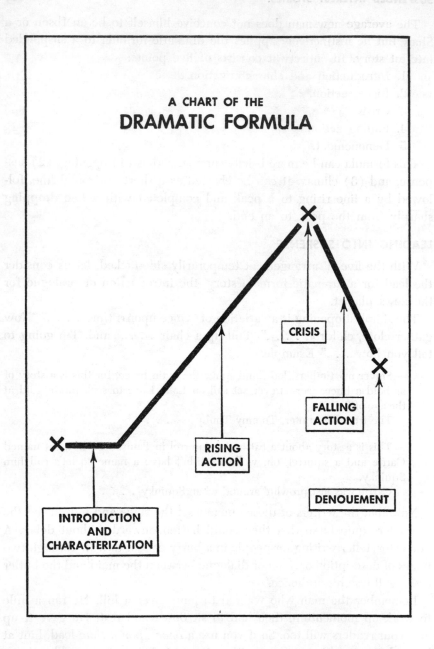

A CHART OF THE
DRAMATIC FORMULA

CRISIS

FALLING
ACTION

RISING
ACTION

DENOUEMENT

INTRODUCTION
AND
CHARACTERIZATION

A Plot Structure

Patrick Mahoney, of Oakton, loves a parade and he just couldn't resist a chance to march in one yesterday. Today he wishes he had stayed at home.

While carefully keeping the cat in the bag, a dramatic writer still should twist into his lead an oddity or enigma to arouse curiosity. He knows, for example, that Mrs. Pratt used peach pickle syrup for a vinegar rinse, but he begins: "Mrs. Peter Pratt's freshly shampooed hair stood straight up." He knows that Mrs. Holt won three bushels of apples in a pie-baking contest, but he begins: "Harry Holt came to the Timber County Fair to sell some of his surplus apple crop." He knows Powell died of a heart attack when he saw his cards, but he begins: "The odds against drawing a straight flush on the first deal in poker are 64,999 to 1."

THE SHORT, SHORT STORY

The most welcome contributions that reach the desk of a makeup man are three-or-four-line items known as *brighteners* or *shorts*. They fill up chinks in a column, dress up a page and offset the weightier articles around them.

Nine out of ten of these gems are bits of humor with surprise last lines. They are, in fact, midget but genuine suspended interest stories. Here are a few:

Raymond Scott, 20, paid a $10 fine in Traffic Court yesterday for driving with an obstructed view. The obstruction—a girl sitting on his lap.

Two teen-age boys were caught here today letting the air out of the tires of a dozen parked cars. Police Sgt. Ben Farrell fitted the punishment to the crime. He made the kids pump up the tires again—by hand.

Today's issue of the school newspaper at Midland High reports that Lucinda Lee won an essay contest in her sophomore English class. Lucinda's subject: "Why I Hate English."

Sam Thurston reported today that there will be no more "Buck Nights" at his drive-in theater west of town. Every Monday each vehicle was admitted for a dollar, regardless of the number of its passengers. Last night a trailer truck pulled in with 17 people aboard. Tab for all—one buck.

"Twenty-one years and some months." So answered a woman in an accident case here today when asked her age. "How many months?" asked Judge Clarence Hays, adding, "Remember, you're under oath." "Well," she replied, "if you must know—117."

There is an incessant demand for short, short stories of this variety and an alert reporter never misses a chance to turn one in. They count up on his production ledger.

KEEPING THE READER DANGLING

Scheherazade, the storyteller in the "The Arabian Nights' Entertainments," saved her life because she kept the Sultan guessing. He had to know what was coming next. In the same way, a news writer follows up his come-on opener in a longer suspended interest story as he moves into the narrative.

Note here how this writer baited his hook with a human interest situation which catches the interest of any woman with a perambulator or any man with a workshop, then bit by bit let out his line:

> Joseph Martin's wife got tired of pushing the baby carriage of her 2-month-old daughter, Ellen. So Joseph put a lawn mower motor in it.
>
> That was a week ago. Mrs. Martin, who lives at 516 Tremont St., tried it out. It put-putted along just fine at three miles an hour. She showed other mothers how easy it was to carry 10 pounds of potatoes and the baby, too.
>
> Her friends told their husbands, who asked Martin how to install motors for their own wives. Martin was filled with pride.
>
> This morning Mrs. Martin took Ellen into the Supermarket at 201 14th St. and left the motor running.
>
> All by itself, the empty carriage started going places. It upset fruit baskets. It banged against other carriages. It backed up, jumped the curb and chugged into a parked car owned by Len Liggett, a salesman. Liggett reported his dented fender to police.
>
> This afternoon Martin paid for the fender. Then, said the sergeant at Central Station, he needed license plates for a self-propelled vehicle, and lights and brakes. Oh, yes, and Mrs. Martin would have to pass a test and get a driver's license.
>
> Tomorrow, said Martin, his wife will be pushing the carriage again. The motor is back in the lawn mower.

The reader begins to suspect the truth halfway through this story but isn't quite sure until the end is reached:

> It was an odd operation—the one performed yesterday afternoon in the emergency ward at Haven Hospital. A surgeon, Dr. Lawrence Hill, bent over a boy patient with a nurse and a janitor as his assistants.
>
> "Hacksaw," demanded Dr. Hill. Then, in order: "Pliers—metal shears—can opener."
>
> The patient mumbled in a muffled voice.
>
> At last it was over and 8-year-old Kenneth Stetson, son of Mr. and Mrs. S. M. Stetson, of 290 Taft Ave., arose without a scratch on him. He had been brought to the hospital by his parents.
>
> Kenneth, said his mother, was playing soldier. For a tin hat he borrowed her aluminum kettle. It slipped down over his ears and nobody could get it off.

A DIAGRAM OF THE
DRAMATIC PLAN

LEAD

It looked like a tough job for the boys at the West Side fire station when they rushed to the home of W. A. Hestberg, 172 Pine St. yesterday. But they did their duty in fine style.

NARRATIVE

"Come quickly, the attic's on fire," Mrs. Hestberg's maid telephoned in a frantic voice. A pinochle game in the shady station yard ended abruptly.

"Let 'em roll," roared Capt. James (Smoky Jim) Flanagan, veteran of a hundred thrilling battles with the red demon. He jerked on his helmet.

Bells clanging, the three trucks thundered out on their race against time. In seven minutes flat three hose lines uncoiled along the pavement at the Hestberg home.

"This way," the maid beckoned Captain Flanagan and a half dozen aids, fire extinguishers and axes in hand. She pointed upstairs with a trembling finger

Rushing to the third floor they saw through a crack in the ceiling what appeared to be flames in the attic The captain bellowed orders. Two stalwart firemen leaped forward.

"Open it up, boys," shouted Flanagan. A pair of axes swung lustily, splintering the ceiling like matchwood. Lath and plaster clattered to the floor. Fireman Thomas Moser climbed through the hole.

SURPRISE CLIMAX

"Well, I'm a son of a sea cook," he muttered. He found only a blazing patch of sunlight.

Surprise at the End

"Now," said Mrs. Stetson after the operation, "I'll have to buy a new kettle."

CUMULATION CREATES SUSPENSE

As a magician pulls one rabbit after another from his top hat suspense accumulates. After three or four bunnies come out, the live duck is a real surprise. A similar pull is exercised by using the 1–2–3 arrangement like this:

> What do you think are the nicest—the very nicest—words in the English language? A television station here has just awarded prizes in a contest to find out.
> The runners-up:
> "I love you."
> "All is forgiven."
> "Drinks on the house."
> "Dinner is served."
> "Sleep until noon."
> The winning words:
> "Here's that five bucks I owe you."

An analysis of the following story will reveal the structural characteristics of both narrative and dramatic stories, with the 1–2–3 arrangement used to good effect:

> Maybe he was fed up with going by a sissy girl's name. Anyway, Mrs. Edward Everett's parrot made it plain that he was plenty mad about something.
> Two days ago he escaped from his cage on the Everett porch at 617 Grove Ave. and took to the trees. Wing-loose and feather-free, he flew from branch to branch in the back yard in disdain of would-be catchers.
> Aided by Fire Chief Ralph Chambers, Mrs. Everett tried a lot of things Monday and Tuesday, among them:
> 1. They squirted water from a fire hose. That sent Polly scooting to another treetop.
> 2. They rigged a perch on the end of a fishing pole, baited with food. Polly spurned it.
> 3. They set up a 75-foot aerial ladder. Polly kept one tail feather ahead of it.
> 4. They placed a caged parrot outdoors as a decoy. Polly screamed "Hello" from a treetop.
>
> Finally it got to the point where Mrs. Everett offered a $5 reward for an idea that would land her feathered pet back in his cage.
> Yesterday came Samuel Carson, owner of the pet shop where Polly was bought. He smiled with the wisdom acquired in a chat with Polly's previous owner. Standing under the tree he clucked gently several times, "Butch want a cracker?" Butch promptly settled on his shoulder and Carson plopped him into the cage.

THE PUNCH LINE AT END

A dramatic news writer incurs the same obligation as the playwright to wind up with a wallop. That means he must know, and mentally write, his last lines first, and build up to them. If he creates the anticipation of a bombshell at the end he must explode it.

Nursing along the gag or tag line—arousing anticipation without giving satisfaction—is the most difficult part of dramatization. Keep the secret under cover until at last you reveal that:

. . . By the way, the gun really wasn't loaded.
. . . On the back seat lay the baby, peacefully snoozing.
. . . Yes, the black powder was dirt—just plain black dirt.

Glance back now at some of the last lines used in our samples:

. . . It's an old custom with wooden Indians.
. . . had punched through a six-inch water main.
. . . girl sitting on his lap.
. . . "I Hate English."
. . . pump up the tires again—by hand.
. . . tab for all—one buck.
. . . if you must know—117."

The denouement of the Linotype drama comes quickly after the climax and falls with the finality of an auctioneer's hammer. After the whip is cracked there may be a slight echo, but then it's time to cut the story off.

It is permissible to tack on "The motor is back in the lawn mower" or "I'll have to buy a new kettle" but nothing more. There is no epilogue.

The copyreader must be an accomplice when the writer tries a dramatic story with a surprise climax. Stupidity spoils suspense if the writer begins his story, "Accustomed as he is to queer goings-on . . ." and the headline reads, "Wooden Indian Lands Baseball Fan in Jail." A good headline writer never spills the secret. He joins in the conspiracy to conceal the climax. It is a cooperative enterprise.

SHOP TALK

1. Distinguish between human interest and suspended interest. Define and discuss each.
2. How does the suspended interest story upset the structural arrangement of straight news stories? Diagram it.
3. How do narrative and dramatic structures differ?
4. Specify and discuss the essentials for a suspended interest lead.
5. Sketch the dramatic formula on the blackboard. Apply it to the structure of suspended interest stories in this chapter.

CHAPTER 20

Give It to a Rewrite Man

THE REWRITE BATTERY IN ACTION

Idly shuffling through an afternoon newspaper Jefferson Harris, rewrite man for the Midland *Times,* slouched low in his chair, obviously killing time. He looked up once to observe to Leo Burke, his partner at a nearby desk, that things were pretty quiet. Burke nodded and continued to stir a container of coffee with casual unconcern.

A telephone jangled stridently. Harry Baxter on the city desk answered. The phone conversation ended with the assistant city editor saying: "Okay, give it to Harris."

"Hey, Jeff," Baxter called to Harris, "here's Dave Jordan out at the airport with a piece about a plane upsetting. He's got another job to do before coming in. Take it for about 200 words."

As Harris pulled down his eyeshade and adjusted his telephone headset, Baxter switched the call to him, then turned his attention to several clippings from the afternoon *Herald* and *Gazette.* He summoned Burke and handed him two of them together with several publicity releases.

"Do about half a column on the barbershop strike and a couple of sticks on the flower show," he ordered. "Slug 'em BARBER and BLOOM. There are two or three shorts in these handouts." Burke nodded, picked up the clips and mimeos and returned to his desk.

Within a few minutes Harris and Burke, bent over their typewriters, were steadily pounding out stories for the Early edition of the *Times.* Now and then one of them pulled a sheet from his machine, called out "Copy boy!" spiked his raw material with a dupe for the alibi file and pulled over data for the next story.

The rewrite battery had gone into action.

DUTIES OF THE REWRITE MAN

Rewrite men, like copyreaders, often feel that they are the unsung heroes of the city room. In some offices rewriters get bylines or share them with reporters, but most of their work is behind the scenes and anonymous.

While his credit may be scant and he may win no awards, the rewrite man is a highly skilled artisan, paid as well or better than the average reporter. He is almost always a graduate reporter with several years of street or beat experience. He knows the city and the news sources in it. He can judge news values, sense human interest and organize facts. Above all, he is chosen because of extraordinary ability to make words do his will.

He writes about many events he never sees except as he visualizes them in his mind's eye. But, as the daily dramas of life—tragedy and comedy—pour into his ears or pass on paper before his eyes and are shaped swiftly by his fingers into cogent and colorful copy, he knows that he is a creator. And he enjoys the same feeling of satisfaction as the writing reporter when his product comes up from the pressroom with the ink still wet and the paper warm.

As we have pointed out previously, a leg man covers news but does not write it, a staff reporter does both, and a rewrite man devotes his time exclusively to writing and rewriting.

A half dozen or more "rewrites" function on the metropolitan dailies and the big bureaus of the wire services, whereas on smaller papers reporters frequently rewrite as well as report. Even in the cities, reporters pinch-hit for rewrite men when the day's run of news is heavy and their own stories are safely out of the way. And a reporter may act as a rewrite man if he is being assisted by another reporter or leg man by telephone. Thus the jobs of writing reporter and rewrite man are more or less interchangeable.

The major duties of rewrite men are:

1. To take news by telephone from leg men, and from other reporters when time and distance prevent them from writing their own stories.

2. To rewrite stories from other papers.

3. To improve copy written by reporters and to add new developments to stories in editions already printed.

4. To localize wire service copy and news from papers outside the city.

5. To interview office callers and, at times, conduct and write telephone interviews.

6. To transform into news copy publicity releases, letters and other written or printed documents as selected by the city desk.

First aid to the city editor, the rewrite man performs the nimble function of a Jack-of-all-stories, often turning out some of the day's featured articles and also serving as a literary handy man. On a busy day he may

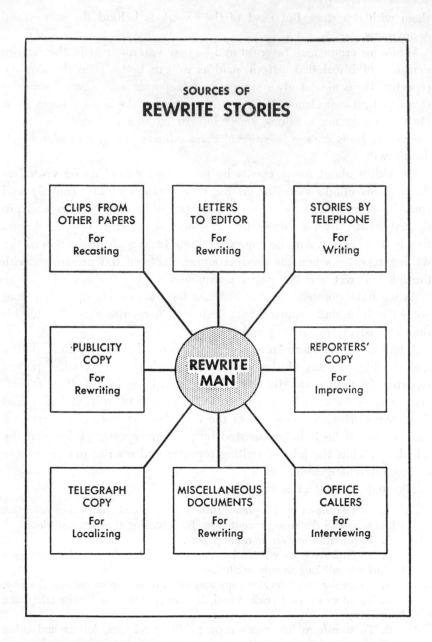

SOURCES OF
REWRITE STORIES

| CLIPS FROM OTHER PAPERS | LETTERS TO EDITOR | STORIES BY TELEPHONE |
| For Recasting | For Rewriting | For Writing |

| PUBLICITY COPY | **REWRITE MAN** | REPORTERS' COPY |
| For Rewriting | | For Improving |

| TELEGRAPH COPY | MISCELLANEOUS DOCUMENTS | OFFICE CALLERS |
| For Localizing | For Rewriting | For Interviewing |

Rewrite Man—Jack-of-All-Stories

write continuously for four or five hours with hardly a pause except to listen to a reporter or to change the paper in his typewriter. He is a one-man band playing many tunes—off stage.

Like the copyreader, a rewrite man is not always in the good graces of reporters, especially when he is called upon to revise the copy they have written. But despite this traditional friction, the relationship is usually good-humored and friction vanishes when teamwork is urgent—a peculiarity of the American press.

After a newspaper tour in this country, a foreign editor expressed amazement at the coordination he observed. "Instead of vying with each other as we do," he said, "your reporters assist each other, rewrite men collaborate with leg men, copyreaders retouch stories they know other names will byline and newsmen supply the city editor with tips other writers will follow."

THE TECHNIQUE OF TELEPHONING

We have seen how technological advances touch the work of newsmen in several ways. The Teletypewriter is standardizing style sheets. Tape recorders are used in some interviews. Radio and television apparatus have invaded the press conference.

However, none of these has affected the reporter as much as have two inventions nowadays taken for granted—the typewriter and the telephone. All reporters except leg men must use typewriters and all—no exceptions—telephones. Just as valuable as speed and accuracy in typing is skill in giving and taking information by phone. Some journalism schools have recognized this by giving special training in telephoning technique.

Alexander Graham Bell's ring-and-talk device has developed into a worldwide web of wire and wireless communication. It gives a newsman immediate entry into homes and offices, eliminating time-consuming travel, and connects him with isolated points where news events are going on or have just been completed. The long legs of the telephone bring in perhaps half of a newspaper's editorial content.

The first lesson learned by a cub talking to an outsider is the finality of hanging up—the need to have ready in his mind, if not in writing, a complete set of questions covering the essentials of the story he is seeking.

A rewrite man knows full well the frustration that can follow the ending of a conversation with a street number, an age, or a *Miss* or *Mrs.* missing. He pins down each precise point on the first call.

Talking by phone to a non-newsman can be tricky, especially if he is hostile, adamant or hard to understand. Usually the best approach is the same as in a face-to-face interview. Say plainly who you are and what you want, then courteously and patiently ply your questions until they are all answered.

No such prompting should be necessary when a newsman himself is on the outside end of the line. Out on an assignment, the leg man should be well prepared to deliver the facts into a mouthpiece *before* he starts talking. His notes should be arranged so they can be transmitted without fumbling, repetition or delay.

Occasionally an outside man may be handed a lengthy document or release of urgent news importance and be compelled to digest and dictate from it simultaneously. This is a brain-twisting operation. However, there usually is time at least to glance through the material before telephoning.

Old-time reporters usually deliver their facts in the order the story will be written—lead material first and other points in order of descending interest. This practice prevents the omission of vital points and facilitates the casting of the rewrite man. Some experienced reporters can dictate creditable copy word for word and some rewrite men can take it in shorthand, but neither procedure is common. Customarily the conversation is an oral transfer of the reporter's notes into the typewritten notes of the rewrite man.

Time can be saved if you skip the words *hello* and *yes* and answer a call by giving your name, thus: "This is John Jones" or "John Jones speaking." The British version is "John Jones here."

The Bell System advises its operators to speak at a lip distance of about one-half inch from the telephone mouthpiece and at an approximate rate of 126 words a minute.

AN EXCHANGE OF ADVICE

One day on a bulletin board in the *Times* office an irate rewrite man posted a "Memo to Reporters." Underneath there appeared an answering "Memo to Rewrites" compiled by a reporter. Others joined in and from day to day more seriocomic "diplomatic notes" were added. We present them here for they contain clues to improvement of telephoning technique:

Rewrites to Reporters

When the desk tells you to give enough for a hundred words, don't give enough for a thousand. Condense!

Never say "just a minute" and then take five. Have your notes ready. Our time is valuable.

Don't hem and haw and repeat the same fact three or four times.

You don't whisper to others; why whisper to us? And don't shriek; excitement ruins our peace of mind. Talk in normal tones.

Remember that rewrites are not shorthand experts and cannot take such names as Proskoskoskiewitz as fast as you reel them off.

When you give the name of a street or avenue, don't make the rewrite ask you whether it is a street or avenue.

When giving a follow-up story, don't say: "Remember what we had in the paper two days ago?" Review the facts.

Call once on a story. Don't come back on the phone every few minutes with things you forgot the first time.

If the desk said to turn in one or two stories, don't try to add six or seven others that just popped into your mind.

Don't eat your lunch in the telephone booth. Words chewed between bites on a sandwich have little meaning for us.

Reporters to Rewrites

Don't make the reporter feel that you are excessively bored by the stuff he is giving you.

Keep an extra sheet of paper handy. Don't ask the reporter to wait while you get one.

Don't hurry a reporter. He may be in a drugstore booth balancing his notes on his nose, mopping his face and looking for another dime.

Don't catch up the reporter with a snappy, "Well, where does he live?" or greet him with, "Yes, I know, what about it?" before he has a chance to tell you.

Refrain from wisecracking if the reporter presents you with a bright word or phrase. The boss will think it's your own brain child.

Don't try to tell a reporter your pet theory of the crime. He's on the scene and knows more about it than you do.

Look up the clippings in the morgue for last week's developments. The reporter is no encyclopedia.

Adopt the reporter's suggestions for a lead once in a while. You should be glad to get them.

Stick to the facts the reporter gives you. Don't twist them to suit yourself.

Light your cigarette before you start talking, instead of stopping the dialogue to borrow a match.

A STORY IS TELEPHONED

Let us now listen in as Jordan, a trained reporter, talks to Harris, an experienced rewrite man. This conversation ensues:

HARRIS: Hi, Dave. Jeff Harris speaking.
JORDAN: Hi, Jeff. All set?

HARRIS: Go ahead.

JORDAN: Okay. Plane turned over out here at the Municipal Airport—private
plane—making a landing. The pilot was hurt. His name is Robert, middle
initial H for Henry, Sobol. S for Sam, O for Oscar, B for Ben, O for Oscar,
L for Lucy. Forty-two years old. Married. No kids. He lives at 1742 17th St.
Architect. Office at 317 Center St. in the White Bldg.

HARRIS: What building?

JORDAN: White, like the color—red, white and blue.

HARRIS: Yeah, go ahead.

JORDAN: Sobol flies his own plane, twin-engine Samson, wasp engines. He
was flying back from a business trip to Metropolis. It was foggy out here.
Visibility poor. He came in at 1:15 and overshot the east-west runway.
Skidded into a fence and turned turtle. Sobol stumbled to the hangar. The
airport manager, G for George, A for Adam, Stewart, spelled like Jimmy
Stewart, called an ambulance. Sobol had two broken ribs, cuts and bruises.
He went to Mercy Hospital.

HARRIS: What did he say about it?

JORDAN: He told Stewart, quote, the fog started closing in on me over Mercerville. I didn't have enough gas to get back to Metropolis, so I had to try it.
The runway was slippery and I went over, unquote. Incidentally, all flights
out here are canceled until the fog lifts.

HARRIS: What happened to the plane?

JORDAN: One wing ripped open but mechanics were able to taxi it into the
hangar. By the way, tell Baxter I'll be in by 6 and I'll check to see when
flights start again. Fog's lifting now.

HARRIS: All right, is that all of it?

JORDAN: That's all.

HARRIS: So long.

JORDAN: Goodby.

You will note that Jordan specified with exactness times, names and
addresses, made his quotation marks audible and used a spell-out alphabet familiar to Harris.

The use of unmistakable-sounding words for positive identification
of letters has long been recognized in the newspaper business, by telegraph companies and in military operations. Many names, such as Louis
and Lewis, sound alike and must be spelled and many letters, such as
B, C, D, E, G, P, T and Z, may be mistaken for one another without a
method of separately identifying each one. A listener can identify the
words more accurately if he knows the list from which they are chosen.

In an accompanying chart you will find the complete alphabets as used
by the International Civil Aviation Organization, by Western Union
and by the Midland *Times.*

During World War I the military alphabet was: Able, Boy, Cast,
Duck, Easy, Fox, George, Have, Item, Jig, King, Love, Mike, Nan, Opal,

THREE WIDELY USED
TELEPHONE ALPHABETS

INTER-NATIONAL	WESTERN UNION	MIDLAND TIMES
Alfa	Adam	Adam
Bravo	Boston	Ben
Coca	Chicago	Charles
Delta	Denver	Daniel
Echo	Edward	Edward
Foxtrot	Frank	Frank
Golf	George	George
Hotel	Henry	Henry
India	Ida	Isaac
Juliett	John	John
Kilo	King	Kate
Lima	Lincoln	Lucy
Metro	Mary	Mother
Nectar	New York	Nathan
Oscar	Ocean	Oscar
Papa	Peter	Peter
Quebec	Queen	Queen
Romeo	Robert	Robert
Sierra	Sugar	Sam
Tango	Thomas	Thomas
Union	Union	Union
Victor	Victor	Victor
Whiskey	William	William
Extra	X-ray	X-ray
Yankee	Young	Young
Zulu	Zero	Zebra

Words for Telephone Spelling

Pup, Quack, Rash, Sale, Tare, Unit, Vice, Watch, X-ray, Yoke and Zed.

During World War II every GI learned the revised international code alphabet: Able, Baker, Charlie, Dog, Easy, Fox, George, How, Item, Jig, King, Love, Mike, Nan, Oboe, Peter, Queen, Roger, Sugar, Tare, Uncle, Victor, William, X-ray, Yoke and Zebra. Companies were named *Able, Baker,* and so on. The name *Roger,* meaning "I am reading you all right," went into the new-word dictionaries.

In 1956 a new alphabet developed by the ICAO went into effect. This has been generally adopted for military use among the Western nations. The familiar *Roger* is replaced by *Romeo. Juliett* is spelled with a double-t because certain non-English-speaking personnel cannot make it out otherwise. The old *Fox* and *Tare* were baffling to them, so these were changed to the world-known dances *Foxtrot* and *Tango.*

Fifteen of the Western Union and *Times* words are the same: Adam, Edward, Frank, George, Henry, John, Peter, Queen, Robert, Thomas, Union, Victor, William, X -ray, Young.

The *Times* list, drawn largely from common first names, is one of the oldest in the newspaper business. It grew naturally, was spread by journeymen and can be heard in newsrooms from coast to coast. Sometimes nicknames like *Charley, Danny, Eddie, Ike* and *Tommy* are substituted, and *Mother* may become *Mary,* but by and large the alphabet is standard and serviceable. There is no reason to change it.

LEADS FOR LIFTED STORIES

Each newspaper of general circulation is prepared on the theory that many buyers or subscribers read that paper alone and it therefore prints all news developing in a 24-hour period. However, many other readers of AM papers do see PM papers and vice versa. Hence a heavy percentage of news, especially in first editions, is lifted, revised and usually shortened.

In the chapter on taboos we explained that the copyright law bans only the pirating of literary style, that news facts in themselves, once published, are public property. We also pointed out that newspapers appropriate at will the contents of routine stories which are complete in themselves and require no follow-up assignments.

While news thus is lifted when convenient, it always is camouflaged before it again appears in print. Two papers never publish the same local story word for word and even well-written publicity stuff is recast to avert style duplication unless it has been written exclusively for the one paper.

To the rewrite man is assigned the task of dressing up the borrowed stories in new raiment. Unlike a reporter, he cannot dig up a new angle by personal investigation. There is no new angle. His chore is to substitute synthetic newness for real newness, thereby making aging and worn news *seem* new to the reader.

There are several tricks for freshening wilted news. In the clipping before him the rewrite man may find an angle that was overlooked as an alternate lead or played in a minor key in the earlier version—perhaps a motive or cause—which can be made into a theme. Or a happy new phrase or two may pop into his mind. With no new facts he still can dress up a story with an altered arrangement.

Here are some openers used for second-day stories in an afternoon newspaper by a rewrite man who did not have a single new fact beyond the clippings:

> Funeral services were being planned today for Albert McEvoy, retired head of the McEvoy Shoe Co., who died at his home, 618 Spruce St., yesterday. He was 78 years old.

> An investigation was begun today into causes of a fire which cost the lives of an aged couple and drove several families to the street from an 18-apartment building at 8127–37 Garfield Ave. last night.

> Ten youths were in jail on suspicion of murder today after a 16-year-old bystander to a gang brawl was killed by a bullet fired in the melee. All were held without bail.

> After a brilliant military wedding attended by the elite of Crestwood's social and Army circles, Col. and Mrs. Robert Duncan, the former Evelyn Kale, today were en route to Honolulu for their honeymoon.

> A score of students, charged with resisting policemen who broke up an antiwar protest meeting at Midland College last night, were to be arraigned in Municipal Court this morning.

> Patrolman Nicolas Dunn today was receiving congratulations from his buddies for emergency assistance in delivering an eight-pound son to Mrs. Lester Stern, 257 Clark St., yesterday.

> State highway patrolmen searched today for two convicts who attacked guards and escaped yesterday from lifer cells in the State Prison at Capital City.

How could the rewrite man be *sure* that the events he says are to occur today *will* occur today? He knows either because it is so stated in the earlier story or because the occurrence is inevitable. Re-examine the leads just cited.

A funeral *always* is planned after a death. An investigation *always* follows a fatal fire when the cause is undetermined. Suspects held without bail *necessarily* are in jail today. The wedding story clip said the couple would go to Honolulu by ship and therefore they *are* en route today. Also specified was the time of arraignment for the arrested students. Policemen who deliver babies *always* are congratulated. And a search *always* follows a prison escape.

The rewrite man therefore took no chances on being inaccurate as he brought the *today* angle up into his new leads.

A morning paper writer, of course, uses *yesterday* and *last night* freely but he, too, often tries to restore the immediacy element by leading with the upcoming development *today*.

It is possible to belabor *today* to the point of awkwardness like this: "John Jones is dead today because he was shot to death by his wife yesterday." Compare these alternate leads:

AWKWARD

Mayor Nelson today had been criticized for his sales tax plan by Joel Marshton, president of the Commercial Club, who spoke last night at a meeting of the Midland Merchants Assn. in Community Hall.

"The Mayor has been misguided," he declared . . . . .

BETTER

Mayor Nelson's sales tax plan is unsound, in the opinion of Joel Marshton, president of the Commercial Club.

"The Mayor has been misguided," Marshton declared in an address before the Midland Merchants Assn. in Community Hall last night . . . . .

The principal objective of the rewrite man is to subordinate the *last night* or *yesterday*, rather than accentuate the *today*. This can usually be achieved, as in the better example, without using unnatural and stilted phraseology in the lead.

SHIFTING THE EMPHASIS

Assume now that the rewrite man must recast a PM story from another PM paper and that there is no way to advance the time element. Assume further that no fresh facts, real or synthetic, are in sight. Also assume that he is asked to fill as much space as was taken by the original story.

The rewrite man can still secure a semblance of originality by a rearrangement that will shift emphasis to an angle not played up by the first writer:

ORIGINAL STORY

To the relief of his frantic mother who feared he was injured, Freddy Zengel, 4 years old, was returned to his home at 317 Weston St. today after the police found him in Bayview Park.

"He's been gone an hour and I'm afraid he has been hurt," Mrs. Paul Zengel, the mother, telephoned Sgt. Louis Collier at the 7th District Station. "He's never run away before. What shall I do?"

Twenty minutes later Patrolman Patrick Flynn spied the lad, who had abandoned his red tricycle to chase pigeons in the park. Freddy told the officer he was going to visit "my grammy."

With Freddy restored to her arms, Mrs. Zengel explained that the boy is fond of his grandmother, who lives in Philadelphia.

REWRITTEN STORY

Distance didn't matter much to 4-year-old Freddy Zengel when he started out on his red tricycle to visit "grammy" who lives 773 miles away in Philadelphia.

What upset his plans, when he had only 772⅞ miles left to go, were the pigeons in Bayview Park.

Freddy, who lives with his mother, Mrs. Paul Zengel, at 317 Weston St., two blocks from the park, forgot to tell her about it when he departed today. Mrs. Zengel called the police.

Patrolman Patrick Flynn found Freddy merrily pursuing the park pigeons.

"Where were you going, sonny?" he inquired.

"To see my grammy," Freddy informed him gravely, as he headed his tricycle home with the policeman as an escort.

One safe way to rewrite a story in print is to read it over once, then lay it aside and mentally plan a reorganization. While writing, refer to the original only for specific data. Spin out the story on your own loom. The product will be a newly styled fabric woven from the older threads of fact.

LOCALIZING THE OUT-OF-TOWN ARTICLE

To bring the news nearer home to their readers, papers seize every opportunity to localize stories received by wire or clipped from out-of-town publications. Revision of these articles—carrying out an injunction to "play up the local angle"—falls within the province of the rewrite men. The key to localization lies in rearrangement of the facts so that the point of special concern to the home town is lifted into the lead and the story given a new direction by playing up the community note, minimizing the more general features.

Delegated to localize the following item, a rewrite man merely eliminated the dateline, transposed the units and added a few words from a morgue clipping. The same procedure could be used for papers in any of the towns mentioned in the article:

OUT-OF-TOWN

Capital City, June 4.—Meadville High School captured first honors today in the statewide public speaking contest sponsored by the University of Centralia. Howard Baum, 17-year-old Meadville student, outpointed Merton Sanders of Capital City in the oratory finals.

The winning oration, "Preparing for Peace," drew a 2–1 decision over "The New Economic Era" presented by Sanders. Other participants ranked in the following order:

Judith Mathers, Midland, "The Forgotten Man."

Peter Howell, Clay City, "Our Changing Social Trends."

Grace Pinkney, Southfield, "The Problem of Asia."

Philip Lang, Glen Haven, "The Legion of Hope."

Isaac Greenberg, Junction City, "More Worlds to Conquer."

Each of the seven contestants was chosen as school champion in preliminaries last May. A gold cup went to Baum. Silver cups were presented to the second and third prize winners.

LOCALIZED

A new silver cup for third place in the statewide public speaking contest will be placed in the trophy cabinet at Midland High School within the next few days.

The prize was awarded to Judith Mathers, MHS champion and finalist in the competition held at the University of Centralia in Capital City today. Her oration was entitled "The Forgotten Man."

First place went to Howard Baum of Meadville, whose subject was "Preparing for Peace." Merton Sanders of Capital City placed second with "The New Economic Era." Seven schools were entered.

The other contestants and the order in which they finished were: Peter Howell, Clay City; Grace Pinkney, Southfield; Philip Lang, Glen Haven; Isaac Greenberg, Junction City.

Miss Mathers, 18 years old, is a senior at MHS. She is the daughter of Mr. and Mrs. Thomas B. Mathers, 609 Pierce Ave.

ADVANCES V. FOLLOW-UPS

When lifting from another paper a rewrite man usually is instructed to reduce the wordage, especially if the occurrence is outside the area of concentrated circulation. Here we have an example of localization in reverse—a story in a newspaper published in a neighboring town boiled down for the Midland *Times:*

Booneville *Register*

The boys of Booneville will have to revise their mental picture of a sour-faced, brutal, crabby old dogcatcher.

For this city's new shepherd of stray hounds is blonde, attractive Sybil Saunders, 32-year-old widow and mother of two boys herself. Today she succeeded her husband, the late J. M. Saunders, who died July 16.

Upon assuming office, Mrs. Saunders pledged an efficient—but humane —administration.

"It's not necessary to abuse the dogs," she said. Although the law allows ownerless dogs to be put to death after 72 hours, Mrs. Saunders will give them more than three days' grace.

"We will keep them for a month in the hope that the owners will show up," she promised.

Mrs. Saunders, who will receive $400 a year plus $2 for each dog destroyed, is the first woman dog warden in the history of Booneville.

Midland *Times*

The stray dogs of Booneville are going to be doggone lucky.

There's a new dogcatcher there today—Sybil Saunders—and she likes dogs. Hereafter, she said, strays will be held for a month instead of three days.

Mrs. Saunders, the first woman dogcatcher in the history of Booneville, will be paid $400 a year and $2 for each dog destroyed.

The dogcatcher story really ended with the appointment and statement of Mrs. Saunders. The fact that she is on the job today is purely a device to get rid of *yesterday.*

Now we come to a wholly different news situation. A rewrite man for the Midland *Herald,* a PM paper, has before him the final edition of the morning *Times,* containing complete coverage of a special City Council session concluded at 5 p.m. yesterday—too late for the *Herald.*

The *Herald* yesterday could not predict the Council vote on a major local project. It was uncertain until the last moment. But the *Herald can* predict that Mayor Nelson will sign the bill. In an interview printed a week ago the Mayor outlined the plan he would follow if the Council accepted his recommendation. It did. And the *Herald* city desk man does not propose to let today's story go by default to the *Times.*

With the help of the morgue a *Herald* rewrite man turned last week's interview into an advance and stretched it out as instructed:

With a stroke of a gold-pointed pen, Mayor Nelson today was scheduled to sign an ordinance providing for the construction of a 300-yard viaduct to carry McKinley avenue over the tracks of the Shore Line Railroad at 27th street.

The $350,000 improvement, approved by the City Council yesterday, will break a traffic bottleneck on the North Side of the city. Work is expected to start before Jan. 1.

Nelson announced last week that he would cooperate with a group of North Side civic clubs which sponsored the project in a signing ceremony if the ordinance passed.

The gold-pointed pen has been provided by the civic groups and later will be framed as a memento. Invited to the signing were a dozen representatives of the clubs concerned, as well as a delegation of students from Hillview High School.

A ribbon-cutting ceremony, followed by a parade, is expected to mark the opening of the viaduct about May 1.

Despite the opposition of South Side members, the Council adopted the viaduct ordinance by a narrow majority of two votes at the close of a three-hour session lasting until 5 p.m. . . . . .

Little is left for the *Times* to exploit the next morning. The *Herald* rewrite man has been able to report the news effectually not *as* or *after* it happens but *before* it happens.

OTHER REWRITE TASKS

One of the men in the rewrite battery usually gets the job of interviewing telephone and office callers with tips or data to give the paper and of revising selected communications mailed or brought in—typewritten, mimeographed and printed offerings from ad agencies, publicity and public relations representatives of business concerns and organizations.

It is copy boy's work to open and stack up the material variously called releases, handouts, blurbs or puffs. Then a rapid-reading assistant city editor skims through the thousands of words, searching for nuggets of news. Some items go to reporters for assignments or background. Some go into the future file. And still others go into a basket for the rewrite men.

The problems presented by this kind of press copy will be fully discussed in the chapter on business news. For the present it is sufficient to note that free advertising and propaganda are generally weeded out and rejected while news from schools, churches, libraries, museums and civic organizations which promote education, religion and progress is given space generously. Broadly speaking, the decision to use or discard is based on news value to the public as against value as publicity for the sponsor.

Telephone and office callers are interviewed by a rewrite man in the same way as interviews are conducted by a reporter and are so written.

From the point of view of content and structure, any article prepared from a written communication corresponds closely to the speech story. The rewrite man handles it precisely as a reporter handles the notes or copy of an address. He selects a lead first, then striking quotations to sustain it. Near the top of the story he traces the setting, that is, the circumstances prompting the making of the statement or announcement. Then he continues along the main track, reducing long general passages to compact paragraphs, linking in the best quotations to fill the allotted space.

Both interview and speech story techniques have been outlined in previous chapters.

SHOP TALK

1. Explain how the duties of a reporter, a rewrite man and a leg man differ. How does each fit into the newsroom organization?
2. What is the best arrangement of notes for telephoning information to a rewrite man?
3. How may an article already published by an earlier newspaper be recast to make it appear timely?
4. Do you think too much effort is expended to advance the time element in aging news?
5. Why do editors strive to localize out-of-town stories? Does localization improve the news value of a story?

CHAPTER 21

News from Out of Town

BLAIR GETS A BREAK

One evening a Midland *Times* office boy ushered to the desk of City Editor Mark Mason a young man who carried in his pocket a job résumé and under his arm a scrapbook filled with clippings neatly pasted in double columns on a dozen or more pages. The caller introduced himself as Clinton Blair, editor of the weekly Meadville *Citizen* and correspondent for the *Times*.

"The state editor, Mr. Walsh, referred me to you," said Blair.

"So you're Blair," Mason greeted him. "Yes, the state desk tells me you did some nice work for us last week on the tornado over there. What can I do for you?"

Blair grinned an acknowledgment of the compliment but was not taken by surprise. He already knew it was "nice work." In fact that was the reason for his visit. The storm was the break he knew would come sooner or later. He had telephoned the first report to the *Times,* wired in a complete story with the casualty list, rushed in pictures by bus and cleaned up the story so swiftly and thoroughly that Mason did not send a staff reporter to Meadville. The *Times* left the follow-ups to Blair, paid him well and added a bonus.

This interview was what Blair had worked and waited for. Coming directly to the point, he said:

"I want a job on the city staff of the *Times*. I've been your Meadville correspondent now for a year and I can make good. I'd like you to look over this résumé and some of the stuff I've written for you and other papers."

Mason took the résumé and glanced over it. He then reached for the scrapbook and turned the pages meditatively. He scrutinized several samples carefully and handed the book back with a promise to have a talk with Walsh and let him know. The following Monday Blair received a telegram reading: "Can place you at $85 a week. Arrange substitute at Meadville. Start here noon Aug. 15. (Signed) Mason." That was the beginning of Blair's services as a reporter in Midland.

On arrival he discovered that he had filled a vacancy created by the resignation of Edgar Barton, a *Times* staff man who, as a correspondent, had lifted himself into a higher-salaried position on the *Star* of Metropolis, a larger city 400 miles away.

With the permission of the *Times,* Barton had represented the *Star* in Midland. On several occasions he had mailed feature stories to the *Star* and had sent in a modest stickful of spot news from time to time, especially if it had a Metropolis angle. He had suddenly distinguished himself when a Metropolis-bound passenger plane plunged in flames coming into Midland Airport a half hour before the *Star's* Home edition deadline.

OPPORTUNITIES FOR CORRESPONDENTS

Most publishers permit a staff member to serve as a correspondent for larger papers and with good reason. The work seldom interferes with his main job and adds to his income, lessening the chance of losing him. Others regard it as good publicity for the home town and hence for the local newspaper. Some publishers forbid the practice, however, or restrict the correspondence to noncompeting papers in distant cities.

The experiences of Blair and Barton are in no way unusual, for alert editors keep an eye on promising men and women with experience obtained on smaller papers. Ask a dozen successful big city newsmen how they won their first advancements and half of them will say that they were graduated from small town newspapers where they acted as correspondents for wire services and for city newspapers that circulated in their communities.

Perhaps a first-class story unexpectedly broke in the reporter's home town, bringing him recognition overnight. And even if no such spectacular incident spotlighted his ability, the chances are that he kept plugging away, making himself useful, and was given a tryout when a new man was needed to fill a vacation gap.

There is no surer way to prepare for larger responsibilities than by breaking in on a small paper and serving as correspondent for a larger one.

Not all small town newsmen are striving for a job on a larger paper. Many of them are happy where they are and stay there. But these, too, frequently supplement their incomes by sending copy elsewhere by phone, wire and mail.

Almost all reporters at some time meet the problems of covering news away from home and transmitting stories by telephone and telegraph. Frequently a local story leads one to an out-of-town assignment. It follows that the beginner should have at least a nodding acquaintance with the work of the correspondent.

NEWS FROM A DISTANCE

Newspapers obtain their nonlocal news from press services, foreign correspondents, correspondents in other cities or towns, rural correspondents, and regular staff members sent on out-of-town assignments.

Only a few metropolitan dailies can afford to send correspondents overseas or maintain outside bureaus. There is a unanimity of interests within a state and a medium-sized daily may have a state editor and post a man in the state capital or send a man there during a legislative session, but a vast majority of papers rely on the wire services for out-of-state news.

At the Midland *Times* the city's suburbs are assigned special pages, but the suburban editor and beat men are under the direction of the city editor.

Beyond its immediate environs the *Times* has 16 town correspondents in sizable neighboring communities, including county seats. These reporters are affiliated with small dailies and weeklies. In addition, the *Times* has 50-odd rural correspondents—amateurs scattered over 10 counties in which the paper circulates—who send most of their copy by mail. All are paid on a space basis.

The *Times* and the afternoon *Herald* are members of the Associated Press, which is owned and cooperatively controlled by its members. The *Gazette* secures its foreign, national and part of its regional news from United Press International, a privately owned agency that sells news to any who will buy.

The AP, older of the two organizations, was founded by a group of New York editors in 1848. The United Press, created in 1907 by the merger of two groups serving the E. W. Scripps chain, and International News Service, established by William Randolph Hearst in 1909, merged in 1958 to form a single agency—UPI. Both AP and UPI provide syndicate, picture and allied services in addition to the distribution of news to newspapers, radio and television stations and news magazines. Each employs a vast corps of correspondents and maintains bureaus in the main news centers around the world.

The way Midland's newspapers bring nonlocal news into their columns is typical of a system which varies in accordance with conditions in a given circulation area. Distance, population distribution and competition regulate the news demand and supply.

A small paper competing with nearby metropolitan dailies contents itself with little world and national news, whereas a large daily in sparsely settled territory carries much nonlocal news and may use as many as 100 or even 200 regional correspondents. Urban dailies and press services keep staffs stationed in key American news centers such as New York, Washington and Hollywood as well as in foreign capitals.

Few news events of significance slip through this vast and intricate net that stretches from your own neighborhood to the remote outposts of civilization. At its interstices are reporters—thousands of men and women with alert eyes and ears and the know-how of writing.

CLASSIFICATIONS OF CORRESPONDENTS

As shown by the discussion so far, the term *correspondent* is applied loosely and indiscriminately to reporters who gather and transmit nonlocal news copy.

These people range all the way from farm wives to celebrated by-liners on missions abroad. Their stories run from brevities to battles, from personals to peace conferences. They transmit them by telephone, telegraph, wireless, mail, automobile, oxcart and dog sled.

In order to focus attention on practical techniques of value to a beginner we shall omit the foreign and metropolitan experts and rather arbitrarily classify correspondents as follows:

1. *Town correspondent.* Attached to a neighboring town newspaper. Sends spot news by telegraph.
2. *Rural correspondent.* No professional experience. Mails in news letters.
3. *Wire service correspondent.* Attached to newspaper or free lance. Sends spot news by telegraph.
4. *Staff correspondent.* On the staff of a newspaper. Sends spot news by telegraph or returns to office to write.

Again we point out that the classifications overlap and intertwine as to personnel, employment and methods of news transmission. Thus, a town correspondent frequently sends a weekly column of personals to another paper and a rural correspondent may telegraph spot news. Also any correspondent paid on a space basis may serve several noncompeting news outlets including a press service and several newspapers.

Within the editorial departments of newspapers there are several ways of handling wire and mail copy and supervising out-of-town writers. The simplest division of editorship is into two parts—the local or city desk in charge of staff reporters and the telegraph or wire desk in charge of news from out of town. But if the paper has numerous correspondents, as the Midland *Times* does, the common practice is to set up a regional or state desk to deal with them.

The *Times* state desk is manned by William Walsh, the state editor, and two assistants. They direct rural and town correspondents, order stories from them and handle their copy. They have access to AP copy and are responsible for news originating anywhere in the state of Centralia—outside of Midland and specified suburbs—except that covered by local staff men sent out and controlled by the city desk. Stories from outside carry a distinguishing dateline.

There must be and is the closest coordination between city and telegraph or state desks, as well as between the copy and makeup desks. The desks are within easy reach of one another and conversations among the editors manning them are frequent.

THE JOB OF THE RURAL STRINGER

Country correspondents are called *stringers* because few of them are paid weekly or monthly salaries. They clip their articles and send them in for payment at so much an inch or column. The pasted-up clippings are traditionally known as *strings*.

Later on we shall discuss the correspondence work of local newspapermen like Blair of the Meadville *Citizen*. Right now we are dealing with amateurs in smaller places. While newsmen generally telegraph or telephone their reports, rural stringers usually mail them on a daily, weekly or semiweekly basis.

No one ever became rich as a rural correspondent but just about everyone is willing to try it. The work has compensations other than the few dollars a month that it pays. It gives a person prestige among his neighbors, especially if he has a byline or a thumbnail cut, and makes him welcome among the people whose names he puts into print.

Nevertheless, finding suitable correspondents who will work for small pay, keeping them on the job and putting their contributions in shape to print is a difficult and sometimes provoking task. A good state editor is a patient teacher of journalism as well as a buyer of news.

At least two-thirds of country news getters are women because they visit, telephone and write more than men and have more spare time. Correspondents may be housewives, telephone operators, store clerks, students, clergymen or farmers. The ideal one, perhaps, next to a retired newspaperwoman, is one with college training and schoolteaching experience. She has a sound background, an interest in people and time on her hands.

While dormant, dull and dangerous writers are quietly weeded out, the better country correspondents are complimented or rewarded with bylines and bonuses for exceptional effort. Harsh criticism does not work with people paid in pin money, but if a recruit blunders too often he is replaced.

A typical yarn concerns a correspondent who dropped in to tell the state editor that nothing ever happened in his village. As he left he added sadly: "It's about gone, anyway, on account of those old mine tunnels. Three houses caved in this morning."

Failure to recognize news is not so common as failure to recognize what is *not* news. For example, a one-day visit is of slight value. It is hardly more important than the fact that the Smiths had ham and eggs for breakfast.

Other common faults among contributors from rural areas are poor grammar and spelling, illegible handwriting, failure to include full identifications and delay in sending copy.

An efficient correspondent knows when the mails close at his post office and sees to it that his stuff is posted in time to make a certain train or bus and yet not be so early that he will miss late news items.

A GUIDE FOR CORRESPONDENTS

Many newspapers carry on a constant program of education for rural correspondents. Part of the *Times* program consists of sending to each new one a set of instructions and suggestions. This list of do's, don'ts and maybe's follows:

Be Factual

Don't let personal feelings affect your selection of news items.

Be accurate. Shun gossip and hearsay. Go to the people who know the facts.

If a story may hurt somebody, be sure it is based on official information.

Don't exaggerate. Understate rather than overstate your case.
Write without editorializing.

Names

Get first names or initials right. Write a person's name as he signs it.
Do not repeat the same name in two items if you can avoid it.
Try to get the name of each person in your community in a newsworthy story at least once a year.
Do not use time after time the names of those attending the same regular meetings.

Mail News Not Wanted

Don't send items about routine family visits or small social events.
Don't send lengthy marriage or death items unless the principals are well known.
Don't send stories of wedding anniversaries below the 50th.
Unless they are unusual, omit stories of illnesses and nonfatal accidents.

Mail News Wanted

Cover all large assemblies with 100 or more present.
Send stories on town meetings, fairs and parades but not too many details.
Civic improvements and highway developments are mail news.
Anything odd or unusual in your community may make a story.
Look for short human interest stories with a laugh or a sob.
Send all notices of coming events by mail.
We allow three days from the time an event occurs until it reaches us—but mail your letter as soon as possible.
Your mail items are needed most on Saturdays, Sundays and Mondays.
Watch the stories sent in by other correspondents. They may give you ideas.

News to Rush

Tips are valuable. The minute you get word of a big story, phone or wire such information as: "Man and woman found shot in motor court here. Registered as Mr. and Mrs. L. A. Parks of Midland." Then follow the instructions you get from the state desk.
Here are examples of events to report immediately:
Fatal accidents.
Plane and train wrecks.
Storms and floods causing deaths or heavy damage.
Major crimes such as homicides or bank robberies.
Any major event which might lose its news value if delayed.

Get Pictures

The *Times* is always in the market for pictures. When you hear of a story, think: "Is there a picture in it?"
If you have a good camera, use it. If not, hire a local photographer.

Rush important pictures, plates or negatives by air mail, special delivery or in care of a bus driver or trainman. Give us his name and number.

General

Keep in touch with your local officials and have them call you when anything unusual happens.

Let people know you are a *Times* correspondent. It will help you get the news.

Send the news regularly. If you are away, get a substitute and notify us.

Don't force us to call you day after day for developments of a story. Follow them yourself.

Come in and visit us when you can. You are welcome.

Remuneration

The *Times* pays 10 cents a column inch for all news and pictures printed. You will get your check about the middle of the month for the preceding month.

The *Times* does not object to extraordinary expenses when authorized or in an emergency. Send us an itemized bill.

THE QUERY AND WORDAGE ORDER

As noted in the "News to Rush" section, a big story may drop into the lap of a rural correspondent and he may be instructed to telephone or telegraph developments until a more experienced man can reach the scene. This, however, is a rarity.

On the contrary, newsmen serving as correspondents in sizable communities customarily use Western Union and phone if the news is urgent. But they quickly learn that telephoning and wiring costs money.

Western Union offers special rates to the press. Press rates average about one-third of public rates in the daytime and one-sixth of the regular rate at night. Nevertheless, the charge per word in a dispatch inevitably piles up the expense. The whole system of news transmission by telegraph is arranged to reduce tolls as far as possible, so brevity becomes more than an office byword.

Allotting story space is accomplished in large part through the *query*, a brief notice sent by the town or wire service correspondent indicating the content of the story he has in hand and the suggested length. If the editor wants the story he transmits a message to that effect, ordering so many words.

Other considerations, aside from economy, account for the query. The correspondent's article may already have been received from another source or it may not make the same appeal to the distant editor as to the local reporter. Again, the paper's schedule may be tight, with space at a premium. These things the correspondent, miles away, cannot determine. It is therefore necessary for him to forward a thumbnail version of the news and on the basis of that bulletin the editor decides how much of the story he requires.

If the reply says to forward 500 words, the editor means 500, not 600 or 1,000. If no reply is received by the correspondent, the story is not wanted.

To illustrate, assume that a Metropolis society couple elopes to Midland and is married there. Barton, the Midland correspondent for the Metropolis *Star*, is confident that the *Star* will print a story and flashes the following query:

> HAROLD MILES, ARTIST, WED HERE TO CAROL KANE, DAUGHTER E. O. KANE, OWNER CRESCENT MOTOR COMPANY, METROPOLIS. BELIEVE SECRET WITHOUT KANE'S CONSENT. FOUR HUNDRED.

A half hour later Barton receives this reply:

> SEND THREE HUNDRED WEDDING. IF INTERVIEW WITH BRIDE UP TO SIX HUNDRED. WHERE FOR HONEYMOON.

The correspondent is naturally anxious to make the most of his story and endeavors to sell it by dispatching the most attractive query possible. No salesman submitting a sample of his goods will display a shoddy, unattractive piece of material. He selects his best. Similarly, the alert correspondent compresses the most engaging facts of his story into his query remembering, of course, that the bulletin must be accurate, brief and give the high lights of the news.

Imagine yourself a state or telegraph editor allotting space with the following queries before you. Which one in each pair would induce you to send an order for the complete story?

(1)

> Spelling contest held here today with all elementary schools participating. Grace Blake, Washington School, winner, with John Westerly, Bryant, second.

> Three pupils stumped by antithesis in county spelling bee. Grace, 12, downed Johnny, 15, on sauerkraut. Hundred participated. Winner to state finals.

(2)

> Fortune found by Lawrence Roberts, 15 years old, near here this afternoon. Whole town talking about it.

A CORRESPONDENT'S
QUERY AND REPLY

WESTERN UNION

JOSEPH L. EGAN
PRESIDENT

CLASS OF SERVICE		SYMBOLS
This is a full-rate Telegram or Cable-gram unless its deferred character is indicated by a suitable symbol above or preceding the address.		DL = Day Letter NL = Night Letter LC = Deferred Cable NLT = Cable Night Letter Ship Radiogram

The filing time shown in the date line on telegrams and day letters is STANDARD TIME at point of origin. Time of receipt is STANDARD TIME at point of destination

```
METROPOLIS STAR                        DPR COLLECT

METROPOLIS U S A

DANIEL FOLEY METROPOLIS JAILBREAKER CAPTURED BY SHERIFF

FISHER AND POSSE HERE STOP FOLEY WOUNDED IN GUNPLAY

STOP FISHER BRINGING HIM TO METROPOLIS FRIDAY STOP

SEVEN HUNDRED

                           BARTON
```

WESTERN UNION

JOSEPH L. EGAN
PRESIDENT

CLASS OF SERVICE		SYMBOLS
This is a full-rate Telegram or Cable-gram unless its deferred character is indicated by a suitable symbol above or preceding the address.		DL = Day Letter NL = Night Letter LC = Deferred Cable NLT = Cable Night Letter Ship Radiogram

The filing time shown in the date line on telegrams and day letters is STANDARD TIME at point of origin. Time of receipt is STANDARD TIME at point of destination

```
FRANK BARTON

MIDLAND TIMES

MIDLAND CEN

SEND FIVE HUNDRED FOLEY EARLY EDITION

                       WATROUS STAR
```

How a Story Is Offered and Ordered

Gold bars worth $5,000 dug out of "Witches' Cave" by Boy Scout. Thought loot from Midland Express robbery in 1882.

(3)

Thrilling basketball game won by Hillview team over Lincoln High School. Big noisy celebration causes trouble.

Snake dancers jailed for building street bonfire and chopping fire hose after Hillview High beats Lincoln 39–38.

MORE ABOUT QUERIES

In his zeal to "sell" a story a correspondent sometimes yields to the temptation to send a *blind query,* that is, one which exaggerates the story by the use of such phrases as *prominent man, disastrous accident* and *tense excitement.* Such generalities make it difficult for the editor to weigh the exact news value of the occurrence. Here is a specimen:

MANY LIVES ENDANGERED BY STORM HERE. IMPORTANT BUILDING BADLY DAMAGED. CITY OFFICIALS GREATLY CONCERNED. FEAR LOSSES WILL RUN HIGH. ONE THOUSAND.

The foregoing query would probably be cast aside because of its vagueness. It would have been much better to crosscut the news in this fashion:

FIFTY-MILE GALE RIPS ROOF FROM OPERA HOUSE. DAMAGE IN CITY TWENTY-FIVE THOUSAND DOLLARS. TWO HUNDRED.

Queries deliberately aimed to trick an editor usually bring a kickback. For example, the *Times* received this one: "Clay City woman tops 5,000 entries in nationwide contest." She received honorable mention, as did about 500 others. City Editor Mason notified the Clay City correspondent that any more such misleading queries would result in refusal to pay wire charges.

Orders for an article desired by the paper may be wired to the correspondent, although he has not sent a query previously. He should execute such orders promptly and in exact accordance with directions.

Is a correspondent at any time justified in wiring a story without first sending a query? Yes, if the story is unquestionably an urgent one and the time is short. In that event toll charges mean relatively nothing. Use of a telephone is warranted if wire facilities are not available. To be on the safe side, however, the reporter may make his query long enough to be used in bulletin form and then wait for an order before filing more.

Of utmost importance to the out-of-town reporter is exact knowledge of edition deadlines. A list of the deadlines usually is forwarded to him when he assumes his position, and he should consult it to gear his filing to office procedure.

FILING TELEGRAPH COPY

Telegraph dispatches should be filed at the earliest possible moment —for an edition, at least one hour before a deadline—so that there will be enough elbowroom for transmission and editing.

If the deadline is imminent and the story extremely important, the dispatch should be sent in takes or handled in running form. A correspondent can save precious minutes by using a typewriter in the telegraph office when a sending operator is not available in his own shop rather than carrying or sending his copy across town after it is finished.

Telegraph news may be sent to a newspaper by automatic printer-telegraph machines or hand-operated Morse instruments. The code-clicking Morse instruments are disappearing. They now are used mostly for such special events as football and baseball games when material is wired from a press box. Most press service and Western Union wordage goes by Teletype.

A correspondent without a direct office-to-office connection files *overhead*, meaning that he sends via Western Union. Messages and copy are marked *DPR* or *NPR*, meaning day or night press rate. NPR is cheaper and both rates are much less than those for private or commercial messages. Press messages go collect.

At the right top of page one the sender types DPR COLLECT or NPR COLLECT. Unlike a local story, the telegraph story starts with a dateline:

(*Special to the Midland Times*)

Meadville, Sept. 3.—

Telegraph stuff is written in complete sentences just as it appears in the paper, including the articles *a* and *the*. Queries may be shortened by skeletonizing, but abbreviated copy is employed only in sending foreign cables. Time is required to build up a complete narrative from scattered facts supplied by wire and translating "cablese" does not save enough money in telegraph tolls to make the practice economical.

The correspondent must know the number of words wanted and keep within that limit. If he runs over repeatedly he invites a reprimand. Generally speaking, he should follow the inverted pyramid structure which, as we shall see, is virtually mandatory in wire service copy. Unless the story is brief or his query indicates suspended interest he should beware

SAMPLE PAGE OF
TELEGRAPH COPY

```
                                              6 15 P M
METROPOLIS STAR                           D P R COLLECT
METROPOLIS U S A
               (Special to the Star)
          Midland, Cen., Nov. 12.--With two bullet wounds in
     his left arm, Daniel Foley, suspected burglar, tonight was in a
     Midland hospital awaiting return to the Metropolis jail from
     which he escaped Wednesday morning. His wounds are not
     serious.
          Foley was shot and captured this afternoon by Sheriff
     John E. Fisher and a posse near the Midland Shore Line railroad
     junction two miles north of here after he jumped from a
     southbound freight train. Deputy Sheriff John Shanks shot him
     when he drew a pistol instead of obeying an order to raise
     his hands.
          Sheriff Fisher said that if Foley is able to travel
     he will bring him to Metropolis Friday. At that time Fisher
     expects to collect the $500 reward offered for his capture.
          At the hospital tonight Foley refused to talk
     except to say that he intended to make his getaway into
     Oklahoma. When asked how he obtained the saws with which he
     cut his way to freedom, Foley said to "find out from the jailer
     in Metropolis."
                                              2 Foley follows
```

First Page of Wired Story

of narrative or dramatic construction which might lop off the climax of the story.

A wordage order specifies the maximum, not the minimum, and is subject to last-minute revision. If space suddenly shrinks, the state editor may choose to cut off a story even after filing has begun.

There is no justification for padding which adds unnecessarily to the telegraph toll, especially if the extra material can be clipped from other papers or obtained from the morgue.

LOCALIZING OUT-OF-TOWN NEWS

We have discussed the localization of outside stories by staff reporters and rewrite men. A wise correspondent filing a story anticipates and, if possible, averts the overhauling of his contribution by localizing as he writes.

A newsman localizes not in relation to himself but in relation to his readers. If a correspondent for the *Times* is writing for a Clay County column or page, his readers live in that county. Most Midlanders will pass it up. But if the story is of wide interest, likely to go into the general news columns, the sender skips over Clay County detail and plays up the angle with strong appeal to readers in Midland or the entire *Times* circulation area.

Note how the following story, sent to the *Times* by its Southfield correspondent, emphasizes the Midland angle:

(Special to the Midland Times)

Southfield, Oct. 30.—After a midnight raid on the Midland College campus, students at Fairmount Teachers College today staged a tumultuous celebration over recapture of the famous "Jinx" stone held by MC for the last two years.

Classrooms were empty during an impromptu half holiday this afternoon as the students planned a torchlight parade in honor of three seniors who slipped the stone out of a trophy case in Shield Gymnasium in Midland last night.

The "Jinx" stone, planted in a mock cemetery after a football victory by a Yellow team over Midland seven years ago, has since been a token of rivalry between the two schools.

"We arrived in Midland about 2 a.m. and found not a soul on the campus," Dick Perkins, one of the Fairmount raiders, related today.

"We found an open window in the gym basement and the trophy case on the third floor was unlocked, so we just helped ourselves to the 'Jinx' and slid it out the window. Once the caretaker passed by, but he didn't notice us."

The Fairmount students plan to bring the "Jinx" to Midland next Saturday for the MC game, but it will be under a heavy guard of rooters to prevent the Midlanders from recovering it. Later it will be locked up in a Southfield bank vault.

AFIELD ON AN OUT-OF-TOWN ASSIGNMENT

A reporter accepts as an honor any assignment that moves him to another city on the trail of a story, for such a foray gives him greater responsibility than is ordinarily enjoyed in the local room. In large measure the writer becomes his own editor, working without supervision.

His travel, hotel, food and other expenses, including tips, are repaid to him. If wise, he records them carefully or estimates them fairly. He can lose half his salary by carelessness, and when expense accounts turn into "swindle sheets" they can cause him trouble, perhaps lose assignments for him in the future.

On arriving at the scene of action it is expedient that a reporter promptly orient himself. He should determine how he is to move about —afoot, by car or by taxi—and how he is to transmit his story—by telephone or telegraph. If by wire, he should find the local telegraph office, ascertain its closing hours, identify himself and make arrangements for filing. Otherwise he may find himself near a deadline without an operator or with the door locked.

Local newspapers, if any, may prove of great value. He should buy all in sight and immediately read anything they have printed on the story assigned to him.

If his paper has a correspondent on the spot and especially if that correspondent has originated the story, the visiting staff man should at once contact and cooperate with him. If staff men attached to other outside newspapers or writers for the local press are on hand, he will work with them, pooling information unless specifically instructed to keep his stuff exclusive.

In the absence of fellow newsmen, the most likely place in town to get help is a local newspaper office. The editor is familiar with the community and its personalities if not the background of a particular news development. Nine times out of ten he willingly helps out the visitor with information or introductions, sometimes offering him a desk and typewriter and may even print a piece about him and his visit.

Above all, the man on an out-of-town quest should remember the purpose of his trip—to serve his own newspaper, not to enjoy a vacation. He must keep constantly in mind the instructions of his superiors and the kind of story they want if he expects to be commended when he returns to his home office.

PRESS SERVICE COPY

In our analysis of the correspondents' work we have covered all types of news except that sent to a press service by a free-lance or regular correspondent or an out-of-town staff man.

In most essentials, press service news parallels that handled by newspapers for themselves but there is one difference. The rule of inverted pyramid structure applies far more stringently to wire service than to individual newspaper stories.

The services have many circulation areas. They cover the world, serving thousands of newspapers large and small, near and far. One paper may want a column about a certain event of interest in its section while another will use only half a column, a third only a paragraph. For example, a story of a fire in Midland would be worth 1,000 words in Midland, 500 in Capital City, 100 in Metropolis and nothing at all in New York.

It is evident that a wire agency cannot furnish a dozen or more different versions of one event to fit the particular interests of as many papers. It is essential therefore that the dispatch be so written that the upper part may be printed, the rest thrown away. Such a story may be cut at any place following the first paragraph without leaving a loose end. If it is not so written at the start it will be overhauled by a rewrite man in the AP or UPI bureau where it is received.

Another reason for the more rigid structure of wire service stories is that a press agency serves many newspapers with different deadlines. This calls for frequent revisions. A fast-developing story may in the course of an hour have two or three new leads with pickups from earlier dispatches plus inserts and additions to bring it up-to-date. Such swift patchworking is impossible unless there is an orderly arrangement.

Place a piece of paper over the following dispatch, uncovering and reading a paragraph at a time. You will note that each division may be used to finish the story.

Midland, Cen., Nov. 2.—A Midland architect shot and killed his pretty estranged wife here today so she "wouldn't ever hurt anybody else." The victim was 23-year-old Wilma Braden. Her husband, Boyd, shot her six times with a new .38 caliber pistol.

"I didn't want her to have the kids," he said.

The shooting occurred in midafternoon while Mrs. Braden, the mother of two sons, 3 and 4, sat alone in the office of a real estate company where she worked as a stenographer.

Braden said he and his wife separated a week ago and that she had started divorce proceedings.

He calmly told police that he talked only briefly with his wife.

"Then I shot her so she wouldn't ever hurt anybody else," he said. "I just couldn't stand losing the boys."

Occupants of other offices heard the shots. As they rushed into the hallway, Braden came out, gun in hand.

They quoted him as saying: "Call the police and maybe an ambulance, although I don't think that will be necessary."

Braden was booked on a homicide charge and held without bail in the City Jail. County Attorney Howard Ford said he will be arraigned for first-degree murder.

Neighbors of the Bradens told police the couple quarreled frequently . . . . .

Press services, like newspapers, often carry one-, two- or three-paragraph suspended interest stories to spice the day's news budgets. Indeed these brighteners are in great demand.

If a correspondent is certain that he has a superior human interest or dramatic formula story he may develop it at some length and risk the wordage on the wires. But it must be exceptionally good to be acceptable. All standard straight news wire service stories follow the order of descending news importance.

SHOP TALK

1. Go through a newspaper and see if you can list the sources of all nonlocal stories.
2. Discuss fully the organization, ownership and history of press services.
3. Devise and criticize queries based on several stories in current papers.
4. Criticize the volume and value of rural correspondents' columns in your local newspapers.
5. If you were sent out of town to cover a convention attended by prominent people from your city, what steps would you take upon arrival?

CHAPTER **22**

Catching the Deadlines

SPEED IN THE NEWSROOM

A glance at the big clock over his desk told City Editor Mark Mason that it was 7:03 p.m.—57 minutes before the 8 p.m. Early edition copy deadline—as he answered a telephone call from police headquarters.

"Maxwell," said the other voice crisply. "Something up at City Jail. All squad cars called. Looks serious. I'll have more in five minutes."

"Okay, feed it to Harris as fast as you get it," ordered Mason. "Stay there. We'll cover the jail."

Mason looked again at the clock, swung around in his chair and called to Harris: "Give your stuff to Burke. Stand by for Maxwell." Noting that Markham was free and McConnell was writing a second-rate story, Mason summoned them both, signaled for a photographer and dispatched the three to the jail with no instructions except: "May be a jailbreak. Keep moving."

Every man in motion—Mason, Maxwell, Burke, Markham, McConnell and the photographer—was fully aware of the time situation without further talk. Fifty minutes remained before the deadline. It was a race against the clock, with the outcome uncertain but the procedure as practiced as a fire drill.

Before 7:10 Maxwell was back on the phone. It was a jailbreak during a dinnertime riot, according to a phone report to police by Warden Wilkins. Deputy Warden Stone, bludgeoned with a piece of pipe, was critically injured. At least two prisoners, so far unidentified, had escaped.

"Take Maxwell," Mason told Harris. "Five hundred for this run. Slug it JAIL. Let me have it in takes."

A story was on the copy desk at 7:37 when Markham called from the jail. Five prisoners were gone—he had names. They included a widely publicized convicted killer, apparently the leader. An ambulance had arrived for Stone.

"Give it to Harris for a new lead and an insert on the names," the city editor told Markham. "Stay at the jail. Tell McConnell to follow up on Stone."

Hastily Harris, the rewrite man, revised his story and with five minutes to spare sent over the last of the insert. But the story was breaking unexpectedly fast. Once more Harris was called back on the phone by McConnell reporting the death of Stone on the way to a hospital.

"Make it a bulletin," came the order from Mason.

Precisely at 8 p.m. Harris jerked a two-line bulletin from his typewriter. A copy boy rushed it to Mason for approval and the copy desk relayed it to the composing room. The jailbreak story for that edition was completed and ready for the presses. The *Times* hit the street with the major news facts on page one.

LITERATURE IN A HURRY

To anyone unacquainted with newsroom talk and procedure this episode might appear to be a jumble of hit-or-miss activity with a lucky outcome. To a newsman it is routine long since established to ensure speedy publication of a fast-breaking story.

It has been said that news is literature in a hurry. This is merely another way of redefining the first and primary requisite of news—immediacy. By nature news is a perishable commodity, losing its salability as the clock goes around. Few spot stories are worth anything 24 hours after their entrance into print. Once published, they are crowded off the boards by more youthful candidates and left to the magazines and history books or to oblivion.

It is true that radio put an end to newspaper speed supremacy. For example, the *Times* radio station, MIDT, and its television station, MITV, bulletined the jailbreak developments before they reached the composing room. Presses and trucks cannot keep pace with the lightning delivery of radio and television microphones. This competition has all but silenced the cry of "Extra!" and has shortened the lives of exclusive stories. However, while extra editions and scoops are rarer, there is no letup whatever in the pressure to cover and print the latest news in the regular editions with all possible speed.

Work in an editorial room would be simple indeed if a newsman, like Joshua, could command the sun to stand still and allow himself the time necessary to complete and polish his handiwork without molestations. But the clock runs on relentlessly, and frequently newsmen must forge fast with the furnace at full draft.

Readers little know nor care whether 10 minutes or 10 hours go into the preparation of a news story but they expect the paper to be up-to-the-minute and they expect it to arrive on time every day.

In all modern newspapers of any size editions go to press on the minute. It is only in the movies and in fiction that an editor shouts, "Hold the presses!" Trucks, trains and planes operate on schedule time and the type forms cannot and do not wait. Extremely important news stories are *replated*.

By and large the local room staff is geared to deadlines, that is, the stated hours when copy must be cleared in time to make regular editions.

Pressure increases as a deadline approaches. With a deadline several hours away, the reporter has a reasonable amount of time to gather material and write a story. Usually, even after it is finished, he may furbish it to include later happenings. But sometimes all plans are upset in a split second. Stories may not break until a deadline is perilously near or unexpected developments may come so fast that time does not permit the overhauling of an early version. Thoroughness must be sacrificed to speed and short cuts are in order.

Perhaps half the stories in an afternoon newspaper and two out of three in a morning paper remain intact through all editions. The others are removed, patchworked or rewritten during the period of publication.

The mortality of PM paper news is higher for the reason that more news develops and changes during waking and working hours—daytime—than during relaxation and sleep hours—nighttime. Hence afternoon paper reporters are more accustomed to quick changes than morning paper men.

THE NEWS ASSEMBLY LINE

This is a book about news gathering and writing—not copyreading, makeup, typesetting or proofreading.

No reporter needs to be an expert in the operations of the composing and pressrooms. However, as one workman in a shop operated on a production line schedule, he should be well enough acquainted with them to coordinate intelligently with those who carry his words on to their final form in the newspaper.

If he has written a complete and acceptable article the reporter or rewrite man has nothing to do with it after it leaves his desk. He has only to slug and type it properly in accordance with the paper's copy rules and style sheet.

But if a running story is coming in piecemeal and requires revisions after the first draft has moved on down the assembly line, then the writer must understand how the work of others bears on his own.

After passing over the city desk in pages or takes, copy goes to the desk of a man who evaluates the various stories and determines the display each is to receive. He specifies the headline and type sizes and widths and lays out the news pages in *dummy* form. This man at the Midland *Times* is called the *makeup editor*. In many offices his title is *news editor* or his work is done in part or whole by the *managing editor*.

From him copy goes to the copy desk chief, who passes it to a copy-reader to edit and headline in accordance with the instructions of the makeup editor.

Any one of these three—makeup editor, copy desk chief or copyreader, but usually the last—marks down instructions for the typesetter. After the story is set in type *galley proofs* are pulled. One of these goes to the makeup editor and another to a proofreader who corrects typographical errors.

Meanwhile the story may be developing and require one or several rapid changes. These are initiated at the source of the news. They go through a typewriter and then again down the assembly line with the proof being marked to accompany the typewritten copy.

PATCHWORK WITH PRECISION

A story revised from edition to edition is called a *running* story because the copy usually runs in *takes,* that is, one or two paragraphs at a time as the news moves forward. Running stories almost invariably are spot news that arouses keen public interest. Wrecks, fires, sporting events, elections, trials, sessions of legislative bodies, and conventions often call for running story treatment with corrections, additions and substitutions crowding for attention into the last hour before the presses whine.

Running stories may be written by reporters at the scene, say in a press box at a football game, and telegraphed or they may be telephoned by leg reporters to rewrite men. Frequently several reporters and rewrite men are assigned to the same running story.

There is nothing haphazard in the work of keeping this freshet of news under control. In the newsroom it is received, written, sorted, slugged and moved systematically and swiftly from source to press.

On the assignment and schedule sheets each story has an identifying label or title given to it by the city desk man. This is usually one but sometimes two words. Examples: JEWELS, PARADE, CITY COUNCIL. Some papers distinguish between a train WRECK, plane CRASH and motor vehicle SMASHUP. Others abbreviate Supreme Court of the United States as SCOTUS, Congress as CONG, politics as POL, holiday as HOL, and so on.

If an event is *sectional* and separated into related stories under different headlines, the related stories may carry double slugs such as WRECK-Casualties, WRECK-Rescue and WRECK-Eyewitness.

This label typed at the top of his first page of copy by the writer is generally known as a *slug* but sometimes is called a *guideline*. It stays with the story from start to finish.

One of two devices is used to tell compositors there is more than one page to a story. The writer usually types the word *more* at the bottom of each sheet except the last one, which closes with an end symbol, # or 30. The makeup man or copyreader may change the *more* to *t.r.*, which means *turn rule*. A turned rule is a type slug turned face side down so that it appears as a heavy black line on proofs.

Keeping in mind these mechanical pointers, let us now analyze what we have called the short cuts as they are applied in typical near-deadline operations. These, in brief, are:

> *Bulletin*—a brief one-or-two-sentence report of urgent news value.
> *Insert*—new material placed in the body of a previously written story.
> *New Lead*—the fore part of a standing story rewritten to cover late developments.
> *Add*—new material added to the end of a previously written story.
> *Sub*—new or revised matter which replaces earlier copy.
> *A-matter*—early or detailed material written and set in type in advance of the lead or body.

It will be seen that these six basic devices enable newsmen to work their will with stories at any point along the production line from typewriter to the lockup of the type in a page form.

The terms are used in combination forms such as:

> *Bulletin to lead all*—to be placed immediately under the headline.
> *Kill for Insert B*—drop this paragraph or these paragraphs and substitute Insert B.
> *Add 1 on the sub*—to be placed at the end of the sub.

The terms and their combinations sometimes are shortened. As *turn rule* may become *t.r.*, *new lead* may be abbreviated to *n.l.*

The short-cut devices vary somewhat in accordance with the size and organization of the newspaper shop but in essentials they are the same everywhere. Once understood through definition and practice, the news-room speed-up process loses much of its complexity.

BULLETINS AND FLASHES

Fastest and briefest of all news forms is the *bulletin,* a short but complete report of a sudden news development which is given the right of way and hurried to press because of its urgency.

A term closely associated with bulletin, but less frequently seen, is *flash.* The word *flash* is heard in some dramatized radio newscasts. Newspapers occasionally use bulletin and flash interchangeably. However, in general press usage the word *flash* means a device used in telegraph or Teletype copy to expedite transmission—a spot news fact of top news value, written in condensed style, as "Dawson concedes," "Stoneham dead" or "Kelly by kayo in third." Such flashes are standard tools in wire service copy. Newspapers translate them into full-sentence bulletins before putting them into print.

Typical examples of bulletins in the three Midland newspapers follow:

> Two drivers were killed and four passengers injured in a head-on collision of two cars at Douglas Ave. and 10th St. just before noon today. Police identified the drivers as Vernon Hewitt, 27, of 408 Hester St., and K. L. Leach, 43, of Larchmont.

> Leonard E. Cole, head of the Midland Securities Corp., was found guilty of embezzlement by a jury in Circuit Court today.

> Mayor Nelson last night announced the settlement of the three-day bus strike. Service will be resumed on all lines at 6 a.m. Tuesday.

> A four-alarm fire broke out at 10:15 p.m. last night in the main plant of the United Products Co., at Main St. and 14th Ave. No one was injured. At 10:30 three upper stories of the seven-story brick factory were ablaze. Six fire companies fought to save nearby warehouses and homes.

> The Midland Blue Sox won the intercity pennant today by defeating Junction City 3–2.

> Three masked and armed men escaped with a $4,000 payroll after a daylight holdup of a Midland Savings Bank messenger on the bank steps at 3 p.m. today.

Such bulletins may be marked into page makeup in various ways. If it represents a new angle of a story already in print a bulletin customarily is wedged between the headline and lead or boxed near the top of the story. If it reports an isolated incident it may be set in boldface or 10-to-12-point type under its own headline anywhere on page one.

Many newspapers, especially those with afternoon editions, reserve a special *fudge* column on the first page in which bulletins are inserted or fudged without disarranging the makeup of other columns. Late market reports, racing results and other spot news summaries, as well as bulletins, are jimmied into or yanked out of a fudge column within a few minutes of edition deadlines and can be changed quickly in replates during press running time.

HOW BULLETINS ARE HANDLED

Like any other news story, a bulletin passes through several hands from source to publication. It differs only in that it travels more swiftly through the processes of transmission, writing, editing and printing.

A trained reporter knows instinctively when he has in hand a fact, statement or incident of true bulletin caliber. It shouts for action. But he is careful not to "play newspaper" by trying to pump up a trivial incident into a synthetic scare-type bulletin. Attempts to put through essentially unimportant news as bulletins are just as embarrassing as missing really big news breaks.

Nor may the reporter safely sacrifice accuracy for speed. Many a newspaper has been humiliated by a reporter's attempt to beat the gun a few seconds by taking a chance. Don't gamble. Wait until the verdict is read, the last batter is out, the release time is reached—then move fast. Get it first if you can—but first, get it right.

If a bulletin event is expected, a writer may gain time by shaping alternate bulletins in his mind or on paper. For example, he may be able to foresee the outcome as win, lose or draw or as guilty, innocent or hung jury, and be ready to phone or write one of the prepared bulletins intantly.

As written, a bulletin closely resembles a summary lead. It attempts to telescope into a few forceful words the answers to the five W's. However, it does not wait for complete answers or for dressing up of any kind. Note the slight differences here:

Bulletin

A huge water tank crashed at 10:18 a.m. today on a building at 915 Clinton St. Fire apparatus and ambulances were rushed to the scene. At 10:45 Fire Chief Chambers reported two men injured.

AN AFTERNOON PAPER

FUDGE COLUMN

LATE NEWS BULLETINS

WOMAN CRITICALLY BURNED

Mrs. Harvey Knox, 65, was severely burned at 9 a.m. today when her clothing ignited while she was firing a furnace in her home at 391 Ash St. Her condition is critical.

COE NAMED FAIR CHAIRMAN

Capital City, May 9.—Governor Boland today appointed F. R. Coe of Midland as chairman of the State Fair Commission. Coe will succeed Charles Racine on July 1.

WINS SPELLING CONTEST

Theresa Wilks, 10-year-old pupil at Bryant School, is Midland's champion speller. She won top honors in the citywide finals at Center High this afternoon by correctly spelling "anesthesia."

DRIVER KILLED IN CRASH

One man was killed and two injured at 2 p.m. today in a head-on auto collision on Highway 77 three miles east of Midland. State police identified the dead man as J. P. Wren, 42, of Fairfield.

WRIGHTMAN SIGNS RIVER BILL

Washington, D. C., May 9.—President Wrightman today signed the Rivers and Harbors appropriation bill which contains an allotment of $750,000 for Timber River flood control.

Literature in a Hurry

Lead

With a roar like the rumble of an earthquake, a 5,000-gallon tank collapsed today on the roof of a shoe factory at 915 Clinton St. Two men were hurt as water cascaded through five stories to the street below.

While a wire service flash, like a telegram, omits articles and verbs in order to save words and gain seconds, the bulletin as written for a newspaper is not skeletonized. No matter how scanty the information, it must consist of at least one complete sentence as it leaves the typewriter. Examples:

WRONG

Plane crashed Municipal Airport 4:45. Pilot, two others killed. Belonged Skyway Co. Motor trouble. Fell 500 feet.

RIGHT

The pilot and two passengers of a Skyway plane were killed at 4:45 p.m. today when the ship crashed at the Municipal Airport. The plane fell 500 feet after developing motor trouble.

WRONG

Jacob Robbins resigned. Was School Board head. Politics blamed.

RIGHT

Jacob Robbins, president of the Board of Education, resigned at a meeting of the board this morning. He said: "The political pressure is too strong for me."

Exact clock time is cited more often in bulletins than in leads. Specification of the time impresses readers with the newness of an occurrence. As a late afternoon paper bulletin subsides into a morning paper lead, *4:45 p.m.* is likely to be loosened into *late yesterday* and in still older versions merely *yesterday*.

FROM BULLETIN TO LEAD

A bulletin is merely the starter's gun in the race to put an important story into print. If a replate is called for or if another edition is coming up, a bulletin is automatically transformed into a complete story or a new lead on the standing story. No bulletin is allowed to remain without elaboration through more than one run of the paper. The old lead, if there is one, is stricken out and subbed or it is amended and sunk under the new copy.

Presume, for illustration, that rescue forces are digging for a group of miners trapped underground the previous day by an explosion. Their fate is uncertain. A complete account of the accident is already in editions of a PM paper on the newsstand under a lead like this:

> Rescue squads this morning were digging desperately in the upper shaft of Wilson Mine No. 3 in an effort to reach 22 miners buried by an explosion yesterday.

Now comes a telephone report from the mine that the rescuers, nearing the men, have received signals that indicate some of them are alive. A bulletin is inserted over the top of the story:

> Faint rappings, heard by rescue workers at 10:15 a.m., indicated some of the miners entombed in Wilson Mine No. 3 still are alive.

No sooner has this bulletin sped to the Linotype than a second follows:

> All 22 men trapped in the Wilson mine were found alive at 10:25 a.m.

With the last-minute news now covered in the bulletins, the reporter on the assignment has a few minutes' breathing spell. During that time he may or may not receive new information. If so, it is incorporated with the substance of the bulletin matter in a new lead, slugged NEW LEAD—MINE:

> Every one of the 22 miners entombed by an explosion in Wilson Mine No. 3 yesterday was brought safely to the surface this morning. Although chilled, weak and exhausted, they were otherwise unharmed by their harrowing experience.
>
> Squads of rescue workers, who for 16 hours had dug frantically in the upper shaft, located the men at 10:15 a.m., and 10 minutes later broke through the wall of slag enclosing them.

If there are more editions to follow, the writer may revise the story several times, including additional details and discarding or sinking still farther the earlier paragraphs about the explosion. After the last run any fresh data will be handled in ordinary follow-up stories.

INSERTS, ADDS AND A-MATTER

An *insert,* as the term indicates, is copy inserted in the body of a news article, whereas an *add* is an addition placed at the end. Like the bulletin and new lead, they are devices used to incorporate new data into a standing story without the necessity of a complete overhauling or rewriting.

Developments and details not important enough to warrant reshaping the lead are handled as adds and inserts. By scanning the printed story a rewrite man or copyreader can pick out the logical place for the insert or add, indicate it with a pencil, then send the corrected clipping with the insert to the copy desk. If the story is not yet in the paper, the copyreader marks news leads, inserts and adds on the proof.

Usually the writer, city editor and copyreader agree upon the point where an insert is to merge with a story or whether the new material is to be an add, thereby making it possible for the writer to type his own slugs and see that the subject matter dovetails into the separated portions. Inserts and adds, of course, must be properly slugged by someone. Otherwise the smooth flow of reading text may be abruptly broken, or phrases and words repeated in successive paragraphs.

Inserts carry alphabetical and adds numerical slugs, thus: INSERT A, INSERT B; ADD 1, ADD 2.

An add is an angle of the story, sometimes lengthy but never of urgent news value, which is tacked onto the spot news lead and body. It may consist of an interview, statement or background.

An add differs from A-matter in that the add usually is written coincident with or after the spot news portions of the story whereas A-matter is prepared in advance and in anticipation of a lead to come. For example, during the early afternoon an AM paper writer may prepare A-matter, say on the morning developments at a trial. This is edited and set in type before or as the afternoon developments are processed. B-matter follows A-matter, C-matter follows B-matter, and so on indefinitely.

Background material prepared hours, days or even weeks in advance of an anticipated news development is A-matter. A clear example is the chronology of a man's life shaped into a prepared obit. Some papers have scores of these obits in type awaiting the person's death. Such A-matter is ready to go under a death bulletin or be tacked to a death lead without the delay of typesetting.

APPLICATION OF THE SHORT CUTS

Return now to the mine story as rewritten with the rescue lead by Ralph Jones, afternoon paper rewrite man. This story has been on the street for an hour when a reporter at the mine telephones the information that six of the victims have been hospitalized. He also submits an interview with one of the miners and a statement from a mine official.

Obviously, the fact that the men are safe remains as the lead, but here is fresh material to improve the story. The rewrite man writes three pieces of copy, slugging them MINE—INSERT A, MINE—INSERT B and MINE—ADD 1, as follows:

Jones—MINE—INSERT A

Within a few minutes after their rescue, six of the men were removed in ambulances to Haven Hospital where they were placed under the care of physicians. They will be given specially prepared food and kept in bed, with visitors excluded for the present. Dr. Hugh O. Branson, head of the Wilson Mining Co. medical staff, said none of the 22 men would be allowed to return to work for at least a week.

Jones—MINE—INSERT B

The story the men told of their imprisonment was one of long hours of fear and uncertainty as to their chances for life. Although none was hurt when the walls of the shaft crumbled, they had no idea how many tons of slag had piled up in the passage or how long it would take to reach them.

"We had two shovels and for several hours we took turns digging," said Bert Kominski, foreman of the crew. "Then we gave it up as hopeless. After that the men tried to keep up their spirits by talking. A few prayed. None of us slept.

"We had about given up hope when we heard noises down the shaft and knew that they had found us. We shouted ourselves hoarse and pounded with our shovels to attract attention. It seemed like a century before they broke through finally, but I guess it was only 10 or 15 minutes."

Jones—MINE—ADD 1

R. H. Leeds, superintendent of No. 3 mine, announced that the mine will not be reopened until it is equipped with the latest safety devices to prevent a repetition of the near-tragedy.

"We expect to make a thorough investigation into the causes of the explosion," Leeds said. "Certainly the company will spare no expense to make it safe in the future. All of us, of course, are overjoyed that no lives were lost, but we realize that good fortune was on our side."

During the six months or more that the mine is shut down, Leeds said, its crew of 75 men will be given employment in Wilson No. 1 or No. 2.

Probably Insert A would be placed near the lead and Insert B farther down in the story, while Add 1 would go at the end.

During the hour he waited for the insert and add developments to be phoned in Jones wrote several pages of A-matter from library clips. This, a review of previous mine accidents, began:

Jones—MINE—A-MATTER

The cave-in marked the second such incident at the Wilson mines since No. 1 was opened 12 years ago. A similar accident took the lives of three men in mine No. 2 last April.

When the writer, copyreader, proofreader and compositor completed their work, the story as printed—a combination of old story, new lead, insert, add and A-matter—was blended into smooth, coherent form as

SHORT CUTS IN A
RUNNING STORY

TWENTY-SEVEN

Shoot—H T K......................

~~With a bullet hole in his head, the body of~~
Maurice L. McMahon, manager of the Mc-
Mahon hardware store, 1323 9th St., was
~~found in the rear of the store this morning.~~

Turn Rule for New Lead

The police were notified by Albert Dorr, a
clerk, when he arrived at the store at 7 a.m.
After a preliminary examination, Lt. Raymond
Flynn said he believed McMahon was shot by
holdup men, as the safe swung open on its
hinges. It contained only $3.10.

A .32 automatic pistol with one cartridge
fired lay about five feet from the body. The
gun is being examined for fingerprints.

Turn Rule for Insert A

McMahon, who was 47 years old, lived at
761 Banks St. He was married and the father
of three children, Maurice Jr., 14, Joseph, 10,
and Emma, 7

Mrs. McMahon said her husband went to
the store at 10 o'clock last night, explaining
that he intended to go over some inventory
sheets.

"I was not worried about him because he
sometimes stops at the Elks' Club on 6th street
on the way home and I thought he might have
gone over there," Mrs. McMahon said. She
retired at 11 p.m. and did not miss him until
this morning. She had started to telephone
friends and relatives when she learned from
the police of his death.

Turn Rule for Insert B

McMahon, who had operated the hardware store for the last ten years, was a past
president of the Midland Hardware Dealers
Assn.

How Proof Is Marked

though it had been fashioned by one man at a single sitting. None of the short-cut devices were visible to the average reader in the finished product.

REVISION WITH SPEED

To illustrate further the short-cut devices for catching deadlines let us follow another running story through a PM paper's publication period.

It is 7:50 a.m., ten minutes before the first edition deadline of the Midland *Gazette*, when a police report arrives that employes have found the body of Maurice L. McMahon, manager of the McMahon Hardware Store, 1323 9th St. There is a bullet hole in the right temple. A rewrite man types a 50-word BULLETIN.

Reporters are now dispatched to the store, the McMahon home and the coroner's office. At the home Mrs. McMahon says that her husband went to the store at 10 p.m. to check some inventory sheets. Knowing that he sometimes stopped at the Elks' Club on the way home she was not alarmed when she retired at 11 p.m. and did not miss him until morning. At the store police find a gun near the body and the safe open. They are working on a holdup theory. Meanwhile the coroner removes the body and orders an autopsy. One reporter hears that McMahon was heavily in debt. This is confirmed at the Midland Savings Bank. It is now 11 a.m. and the next deadline is at noon. A rewrite man puts together a half-column story slugged SHOOT.

Already in the composing room is an obit slugged SHOOT—A-MATTER.

At 2 p.m., with a 3 p.m. deadline coming up, police identify the gun as one taken from a display rack at the McMahon store. This development warrants the preparation of SHOOT—INSERT A.

Meanwhile it is learned from the bank that McMahon recently invested $100,000 in an Oklahoma oil company. A wire goes to a correspondent in Oklahoma for information about the concern. At 2:45 p.m. a short dispatch from him states that McMahon lost $100,000 in the concern, which became insolvent three days ago, and that he was subpoenaed to appear in court at the bankruptcy proceedings next Monday. At once the story gets SHOOT—NEW LEAD.

Just before the next deadline at 3 p.m. police report that Mrs. McMahon has found a note from her husband revealing his intention to commit suicide. This calls for a BULLETIN.

While the presses are running, the writer has overhauled the story completely, leading with the disclosure in the note and linking this conclusive suicide angle to other points which have developed during the day. This story is replated. Thus the day's work is completed, leaving little for the morning papers.

SHOP TALK

1. What are deadlines and why are they inflexible? How do morning and afternoon paper deadlines differ?
2. Point out in current newspapers happenings likely to be handled as running stories.
3. Which of these stories might call for bulletins? How is a bulletin written?
4. Show how the following are used in a running story: new lead, add, insert, sub, A-matter.
5. Outline an illustrative running story, tracing developments that would demand each of the news writer's short-cut devices.

CHAPTER **23**

Policy, Crusades and Exposés

VIEWS IN THE NEWS

"So the Mayor says, 'No more ball playing in Island Park,' does he? No wonder the teen-age gangs are running wild in that part of town. There aren't enough playgrounds now. Let's give it a ride—editorial, cartoon, a couple of pictures. Tell one of your reporters to go after it."

Publisher Thomas Putnam of the Midland *Times* was speaking at his daily conference with department heads. A few minutes later the managing editor had an earnest talk with his city desk man who, in turn, gave instructions to Reporter Paul Wilson on the City Hall beat and to a photographer.

Meanwhile, Publisher Frank Fieldstone of the *Herald* had conferred with his own editorial executives. He told them: "Nelson says he's going to put some greenery back in Island Park. Good idea. Give old folks and women with babies a place to relax without dodging baseballs and choking up with dust. Let's give him a pat on the back."

Wilson of the *Times* and Joseph Jacobs of the *Herald,* comparing notes in the City Hall pressroom, discovered they were working on the same story—a follow-up on Mayor Nelson's park-playground decree.

Said Jacobs ruefully: "Your boss is right. My boy, Bobby, plays out there on a Little League team. Now he'll be on my neck every Sunday or get killed playing in the street."

With a wry grin, Wilson replied: "You fellows with kids just want to get rid of them. What about a guy like me? I take my girl walking down there—like to have a bench or two to sit on. We want some place to have peace and quiet. That's what a park's for."

Each out of sympathy with his own publisher but each with a job to do, the two reporters good-naturedly joined forces and worked on the assignment together. Wilson started his story:

Midland's play-starved youngsters, ordered off the sacrosanct east lawn of Island Park by Mayor Nelson, watched with heavy hearts yesterday as workmen replaced their baseball backstops with "Keep Off The Grass" signs.

An accompanying photograph in the *Times* showed a wistful, ragged little boy and his dog disconsolately gazing at a "Keep Off" sign. The caption read: "Evicted By Mayor."

Alongside of a picture of a gardener planting fresh flower beds the *Herald* carried a story by Jacobs which began:

Midlanders seeking an oasis of escape from the city's noise, heat and traffic found it today as grass, flowers and shade trees were restored to the east lawn in Island Park.

Each reporter wrote his story from the point of view of his publisher. In short, he *interpreted* the facts and *slanted* his story in accordance with *policy*—a fact of newspaper life to be recognized and faced philosophically by men who write and edit the news.

POLICY AND THE REPORTER

The student at this point most certainly will recall earlier warnings that a reporter must be accurate and objective, especially that he must not editoralize, that is, he must keep himself out of his report, avoiding words that throw a favorable or unfavorable light on an event.

On its face this is sound advice. Nothing will bring down the wrath of a city editor upon a cub more quickly than for him to inject his own bias into a story. But here an important distinction must be made between editorializing and policy writing. The first—coloring news to fit the *writer's* own personal opinion—is taboo if his opinion does not coincide with that of the publisher. The second—slanting news to fit the *publisher's* point of view—is approved in greater or lesser degree on all newspapers.

It is not long before the observing beginner notes that his paper, no matter how ethical the management, *does* inject its views on certain public questions into its news columns in the style and arrangement of stories as well as in their selection, length and display.

Some subjects are chosen as topics for assignment and some are ignored. Some are given plenty of space and some cut short. Some stories are rewritten to make a policy angle more conspicuous. Some go on the front page under heavy headlines while others land back with the want ads or wind up in the wastebasket—for the sole reason that they do or do not conform to the paper's policy.

It also becomes clear that his paper, if it is a leader in the community, gives space in its news columns generously to the promotion of civic projects, cultural events and charitable campaigns, sometimes engaging in constructive *crusades*. At other times investigative reporters may be assigned to ferret out facts for an *exposé* of corruption, crime or some other condition which the newspaper's management views as venal or evil.

Impressed by these things, the new reporter sometimes decides to introduce policy deliberately into everything he writes, confident he will please his superiors. Often the result is that he picks the wrong stories to slant and by wrenching them out of perspective succeeds only in drawing a reproof from the desk for his well-intentioned efforts.

Finally it dawns upon him that policy affects comparatively few of the day's stories, mainly those dealing with public affairs. He discovers that it is wiser to write straight copy unless he has instructions—expressed, implied or learned by long experience—to angle, and to what degree, specific stories on specific subjects.

Also he learns that even in news reports where policy is purposely pounded there is no falsification of facts. Slanting does not include inaccuracy. No newspaper, however militant, can afford to let policy interfere with the clear and truthful presentation of important news.

ETHICS IN NEWS TREATMENT

We now have stepped into the center of an arena where controversy rages among teachers, authors, publishers, editors, critics and defenders of the press.

You can start an argument among them anywhere—in the classroom, newsroom or living room—over the fighting words *objective* and *interpretive* reporting, news *slanting* and *coloring*, newspaper *policies, platforms, crusades* and *exposés*.

On the one hand it is contended that the obligation of the press is to be strictly objective, to keep its news and editorial columns separate and never to slant news to promote the pet projects or private whims of anybody, including the publisher. Policy writing is regarded from this point of view as something synonymous with propaganda.

On the other hand it is argued that the public demands from a newspaper—and is entitled to—something more than mere parrot-like transmission of bare facts without explanations. This group holds that a newspaper, as a wide-awake community leader, should use its news as well as its editorial columns to stimulate thought, provoke action, expose wrongdoing and promote progress.

Two simple situations will bring into focus the pro and con of the policy issue.

Publisher Putnam of the *Times* is thoroughly convinced that the city administration is corrupt and should be ousted. By slanting City Hall news Putnam believes that the *Times* can serve the community. Should it launch the attack or keep its role of impartial observer?

Again, Putnam looks with favor upon a worthy charitable enterprise, for instance, a drive for funds to aid crippled children at Christmas. The news value of such a drive is scant. Its success hinges upon favorable publicity—a policy which promotes the drive at the expense of other news. Should the *Times* treat the drive as minor news—which it is—and allow children to go hungry?

These are controversial questions. No attempt is made to answer them here or to enter the free-for-all over objectivity, interpretation, policy, slanting or the crusade and exposé issues. This is a textbook on newspaper reporting, not journalism ethics, and its aim is to teach reporters their trade as they find it.

It may be observed, however, that much of the heat in discussions of news treatment is generated by a variation in definitions which, when clarified, bring most newsmen into agreement.

The debate over objective v. interpretive reporting, for instance, dissolves if *objective* is defined as fair and full rather than flat and flimsy and *interpretive* as clear and carefully explained rather than editorializing and moralizing. Good copy, then, is both objective and interpretive.

As for policy writing, the reporter has little voice in the matter anyway for he is a paid craftsman who receives, not gives, orders. His employer, not he, takes the responsibility. He writes what his superiors instruct him to write, in the way they want it written, with as much skill and conviction as he can. If he is unwilling to do so his only alternative is to quit and try to find work on a paper more suited to his tastes. Such revolts seldom occur. Most realistic reporters do not let ideological differences with their employers stand in the way of getting or holding a good job. When assigned to stories they do not like they simply shrug their shoulders and go to work.

CRUSADES, EXPOSÉS AND PLATFORM

The policy of a newspaper is its position on a specific current public issue or its long-range attitude toward a continuing situation. For example, a newspaper's policy may favor a bond issue for schools and oppose a tax increase for a new courthouse; to continue its traditional political independence and its support of foreign aid.

TYPICAL TOPICS IN
NEWSPAPER PLATFORMS

LOCAL

Prevention and punishment of crime.

Management of public schools.

Civic enterprises such as the support of local institutions.

Promotion of better sanitation, housing, parks and playgrounds.

Regulation of public utilities.

REGIONAL

Construction of roads, waterways, airports and other transportation facilities.

Conservation of natural resources and wildlife.

State laws on controversial issues such as capital punishment, divorce and gambling.

Development of industry and agriculture.

Relationships of the community with neighboring communities.

NATIONAL

Governmental taxes and expenditures.

Legislation affecting business, labor and agriculture.

Civil rights and protection of minorities.

Extension of privileges and benefits to special groups.

Preparation for war and attempts to insure peace.

INTERNATIONAL

National sovereignty and world relations.

Forms and operations of other governments.

World trade and commerce.

Military actions affecting other nations.

Advancement of American interests abroad.

Public Policy Issues

Some newspapers set forth their policies in a platform printed under the masthead or at the top of the editorial page. From time to time planks are removed and new ones inserted. A platform may be restricted to local matters or extend to regional, national and world affairs.

A platform representing the principles of a publisher, whether or not put into print, is broad and enduring as contrasted to the more specific and briefer crusade or exposé.

As the words themselves indicate, a crusade is intended to achieve, accomplish or build something regarded as in the public interest—to promote a worthy cause—while an exposé is an investigation and disclosure of a condition, such as malfeasance in office, which is considered against the public interest.

The frequency and vigor of crusades and exposés conducted by newspapers vary widely and depend upon the aggressiveness of management. Broadly speaking, smaller papers are more inclined to crusading, larger ones to exposing. Some publishers and editors are content with moderation and mildness; others are full of fight and fire. Some are fairly satisfied with things as they are; others are almost constantly seeking changes. Some are satisfied with pinpricks; others throw power punches.

Typical campaigns last from a few days to several weeks. Often they take the form of a survey or inquiry resulting in a series of articles printed in installments. Usually they carry the byline of the writer who may or may not be assisted by other staff members.

Typical local crusades concern highway safety, better transit service, jobs for the physically handicapped, smoke abatement, Community Chest and other fund-raising drives, and public improvements such as schools, parks and bridges.

Newspapers themselves sponsor golf, boxing, baseball, bowling and marbles tournaments, soapbox derbies, model plane contests, swimming meets, summer camps, talent and hobby shows, music, drama and art programs and festivals, spelling bees, town meetings, home and fashion shows, cooking and garden contests. All these promotions are properly classified as crusades.

Exposés may be to stop public graft, favoritism or payroll padding; to reveal vote frauds; to uncover the menace of factory firetraps; to clean up streets, beaches, hospitals or restaurants; to uncover vice and crime in all their ramifications.

An exposé may blend into a crusade. For example, a newspaper may first describe slum conditions and then report what other cities are doing about public housing.

The campaign may not necessarily be either supporting a cause or attacking an evil but, rather, explaining a situation or giving both sides of an issue. Series of articles on such questions as school segregation, water fluoridation and fair trade laws may be purely analytical.

Crusades and exposés may follow one another in an almost continuous chain. At the moment, perhaps, the Midland *Times* is firing at a proposed city sales tax and exposing quack doctors. Last month it was campaigning for quick completion of the state turnpike. Next month it will stage a drive for a new municipal auditorium and then try to bring a nuclear energy plant into the city to supply cheaper electricity.

COVERING POLICY ASSIGNMENTS

The Midland *Times* is a wide-awake newspaper with a lively curiosity about everything that involves the welfare of its community. Its reporters investigate everything Publisher Putnam thinks should be exposed, censured or applauded. Hence from time to time orders like these appear on the city room assignment sheet:

> *Home.* Visit the County Home for the Aged. Describe the poor facilities and improper care of inmates. Report on plans for a new building.
>
> *Traffic.* Keep working on series showing need of proposed law for compulsory inspection of automobiles.
>
> *Scouts.* Boy Scout campaign starts tomorrow. Write 50 per cent why public should contribute to fund.
>
> *Lunch.* Keep pushing plan for free lunchrooms in grade schools. Interview Superintendent McClure. Get some teachers and parents to boost the idea.

The foregoing are specific policy assignments. At the outset the wise reporter senses the exact kind of story wanted and he immediately begins to collect data to give it foundation. Like a debater, he has been assigned to one side of the question and he searches for suitable facts to prove it. He selects for prominence data that most fully supports the policy held by his paper.

Reporter Michael McCauley, let us say, receives the County Home assignment. After inspecting the home he interviews Superintendent Follmer, who tells him that conditions are really excellent. Will Follmer's statement be included in the story? Yes, but not as a statement that carries much weight. McCauley will quote copiously from Health Commissioner Flint, who says that conditions are really bad. McCauley will also obtain statistics compiled by the Chamber of Commerce showing how a new building can be financed without heavy drain upon the county treasury, to give authority to the contention of the newspaper that the home needs overhauling.

Observe the way McCauley writes the story as contrasted to the way it was written in the *Herald,* which is satisfied with conditions and supports Follmer:

Times

Crumbling walls, improper ventilation and poor sanitary facilities mark the County Home for the Aged as a "public disgrace."

This was the assertion yesterday of Health Commissioner Charles H. Flint after an inspection of the 50-year-old structure at Highland.

The statement of Dr. Flint added impetus to the movement for a new $50,000 building sponsored by the Midland Chamber of Commerce, which will seek a county appropriation for the purpose.

Supt. E. J. Follmer, insisting there is no need for a new building, called criticism of conditions "rank sentimentalism". . . . .

Herald

The County Home for the Aged at Highland still is in good condition and will be adequate for several years more, Supt. E. J. Follmer declared today. There is no immediate need for a new building, he said.

"All this talk about terrible conditions out here is rank sentimentalism," he asserted.

"No institution in the country is more carefully operated than this one. Of course, the building isn't modern, but it is suitable for its purpose."

Health Commissioner Charles H. Flint, meanwhile, approved the plan of the Midland Chamber of Commerce to ask an appropriation for a new $50,000 building. . . . .

In writing his story, Reporter McCauley followed instructions. He emphasized the facts supporting the assignment but gave the story a cloak of objectivity by presenting the other side, although in a subordinated and abbreviated form.

SLANTING WITHOUT INSTRUCTIONS

Reporters on regular beats which turn up policy news, especially those covering politics and public affairs, automatically slant stories involving issues on which their paper's stand is well known.

Reporter Wilson covers the City Hall beat for the *Times,* which is at odds with the mayor and is seeking to defeat him for reelection. A dispute involving the mayor's attitude toward a pending ordinance arises at a City Council meeting. Familiar with the *Times'* policy, Wilson will, without specific instructions, emphasize the attack upon the mayor and minimize the defense. If the defense has the best of the argument, Wilson may

PLATFORM OF
THE MIDLAND TIMES

FOR MIDLAND

Build a new municipal auditorium.
Modernize Midland airports.
Raise study standards in the public schools.
Stop drunken driving.
Clear out Midland's slum areas.

FOR CENTRALIA

Control Timber River floods and pollution.
Revise the prison parole system.
Abolish the state income tax.
Complete the Centralia Turnpike.
Provide more state parks.

FOR THE UNITED STATES

Treat agriculture on a par with business and labor.
Balance the federal budget.
Preserve our natural resources and wildlife.
Provide for adequate national defense.
Protect the civil rights of minorities.

FOR THE WORLD

Cooperate for world peace but keep our powder dry.
Extend fundamental human liberties to all peoples.
Encourage the international exchange of students.
Cultivate good relations with Pan-American nations.
Eliminate barriers to trade and travel.

What the *Times* Stands For

even bolster up the other side through interviews obtained after the Council session.

Ann Kemp is assigned to cover a Chamber of Commerce luncheon at which the question of a new municipal auditorium arises unexpectedly in extemporaneous talks. Well aware that her paper advocates the project, she automatically leads her story with that development, placing stress on the words of the pro-project speakers.

A drunken driver runs down and kills a child playing in the street. On the same day two other persons, one of them prominent, lose their lives in a spectacular automobile accident. The *Times* is engaged in a campaign for stiffer punishment of drunken drivers. Leo Burke, rewrite man handling a composite accident story, knows how his paper stands on reckless driving. Consequently he centers his verbal batteries on the child's death, keeping the other deaths, despite their greater news value, in a secondary position.

An experienced reporter remembers not only the broad and general policies of his paper but the specific crusades and exposés in which it has been engaged and by logical deduction determines whether to slant a story and how. If in doubt he asks a superior. Closer to the management than the reporter, the city editor guides the latter with such advice as:

"We don't like that racket. Let's hit it."

"The old man says to leave it alone."

"Better play it straight. We haven't taken a position."

"Yes, we had an editorial on that last June. Give it a couple of cheers."

Keeping in mind the Midland *Times* platform and its crusades as mentioned in this chapter, note how the following leads are fashioned so as to slant toward policy:

Firetraps in tenement districts took two more lives yesterday, swelling the tragic toll of flames among the poor to seven this year as the city delayed the slum clearance program.

Failure of the state to stop pollution of the Timber River by upstate industrial plants is again menacing Midland's supply of drinking water.

Illegal parking by motorists on vacant lots in the Greenview Gardens section was blamed yesterday for forcing hundreds of youngsters to play ball in the streets.

In a final appeal for subscriptions to the Midland Boy Scout fund, Walter Simmons, chairman of the Scout finance committee, yesterday stressed the need for more camp facilities.

Will you go hungry on Christmas Day? Scores of children in Midland face that bleak prospect unless you and others give your dollar to the *Times* Christmas Basket fund this year.

THREE STORIES ABOUT "THE CAT"

To illustrate policy treatment further let us compare stories in three newspapers. Just now the management of Paper One is on good terms with the police department. Paper Two regards it as corrupt and inefficient. Paper Three occupies a neutral position.

During the evening and night the following events take place:

1. A gang of bandits held up the owner of the Uptown Pharmacy, one block from a police station. The bandits' car passed the station and disappeared.

2. Sgt. Thomas Naughton, a motorcycle policeman, wounded and captured an automobile thief after an exchange of gunfire.

3. Mrs. John L. Kirk, wife of a businessman, was bound and robbed in her home by a criminal whose activities have startled the city. As usual, he left a calling card inscribed "The Cat."

Here are three incidents, the facts of which are obtained by reporters for three papers. Each man submits his version of the evening's criminal activities in a composite story. Keeping in mind the respective policies, observe the way each paper treats the three crimes:

Paper One

Shooting it out in a running gun battle, Motorcycle Officer Thomas Naughton last night wounded and captured a suspected automobile thief after apprehending him in the act of removing a car from the garage of its owner, Justin E. Burgess, 1826 Douglas Ave.

The man captured gave his name as Luke Larkin of Detroit. With two of Naughton's bullets in his left side, he was taken to St. Mary's Hospital where physicians today said he has little chance to recover.

Riding by the Burgess home on patrol duty near midnight, Officer Naughton noticed Larkin trying to back the machine out of the driveway and drew alongside to investigate. Larkin straightened out the car and sped forward, ignoring the policeman's order to halt. When Naughton followed, he drew a revolver and fired back twice, then sought to outdistance the motorcycle. Naughton returned the fire and a dozen shots were exchanged as the machines raced south on Douglas avenue.

At Adams street the automobile swerved into the curb with Larkin slumped over the wheel in a faint. Naughton took him to the hospital.

"A first-class piece of police work," commented Capt. Hugh O'Malley upon receiving Naughton's report. The officer will receive extra compensation, Captain O'Malley said.

Two other crimes engaged the attention of the police during the evening, one of them another daring holdup by the "Cat" bandit, who entered the home of John L. Kirk, 1470 Harrison Ave., bound and gagged Mrs. Kirk and ransacked the house, escaping with $400 worth of valuables.

Kirk is out of the city and the "Cat" apparently knew Mrs. Kirk was alone. He entered by a dining-room window, accosted her and tied her to a chair. As usual upon his departure he left a card inscribed "The Cat." Mrs. Kirk was released by her son, Walter, when he returned home an hour later.

James Millikin, proprietor of the Uptown Pharmacy, 203 Main St., reported he was robbed by four unmasked men who entered the store just before closing time at 1 a.m. The police were combing the district for the gunmen early this morning.

Paper Two

A stone's throw from the Central Police Station where a dozen policemen warmed their feet at a comfortable stove and played pinochle, four unmasked bandits last night held up the proprietor of the Uptown Pharmacy, 203 Main St., and escaped with the day's receipts.

The police were not aware of the crime until 15 minutes later when the victim roused them with a telephone call. By that time the robbers had disappeared.

James Millikin, the man robbed, said he had dismissed his clerks and was counting his money preparatory to closing up when the four walked in, pretending to be customers. Two of them drew guns and covered him, he said, while the other two rifled the cash register and the safe. They remained in the store 15 or 20 minutes, he estimated.

"I always have felt perfectly safe before because the police station is so near," Millikin said.

At about the same time the drugstore holdup was in progress the "Cat" bandit, whose activities have had the police running in circles for a month, struck again on the North Side. He invaded the home of John L. Kirk of 1470 Harrison Ave. and carried away jewelry valued at $400, after binding and gagging Mrs. Kirk. Hours later a half dozen detective bureau squads were searching for him in vain. Their only clue was the usual calling card bearing the words "The Cat," left by the bandit on Mrs. Kirk's dressing table.

Earlier in the evening, Sgt. Thomas Naughton, a motorcycle officer, shot and wounded an alleged automobile thief, identified as Luke Larkin of Detroit, after he had removed a car from the garage of Justin E. Burgess, 1826 Douglas Ave. Larkin was taken to St. Mary's Hospital, where his condition is serious.

Paper Three

In the same stealthy, feline fashion that he has entered a dozen North Side homes recently, the "Cat" bandit, whose depredations have terrorized the women of that district and baffled the police, last night entered the home of John L. Kirk, 1470 Harrison Ave., bound and gagged Mrs. Kirk and ransacked the house.

As customary he left his neatly lettered card inscribed "The Cat." It was found on the dressing table in Mrs. Kirk's bedroom.

The "Cat" apparently had prowled around the Kirk home until he made certain Mrs. Kirk was alone and then slipped through a dining-room window. Silently he made his way into the living room and confronted his victim as she was reading a newspaper. Before she could scream, he seized her and clamped his hand over her mouth. After gagging her with a handkerchief and tying her in the chair, he warned her not to move and proceeded to go through the house. He took about $400 worth of jewelry.

Mrs. Kirk was not released until an hour later when her son Walter, 20 years old, came home. He called the police. The elder Kirk is in the East on a business trip.

Mrs. Kirk's description of the "Cat" tallied in every particular with descriptions given by his other victims, most of them women. He is a slim youth, 22 to 23 years old, and dark-haired. He wears a cap, a mask and gloves.

"He nearly frightened me to death," Mrs. Kirk told the police. "I was sitting there reading and suddenly I realized someone was standing in front of me. He had a knife and warned me to keep quiet. I would have screamed anyway, but he seized and gagged me.

"'I'm not going to hurt you,' he said, 'unless you try to get loose.' Then he went through the house. I could hear him walking upstairs for a few minutes. He came into the living room again, looked at me and slipped out. That was the last I saw of him."

Six detective bureau squad cars early this morning were cruising the North Side looking for the "Cat." Fingerprint experts meanwhile searched the house. They found only glove marks.

Last night's raid by the "Cat" was his second this week. Tuesday night he burglarized two apartments at 2003 E. 17th St. while their occupants were at theaters. He had left his card after four other holdups of women in their homes.

Another crime which kept the police on the jump last night was a holdup by a gang of four men who took $350 from James Millikin, proprietor of the Uptown Pharmacy, 203 Main St. Walking into the store while Millikin was alone, two of the robbers threatened him with revolvers, while the other two removed the contents of the safe and cash register.

An alleged automobile thief, identified as Luke Larkin of Detroit, was in serious condition at St. Mary's Hospital this morning following a shooting affray with Sgt. Thomas Naughton, a motorcycle officer, who wounded and captured him after he attempted to escape with a car belonging to Justin E. Burgess, 1826 Douglas Ave. Sergeant Naughton and Larkin shot it out in a running battle along Douglas avenue, two of the policeman's bullets taking effect. Capt. Hugh O'Malley promised extra compensation for Sergeant Naughton.

How well each writer carried out the policy of his paper may be readily demonstrated in the three specimens printed. Presenting the same set of facts, Paper One emphasized the episode reflecting credit upon the police department. Paper Two presented facts disparaging to the department and the neutral Paper Three made the most of the "Cat" affair, obviously outweighing the other two events in news value.

Once more the distinction between accuracy and impartiality needs to be emphasized. As the examples of policy stories show, the reporter in each case has presented unimpeachable facts. At the same time he has arranged those facts with a decidedly partisan bias, intending to cause the reader to draw a desired conclusion.

The secret of policy writing does not lie in open argumentation but rather in selectivity, arrangement and inference. First the reporter uses discrimination in obtaining his material. He seizes and develops facts and statements that will sustain the view of his paper, balancing those facts against others that seem to contradict it. Next he emphasizes in the lead the strongest and most significant aspects of the favorable evidence, subordinating but not omitting less favorable evidence. And finally he chooses his words with care so that the reader is encouraged to draw certain conclusions from the premises outlined in the story.

SHOP TALK

1. What is newspaper policy? Point out public questions in your community upon which a newspaper might establish policies.
2. Differentiate between editorializing and slanting the policy story.
3. Debate the ethics of policy writing. If you were a publisher and aware of an epidemic in a city where a convention was in progress, would you publish the facts?
4. Should a newspaper give special prominence to a story concerning, for example, a Christmas basket program because the publisher believes it worthy?
5. If you were a reporter assigned to a policy story in conflict with your own views, how would you proceed?

CHAPTER 24

Sports from the Press Box

NEWS FOR MEN AND WOMEN

The aim of this textbook is to teach apprentice reporters basic methods of covering and writing the news to which they are most likely to be assigned in the first few months of their careers.

We are not warranted, therefore, in studying comics, pictures, editorials, commentary columns and other such specialties except insofar as they touch the work of the young local staff reporter. Nor should we discuss in any detail departmentalized news of antiques, art, automobiles, aviation, books, education, farming, finance, gardening, hobbies, movies, music, pets, photography, radio and television, real estate, religion, science, shipping, stamps, theater, travel and resorts.

However, there are two classifications of departmentalized news so strong in appeal that they appear in every newspaper, large and small. Frequently they show up on the local room assignment sheet and move from their own pages into the general news of the day. These are sports and news for women, especially society. This chapter and the next are devoted to them.

Surveys show that 80 to 90 per cent of male readers are sports followers while 75 per cent of the feminine readers turn to the women's pages. Nearly half the women take some interest in sports while one-third of the men run through the sections for women. No other kinds of specialty news attract anywhere near such volumes of reader interest.

Critics of the press often deplore the heavy coverage of athletics and look with slightly less disfavor on the space devoted to accounts of weddings, society chitchat and recipes. Circulation and advertising figures supply the answer. Such news means more readers and revenue.

Customarily sports are reported by men and women's activities by women. But it is not at all uncommon, especially on the smaller papers, for these sex lines to be crossed. A well-trained woman reporter should be able to cover a baseball game competently while a man should be ready at any time to handle a wedding.

THE FIGHT'S THE THING

The powerful news element in stories of physical prowess is conflict and, to a lesser degree, drama and emotions. Any contest or struggle exerts a magnetic pull, especially on men.

All people—men, women and children—live in two worlds. One is a world of fantasy or make-believe and the other a world of reality. In his world of fantasy a man inevitably identifies himself with combat. He imagines himself a combination of Sir Galahad, Robin Hood and Daniel Boone—a fighter crafty in strategy, daring in defense, valorous in attack, always victorious against the odds—in short, a hero.

In primitive life men were the warriors and hunters, and our modern sports are merely new versions, refined through the ages, of the earlier and bloodier encounters. Baseball, for example, is throwing as with a rock, hitting as with a stick and running as from a pursuing enemy. Hunting and fishing have changed but little since prehistoric times.

A man therefore has no trouble as he reads in projecting himself into the role of star hurler, home run hitter, canny captain, broken-field runner, knockout king, triumphant jockey, crack marksman or prize-winning fisherman—a courageous challenger and coolheaded champion.

In every instance the fight's the thing in sports, and Americans are sports-loving people. Thousands throng the gridirons, diamonds, links, tracks and rings to witness contests of strength and skill. They are but a handful compared to the millions, many of whom never have witnessed the sports they read about, who vicariously participate via the newspapers, radio and television. The fact that some sports are amateur and others professional seems to make no difference to readers or editors. Pro baseball, basketball, horse racing, football and hockey are big business but the taboo against free publicity for money-making enterprises is steamrollered in the sports columns by the demands of avid rooters, hot-stove league experts and Monday morning quarterbacks.

Suspense and emotions more than conflict engage the interest of many women in sports. Plenty of the booing is soprano. Her chrysanthemum and fur coat or her date at the homecoming prom may concern her more, but a coed will scream just as excitedly as her escort when the home team reaches the one-yard line with a minute left to play. And she will look for her alma mater's score on the sports pages as long as she lives.

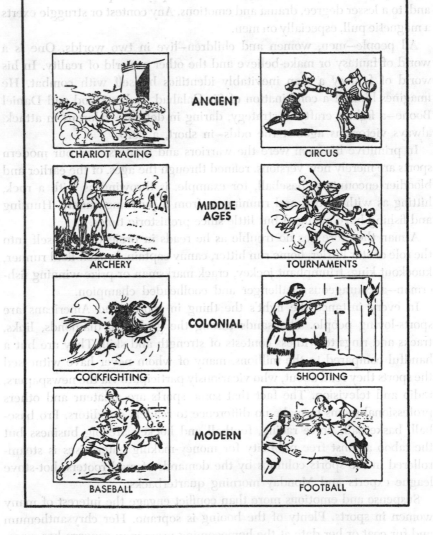

THE POPULAR PULL OF
SPORTS IN HISTORY

ANCIENT — CHARIOT RACING — CIRCUS

MIDDLE AGES — ARCHERY — TOURNAMENTS

COLONIAL — COCKFIGHTING — SHOOTING

MODERN — BASEBALL — FOOTBALL

The Fight's the Thing

SPORTS THAT MAKE NEWS

Sports are divided roughly into two groups, participant and spectator. Although the former, such as fishing, hunting, bowling, golf, swimming and roller skating provide exercise and fun to vast numbers of people, they occupy little newspaper space as compared to spectator sports, such as football, baseball, boxing and horse racing, in which a few participate and many watch.

The great American spectator sports are baseball in the spring and summer, football in the fall and winter and basketball in the winter and spring. These consume more newspaper acreage than all the others combined. They demand skilled and speedy coverage, especially in the afternoon papers, but more and more in the morning papers as night events increase.

Sports that make news are so many and so varied that even a complete enumeration is impractical. In all the following there are official champions:

Archery	Dogs	Rodeos
Auto racing	Fencing	Rowing
Badminton	Football	Shooting
Baseball	Golf	Skiing
Basketball	Gymnastics	Soccer
Billiards	Handball	Softball
Bobsledding	Harness racing	Squash racquets
Bowling	Hockey	Squash tennis
Boxing	Horse racing	Swimming
Canoeing	Horse shows	Table tennis
Casting	Horseshoe pitching	Tennis
Checkers	Ice skating	Track and field
Chess	Lacrosse	Volleyball
Court tennis	Lawn bowling	Water polo
Cross-country	Motorboating	Weight lifting
Curling	Polo	Wrestling
Cycling	Racquets	Yachting

Special branches of sports writing are the hunting, fishing and boating columns, usually headed by some such title as *Rod and Gun, Hooks and Bullets, Afield and Afloat, Fur and Fin, Wood, Field and Stream* or *Nautical Notes,* and the outdoor and wildlife columns appealing to campers, trappers, canoeists, hikers, photographers, bird watchers, Boy and Girl Scouts, botanists and other nature lovers.

By reason of climate or custom, certain sports are more popular in one region or another. Hockey, ice skating, skiing and other winter sports are concentrated in the North, golf, boating, swimming and skin-diving in the

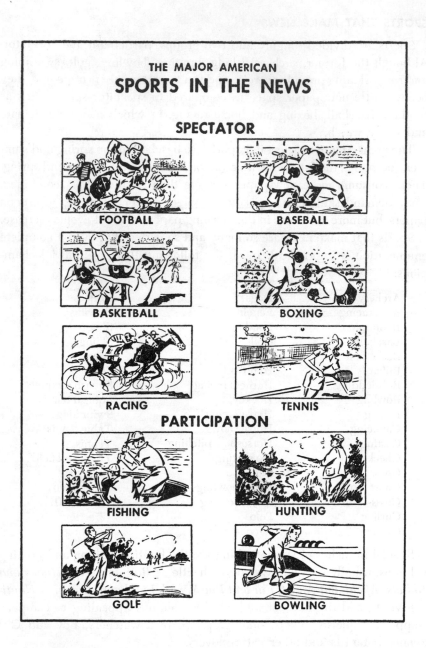

THE MAJOR AMERICAN
SPORTS IN THE NEWS

SPECTATOR

FOOTBALL

BASEBALL

BASKETBALL

BOXING

RACING

TENNIS

PARTICIPATION

FISHING

HUNTING

GOLF

BOWLING

Sports Page Leaders

South. Rodeos draw crowds in the West and Southwest while soccer and rowing indicate the European influence in the East. Jai alai from Cuba has taken hold in Florida.

A comparatively new sport, basketball, spread like wildfire through the Midwest and now has invaded all sections of the country while major league baseball has extended to the Pacific coast.

The popularity and newspaper coverage of sports change with the times. Professional wrestling, in recent years, has come to be regarded as entertainment rather than a true sport. Harness racing, once a county fair feature, has become a nighttime attraction in the big cities. Despite the fact that its basic lure is betting, it wins space on the sports pages.

How has television affected the sports pages? The answer is—not much. When radio came on the scene and began to broadcast boxing, baseball and horse racing, some sports editors feared the competition as they did TV later on. They did not fully understand the nature of news.

Radio and TV have made millions of new fans, especially women, who want to read about as well as see and hear about sports as they do about any other personally interesting news. For the same reason that you are eager to read about the wedding or game you attended so you want to read about the event you saw on your TV screen.

How did the experts see the touchdown play? What caused the rhubarb? Who is the favorite in tonight's fight? Radio and TV help to raise the questions. Newspapers answer them.

We shall discuss the interrelation of the news media more fully in our final chapter. It is sufficient to note here that they complement and boost one another.

WHO ARE THE SPORTS WRITERS?

The size and makeup of the sports reportorial staff depend largely on the circulation of the paper. Metropolitan dailies maintain well-manned sports departments which constitute separate news-handling units with as many as a score of writers, their own editors and copyreaders. Medium-sized papers like the Midland *Times* employ two or three regular sports reporters, one usually serving as editor. In smaller towns the general assignment and school men cover local sporting events in connection with their other duties.

During recent decades sports news coverage has expanded steadily and the tendency is toward special departments and heavier use of wire copy and pictures.

Highly specialized sports stories in the larger papers are handled by experts with background and training analogous to that required for expert financial or political reporting.

However, the apprentice on medium- and small-sized papers must expect to be assigned to sports events at any time, especially on weekends when the regular writers are crowded. Almost the entire local staff may be tied up on a November Saturday afternoon when collegiate and scholastic football games become major news.

A beginner is expected to handle routine contests with accuracy and skill. Certainly he needs to know how to score football, baseball and basketball games. Even a copy boy is expected to know a lateral pass from a field goal, a strike-out from an inning, a jump ball from a personal foul.

It looks easy but it isn't. Everybody, it seems, envies a reporter at a sporting event. He carries a pass, occupies a front-row, ringside or press box seat, invades the dressing rooms, hobnobs with stars and coaches and knows all the dope. Even among newsmen the feeling persists that sports writing is a cinch. Imagine being paid for going to a ball game! Think of bylining a few big football games in the fall, mooching off a baseball team in the summer and turning in whacking big expense accounts just for having fun!

Sports coverage and writing have their woes and problems exactly like any other news work—odd working hours, nerve-straining deadlines and the drudgery of statistical tabulation.

Others are in the stands for the fun of it. The writer is there to work at his trade. He dares not relax for long. He must be constantly on the watch and simultaneously keep scores, take notes on plays or write.

Experience soon teaches the beginner that he must discount the crowd—except to get an accurate count—forget the excitement and keep his attention frozen on his business. He is expected to extract not thrills but cold facts. When the spectators roar he must remain calmly methodical. A press box is not a cheering section; it is a workroom. When the game is at an end and the desk is demanding a story, hullabaloo produces little copy.

While the writer's range of observation must necessarily include the crowd and the spirit of the occasion to give his report atmosphere and color, it requires, first of all, factual data in orderly array.

He does not take sides nor does he cross over the bounds of fair comment into criticisms of personal reputation or conduct, thereby forfeiting his legal protection. Newspapers have been sued because a writer said a player muffed because of worry over his wife's infidelity.

FINDING OUT THE FACTS

"Want to go out to the ball game this afternoon?" That casual question from a city desk man may be the introduction of an apprentice reporter to sports writing.

Too often the assignment is given as a sort of holiday trip—a reward for duller labors—and happily accepted as such by a beginner. Like Conway, the cub at the train wreck, he finds out to his sorrow that breezy descriptions of crowds and cheers don't make a story. He needs hard facts, cold figures and a clear style.

His best advice is to cover the event exactly as he would a fire, wreck, speech or funeral. The reliable five *W's* and the inverted pyramid are safe guides to at least reasonable success.

Unless he is familiar with the participants and the immediate background of the contest, the reporter has a preliminary mission to the morgue to read up on them. There and at the scene he needs to acquire the following factual information:

1. *The score or outcome.* Who won? That, of course, is the crux of the game. Should it end in a tie score, a riot or be called off on account of rain, the outcome is always important.

2. *Significance of the outcome.* Was the championship at stake? Do team standings change? Who gets the cup? Is a grudge wiped out?

3. *Spectacular plays.* Tell about the last-minute fumble, the three-bagger that won the game or the basket from mid-court.

4. *Comparison of the teams.* How did the weights compare? Were the visitors better trained? In what departments of the game did the winners excel? Where were the losers weak?

5. *Individual stars.* Who were the stars and how did they star? Was the pitcher steady or the right halfback extraordinarily speedy?

6. *Weather conditions, if outdoor.* Mud, sunshine, heat, cold or wind may be important.

7. *Crowd and celebration.* Don't forget the spectators. Was it a record crowd? How did the spectators behave?

In addition to these basic points applicable to all sports the reporter may need to gather certain statistics and present them as a part of the story. We will illustrate these shortly. At the start the neophyte can do no better than imitate those printed previously.

PIECING THE STORY TOGETHER

With accurate and adequate notes covering the seven points the reporter is prepared to build an intelligent, if not brilliant, story. There follows a standard account of a game. Thousands like it have been written

and thousands more will be turned out. Watch how the seven points are
built into the story structure:

(1)

With Harry Sullivan, rookie southpaw from Dallas, pitching almost hit-
less ball, the Midland Blue Sox downed the Booneville Boosters by a score
of 7–1 at Midland Field yesterday.

(2)

The victory gave the Sox a clean sweep of the four-game series and they
will go on the road tomorrow safely berthed in second place in the Timber Valley League. Friday they will bump into the league-leading Capital
City Oilers for the first of three games. Two out of three would put the
Sox on top of the heap.

(3)

The Midlanders knocked the bottom out of the contest in the seventh
frame by scoring five runs, making the count 5–0. With two on base, Kerr
lifted a homer into the left bleachers. A double steal of third and second
by Kribs and Hoffman and a three-bagger by Byrne in the seventh accounted for the other two runs.

(4) (5)

Crippled by the loss of Grimes and Williams, their two heaviest sluggers,
both laid up with injuries, the Boosters were completely at Sullivan's mercy.
For eight innings he baffled them. In the ninth, under the protection of a
seven-run lead, he eased up and Booneville slipped over one run, its lone
tally of the game.

For the first six innings neither nine got a man farther than second. Then,
in the seventh, the Sox went on their rampage, hammering Connelly (details of game). . . . .

(6) (7)

The game was played under almost perfect weather conditions which
brought out the biggest attendance of the season. It was Ladies' Day and
3,000 spectators, half of them women, filled the grandstands to capacity.

Apply the observation test again but notice how the essentials, although
unchanged, have combined and shifted position:

(1) (2) (5)

Dick Cook's field goal in the last two minutes enabled Midland College
to beat Larchmont at Shield Gymnasium last night, 31–29, and extend the
Purple winning streak to five in a row.

(3)

With the score knotted at 29–29, the former Meadville High star drib-
bled through the Leopards' defense and sank a field goal after the hard-
fighting Midland forwards had staged a rally in the last half.

(4)

An airtight Larchmont defense, its strongest asset in previous games, crumbled under the fast attack of Red Stone and Garry Holly after the Leopards led at the half 20–16.

(7)

Six hundred enthusiastic Purple supporters staged a parade through the downtown section in celebration of their victory. . . . .

HOW TO WRITE THE LEAD

Among his seven essential points the writer has a choice of one or several facts for his lead. When in doubt it usually is safest to play the score, or at least include it, in the lead. Four times out of five the outcome is the nub of the story, although any combination of the seven points may be used to bring the most spectacular to the top, as in these examples:

(2) (1) (7)

Ridge Normal's league-leading basketball team scored its eighth victory in 10 starts last night by overwhelming the University of Centralia, 43–20, before 1,500 fans in the Redskin gymnasium.

(1) (7)

Five records were broken in one of the best-attended track meets of the local indoor season in the seventh annual renewal of the Midland Public School League meet at Memorial Stadium today. More than 1,700 watched the contests.

(5) (1) (2)

Harry Sachs, the Timber Valley League's champion batsman last season, found the range at Midland Field today and slugged the Larchmont Lucifers to a 5–2 victory over the Blue Sox, squaring their two-game series.

(3) (5) (1) (2)

Running 52 yards for a touchdown three minutes before the final gun, Johnny Ripley gave Larchmont College a 7–6 victory over its ancient rival, Holbrook, at Harrison Field yesterday.

(6) (5) (1)

On a bleak battleground the touring golf professionals began their last stand of the winter today in the Hillsdale Open with veteran George Croft and young Allen Lister leading the way through the first 18 holes with 69s.

Action verbs add strength to any news lead and in none are they so valuable as in the sports story opener. By its nature the account of an athletic contest is one of motion.

While there is nothing wrong with the solid words *won,* *beat* and *defeated,* there are a thousand and one variations such as pummeled, trounced, licked, sank, whacked, nipped, wiped out, downed, blasted, thrashed, overwhelmed, shellacked, subdued, edged out, trimmed, polished off, set back, stopped, outdistanced, toppled, walloped, whipped, torpedoed, upset, overpowered, swamped, outlasted, trampled on, dumped, belted, outplayed.

Here are a few phrases taken at random from sports story leads to illustrate the value of action verbs:

clicked off pars like clockwork	snapped a 10-game winning streak
broke a 14–14 deadlock	racked up a 5–4 victory
ran and passed to a 42–13 triumph	cracked a stubborn defense
exerted a steady last-half drive	tugged to a 1–1 tie
turned back the favorites 57–53	blasted his way into the finals
survived a stretch duel	nipped their traditional rivals
led from flagpole to wire	took its worst whipping
kept their perch atop the league	stroked a magic putter to card
scored a major upset	slammed out a 5-under-par 66
remained in the undefeated ranks	ran a front race from gun to tape
waged a terrific uphill struggle	romped to its third straight win

Your lead is likely to pass muster if you report the outcome of the contest in words that move. But don't overdo, either. It is far better to say simply that Sam Sanduski won a 10-round decision over Herman Hopper last night at Sportsman's Arena than to gush forth with:

> Sam Sanduski, the coming glove artist from Timberton's Cauliflower Alley, had the roar of the crowd in his ears—the roar the fans give for a champion—as he waltzed through 10 rounds with the precision of a veteran ringmaster to take a well-earned unanimous decision of two judges and the referee over Herman Hopper, the hope of Holbrook, at Sportsman's Arena last night.

SPORTS SLANG AND VERNACULAR

The sports writer, like a drama or music critic, enjoys comparative freedom as a free-swinging stylist. While his primary obligation is to make himself clearly understood by his readers, there are several sound reasons why he must venture into vernacular more picturesque than his colleagues writing other types of news.

First, conflict—the main news element in sports—is synonymous with fast-moving action as contrasted to the consequence element in the account of, say, a medical discovery or plans for a new building.

Second, the audience of the sports writer, while a large bloc, still is a segment which divides into smaller segments of readers, each regarding himself as somewhat of an expert acquainted with the jargon of a fan.

Finally, whereas other beat and special assignment men like police or courthouse reporters don't have to write anything unless something happens, the sports writer has to turn out copy daily. One game is much the same as another. Stories about a half dozen printed on the same page would be dull indeed if all were cut in the same pattern.

Does the sports writer revel in slang? He certainly does. But here once more close scrutiny dispels the popular belief that the sports page is a hodgepodge of trite, vulgar and cheap-Jack expressions meaningless to the uninitiated. Only in a story produced by an amateur will you find such silly symphonies as these:

banged the apple	lammed the pill
booted the pigskin	scorched the cinders
caged the spheroid	split the ozone

Worn-out slang and breezy colloquialisms belong to quite different families. It has become wearisome to call a home run a *circuit clout, round tripper* or *fence-topper;* basketball players *knights of the waxed courts* or *casaba artists;* a crowd the *faithful, rabid rooters* or *cash customers* who *witnessed the proceedings.*

To continually call football a *grid game,* basketball a *dribble derby,* a game a *tilt* or a *tiff,* a team an *outfit* or *machine,* a diamond a *pasture,* a goal a *bucket,* a hit a *bingle,* an error a *bobble,* and so on becomes as foolish as always describing a sports reporter or writer as a *scribe.*

However, there is touch and go in the statement that "the southpaw pitched airtight ball," whereas "the left-handed pitcher threw the ball so well that his opponents were unable to strike it" is laborious and flavorless. "A hard uppercut to the jaw and a left hook to the belt line" is certainly preferable to "a severe blow administered to the face and another, with the left hand, to the region of the stomach."

Such phrases as *struck out, kicked goal, won the toss, a birdie, a love set* and *knockout* clarify rather than corrupt sports writing. They are in fact perfectly proper terms used for explicit situations.

And certainly a racing writer can expect his readers to know what he is talking about when he uses terms like *across the board, daily double, going away* and *tote board.* Indeed to interpret them in his copy would be a waste of words and a theft of space.

To call a rhubarb a rhubarb is just as sound as calling a spade a spade. You don't have to tell sports fans that it is a misunderstanding on the diamond in which the umpire and one or more players engage in a verbal or physical contest. Certainly it is as legitimate for the sports writer to mention the catbird seat as for the financial reporter to mention fiduciary returns and the music critic prestissimo and adagio.

The conclusion is that sports writers can and should be both clear and colorful, factual and fresh, right and racy.

FROM THE LEAD DOWN

We have seen how the seven-point formula is applied to the structure of a brief account of a sports event. Assuming that he has a column or more to fill, how does the writer proceed?

For assistance we may fall back on the diagram of the action story illustrated in Chapter 9. Although the writer needs to cover most if not all of the seven points in the fore part of his story, he may safely follow the tell-retell diagram as he lengthens his copy.

Note how the diagram is applied to the following account of a football game:

Lead—Incident Told

An 11th-hour field goal by Fairmount's fighting Teachers today broke a 14–14 deadlock with the Midland Panthers and gave the visitors their first victory over the local eleven in three years.

Retold—More Detail

With one minute and 45 seconds left to play, the adroit toe of Fairmount's Ken Kruger kicked the ball 29 yards between the uprights to produce a thrilling 17–14 margin in a contest that was tied in the third period.

An all-time record crowd of 12,854 watched the 21st annual battle at Midland Stadium in chill, gray weather.

Retold—More Detail

Most of the spectacular play was concentrated in the pyrotechnical third period. The two teams, with Midland a seven-point choice, boxed each other around inconclusively during the opening quarter. The Panthers scored first in the second period and held their 7–0 margin to half time.

In the middle of the third quarter, however, Jack Jefferson's backfield struck back, tying the score, and three minutes later they counted again. But before the period ended the Purple men reasserted themselves, establishing the tie.

Spectators already were leaving their seats as the tie held to the closing moments of the game. A fumble gave Fairmount the ball on its own 30. Three line plunges gained only a yard. Then came Kruger's boot.

Retold—More Detail

During the first period the ball remained in mid-field for a full five minutes before a Midland punt sent it soaring. . . . .

The writer has now begun all over again and, closely following his notes, he chronicles the game period by period and play by play in narrative form. From time to time he weaves in references to the crowd, the weather, individual stars and spectacular plays. But in the main the re-telling is chronological.

Once the story is charted in this fashion it is fairly simple to estimate space by quarters and to write accordingly. It is necessary only to leave space for the statistical summaries if they are to be included in the story proper.

STATISTICS IN SPORTS

A surprising amount of sports writing is nothing more or less than bookkeeping. Box scores must balance, league standings must check, the hitting averages must be up-to-date. Metropolitan sports pages are clut-tered with figures representing averages, percentages, breakdowns and assorted totals. So important are mathematics in sports that the larger papers employ special men whose job it is to tabulate these ciphers and digits.

As a means of economizing on space, certain standard devices for listing players and scores are universally used and should become familiar to the sports reporter. These forms include lineups of players, box scores and score summaries.

The baseball box score tells the whole story in a fraction of the space re-quired for a full account. If space is scant, a single paragraph lead and the box score will cover the game. A box score follows:

LARCHMONT								CLAY CITY						
	AB	R	H	O	A	E			AB	R	H	O	A	E
Messenger, 1b	4	0	1	10	1	0	Savage, 2b ...	3	1	0	1	0	1
Brayman, 2b .	4	0	2	2	4	0	Orr, rf	4	0	1	4	0	0
Tripp, cf	4	0	1	2	0	0	Winkler, lf ...	2	0	1	0	0	0
Groves, rf	4	0	0	1	0	0	Reid, cf	4	1	1	6	0	0
Lacy, lf	4	0	1	1	0	0	Martin, 1b ...	3	0	2	10	2	1
Goldman, 3b .	4	0	2	1	0	1	Murphy, ss ...	4	0	2	2	4	0
Ramsdell, ss ..	3	0	0	5	5	0	Olson, 3b	3	0	0	0	1	0
Trueheart, c ..	2	0	0	3	0	0	Schaefer, c ...	3	0	0	3	2	0
Sherman, p ...	2	0	0	0	4	0	Kenmore, p ...	3	0	2	1	0	0
Lord, p	0	0	0	0	0	0							
Parks, c	1	0	0	0	1	0							
xHanson	1	0	0	0	0	0							
Totals	33	0	7	25	15	1		29	2	9	27	9	2

xBatted for Sherman in 8th.

Score by innings:

Larchmont	0 0 0	0 0 0	0 0 0—0
Clay City	1 0 1	0 0 0	0 0 x—2

RBI—Murphy, Reid. 2B—Murphy, Martin. S—Ramsdell, Winkler. DP—
Brayman, Ramsdell and Messenger 2; Ramsdell and Trueheart. Left—Larch-
mont 7, Clay City 7. BB—Sherman 2, Lord 2. SO—Kenmore 4, Sherman 1.
HO—Sherman 8 in 7; Lord 1 in 3; Kenmore 7 in 9. R-ER—Sherman 2. WP—
Kenmore. W—Kenmore (8–2). L—Sherman (3–2). U—Cranston and Mayer.
T—2:32. A—3, 618.

A typical basketball lineup and summary follow:

MIDLAND	G	F	P	T	JUNIPER	G	F	P	T
Ruffner, f	5	3	2	13	Burbank, f	5	2	2	12
Lovelace, f	0	0	1	0	Kitchner, f	1	1	0	3
Riggs, c	5	2	2	12	Walters, f	1	0	0	2
Davis, c	3	0	0	6	Marks, f	2	1	0	5
Smith, g	6	6	1	18	Swanson, c	4	3	2	11
Timkin, g	2	1	0	5	Ames, g	1	0	0	2
Rich, g	1	2	0	4	Schultz, g	4	1	1	9
Powers	0	0	0	0	Walker, g	0	6	0	6
Lewis	1	0	0	2	Turner	0	1	0	1
					Marshall	1	0	0	2
Totals	23	14	6	60		19	15	5	53

Referee—Ross. Umpire—Young.

Similar summaries, not used so universally, can be devised for any kind
of athletic event. This short cut deals with a series of gymnastic contests:

> *Horizontal Bar*—Won by Waltham, St. Anthony's, 565; Jones, Midland,
> second, 527; Mullins, Ridge, third, 485; Frank, Fairmount, fourth, 450.
> *Side Horse*—Won by Hull, St. Anthony's, 554; Kincaid, Midland, sec-
> ond, 541; tie for third between Simms, Midland, and Waltham, St. An-
> thony's, 514.
> *Parallel Bars*—Won by Burton, Midland, 551; Frank, Fairmount, sec-
> ond, 506; Waltham, St. Anthony's, third, 504; tie for fourth between
> Arden, Larchmont, and Reid, St. Anthony's, 498.
> *Flying Rings*—Won by Tyler, St. Anthony's, 578; Lutz, St. Anthony's,
> second, 572; Harmon, Larchmont, third, 569; Bruno, Fairmount, fourth,
> 551.
> *Tumbling*—Won by Starr, Fairmount, 592; Arden, Larchmont, second,
> 589; Ives, Holbrook, third, 536; Mullins, Ridge, fourth, 517.

The sports-writing apprentice will rarely cover such sports as horse
racing or major golf tournaments, where expert knowledge and treatment
is demanded. He may be assigned to a minor football game but the important contests and the bowl games will go to a topnotch reporter. However,
such sports as track, bowling and swimming are very likely to be his prov-
ing grounds. The following is a typical summary of a college track meet:

100-yard—1. Sam Denton, Holbrook. 2. Sal Parilli, St. Anthony's. 3. Mark Sloan, Midland. :9.8.

440-yard—1. Cliff Baker, Fairmount Teachers. 2. Mike O'Donnell, St. Anthony's. 3. Luther Kraus, Midland. :49.6.

880-yard—1. Duane Davis, Fairmount Teachers. 2. Guy Henderson, Midland. 3. Kyle Bonney, Larchmont. 1:59.

Mile—1. Kevin O'Shea, St. Anthony's. 2. Jepson Robinson, Fairmount Teachers. 3. Ed Ringley, Holbrook. 4:11.

High Jump—1. Leo Speaker, Midland. 2. Bart Diamond, Larchmont. 3. Frank Silvers, Fairmount Teachers, 6 ft. 3 in.

Broad Jump—1. Sal Parilli, St. Anthony's. 2. Sam Denton, Holbrook. 3. Mark Sloan, Midland. 23 ft. 8 in.

Various other devices for condensation may be clipped from the sports pages and used as models for practice. These include tables to show league standings, the compilation of which requires only the inspection of a standard form, coupled with arithmetic.

RUNNING STORIES OF SPORTS

Since most outdoor sporting contests take place in the afternoon, reporters for PM papers are called upon to write running accounts. Morning paper men do the same in covering evening events. Where the utmost speed is demanded, the press box expert dictates detail after detail over the telephone or gives the copy, page by page, to a telegraph operator.

The technique of handling running accounts for the more common contests is well established and easily learned. Before he leaves the office or in the press box before the start of the game or match the writer produces a brief *bunk* or throwaway lead which indicates the game has started and may contain a few lines about the crowd or weather. Examples:

Morton Mercer sought his third straight victory this afternoon as the league-leading Blue Sox met the Capital Oilers in the opener of a two-game series at Midland Field.

Two thousand fans were in the stands at game time on a warm, sunny day.

With the championship of the Centralia Conference at stake, the Purple Panthers met Fairmount's Terrible Teachers at Midland Stadium today in the final game of the season.

Slugger and boxer collided tonight as Kid O'Hara, with a record of five straight knockouts, pitted his fists against the fast footwork of Micky Malloy in a heavyweight 10-rounder at Sportsman's Arena.

From the scene the reporter, or perhaps an assistant if he has one, phones or files the running account divided into periods as follows:

BASEBALL—INNINGS

First Inning

SOX—Sullivan walked. Kerr hit into a fast double play, Lance to Peters to Graham. Hoffman flied to Pitts. No runs, no hits.

OILERS—Mercer grounded out to Larson. Lance was hit by a pitched ball. Kerr threw out Pitts. Peters lifted to Hoffman. No runs, no hits.

Second Inning

SOX—Simms was called out on strikes. Mercer threw out Arden. Larson singled to center. Walker flied to Blake. No runs, one hit.

OILERS—Blake walked. Stone singled and Blake went to third. Larson made a nice stop of Graham's grounder to retire him, Blake scoring. Garner walked. Kerr tossed out Banks. Mercer flied to Arden. One run, one hit.

FOOTBALL—QUARTERS

SECOND QUARTER—Davis kicked off to Martin who returned 32 yards. Watts plunged three yards through left tackle. Midland fumbled and recovered. Morris gained three yards. Davis punted 37 yards to Green.

Franks lost five yards. Fairmount lost another five as an offside penalty. Skaer broke through right guard for a 26-yard run.

Morris intercepted a pass and dodged through 41 yards to Fairmount's nine-yard line. Midland gained four yards on line plunges. Burns carried the ball around left end for a touchdown. Davis kicked goal.

BOXING—ROUNDS

ROUND SEVEN—They danced about in the center of the ring. Malloy swung to the Kid's jaw. O'Hara missed two rights and landed a left body blow. Both pounded body blows at close quarters and went into a clinch. Referee Wilson parted them. The Kid got in a pair of lefts to Malloy's side, then hammered with lefts and rights to the body. Spike retreated. O'Hara hammered down his guard and bored in. Malloy retaliated with wild swings. They were in a clinch at the gong. O'Hara's round.

Running chronicles of other contests are treated similarly, tennis by games and sets, golf by holes, track meets by events. Examples are readily available in the papers and may be used as guides.

Time permitting after his running story is in print, the reporter flashes the result, produces a new lead, or rewrites the entire narrative in comprehensive style.

The latest available score at the end of a period is inserted immediately after the lead, thus:

At the end of the fifth inning the score was Sox 3, Oilers 2.

Score at end of first half: Fairmount 7, Midland 6.

After eight rounds the *Times* gave O'Hara four, Malloy three, one even.

Some papers may include in the score insert the phrase "when this edition went to press" to explain the incompleteness of the story. For the next edition, of course, a new lead based on the final outcome is substituted for the bunk lead, which is discarded.

Another method of keeping even closer up-to-the-minute with a sports story is to replate bulletins of scores in a fudge box on page one or at the top of the running account.

DOPE AND GOSSIP STORIES

The appetite of sports page followers for reading matter is enormous—far too sharp to be met with spot stories of specific contests. There are seasonal lapses between sports. The early editions of afternoon papers have virtually no spot sports news to report, but the yawning pages must be filled.

The answer to the problem is provided by stories and columns of gossip and dope. These consist of forecasts and follow-ups.

The dope story offers a blend of fact, gossip and guesswork based on the writer's experience, conversations with authorities, library clips, statistical analyses, observation of practice and workouts—anything and everything bearing upon leagues, teams, players and records which will give the readers material for speculation and aftermath conversation.

With a major football game coming up, a dope writer may visit the opposing camps, compare the weights, experience and records of the teams, interview the coaches and the players and turn out a series of advance stories.

Again, after a title boxing bout a follow-up writer may talk to the fighters and their managers, listen to and record the alibis of the loser, the plans of the winner, integrating his own expert knowledge and judgment.

The dopesters of the sports section are the regular sports writers and columnists. It is seldom that a general assignment man is called upon for such writing and therefore it is not discussed in detail in this chapter. On the occasions when a city room reporter needs to pinch-hit he may well fall back on the familiar techniques of writing forecasts and follow-ups just as he does on general news topics.

SHOP TALK

1. Why is so much newspaper space devoted to sports? Do you think intercollegiate football deserves more press prominence than intercollegiate debating?
2. Discuss the questions: Should the sports writer use slang? What is legitimate sports phraseology?
3. List the essential facts necessary to write a football, baseball or basketball story.
4. Suppose, as a reporter assigned to cover a professional football team, you were offered an envelope containing a $10 bill by the manager after each game. He asks no favors. Would you accept?
5. What is a sports dope story? Are advance dope stories on important athletic events overplayed?

CHAPTER 25

Writing News for Women

WOMEN FINANCE THE PAPER

This may or may not be a man's world but one thing about it is certain. The woman pays—that is, she does most of the spending.

Newspapers are printed for profit and the bulk of it comes from advertising products and services for sale. Women do 85 to 90 per cent of the buying and no newspaper can be successful unless its reporters and editors know how to attract and keep feminine readers.

A man may read a morning paper at breakfast, on the way to or at his place of work. As he scans the general news, sports and business pages, perhaps he makes a mental note to buy cigars or razor blades. But the paper that remains at home or goes to work with his wife is the one that moves merchandise. Again in the evening the man may buy at a newsstand or bring in from the doorstep an afternoon newspaper and read it first. But it is when the kitchen is cleared, the children are off to bed and the woman of the house peruses her favorite pages that the next day's shopping is planned.

While they earn much, men spend little except for their own personal needs. As purchasing agents for the family, wives and mothers virtually dictate the choice of food, furniture, automobiles, apparel, insurance, pianos, cosmetics and pills—the layette for the baby, new shoes for junior, frock for sister, ties, shirts and shoes for hubby.

These facts are well known to every sales manager, ad writer and space buyer. They should be better known to editorial men whose pay checks, like those of every newspaper worker, come largely from women readers.

It was a wise city editor who tacked on the bulletin board a letter from a woman reader with these notes:

WRITE IT FOR HER

This letter is from Mrs. John Meredith.

She lives in a modest, rented home at 1429 W. 13th St.

She has two children: Lucy, 2, John Jr., 9.

She works part time.

Figure out a lead for your story that will interest Mrs. Meredith. She is your average reader—one of the thousands with whom you seldom come into contact. Forget the man. Write your story for the woman. The man probably will read it anyhow.

Write it for Mrs. Meredith.

BY, OF AND FOR WOMEN

The title of this chapter is "Writing News *for* Women." It is important to distinguish between news written *by* women or *about* women and that written *for* women. These overlap but do not coincide.

We have seen that women work in every corner of journalism. Many cover and write news exactly like men, and there is no logical reason why, with training, both sexes cannot handle news for both sexes equally well.

However, it is true that more men are assigned to topics primarily of male interest such as sports, business, labor and politics while more women deal with society or social activities and such distaff specialties as homemaking. But this natural division is merely numerical and by no means complete or sharply defined.

Our discussion now turns to what women want to read in newspapers —and why.

It is a psychological fact that women tend to be subjective and men objective. Women are the more self-centered sex. They promptly personalize almost everything. Men are more impersonal. This difference underlies sex attraction in the general news of the day.

Gentler they may be but a higher percentage of women than men read stories of accidents and disasters, violence and crime, poverty and suffering—of human beings caught in the throes of their own misdeeds or misfortune. Women are deeply concerned with the fundamentals of life—birth, disease and death. They like to read about the arrival of triplets, a health advance, illness and funerals. They also note weather news carefully in order to dress themselves and their children properly.

Men will pay attention to and discuss foreign news, governmental affairs and technology, but you cannot hold a woman's interest long with abstractions, logic, inanimate things and processes. To win and keep her attention your story must have a human touch.

THE TWO WORLDS OF WOMEN

In the preceding chapter we pointed out that a man lives in two worlds—a world of reality concerning himself and his own activities and a world of fantasy concerning the doings of others in which he participates vicariously. In his mental world a male identifies himself with combat. Hence sports are the most distinctive man-interest news.

A woman likewise lives in the two worlds of practical things and make-believe. Like a man, she is interested in her own personality and work, chiefly that of a homemaker. In her mental world she identifies herself with glamour, romance and the relations of other people. While the news element of conflict appeals most strongly to men, the news element of emotions exerts the strongest pull on women.

The deepest desire of a woman is to be wanted, sought after and cherished. How to make herself attractive is a question of absorbing and never-ending interest to her. It is uppermost in her realm of reality. A woman spends countless hours in beauty shops, before mirrors, reading and talking about the art of adornment. She spends billions of dollars for fashionable clothing and cosmetics. Her health and etiquette are inter-locked with her search for the secrets of beauty. She wants to reduce or gain weight, attain vim and vitality and behave properly in company.

Within her world of reality a woman, next to herself, is concerned with her day-to-day responsibilities. Primarily she must be considered as a wife and mother caring about her husband, children, food and meals, home furnishings and decoration, child raising, sewing, knitting, mending, bridge, music, books, gardening, entertaining and participating in the activities of clubs and other organizations.

With modern household facilities, such as ready-cooked meals, vacuum cleaners and electric dishwashers, making more free time available, an increasingly large number of women have joined the labor force. How-ever, there is evidence that this is motivated not only by the advantage of multiple incomes but also to escape the loneliness of an empty home in daytime.

In her world of fantasy a woman moves into the company of fascinating and romantic characters she can identify with herself. Effortlessly she steps into the shoes of Cinderella and Snow White with Prince Charm-ings and Beau Brummels at her feet. She may never be a Hollywood glamour girl, a Miss America, one of the ten best-dressed women, a queen or even a princess, but she lives their lives in her imagination.

Feminine Reader Attractions

PAGES FOR WOMEN

Ask an adolescent girl what she wants to be and do as a grownup and she will think, if not say: "I want to be beautiful and loved and marry a handsome and wealthy man and have furs and jewelry and go to lots of parties and have two or three cute babies."

The Buffalo, N.Y., *Courier-Express* printed this "Valentine" to its women readers:

> We just love to serve you and think up things to do
> To keep you right in style and march you down the aisle
> To make your housework easier and make you even squeezier
> To make your children sunnier and make your husband honeyer.

In different words these two passages translate our analysis of feminine desires into specific topics of news and features devised by newspapers to fulfill them. To bring these topics into closer focus examine any number of women's pages and you will find them replete with articles on these subjects:

Advice to the lovelorn	Gardens and flowers
Antiques	Health advice
Beauty features	Household hints
Book reviews	Interior decoration
Child care	Movie criticism
Club activities	Music and art
Etiquette	Sewing and knitting
Fashions and patterns	Shopping services
Food and recipes	Teen-age news

There are as many variations of these topics as there are newspapers. How they are received or prepared depends on the size and staff of the paper.

Small town papers with only one so-called society editor or writer busy with hometown personal items and social news obtain all such material from syndicates. As the size of the paper increases, the women's pages omit local items with limited reader interest in order to make room for their own magazine-type features and weave into the women's section semi-news stories and series with feminine appeal.

Metropolitan papers can afford to and do produce articles on such diverse subjects as women's position under Social Security, women and the stock market, how women protect themselves with jujitsu and problems of women drinkers; exposés of the rackets of marriage brokers, baby photographers, charm schools, door-to-door peddlers and baby-selling agencies; and the adventures of airplane stewardesses, fashion models and hat-check girls.

THE SOCIETY EDITOR AT WORK

Society editor is an old-fashioned, time-honored term for a newswoman whose usual job it is to get into the paper news about social events largely of interest to women readers.

The position takes various forms. On a small paper the society editor may well be the wife of the publisher doubling in brass as the conductor of a personals column, mail and correspondence editor, want-ad taker and perhaps bookkeeper. On a medium-sized paper she may be fashionably streamlined into a club editor. In a metropolis she may be a true editor of women's pages with a staff of experts working under her, or a topnotch reporter specializing on the doings of society with a capital S as well as so-called café society.

"Society" in a hamlet consists of almost everyone living in it. In a medium-sized town it consists of members of pioneer or otherwise well-known families. In a big city it is the extremely wealthy, the social regis-terites—the haut monde—reaching out into foreign royalty.

On the Midland *Times* Miss Ruth Ramsey is classified as a special assignment reporter assigned to society but she is generally known as the society editor. She finds, develops and writes her own stories, ranging from social brevities to the governor's inaugural ball at Capital City. She attends some but not all of the functions she writes about. She secures most of her copy in telephone conversations with the persons involved, relatives or secretaries, from scouts or tipsters, including clergymen, florists, caterers, and especially from club officers and publicity chairmen.

From these sources she garners her material on visits, week-end and house parties, showers, engagements, weddings, births, christenings, luncheons, teas, dances, debuts, musicales, receptions, balls, benefits, bazaars and the adventures of Midland's smart set.

Her orbit sometimes overlaps that of the other reporters. Occasionally she turns up a top story on business affairs or politics. And from time to time reporters on the general assignment staff, especially the Misses Kemp and Nestor, swing in to assist her. The men, too, may find themselves working closely with her on major social events that are linked with general news such as a convention, crime or celebration.

NAMES IN SOCIAL NEWS

Perhaps no member of the staff is more careful with names than the society editor, for they are the lifeblood of her stories from personal brevities to page one weddings. Around names are built scores of items like these to help fill the columns of the pages for women:

> Miss Bertha Eddy, whose marriage to Albert Gibson Jr. will take place June 14, will be guest at a luncheon to be given tomorrow by Miss Flora Niles at the Rex Hotel.

> Miss Cynthia Vale, daughter of Mr. and Mrs. John R. Vale, of 162 Banks St., is spending the Thanksgiving holidays at home. She attends St. Anthony's University at Mercerville. The Misses Ethel Mae Sharp, Jane Wolf and Helen Stout will be her guests over the weekend.

> Mr. and Mrs. J. Robert Bailey were dinner hosts last evening to Mr. and Mrs. Wallace Gordon and Mr. and Mrs. Thomas R. Downing at their home in Hillview.

The trained society writer makes every effort to find a live news angle hidden in a mass of names, but always the names are waiting for her. In order to make them stand out in relief society writers sometimes group and tabulate them in small type, thus:

Mesdames

James Barr	William R. Stewart
Edwin F. Mullin	Allen Martin
Frank Daniels	John B. Walters
Roger O. Finnegan	E. L. Little

Misses

Anne Marvin	Lillian Sparks
Jeanette Barton	Barbara Ann Rich
Helen Holbrook	Lucy McCarthy

In the metropolitan newspapers, of course, names are news only when their owners have done something legitimately worthy of reporting to the readers, but even in them 10 times as many names will be found on the women's pages as in any other section of the paper.

Society writers are careful with the forms as well as the spellings of names. The title *Miss* always is placed before the name of an unmarried woman. Her first name is used, not initials only. When mentioned a second time she is referred to as *Miss* without the first name. The title *Mrs.* is placed before the name of a married woman followed by the name of her husband. In a second reference to her the first name of the husband is omitted.

Five points usually covered in an account of a society gathering following its occurrence are (1) occasion, (2) names, (3) gowns, (4) decorations and, if unusual, (5) refreshments. Most important, of course, are the names—the priceless ingredient of the society mélange. Note how in this typical story these points are woven about the names:

> Mrs. Jonathan Gainor, the former Miss Daphne Ellen Taggert, was honored with a bridge tea and crystal shower Friday afternoon at the Ambassador. Miss Marie Harley was hostess, assisted by her mother, Mrs. R. M. Harley.
>
> The guests assembled in the Chinese Room. The tea table was decorated with a centerpiece of pink and yellow summer flowers, with pink candles in silver holders.
>
> Mrs. Gainor wore an afternoon frock of black chiffon trimmed in white organdie. Miss Harley received in a frock of pink crepe, with brown and white accessories.
>
> Guests were Miss Eva Simpson, Miss Margaret Baker, Miss Genevieve Stone, Miss Brenda Scott, Miss Rita Marshall, Miss Marcia Owen, Mrs. Willard Fleming, Mrs. Robert Rice, Mrs. Chester Baker and Mrs. Roger Graham.

The society writer, like her sports-writing brother, is a statistician as well as a stylist. She must be accurate not only with names but with specific information, especially in routines advances like this:

> Plans are being formulated for the annual luncheon and card party for the benefit of the Midland Art Society to be given on Feb. 21 at the Hotel Harper.
>
> Mrs. James L. Caleb is president of the society and Mrs. Kenneth P. Garson heads the benefit committee. Miss Thelma Parsons has enlisted the aid of a group of young women to assist Mrs. Caleb and Mrs. Garson.
>
> The organization, maintained by voluntary contributions, has cooperated with the city since 1902 in promoting art and cultural activities.
>
> Serving with Mrs. Garson are Mrs. Herman Bohn, Mrs. Charles B. Wickliffe, Mrs. Henry Chadwick, Miss Katrina Bishop and Miss Patricia Bishop.
>
> Reservations can be made through Mrs. Garson at 1742 Laurel St.

There are so many such advance notices of organization meetings and similar events that they often are grouped together in a column with a standing headline like *Bulletin Board* or *Looking Ahead*. The items may be assembled under such subheads as *clubs, religious, music, youth,* and so on.

SOCIETY CHITCHAT COLUMNS

To add flavor to the society page some newspapers carry a chatter column consisting of news fragments and intimate items unsuitable for

headline news development. The columns may be entitled *Distaff Data,*
Tea Talk, Fashionable Flashes or *Talk of the Town.* These columns,
highlighting names, conform to the tone of the paper. They may be a
series of pleasant personal snippets or a breezy mixture of fact and comment. Examples:

MODERATE

Canasta parties, farewell teas and Sunday night buffets helped fill the
weekend.

Among the guests at the supper given by Mr. and Mrs. Benjamin Winner
yesterday were Mr. and Mrs. Harold Griffin, Mr. and Mrs. T. A. Tyson
and Mr. and Mrs. Henry Tillman.

Mrs. George Berger will be hostess to the Good Neighbor Club at a
bridge party at her home next Tuesday.

Many of the Greenview colony yesterday visited the wild-flower show
held by Mrs. Seth May.

Mr. and Mrs. Edward Cooper will return this week from New Orleans
where they visited their son, Col. John Cooper, who will sail for Japan
Oct. 27.

RACY

In case you did not know it, Betty Hopkins and Ronald Richman are
that way about each other . . . Betty was voted last year's prettiest deb.

Saw Whitney Chadbourne at the Strand last night with—guess who—
Sally Paulson . . . She is wearing her blonde tresses very long with a little wave . . . Whitney's friends were congratulating him on his polo
game Tuesday.

Oh, dear, what to wear these days of uncertain weather? . . . I saw
two fur wraps at the Hillview Horse Show.

Fannie Compton's tea party in her studio duplex apartment was a suc-
cess in a big way . . . Guests admired the deep crimson velvet hangings
. . . Elizabeth Otis was the honor guest . . . She leaves for London
Friday.

Examples like the second one strew romance liberally with such
terms as *dating, going steady, acting daffy, in a daze, blazing, in a huddle,*
twosoming, middle-aisled, upped and did it, called it off, parted company.

On the society pages of smaller papers such columns tend to be moder-
ate. They consist, in part, of a series of straight personal items. In the
larger papers they become racier and shade into the syndicated gossip-

type columns which range out through the entertainment fields and sometimes into sports, business, politics and even foreign affairs.

ENGAGEMENTS AND WEDDINGS

A standard form for engagement notices is followed in most newspaper offices. The parents of the bride-to-be, not the expectant bridegroom's, usually announce their daughter's engagement.

Here are conventional examples containing the pertinent facts:

> Dean and Mrs. Robert E. Chadbourne of 731 Wentworth Pl. announce the engagement of their daughter, Grace, to Bruce McCoy, son of Mr. and Mrs. John B. McCoy of Salina, Kan. Miss Chadbourne is a graduate of the University of Centralia and a member of Gamma Phi Beta sorority. McCoy was graduated from Rice Institute, Houston, Tex.

> At a dinner given at their home in Crestwood last evening, Mr. and Mrs. Fairfax Urban announced the approaching marriage of their only daughter, Carol, to Frank Bell, son of Mr. and Mrs. A. L. Bell, 1432 Cross St. The wedding will take place in the Urban home, 30 Saxon St., in August.

> The Frank Fullers, of 1720 Forrest Ave., announce the forthcoming marriage on Aug. 15 of their daughter, Judith, to Ralph Martin, son of Mr. and Mrs. John B. Martin, of 321 Tyler Ave.

> June 1 has been set as the wedding date of Mildred Kramer, daughter of Mrs. James Kramer, of 532 Locust St., and Joseph Warburton of Chicago.

Engagement items, sometimes printed in a column with a head like *Rings on Their Fingers* or *Orange Blossom Trail*, may be varied by starting, "An autumn wedding is planned by . . . " "Sandra Logan has become engaged to . . ." or "Miss Donna Lee Brooks will become the bride of . . ." In such a column a subhead often links the two names over each item:

Taylor-Garson

> The betrothal of their daughter, Millicent, to Walter Garson, son of Mr. and Mrs. Kenneth P. Garson, is announced by Dr. and Mrs. W. Franklin Taylor of 1702 Willow St. The marriage will take place in June.

After the engagement has been announced and before the wedding there may be in-between items if the bride is prominent, starting like these:

> Several showers are planned for Miss Shirley Spencer whose marriage to William R. Hansen will take place June 15 in the First Presbyterian Church.

Miss Carolyn Jane Carpenter has selected attendants for her wedding to R. George Brown Jr. at 2:30 p.m. Sunday in Bethany Baptist Church.

Probably half the average society page is devoted to weddings, future or past, and probably no member of the news family seems so elementary to the experienced writer, although difficult to the beginner.

The formula of facts is so well defined that some papers simplify the compiling of data by using a questionnaire. The printed blank covers the following:

1. Who were married?
2. When?
3. Where?
4. Who was the clergyman?
5. What did the bride wear?
6. Who are the parents?
7. Decorations?
8. Music?
9. Reception?
10. Honeymoon where?
11. When will they return?
12. Where will they live?

There are further questions to be answered if the wedding is a more pretentious affair. These include: Who gave the bride away? Who were the bridesmaids? What did they wear? Who was the best man? Who were the ushers? Who were the guests?

APPLICATION OF THE FORMULA

Note how the 12 points are packed into this typical wedding story:

The marriage of *Miss Cynthia Raleigh*, daughter of *Mr. and Mrs. William J. Raleigh*, to *Dr. Leland R. Foster*, son of *Mr. and Mrs. H. F. Foster* of Meadville, took place at *11 o'clock* this morning *at the home of the bride's parents*, 906 Birch St.

The Rev. Edward R. Johnson read the service in the living room before the fireplace, which was banked with *palms, ferns and garden flowers*. The wedding *music* was played by Miss Vera Bergman, accompanied by Miss Roberta Craven on the violin. *The bride wore* a gown of ivory satin with a short train. She carried a shower bouquet of gardenias and lilies of the valley.

Following the ceremony *a wedding breakfast* was served. Only the immediate families were present.

Dr. and Mrs. Foster left for a *wedding trip* to Florida and will be *at home after June 15 in Midland*.

FACTS NEEDED FOR
A WEDDING STORY

WHO WERE MARRIED?

WHEN?

WHERE?

WHO WAS THE CLERGYMAN?

WHAT DID THE BRIDE WEAR?

WHO ARE THE PARENTS?

DECORATIONS?

MUSIC?

RECEPTION?

HONEYMOON WHERE?

WHEN WILL THEY RETURN?

WHERE WILL THEY LIVE?

Twelve Questions to Answer

While the wedding story must not omit the essential facts, it need not always be written in the same conventional way. The words *were married* can be alternated with *became the bride of, exchanged marriage vows* or *went to the altar with.* The lead may begin with a description, thus:

> Brilliant early blooms in the cool hues of spring and gowns in equally delicate shades lent their colors yesterday to the fashionable wedding of Lucy Harmon and Gerald M. Morgan at St. John's Church.

> White snapdragons and tulips formed a garden background for the marriage of Miss Janet Curtis and George F. Merrill in St. Luke's Lutheran Church this afternoon.

> Happy music in a bright major key yesterday enhanced the picturesque wedding here of Susan Manville, daughter of Senator and Mrs. Miles Manville, to Daniel Jordan of the Centralia State Department.

To avoid monotony in wedding reports, look for feature angles. Was the wedding a surprise? Did the bride wear an heirloom? Was the wedding the culmination of a childhood or school romance? Has it any other news significance? A story with this lead was lifted to page one:

> The best man was a grandfather and his mother was the bride at a wedding ceremony yesterday in Southfield. Charles Meyer, 76, and Mrs. E. Langley Carver, 70, were married "because we were both lonely and had many memories to share."

Seldom is the bride left waiting at the church but if she is—and it has happened—and the couple are prominent, you have not lost your story. You have one that will rank with the primary news of the day.

STYLE IN SOCIETY STORIES

To a certain extent the society writer, like the sports writer, has leeway in her style. It has been said that women adore adjectives, using them heavily in their speech. Hence they appear frequently on the society pages.

It is necessary for the writer to acquire a diversified vocabulary which will enable her to please her readers and at the same time write with dignity and restraint. Every hostess would like to have her party described as the loveliest of the season, but such superlatives need to be subdued. Also avoid bromides like:

a good time was had	nuptials were consummated
beautiful bouquets	plighted their troth
delicious refreshments	render a program
exquisite taste	tender a surprise
gorgeously gowned	united in holy wedlock

Constrast the following two stories, one gaudy and stereotyped, the other restrained by a delicacy of expression:

POOR

Amidst a spectacular array of floral offerings and gifts two prominent young people of Midland society were united in holy wedlock today in one of the loveliest weddings of the season. The blushing bride was Janet Jarvis, talented and accomplished daughter of Elmer E. Jarvis, the banker. John Knight, the groom, is an aspiring young attorney.

The Rev. George M. Crandall, pastor of the First Methodist Church, tied the nuptial knot while a host of friends gathered around to tender felicitations.

Janet was radiant in white satin and carried a beautiful bouquet, while John wore the conventional cutaway. The couple departed for White Sulpher Springs, Va., after a reception given at the home of the bride's parents at 4984 Jackson Ave.

BETTER

One of the important weddings of the midsummer season took place this afternoon when Miss Janet Elizabeth Jarvis, daughter of Mr. and Mrs. Elmer E. Jarvis of 4984 Jackson Ave., was married to John Randolph Knight in the First Methodist Church.

The Rev. George M. Crandall read the service. Miss Harriet M. Jarvis, cousin of the bride, was maid of honor and Thomas H. Grierson was the best man. Roger B. Payne and Charles S. Green were ushers.

The bride was gowned in white satin and carried a bouquet of white roses. The maid of honor, Miss Irene Arnold, wore pink chiffon and carried a bouquet of tea roses. The bridesmaids were Miss Agnes Ryan and Miss Nancy Collins.

After their honeymoon trip to White Sulpher Springs, Va., Mr. and Mrs. Knight will return to Midland.

The bridegroom is the junior member of Duncan, Smith & Knight, Midland attorneys.

The society writer needs to remember that she is writing not only for the immediate participants in a social event but for other readers as well. One sure way to offend them all is to bedeck the story with so many sentimental ornaments that it becomes sticky editorializing instead of factual news reporting. In society as well as other stories stereotypes are a poor substitute for sharp and specific detail.

SHOP TALK

1. Do you agree that general news copy should be written to appeal to women more than to men?
2. Criticize the author's analysis of feminine news interests.
3. Is it true that women prefer to read stories written by women?
4. Do you think your local newspaper carries too much or too little news for women?
5. Should the writer of society news always be complimentary?

CHAPTER **26**

The Business Beat Man

MONEY-MAKING AS NEWS

In a broad sense, and as treated in this chapter, the word *business* covers not only finance and commerce but also labor—organized and unorganized—and extends from the giant industries down through the ranks of all who have an occupation in which they earn a living.

Every normal adult, whether working or not, handles money and is interested at least in his or her own grocery, clothing, utility and rent bills, income tax and bus fare. These are business topics. Thus news of business is to be found on every hand. It is a part of day-to-day living and, as such, is closely integrated with all news as well as being classified in a special category like sports, society or politics.

Although in business themselves, newspapers, before the turn of the century, paid little attention to either industry or labor. The press of the past devoted itself largely to literature, politics and public affairs. Private enterprise was private by choice and both the public and the press permitted it to remain so.

As labor organized, its leaders, too, were secretive and hostile to newsmen, who often were looked upon as spies for the capitalist press.

The World Wars, with their regimentations and controls, and the resultant inflations and depressions jolted Americans in every income group from top to bottom into realizing that "business is everybody's business" —that of the capitalist *and* the laborer, the boss *and* the worker, the breadwinner *and* the homemaker. Business became news.

Too many young thrill-seeking reporters still consider business news something dull as dishwater printed in agate type and quietly buried back with the want ads where only bankers, brokers and bookkeepers look at it. Modern editors—even those who cynically define news as "wine, women and wampum"—recognize the reader interest in money-making.

He may not be buying stocks on margin but John Doe will sit up straight in his chair when a barbers' strike hikes the cost of his haircut or a gasoline war cuts the price of his auto fuel. And Mrs. Doe will think about bread and butter for the children or a new dress for herself if his business prospers or goes bankrupt or if his pay envelope is fat or flat.

Yes, business is news.

WHAT IS THE BUSINESS BEAT?

Once again, as we have repeatedly done before, it is necessary to distinguish among the practices of small, medium-sized and large newspapers in the treatment of a specialized news subject as well as among the communities they serve.

There are no business beat reporters as such on small papers, while a great metropolitan daily may employ a score of experts working with their own editors, copy desk, wires and pages. In a medium-sized city like Midland, the *Times* business reporter, Frank Fenwick, also covers labor —a logical combination. He really classifies as a special assignment man but in his byline is "Business Editor." Midland is a plane-manufacturing city in the heart of an agricultural area, and two other men on the local staff are assigned to motors and aviation and to farming.

This brings us to the diversity of business news dependent on the location and products of the newspaper circulation area.

A seaport city is concerned with shipping, a milling city with wheat, a mining center with coal, a stockyards city with livestock, and so on. Citrus fruit is a topic of interest in Orlando, Fla., but not in Cheyenne, Wyo., or Gloucester, Mass., where cattle and fish are more newsworthy.

These variations bear strongly upon the nature of business news stressed in a specific newspaper and on the makeup of its staff assigned to cover and write it.

BUSINESS NEWS TRAINING

It would be unfair to expect an average reporter to be fully familiar with even the main trunks of industrial and labor organizations—and there are many offshoots. But he doesn't have to be a doctor to cover a medical meeting, a lawyer to cover a trial or a coach to cover a football game. By the same token he need not be an economics expert to write business and labor news.

However, if he is to handle intelligently even the routine assignments

TEN COMMON TYPES OF
BUSINESS IN THE NEWS

1. Extensions, improvements, innovations and personnel changes in business firms.

2. Negotiations and decisions involving wages, hours and working conditions of employes.

3. New and labor-saving ideas, machines, products, systems, adaptations and methods used by business concerns.

4. Public utility rates and services.

5. Plans and progress of public improvement projects.

6. Finances and business dealings of governmental agencies and governmental regulations of business.

7. Taxes and assessments.

8. Real estate and building developments.

9. Activities of business organizations.

10. Business conventions, shows and expositions.

Typical Topics for Assignment

that come his way he should know something beyond how to balance his own checkbook. Any reporter should be able to give offhand, clear-cut definitions of the following terms and employ them accurately in his copy:

amortize	garnishee
arbitration	injunction
asset	inventory
audit	lease
boycott	liquidate
budget	lockout
collateral	mediation
collective bargaining	monopoly
common and preferred stock	open and closed shop
cooperative marketing	option
cost-of-living increase	overhead
depreciation	picket
discount	proxy
dividend	receivership
dues checkoff	shop steward
embargo	strike
equity	voucher
escrow	wage minimum
fringe benefit	workmen's compensation

The wise student who expects to become a reporter will learn in school something about business as well as law, science, sports and the other common fields of human activity into which he will be thrust early in his newspaper career. Courses in economics, marketing, business management, advertising or accounting will help equip him for business writing.

Unless he intends to become a specialist it is not necessary that he be a school of commerce graduate or that he work behind a counter or in an office. Nevertheless, it is necessary for him to build up, one way or another, a practical working knowledge of common business transactions and learn where to go for guidance when he finds himself lost in uncertainties.

BE ACCURATE AND CONSTRUCTIVE

In any kind of news story accuracy is a prime requisite, but with the exception of crime and court news there is perhaps no classification of copy that calls for such undeviating precision as stories about business.

Although the report of a business event can often be humanized and even dramatized, its essential purpose is to be factual and informative. You will hear complaints if you mix up addresses in a fire story, misspell the name of a society matron or bungle the box score of a ball game, but the trouble is liable to be much more serious if you drop a cipher from a real estate sale price or give the wrong date for an auction.

Serious, too, can be your error if in a labor story you loosely toss around such words as *lockout* and *strike*. Find out if it is a *union-authorized* or a *wildcat* strike, or if it isn't just a *work stoppage*—a *sitdown* rather than a *walkout*. Or are the employes merely staying away from their jobs by reporting themselves "sick"?

You will recall that the laws of libel are severe in protecting both individuals and companies from loss of reputation and from financial injury. Obtain typed or mimeographed material for exact reference, if possible, when covering a business story. If none is available, take careful notes during interviews and news conferences—notes that you can read and understand when you are writing your article.

Sometimes you will find on your hands figures and interpretations which are not fully clear to you. It then becomes necessary for you to go to the person or persons who can give you the full muster of facts and to keep asking questions until you can clarify them. Verify every statement and credit a reliable authority whenever possible. Then write as an informed student—not as a critic. Write constructively.

For sound reasons other than the negative fear of complaints and libel, a newspaper and its reporters customarily treat business reports as favorably as the facts warrant.

Except in isolated instances, any direct influence exerted by advertisers on news content is a thing of the past. Deliberate distortion to please space buyers does not exist in modern, respectable newspaper offices, for no newspaper can afford to submit to open coercion based on the use of its advertising columns. Here and there the record may show that an editor has soft-pedaled news—say that of an elevator crash in a department store—but it also shows that newspapers repeatedly have gone after damaging news and printed it in defiance of an advertiser.

However, newspapers generally give business a break. There is no question that news about construction, improvements, expansion and advancement produces copy more welcome to the city desk than news of business failures, bankruptcies and removals to other cities.

The newspaper is part of a community whose people depend upon community industries and payrolls. The paper itself is one of those business enterprises and its employes likewise gain a livelihood only if it is solvent and profitable. It stands to reason, then, that the press can ill afford to undermine public confidence in local business enterprises.

ORGANIZING A ROUTINE STORY

The arrangement of a routine business story consisting of a series of facts and figures, all closely related, offers little difficulty. Such a story conforms to the fact diagram in "The Story Structure" chapter and calls for grouping the data in the order of importance. This story illustrates:

Fact 1

Glenn W. Rawson, a member of the partnership firm of Parks & Rawson, electrical appliance dealers, 2nd and Ash Sts., has organized a new firm under the name of Rawson Appliance Co., to be located at 305 Monroe Ave.

Fact 2

Rawson announced yesterday he has purchased the interest of his partner, Harold J. Parks, in the Parks & Rawson firm, dealer and distributor of Allrite appliances and Perfection radio sets.

Fact 3

Rawson's new firm will open for business Monday in its new location on Monroe avenue. The firm will continue to handle Allrite and Perfection products. It also will be the Midland agency for Victory television receivers.

Fact 4

James R. Malchow, who was connected with Parks & Rawson, will be manager of the new Rawson store. Theodore L. Smithers will manage the service department.

Fact 5

Parks will continue in business at the old location of Parks & Rawson on Ash street and operate under the name of Parks Radio-TV Shop. He expects to announce his lines of appliance, radio and television products next week.

The foregoing report involving a small and ordinary business transaction called for no clarification. The plain facts spoke for themselves.

However, if the reporter has a morass of statistical data, almost meaningless except to a handful of experts, he may well use an expert as a mouthpiece for a well-ordered quote story:

Lead—Summary

Consumers, in most cases, will indirectly bear the new one per cent city sales tax which goes into effect Sept. 1, Thaddeus R. Whitlock, legal expert of the Department of Taxation, declared today.

FACT STRUCTURE OF THE
BUSINESS STORY

By FRANK FENWICK
Times Business Editor

FACT ONE

More than one-half of the funds received by the Midland Shore Line Railroad last year were immediately paid out to 1,400 employes, according to a report issued by the company yesterday.

FACT TWO

The report, entitled "How The Shore Line Dollar Was Spent," showed that out of every dollar received by the railroad during the year 51.4 per cent was paid to labor.

FACT THREE

The second largest slice out of the dollar went for the purchase of materials and supplies used in the everyday railroad operations. This expenditure required 17.07 per cent. Power for the company's system took 7.29 per cent.

FACT FOUR

For taxes paid to cities, states and the United States a total of 4.54 per cent was taken from every dollar received by the road. At this rate, the report pointed out, taxes now are almost equal to the amount of dividends paid to the stockholders.

FACT FIVE

Loss and damage payments, depreciation on rolling stock and rentals absorbed an additional 6.48 per cent of the railroad's dollar and 7.72 per cent was needed to pay fixed charges.

FACT SIX

After making all these payments, the road had left 5.5 per cent of the original dollar from which to pay dividends to the stockholders and to provide for a surplus which would sustain the company's credit.

Routine Business Story Arrangement

Quote

"Although the tax is on the privilege of selling, the prudent merchant will pass it on to buyers," Whitlock said.

Summary

The tax expert conferred this afternoon with a committee of the Midland Merchants Assn. The association members have decided to pass along the tax in its entirety but not to place it on the price tag or sales check as a separate item.

Quote

"The average storekeeper," Whitlock explained, "will spread out the tax over his general stock of goods. He has the right, of course, to absorb the tax himself, but a majority, I believe, will include it in their prices."

Summary

The tax will not be a "nuisance," Whitlock promised, since buyers will not have to pay extra pennies in addition to the prices on their purchase slips except on special items.

HANDLING A STRIKE STORY

Neutrality is the golden rule of the labor reporter. In the midst of a labor dispute it may be easier to get a statement from management, but he must make every effort to get the union side as well. The cause of the dispute is fully as newsworthy as its effect.

A labor reporter, like a man on any other run, needs to make friends among union officials who are his news sources. If he is welcome at their headquarters, the union hall or labor temple, he can make his job pleasant and productive.

Constructive stories of union meetings, items about picnics, benefits and women's auxiliaries of labor organizations help build good will which pays off when bitter and violent industrial warfare breaks into the front page.

The writer's chief obligation, however, is to neither side in a strike situation but to the majority of his readers. Note how this story, although fair to all the parties, appeals directly to the noncombatant public:

> The fur was flying in Midland barbershops yesterday and, for the first time in years, the customers relaxed happily in their chairs.
> A full-scale price war triggered by shorter pay checks and a slump in business cut the price of a haircut to one dollar all around the town. The cost of a shave dropped from 50 to 25 cents.
> Union barbers ordered the cuts at a mass meeting Tuesday after several of their unorganized competitors reduced haircut prices to $1.50.

"We simply can't make a decent living at the $1.50 figure," said John F. Jenkins, secretary of the Midland Barbers Union Local 27. Jenkins declared that prices will be chopped again if necessary to bring the nonunion barbers into line.

A spokesman for a dozen members of that group, David Richfield, whose shop is at 912 Main St., argued that $1.75 is a "gouge on the public" and will cause people to start cutting their own hair or driving to shops in other towns.

Mayor Nelson's labor mediator, L. P. Schmidt, announced that he has invited the leaders on both sides to meet with him in City Hall at 2 p.m. today in an effort to iron out their differences.

Meanwhile the barber business in the dollar shops is booming.

A strike usually is not to the advantage but to the disadvantage of the public. If it involves a shutoff of vital supplies such as milk or bus service, it can be a near-disaster. A settlement then becomes bulletin and replate news.

When a settlement is announced by one side, the covering reporter should be certain that the other side is in agreement. If necessary he should insist on a joint statement of the terms before reporting that a settlement has been reached.

USE THE READER'S TERMS

Despite their vital interest to readers, many accounts of commercial transactions are dull and heavy because the writers have failed to humanize and vitalize them. A writer cannot always make his business story as fascinating as a movie star's divorce but he can go a long way in that direction.

The trick of making any intricate subject understandable is to explain it in terms familiar to the reader. For example, business executives understand what you mean by a nonconvertible debenture, but few laymen do. Technical words are scary. Try not to use one without a definition.

A simile or metaphor is even better than a definition. If a nation has a dollar shortage, you can make the fact clear to a housewife by likening it to a woman with just so much money to spend. Shall she borrow, or buy less? An appropriation bill report becomes meaningful if you can translate the dollars into the cost per capita.

Note how the writer of this business story made an extra effort to inject verve and color into the framework of the factual:

Midland gave a rousing welcome yesterday to R. J. Preston Co. and at closing time Manager John K. Link, smiling broadly, estimated that 10,000 persons visited the new department store during the day.

Thousands of Midlanders were on hand at 9 a.m. for the formal opening of the store at 1020 Main St. Mayor Nelson turned a key that unlocked the front door to the public while Mrs. Nelson clipped a red ribbon stretched across the main entrance.

Surging crowds poured through the doors all day. In the first hour Manager Link estimated that more than 2,000 entered the store. Every town within a radius of 100 miles sent groups of shoppers for the gala merchandising event.

Messages of congratulations were received by the directors of the Preston Co. from business leaders in the city. Huge baskets of flowers were sent by several Midland merchants as gestures of welcome.

Specialties of every kind sold rapidly as the throngs moved through the wide and commodious aisles. Store officials lacked time to total up departmental reports, but Link described the volume of business as "tremendous."

"This is a red-letter day for the entire Preston organization," Link declared. "Midland has given us a great welcome and we intend to show our appreciation by serving Midland to the very best of our abilities."

Not every business story offers the opportunity for description and quotes presented by the opening of a big store. All such stories, however, can be written with clarity if not color.

HOW TO SIMPLIFY STATISTICS

In preparing a business story the reporter frequently collects a mass of statistics, financial statements, reports, audits and similar data, some of it valuable, some practically worthless. His temptation is either to use statistical matter as it stands or to cast it aside. Usually the result is an unreadable dissertation choked with meaningless figures or one entirely lacking in convincing evidence.

Statistics intended for newspaper use should be carefully arranged and, if possible, simplified. For example, it means more to say that "three out of five families in Clay City owns an automobile" than that "Clay City has a population of 31,902 and its residents own 19,380 automobiles." Abstract references frequently need to be humanized, although not sensationalized.

If a concern showed a net profit of $32,000, it only confuses the reader to explain that the gross income was $400,000, of which $368,000 went for overhead, wages and other expenditures. Insert a short cut on figures whenever you can without omitting any vital material. Reduce lengthy tables of figures to short ones, and official summaries to helpful paragraphs of interpretation.

Crosscut and tabulate at every opportunity. The ordinary reader will not forge through a formidable brier patch of figures printed in conventional sentence and paragraph style unless they are extremely significant to him. Arrange the rows of data in tabular form so that the reader will be able to grasp them at a glance, thus making them effective. Mark the advantages of tabulation in the following story:

Midland will pay $1,527,717 to operate its city government next year, an increase of more than $100,000 over last year, if the budget estimates completed yesterday by Controller Burton K. Latham are adopted by the City Council.

Higher outlays for relief take $74,703, or nearly three-fourths of the proposed increase. The bulk of the remainder, roughly $25,000, goes for street cleaning.

The controller's figures represent a reduction of $169,970 from the estimates of city department heads, who asked for a total of $1,697,687.

"It is necessary to cut every expenditure to the limit next year," Latham asserted. "Except for the relief increases, we are slashing to the limit in every department."

Latham summarized the status of the corporate fund estimates as follows:

Surplus, last year	$ 111,830
Surplus, this year	59,943
Revenue, next year	1,330,553
Total resources	$1,502,326
Net expense	$1,527,717

The appropriations for the major departments for this year as compared to the controller's estimates of their needs next year are:

	This Year	Next Year
Mayor	$ 18,160	$ 18,902
Council	39,920	42,613
Public Works	363,684	390,815
Police	420,519	441,498
Fire	198,718	219,892
Health	60,225	57,039
Law	12,556	12,326
Electricity	120,555	120,695
Welfare	354,646	426,076

Latham's estimate of next year's expenditures from the water fund, less salvage, is $432,333, and of resources, $432,618. He estimates the vehicle tax appropriations at $48,795, and its resources at $144,866.

Among the more important expenditures from the bond funds next year will be:

9th Street Bridge	$51,207
Pierce Avenue Bridge	42,863
City Jail	6,600
Soldiers' Monument	33,274
Island Park	21,200

> The controller's report will go next Tuesday to the Council, which will refer it to the finance committee. It is customary for the committee to readjust and slash down the appropriations still further.

The reporter should study the style and sizes of type in his paper, familiarizing himself especially with the spacing of statistical tables. Type can be squeezed or spread only a little, and usually the compilation of figures must be rammed into a single column measure. If the reporter has a list of figures which cannot be reduced to columnar width he should consult his superior on the possibility of displaying the matter in a box set in double or triple column width.

PUBLICITY AND REPORTERS

As both business and labor leaders have become less secretive and more anxious to win public favor, their companies and organizations have employed experts to represent them in contacts with newspapers and other communications media.

The first of these, labeled *press agents*, appeared in the entertainment field to ballyhoo publicity seekers in show business. As they entered business, politics, sports and other fields, the go-between group became *publicity* men, then *public relations* men, *counsels* and *secretaries*. Their titles sometimes are shortened to *PA* or *PR*.

All kinds are well known to newsmen. In fact a majority of them can say truthfully: "I once was a newspaperman myself."

Some newsmen scoff at the *PA's* and *PR's* and contemptuously regard their colleagues who enter the publicity field as turncoats who have sold their souls and dedicated themselves to sneaking free advertising into the news columns. Oddly, the same newsman who rejects a handout about a new business product or service may have no objection at all to publicizing day after day a county attorney with puffs and blurbs as valuable to a politician as an item about a sale would be to a store owner. Nor does he wince at publicizing a professional boxing bout or baseball game, both run for profit.

The only sound policy for both editor and reporter to adopt toward public relations men is to take advantage of their help and print their copy if it is news. Naturally the publicity man's desire is to gain good will and business for the firm he represents. The reporter's duty is to obtain legitimate and complete news for his paper. There is no reason at all that one cannot understand the job of the other and cooperate to mutual advantage.

Modern large industries employ public relations men who understand the needs and obligations of the press and respect them. Such PA's send releases only when they have news. They do not try to cover up damaging news, but help reporters get at the truth. They do not complain about minor errors or go over the reporter's head to the editor or publisher. They believe that truth is the best kind of public relations. With such publicity men the wise reporter can and does work and as a result increases his value to his newspaper.

In one sense the public relations representative serves as a sort of beat man for the newspapers which lack the means of bringing the news of big business and big labor unions to stockholders, dealers, or rank-and-file members. These, after all, form a substantial bloc of readers.

Men and women in the news craft, especially reporters on the business beat or labor run, have a professional reason for cooperating with rather than battling press representatives. The public relations field has opened a vast number of new opportunities to those with journalistic training and experience. These jobs not only pay well but can and do lead to advancement in professional standing and into executive positions of the first magnitude.

SHOP TALK

1. Discuss the news value of business. Do you believe that reader interest in business topics is increasing or decreasing?
2. Do you think a newspaper is justified in giving news about business in its community a better-than-even break? In other words, should it boost home-town business in its news columns?
3. Do you think news of organized labor is treated as fully and fairly in the press as news of business?
4. Debate the questions: Should advertisers receive special treatment in the news? Should news be suppressed merely because it extends free publicity to a business enterprise?
5. A merchant has bought at a discount a large quantity of clothing which he will sell at 20 per cent below the normal price. He is a regular advertiser. He wishes you to write a story about the sale. Will you do so?

CHAPTER 27

The Treatment of Crime

WHY CRIME IS NEWS

"Sin writes histories," said Goethe. "Goodness is silent." Fortunately goodness in living is the expected thing. It goes on with unexciting regularity. And for exactly this reason crime—departure from the usual —is news.

If reporters rushed to the scene when anybody did a good deed, we would see headlines like "Honest Cashier Discovered in Bank" and "Faithful Wife Affectionate to Children." These would be comparable to "Railway Journey Ends Safely" and almost as silly as "Sun Rises in the East" or "Water Runs Downhill." Fidelity and honesty are the rule. Hence newsmen spend a good deal of their time reporting misdeeds and dishonesty.

Despite the threat of exposure and punishment, crime marches on. Trailing the culprit is the policeman and behind the bluecoat is the reporter, while on the sidelines a vast audience of citizens looks on through the pages of the newspapers. Conflict and suspense, as well as oddity, energize the chronicles of crime which must be and are printed by every true newspaper in the land.

To issue a newspaper without covering law enforcement would be almost as difficult as baking a cake without flour or operating an automobile without gasoline.

Reduce the local room staff to a single man and that one man would still have to visit the police station on his daily round. Indeed in small towns the police run is the only beat to which a reporter is regularly assigned. Larger papers keep from one to a score of men constantly on duty at headquarters and frequently put general assignment men on police duty or swing them in to help with a major, multiangled crime story.

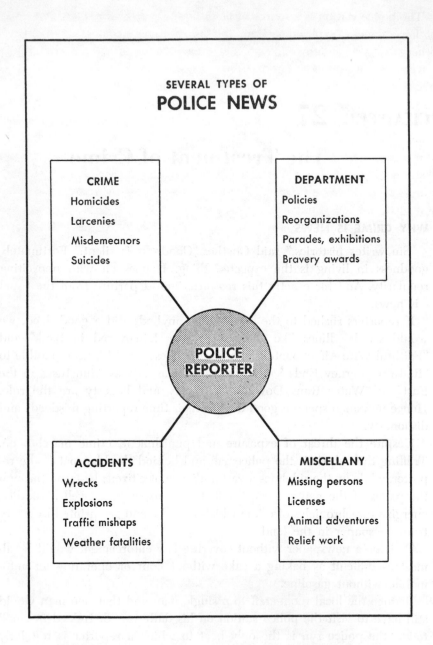

News Sources of the Police Reporter

The police station is a source of news not only of lawbreaking but also of fires, wrecks, explosions, riots, missing persons, accidents and every other variety of villainy, violence and valor plus the sometimes humorous adventures of runaway children and animals. In fact almost any surprising event that upsets the humdrum of law and order comes first to the attention of the police reporter.

As he casually runs down the list of petty crimes on the blotter, listens to short-wave radio calls, inspects Teletype descriptions of wanted men and counts fire alarm bells—tapping his news sources with modern equipment—the police reporter is ever alert for the first word of *the story* which could be the thunderous explosion of an enemy missile with a nuclear warhead.

In many localities the activities of law-enforcement agents other than municipal police are covered consistently. These include state and county police, sheriffs, marshals, constables and their deputies. From the stations, offices and headquarters of all these protectors of the peace flows an endless stream of stories whose subjects range from traffic violations to multiple murders.

CRIME AND POLICY

How much and what kind of crime news should be printed? In any discussion of the newspaper's attitude toward criminals this question is bound to arise.

Newspapers probably are reproached more for reporting crime than for any other reason. The critics say that newspapers make crime by reporting it. Publicity paints crime as attractive and the criminal as a romantic figure, with the result that daredevil youths seek to follow in his footsteps and share glamour and profits of lawlessness. Crime reports injure the innocent relatives of law violators, impair morals and offend good taste.

On the other side of the argument are those who contend that it is the proper province of the editor and reporter not to reform but to inform, that news of crime is vital information, that it is their duty not to appraise news but to determine what is news and to print it. To blame crime stories for crime itself is like blaming antisocial behavior on evil spirits and witchcraft. There is no relation. Wickedness needs to be exposed today just as graphically as it is in the Old Testament and Shakespeare.

Certainly to censor crime news would be to lull the public into a false sense of security. Newspaper readers are entitled to know what is going on in their community even if it is sometimes unpalatable—the stabbings, shootings and poisonings, the brutality and vandalism of juvenile delinquents, as well as the so-called higher class crimes of fraud and embezzlement. Evil unpublicized would be evil flourishing in dark privacy unhindered by public anger.

The second group holds also that the newspaper is a major law-enforcement weapon. The spotlight of publicity serves as a deterrent by warning would-be offenders that crime does not pay. It puts the public on guard against the perpetrators of crime. It aids in the apprehension of criminals. News stories and pictures frequently are their undoing, for they expose the culprit to an army of volunteer intelligence sources. And finally it is only by diligent crime coverage that law-enforcement agencies can be kept on their toes.

On close analysis the dispute between those who would minimize and those who would stress crime reporting is not so sharp as it first appears. The antipublicity advocates admit that all crime news should not be suppressed, and the publicity proponents readily admit that crime should not be unduly glorified or offensively written.

The fact is that some crime news is printed in all newspapers of general circulation. Depending on how it is played, it may be called smut in some papers and sociology in others, but reporters must and do cover it. The argument, then, simmers down to the questions of selection, space and treatment—how many crime stories are printed, to what degree they are displayed and how they are written. These questions are answered by each newspaper for itself.

The policy range on the treatment of crime runs the gamut from the so-called conservative daily-encyclopedia type of paper, which seldom permits a crime to creep onto page one, to the so-called sensational papers, sometimes in tabloid form, which deal dramatically with the blood, mud and ugliness as well as the beauty and occasional sublimity of human life.

Between these two ABC extremes—"Art, Banking and Culture" as against "Adultery, Banditry and Chiseling"—lie the bulk of American newspapers which gather and print crime news on its own merits in competition with other news of the day.

As we have pointed out before, there is little that the beginning reporter can do about his paper's policy except understand and conform to it. He is not likely to influence it greatly until after he grounds himself in the fundamentals of his trade.

POLICE REPORTERS AT WORK

Around the police reporter—as around his confreres who cover sports and politics—has grown a popular mythology which associates him with the heroes of short stories and movie, stage, radio and television dramas who tell off the city editor, solve the crime and win the girl in each whirlwind adventure.

The fiction that a police reporter customarily behaves like Sherlock Holmes or Perry Mason should be shelved at once. Only a few times in his life, if ever, does a reporter sass the boss, catch a culprit or woo the heroine while on duty. He is no such miracle man.

Pressed for time and always confronted with the danger of libel, newsmen rely almost wholly upon tips and statements from policemen, complaint sheets and official records of arrest. Seldom do they scoop the town on news unknown to the homicide squad.

For the most part the reporter follows in the wake of investigations begun by the police department. Development and expansion of a crime story naturally hinge upon the policy of his paper and his own application, but always he is dependent upon official statements, records and actions.

All factors considered, the work of the police reporter probably is more arduous and productive than that of any other man on the local staff. It is true that during some periods when all is quiet he can relax in the pressroom, but he must be constantly on the lookout. When a crime story breaks, he works fast and with painstaking care.

The crime reporter sees and knows the seamy side of life and writes the tales of mean streets. It is one thing to sit at a press table after luncheon and take notes on a speech by a dignitary eager to be quoted and quite another to interview a hysterical and grief-stricken woman about some disgraceful affair in a gambling dive in which her son killed his best friend. Nor is it fun to turn in a story about a drunken driver who will lose his job and shame his family when the case is reported.

Often the hours of the police reporter are irregular, his associations rough and disillusioning. Because of the nature of his work he sometimes encases himself in a shell of cynicism and nonchalance.

The police reporter may not act like a rough-and-tumble character in "The Front Page" but he is undoubtedly the hard-boiled egg of the reportorial nest.

Because it calls for hard and often unpleasant work, for special attention to names, addresses and other facts, for poise and courage, the press coop of a police station is considered a good training school for young

POLICE DEPARTMENT
COMPLAINT BLANK

Received	Where Received	Reported By
Date *June 3*	*Central*	*J. L. Rhodes*

Time	Received By	Transcribed By
7:20 a. m.	*O'Connor*	*O'Connor*

Complainant	Telephone
J. L. Rhodes	*Main 4-6090*

Home Address	Business Address
462 W. 14th St.	*127 Garfield Ave.*

Referred To

Milford and Gates

Nature Of Complaint

Home, 462 W. 14th St. entered. Broke window. Fur coat, value $700, and ring, $350, taken.

From a Police Blotter

reporters. In fact, many newspapers insist on beginners spending a year or two on police news to season them for general and special assignment reporting.

WHAT CRIME IS NEWS?

Why does one crime story emblazon the front pages for weeks, while another expires with a paragraph or two? "That's easy," replies the critic. "To be big news the crime must be bloodcurdling, sensational."

Partly true, but not all that needs to be said. Many a sordid butcher-knife murder is never recorded in print, whereas a penknife scuffle may be given full play with details and photographs. What, then, are the factors which make a crime news? They may be summarized as follows:

1. *Prominence of persons.* Wealth and position count in any kind of story, but especially when there is proof of wrongdoing. If a drunken factory employe kills another in a tavern brawl, the story gets a few paragraphs. But everybody gives heed if a highly respected clergyman shoots a banker's wife. It is a rare departure from the usual when the mayor breaks the speed limit—hence *news.*

2. *Prominence of places.* The same test applies to familiar things and places whenever they serve as background. While a fist fight in a slum district goes unrecorded, a like affray in a millionaire colony brings the reporters on the double-quick. A daylight robbery of the swank Strand Theater on Main street is worth a dozen muggings along the river wharves at night.

3. *Property loss.* Obviously a $10 alley holdup means less than a $100,-000 bank robbery and a $20 check forgery less than the stealing of mail sacks containing $500,000 from a post office truck. If all other factors balance, the property loss gauges the news value.

4. *Action and crowds.* There is little excitement when a dishonest clerk quietly pockets a few dollars from a cash register, but plenty if he waves a gun in a crowded store, starts a panic among the customers and then is pursued through traffic by a shooting policeman. Action and crowds serve to dramatize the story.

5. *Mystery and suspense.* Every detective story writer knows the trick of keeping his readers awake and guessing. So does the police reporter. As long as the police are baffled news interest thrives and expands. The moment the case is solved interest dies out.

6. *Unique circumstances.* The first murderer to inoculate his victim with germs, like the first highwayman to use a helicopter, made a nine days' sensation. A burglar who teaches at college or leaves a note of thanks after ransacking a house reads about his exploits on page one. Anything startling, novel or peculiar in crime, especially if it relates to the motive that prompted the act, strengthens the news bond.

7. *Emotional pull.* Human interest and emotions help to make crime

news. Police reporters probably unearth more human interest stories than do any other members of the staff, with the possible exception of court reporters. All the human emotions reveal themselves in crime stories—love, greed, romance, hate, lust, jealousy, revenge, remorse, self-preservation. A woman may hold the key that will unlock a mystery, and every police reporter worth his salt is anxious to find Madame X and hear her story.

Beyond and deeper than any of these factors, or any combination of them, lie situations which form the mainsprings of the most engrossing crime stories—situations that involve racial prejudice, disputes between capital and labor, political rivalry, marital unhappiness, euthanasia, thirst for power and money. In such cases the leading characters in the crime drama become symbols and are of little consequence in themselves as human beings. They represent the clash of ideas and passions which stirs us all.

CHOOSING A CRIME LEAD

Keeping in mind the seven factors which tend to make lawbreaking newsworthy, let us note how the strongest can be picked out and pointed up in the lead paragraph of the story. Illustrations follow:

Prominence of Persons

The body of Mrs. Calvin Sawyer, 32, socially prominent wife of a wealthy Midland businessman, was found early today lying in an ice-encrusted ditch near Meadville. There was a bullet hole in her left temple.

Prominence of Places

While 50 of Midland's finest stood on the steps of City Hall yesterday watching Mayor Nelson award police bravery medals, a man in the crowd yelled: "Hey, somebody's got my wallet!"

Property Loss

Jewels valued at $100,000, including a $40,000 heirloom necklace, were lifted last night from a wall safe in the Crescent drive home of Mr. and Mrs. J. R. Spencer.

Action and Crowds

A game transit policeman, badly pistol-whipped in a fight with two gunmen fleeing from a $12 change-booth stick-up, shot and killed one of them at 6:30 a.m. today in the Union Bus Terminal.

Mystery and Suspense

A laundry mark "A.R.S." and a ring engraved with a strange Egyptian symbol were the only clues police had today in the death of a man whose body was found last night in Lake Luce.

Unique Circumstances

A quarrel over the ownership of apples on a back-yard boundary-line tree resulted today in the arrest of two neighbors for disturbing the peace.

Emotional Pull

"Turn around," said Nancy Richards, aiming a .22 caliber rifle. "I want you to face me when I shoot you."

Each one of these openers contains a kernel of time-tested reader appeal which sprouts into an attention-pulling story as the details are developed.

CRIME STORY STRUCTURE

Any attempt to chart the structure of a standard crime story would be misleading, for the variations in construction are as diverse as crime itself.

The news factors and leads just illustrated indicate this diversity. Stories of the discovery of bodies conform generally to the fact format, with one circumstance or clue following another until all are set forth. The jewel theft report also adheres to the fact diagram.

After the apple quarrel lead there follows a quote-summary-quote form, with the two neighbors giving their versions of the dispute. The quote format also holds through a large part of the shooting story, with Miss Richards confessing.

It is apparent that only the action structure can be used in the transit-policeman-shooting-affray story or any other narrative-type account of a crime. Since fast-breaking crime stories of the action variety tend to confuse the young reporter, we shall apply the action diagram to one to show its organization:

Lead—Incident Told

A band of armed robbers held up the Midland Savings Bank at Main and 9th streets yesterday morning and escaped with all the bills in the bank's vaults, a total of $16,843.

Retold—More Detail

Working carefully and in no apparent hurry, three of the robbers took possession of the bank for 30 minutes before it opened for business. They kept six employes under control while they methodically cleaned out the bills in the vault. Then they joined two companions waiting outside and disappeared in a green sedan.

Retold—More Detail

The robbery started at 8:30 a.m., when John Davis, 61, the custodian, came to work. As he unlocked the glass door at the front of the six-story bank building, a man shoved him inside. Two other men followed them in. They warned Davis to let in the employes as usual and to greet them as though nothing was wrong.

One by one the six employes, three of them women, came to work. Miss Theresa Youngman, a cashier, said the thieves were polite.

"Would you please join the rest of the party sitting over there?" one of the men said to her.

At 9 a.m. the alarm on the vault door automatically went off. Soon after, the holdup men brought two bank officials to the steel vault door. They were J. L. Lord, assistant manager, and Robert L. Kingston. With a pistol at his head, Lord unlocked the door . . . . .

Following a complete recitation of the happenings in the bank, the story concludes with the statements of witnesses outside who saw the escape car, and a report on the police activities which ensued as the man hunt got under way.

GRUESOMENESS AND MELODRAMA

"Isn't it shocking? All you see in the papers are bloody murders. These reporters! Anything to be sensational." How often one hears such remarks from newspaper readers. The fact is that in the average newspaper no more than six or seven per cent of the space allotted to news is given to reports of crime.

While it is true that the treatment of crime news varies with a paper's policy, the charge that it persistently offends good taste is baseless. As a matter of fact, whatever is merely horrible and shocking seldom gets into print except when vital public issues are involved, and then only in carefully worded form. Readers sometimes get the impression that gruesomeness is stressed in a story when actually it is imagined by them as they mentally fill in between the lines and words.

The first lesson a crime reporter learns is that he must eliminate repellent details from his copy. If he fails to do so, the copyreaders will do it for him.

Contrast the following two stories—one sensational, the other restrained and calmly objective:

SENSATIONAL

Lying in a pool of blood which poured in a crimson stream from his skull, the body of Samuel Whitcomb, a salesman, was discovered today in his room at the Hotel Harper.

That murder had been perpetrated was apparent. Two bullets had torn their way into the left temple and the body was sprawled in a position that showed the victim had fought for his life. His eyes were fixed in a glassy stare.

Mystery shrouded the fiendish affair, the murderer having vanished as though in thin air, and the case probably will go into the annals of the police department as an unsolved outrage.

CONSERVATIVE

Shot twice through the head, the body of Samuel Whitcomb, 37, a salesman, was found late today in his room at the Hotel Harper.

The police, called by employes of the hotel, were investigating the case this evening. No weapon was found in the room and Capt. Hugh O'Malley called the death a homicide. There were evidences that a struggle had taken place.

Whitcomb registered at the hotel Tuesday, giving his address as New York. Papers found in his clothing indicated he was employed by a firm of wholesale clothiers in that city.

Keeping within the bounds of decorum does not mean that a reporter must smother the facts. When necessary even the most sordid particulars may be transmitted to the reader by inference and a discreet choice of words and phrases. However, this does not mean cheap melodrama and excited rhetoric. An effort to dime-novelize only makes ridiculous a news story sufficiently dramatic in itself to stand on its own legs. Compare the following two accounts as to style:

MELODRAMATIC

Gangland's guns barked once more last night!

And when the smoke cleared away, two hapless members of the crime fraternity who dared to "squawk" on a pal, lay stretched in a ditch, stone dead. They had paid for their sins and paid high.

Picture the scene: moonlight . . . the throbbing motor of a high-powered car roaring along Highway 14 . . . a scream of brakes, then a staccato of pistol shots . . . a pair of dark bodies lurching into the road. That, the police say, was the way Frank Foley and Frenchy LaCrosse were dashed into eternity—slaughtered by their own former friends.

It was just last week that these two gunmen spilled in court the telltale evidence that sent Michael (Red Mike) Staley up the river. Staley was their chief. And so they got theirs.

What were their thoughts on that last, long, terrible ride? Did they grovel and beg for their lives or did they face the music like men? Who will ever know?

Hot with anger over this latest outrage of gangdom, Capt. John Trent of the Mercerville police flung five squads into the gang haunts with orders to "bring back the guilty men or don't come back . . . . ."

MODERATE

Two members of the Staley gang early this morning paid with their lives the penalty which police officials say was for betrayal of their boss.

They were Frank Foley, 31, and Jacques (Frenchy) LaCrosse, 32.

Riddled with bullets, the bodies of the two men were discovered in a ditch alongside Highway 14 three miles west of Mercerville by L. T. Hardy, a dairyman, who notified Capt. John Trent of the Mercerville police. Both apparently had been shot and thrown from an automobile during the night.

In one of LaCrosse's pockets was a check for $29.45 paid to him as a witness fee for testifying last week at the trial of Michael Staley, leader of the gang with which LaCrosse and Foley were connected. Both, it was recalled, turned state's evidence and were freed as accomplices in a café shooting in which Policeman Henry Murphy was wounded last summer. Staley received a 15-year penitentiary sentence.

"They were marked men," commented Capt. Trent. "I think they intended to skip town, but either they failed to make their getaway quick enough or they thought they could protect themselves . . . . ."

POLICE BEAT DO'S AND DON'TS

Like other reporters, the man on the police beat must conform to certain standards of fair play as well as accuracy to keep himself and his paper out of hot water.

If the police ask him to withhold the identity of a prisoner until other arrests are made, he usually does so. He keeps confidences and deals squarely with reporters from other papers. And, if his own paper bars the names of juvenile offenders under 18 or the names of women in certain rape cases, he withholds them from the rewrite man or his copy.

He may or may not be tempted to represent himself as a policeman—"Smith calling from police headquarters"—to get information but if he does he uses that information with caution.

Within reasonable bounds the reporter works into his story creditable mention of those who give it to him but not so as to indicate they were bribed by unwarranted publicity.

Far more serious than breaking confidences or offending good taste are the ever-present risks of libel in accounts of lawbreaking, especially when persons of good reputation are concerned. If he is a close student of crime phraseology the reporter knows that such words as *robber, kidnaper, thief* and *arsonist* are dynamite. A suspected slayer is not a killer; a killer is not a suspected murderer; a suspected murderer is not an accused murderer; an accused murderer is not a convicted murderer; a convicted murderer is not necessarily a murderer. Never must a writer presume that a person is guilty of any kind of offense, no matter how damaging the evidence.

Note the safety-valve words and phrases in this account of a police raid:

Six men were arrested and *charged with* gambling last night when a Midland police squad invaded a tavern at 684 Grand Ave. and interrupted *what they said was* a poker game.

J. I. Steelman, 45, *was booked as the proprietor* of the tavern. The other prisoners *were docketed as* Harry Ross, 23, Lawrence Billings, 26, David Jenkins, 42, William Austin, 37, and R. Victor Stern, 56. All were released when Steelman posted surety for their appearance in Municipal Court today.

The raiding squad was headed by Lieut. Frederick Price of the Central Police Station. The officers *said they* seized two packs of cards and several chips.

At the police station *the prisoners said they were engaged in a friendly game* in a private room behind the tavern proper and that the officers entered without a warrant.

In this story the reporter took no chances. He did not allow personal opinion or prejudice to twist his story. He wrote the facts and statements as he received them at the police station and left it for the court to determine guilt or innocence.

Stories about crimes in which no arrest has been made need hardly more than one citation of the source, for an unidentified criminal cannot be libeled. But attribution poses problems in writing crime stories which get cluttered up with *So-and-So said, according to the officer* and *who quoted the prisoner as saying.* One way to clean up such copy is to start a narrative like this:

The sheriff said he pieced together this account from witnesses:
Here is what she said happened:
The report of the arresting officers was this:
Sgt. Johnson told this story of the robbery:

Purported confessions are especially dangerous because they may be repudiated in the courtroom. Some lawyers hold that they should be withheld from print until received in evidence at a trial. Few editors agree but all do agree that they should be attributed to the authorities involved.

TREATING CRIME CONSTRUCTIVELY

If you are working for a newspaper with a policy which calls for the constructive handling of crime news, it is well to emphasize the evil aspects of wrongdoing and the punishment of a vicious act and to bring in, if possible, some reference to its social consequences.

Such a policy can be carried out by the reporter without going beyond the bounds of factual reporting into editorializing. Here are examples of leads on the same stories:

STRAIGHT

Nicholas McGregor, 15, of 1309 Locust St., was taken into custody yesterday on charges of being an accomplice in the holdup of the Colfax Restaurant, 508 Douglas Ave., Saturday night.

Police today were investigating the death of Edward J. Diehl, an electrician, 1703 Poplar St., who was killed by a Midland Shore Line train last night.

SLANTED

A youthful bandit, who thought it would be a thrill to flourish a gun, regretted his folly last night as he sat in a jail cell, charged with robbery and facing the prospect of a term in the state reformatory.

Two small children were left fatherless today after Edward J. Diehl, an electrician, 1703 Poplar St., died last night at a dimly lit railroad grade crossing.

In the following lead the writer deliberately de-glorified the criminal and made it clear that crime does not pay:

The primrose path of lights, tinsel, easy money and the power of the bullet which beckoned two young men ended early today on Main street. One lay dead from a patrolman's gun. The other was captured and jailed on a charge of murder.

Crusades against certain brands of law violation, viewed by a newspaper as particularly menacing to the community, are frequently undertaken and effectively carried out in the news and editorial columns. The Midland *Times*, for example, may wage war on the sale of liquor to minors or set out to clean up a gambling district. At another time it may start a drive to prevent the fleecing of the public by street fakers, and again to drive out loan sharks. These objectives can be accomplished only through the cooperation of the Police Department, bolstered by an aroused public opinion.

At this moment the *Times* is engaged in a campaign to bring about city regulation of the sale of firearms. Investigation of a robbery shows that the robber used a gun easily procured at a local hardware store. No matter how spectacular the crime, the *Times* reporter stresses the purchase of the gun. His story starts something like this:

Using a revolver purchased only a few hours earlier for $6.75, a 15-year old boy last night attempted to rob a gasoline filling station at Elm and

Tremont Sts. Captured by the police as he tried to escape, the youth confessed that he planned the robbery after seeing a firearms display in a hardware store window.

Under arrest is Robert Cramwell, a student at Harrison High School. He said he lived with his widowed mother, Mrs. Ernest Cramwell, at 1123 Harding Ave.

As he walked into the station under the pretext of asking for directions, Cramwell pulled the gun from under his coat and ordered Bert Stacey, the attendant, to face the wall while he rifled the cash drawer. With about $30 in his pocket the boy fled, only to run into Policeman Edward Banks a block away. Banks stopped and searched him, found the gun and money, and took him to the Central Station.

"I needed some cash to pay off a debt and it looked so easy that I bought the gun and tried it," the boy confessed to Lieut. John Wilkerson later. He said the hardware store clerk did not ask him what he intended to do with the weapon.

The holdup lent impetus to efforts of Councilman Otto R. Vincent to secure the passage of an ordinance requiring registration and a city permit before a pistol can be purchased.

"It is entirely too easy for criminals and would-be-criminals to arm themselves," Vincent said, commenting on the incident. "There is no question that my ordinance, had it been in effect, would have prevented young Cramwell from getting into trouble. If the City Council does not adopt it, the city itself will be indirectly responsible for robberies, and perhaps murders, in the future."

SPECIALIZING IN CRIME

From the ranks of the police reporters come the specialists in crime, men who have served their apprenticeship at headquarters and substations, and who know something of the tangled notions that prompt men and women to seek a profitable living as gamblers, racketeers and dope peddlers. These reporters have proved their writing ability and receive only the more important crime story assignments.

The first-class reporting of crime requires more than applied energy and common sense. It demands experience and close familiarity with police methods, with criminal characters and activities in a particular community. The man ambitious to become a specialist in crime should deliberately plan and prepare for such a career. Newspapers employ experts on politics, sports, science, finance, religion and business. Crime likewise calls for the skill of specialists. An important niche awaits the crime expert in the metropolitan newspaper office.

During the past few years papers with an appreciation of the "feminine touch" in crime news have opened opportunities in this field to women. Nearly all the larger papers employ at least one woman crime specialist.

Although the work is rough and sometimes unpleasant for a woman, it is adventuresome and holds attraction for the girl reporter not satisfied with covering society and the doings of women's clubs.

More and more newspapers are going beyond mere reporting of crime news and, together with modern sociologists, trying to throw light on its causes and cures.

A man murders a wife with whom he has lived 30 years. What made him hate her enough to kill her? A 12-year-old boy clubs to death a school chum in a quarrel over a baseball bat. There's more to these stories and situations than the first reports. *Why* did they happen? Trained crime reporters can help to find out and assist, perhaps, in preventing the next one.

SHOP TALK

1. In your opinion, do the present methods of handling crime news make popular heroes out of criminals? How would you change the kind and amount of crime news printed?
2. If you were an editor, would you print the names of boys and girls under 18 who get into trouble with the law? Would more publicity reduce the rate of juvenile delinquency?
3. Does the reporter write a crime story as gruesomely as possible in order to thrill and shock his readers? What are the limits of newspaper good taste?
4. What news other than crime does the police reporter cover?
5. List the factors which make a crime newsworthy. Apply them to specific situations.

CHAPTER 28

Covering the Courts

THE COURTHOUSE BEAT

The courts are focal points of news coverage in every community—from the village police court to the United States Supreme Court in Washington, D.C. Vigilant reporters visit them constantly and they frequently draw the ablest of the star writers.

Courts ordinarily may be classified according to the functions they exercise, as follows:

1. Courts of limited jurisdiction such as police, probate and county courts.
2. Local courts of original jurisdiction:
   a. Criminal courts.
   b. Civil courts.
3. Intermediate appellate courts.
4. Highest appellate court, or supreme court.

In the larger cities and in the state and national capitals, staffs of specialists are assigned to the main tribunals, especially those in the last two categories. The courts in the first two classes are usually covered by local staff reporters. Class No. 1 includes police, municipal, justice of the peace, magistrate, domestic relations, probate and juvenile courts. Those in class No. 2 are known variously as circuit, district, superior and common pleas or *nisi prius* courts. They all derive their powers from the federal, state, county or city governments.

In a village the only court may be that of a justice of the peace. The center of court news interest lies in the county seat, where all the activities of the county government are concentrated in a building commonly called the *courthouse*. If the county seat is a city of considerable size it may have police or other local courts in the city hall or another municipal building. In a metropolis, the ramifications of these and the state and federal courts may be scattered and extend into many avenues.

In Midland, a typical county seat, Reporter Michael McCauley is assigned to the courthouse beat where he gathers news not only from the courtrooms but from a dozen other county offices including those of the sheriff, clerk, treasurer and engineer. He reports news of crime in the county outside the city limits, taxes and assessments, county institutions and welfare agencies, highway improvements and maintenance.

As he makes his daily rounds, brings in and writes his stories, McCauley proceeds in much the same way as Paul Wilson at City Hall and other reporters with regular beats.

In this chapter we shall deal with news of a specific kind—that which emanates from the courts and their adjuncts.

Since Colonial days in America the administration of justice has been a major source of copy for the press. Grave issues of individual right and public equity are weighed and settled in the courtrooms. As carriers of information about these decisions newspapers perform a major public service.

News of the bar and bench is printed not only as an obligation but because it is a highly salable product. It is intimately concerned with the primary news elements, especially conflict, emotions, suspense, sex and oddity. From the courts, as from police stations, come many human interest stories in unadulterated form.

In courtroom coverage newspapers have several distinct advantages over other media. While reporters as well as the public can be excluded by a judge, they seldom are. However, restraints can be placed on picture-taking and on the lights and equipment used in broadcasting and televising, especially during the actual taking of testimony.

Further, a reporter, even though he does not know shorthand, can obtain verbatim copies or extracts from the court stenographer for use by his paper to the extent that they are newsworthy.

The excitement of big courtroom dramas as portrayed in print often leads non-newspaper folk to look on the court reporter with envy. McCauley and his colleagues from other papers grow weary of hearing acquaintances say: "How interesting your work must be. Trials are so fascinating." The newsmen know better.

Most of McCauley's work consists of trudging from office to office, interviewing lawyers, clerks and other attachés, combing painstakingly through dull and highly technical documents and, even during important trials, taking notes with an eye on his watch and his mind ever intent on the dangers of libel.

McCauley knows intimately every judge, prosecutor and attendant in the courthouse. Assiduously he has cultivated their friendship, good will and assistance. Never having studied law, he has been forced to learn about the operations of the courts and the rudiments of legal phraseology by a process of self-education.

TRAINING FOR COURT REPORTING

As has been pointed out, specialists are assigned to the higher courts. However, as in the case of sports, society, business and crime, the beginner is bound to find himself writing chronicles of the courts soon after he starts his first job, for many a general assignment story leads to the courthouse.

Newspaper editors do not expect their reporters to be lawyers any more than they expect them to be financiers, engineers, sports champions or scientists. They do demand intelligent coverage and accurate writing of court news, and this calls for some special skill which must be acquired on the job or, better, in journalism training courses.

Most newspapermen, like McCauley, learn by the trial-and-error method, by gradual absorption of the nomenclature of legal procedure. But those who prepare themselves through study are likely to progress much faster.

In a test of 60 seniors in journalism at a Western university it was found that 47 per cent could not distinguish between a grand jury and a trial jury. Eleven per cent did not know how the government prosecutes a criminal case. Forty-two per cent had never attended a criminal trial. If the foregoing is a fair barometer, reporters-to-be are indeed ill prepared for court writing.

Examine your own acquaintance with the law by defining the following words:

abstract	continuance	injunction
accessory	cross-examine	intestate
accomplice	demurrer	judgment
affidavit	deposition	jurisdiction
appeal	equity	lien
arraignment	escrow	mandamus
bail bond	executor	manslaughter
bailiff	extradition	mayhem
brief	felony	panel
certiorari	habeas corpus	peremptory challenge
chancery	homicide	plea
common law	indenture	praecipe
contempt	indictment	probate

recognizance	talesman	venue
replevin	testate	verdict
reprieve	tort	warrant
subpoena	true bill	writ

While he does not use them in his copy if he can find simpler terms, the court reporter himself needs to learn the meaning of such legal lingo as *ad hoc, quid pro quo, nolo contendere, nolle pros, per curiam, writ of supersedeas* and *writ of certiorari.*

The plan of this book does not permit extended exposition of court practice and procedure. Reporters must acquire such information for themselves through study, by visits to courts and by critical examination of the newspapers. It is sufficient here to indicate some of the main sources of court news and to show how stories can be written to satisfy the copy desk.

NEWS FROM LEGAL DOCUMENTS

Many courthouse stories are based entirely upon documents and papers which, as public records, are available to reporters. These include pleadings in civil cases, wills and estates.

When a person—the plaintiff or complainant—desires to invoke the law to secure his rights, he employs an attorney to file in the court of proper jurisdiction a statement of his case in the form of a declaration, statement of claim, bill of complaint or petition. The attorney for the other party—the defendant—files an answer or reply.

An example of how a reporter prepares a story from such a document follows. Note the italicized words, showing the care taken to base every statement strictly upon the record.

> Miss Agnes Jones today *accused* Dr. Harry Lee, plastic surgeon, of having operated so negligently in a beautifying operation that her face is permanently scarred.
>
> *The charges were made in a complaint* against the surgeon, filed in Circuit Court by Attorney A. S. Howell. Miss Jones asks for $50,000 damages.
>
> *The pleading sets up* that on June 6 Miss Jones, who is 26 years old and lives at 901 Walnut St., asked Dr. Lee to remove a mole from her forehead. He told her, *according to the complaint,* that he could do so and leave the skin unblemished.
>
> "Yielding to his advice and urging," *the document continues,* "the plaintiff on July 11 paid to the defendant the sum of $200 as his fee for the purpose of performing the operation."
>
> *The pleading states* that on July 13 the operation was performed. Later, *it alleges,* her face was permanently scarred.

It is obvious that such a story will cause personal humiliation and embarrassment as well as damage to reputations. While the pleading is privileged, as are all court documents, the reporter must take every precaution to see that his notes are full and accurate and that he does not stray from them when writing. Another example:

If one's wife spends all her time playing bridge, a husband deserves an occasional stag party, *is the contention* of Willard C. Regan, salesman, *in an answer* filed yesterday to his wife's suit for divorce.

Mrs. Emily Smith Regan, the plaintiff, on May 13 *filed a complaint charging* Regan with "habitual drunkenness" and nonsupport. The Regans, until they separated a month ago, lived at 270 Ash St.

"The plaintiff without regard for her duties as wife and homekeeper spent nearly every afternoon and evening at bridge parties, although aforesaid defendant begged her to desist," *the answer states.* "When the defendant, seeking companionship, occasionally went to club and lodge entertainments, said plaintiff objected strenuously and threatened to leave him."

"Several times the said plaintiff actually did leave said defendant for periods of one to ten days," *the answer avers further.*

Denial that Regan "was almost continuously under the influence of liquor" *is vigorously made in answer to an allegation in the wife's complaint.*

The answer asks that the complaint of Mrs. Regan be dismissed, *stating that* "the defendant has been and is now ready and willing to live with and support said plaintiff" if a reconciliation can be effected.

Newspaper readers show a natural curiosity about wills and estates, and reporters watch the probate courts for news of this semiprivate variety. Major points of interest are the amount of an estate, its character, the heirs and beneficiaries, and conflicts arising over legacies. Large sums of money inevitably attract attention. Perhaps a school or charitable institution will receive bequests. The human interest element crops up frequently in wills containing out-of-the-ordinary bequests such as this one:

A Persian cat, Cuddles, and a cocker spaniel, Handsome, are the beneficiaries of $1,000 each left to them by their late owner, Mrs. Arthur Winslow, whose home was at 1457 Jackson Ave.

"They were my best friends in life," declared Mrs. Winslow in her will, filed in Probate Court yesterday. Mrs. Winslow died on Jan. 2 at the age of 82. She left an estate estimated at $3,000.

Mrs. Winslow made provision for Cuddles and Handsome by leaving the $2,000 through her executor, John H. Daley, with instructions to find good homes for the pets and pay for their care until the end of their lives.

Mrs. Winslow had no near living relatives. Her will specified that the balance of the estate, after payment of funeral and cemetery expenses, should go to the Midland Pet Shelter.

Scores of civil actions are instituted at every session of a civil court. Some of them contain strong news interest, especially those in which prominent firms or institutions, large sums of money or broad questions of public equity are involved. However, civil trials furnish little copy as compared to criminal trials. If there is a strong news element such as prominence of persons involved, a criminal trial may provide stories day after day through each step of the proceedings. These vary in different states. The usual stages are shown in an accompanying chart.

EARLY STAGES IN THE TRIAL

After he is arrested and booked, an accused person in a number of states must be indicted by a grand jury before he is brought before the bar in a public trial. The indictment specifies the charge or charges on which he is to be tried. Here is a typical indictment lead:

> A grand jury this afternoon indicted Harold F. Fisher, 43, of Fairfield, for second-degree murder in the alleged "mercy slaying" of his mother, Mrs. Leonard Fisher, 72, last October.

Frequently the pleading of the defendant takes place immediately after the indictment. This may become part of the indictment story. If it occurs later it results in a separate story opening like this:

> Wade S. Fulton, of Clifton, 22-year-old suspended Midland College student, today entered a surprise plea of guilty to a charge of first-degree manslaughter in the fatal beating of a classmate.

A guilty plea ends the court proceedings save for sentencing, whereas a plea of not guilty means that the trial moves to its next stage, the selection of a jury. Although picking jurors may be a long-drawn-out, day-after-day procedure, it frequently requires only one court day. Here the facts are set forth briefly but completely:

> Selection of an all-male jury in the first-degree murder trial of Edwin P. Dunham, 20, accused of fatally stabbing his wife, Sarah, 18, was completed late yesterday in Circuit Court.
>
> When the case resumes at 10 a.m. today, County Attorney Howard Ford will make the opening statement for the prosecution. The state will then call its first witnesses, including a police photographer and a medical examiner.
>
> F. D. Shanks, a Midland feed store owner, of 517 Maple St., was the last juror chosen to round out the 12-man panel. Two alternates were then selected and the court was adjourned at 4:35 p.m.

CRIMINAL TRIAL

1. INDICTMENT.

2. Pleading: guilty or not guilty.

3. Selection of jurors.

4. Opening statement of prosecution.

5. TESTIMONY OF PROSECUTION WITNESSES.

6. Opening statement of defense.

7. TESTIMONY OF DEFENSE WITNESSES.

8. Arguments to jury.

9. Judge's instructions to jury.

10. DELIBERATION AND VERDICT OF JURY.

11. Motions for new trial.

12. SENTENCE BY JUDGE.

13. Proceedings upon appeal.

Steps Likely to Make Major and Minor News

Mrs. Dunham died on Nov. 5 at the Dunham home, 1432 Forest Ave., after being stabbed twice in the throat with a kitchen knife. The stabbing followed what the police described as a quarrel with her husband over money.

The case is being tried before Circuit Judge Edward Smith. Dunham is represented by Attorney Anthony E. Seymour.

DESCRIBING THE TRIAL SETTING

The reporter serves as the eyes of his readers and hence must always keep in mind the necessity for description as well as straight narration. In criminal trials the depiction of action in the courtroom adds to reader appeal. Trace the setting in swift, telling phrases that do not impede the narrative, but remember that scenery is generally incidental to the main issue.

Note in this extract how the writer carries his readers directly into the courtroom with him:

Smiling as ever, sharp blue eyes twinkling behind his gold spectacles, Nixon entered the courtroom to face the charges with every mark of confidence. His wife, his son, his son's wife, the battery of expensive counsel, followed in his wake.

Jackson, the codefendant, stooped, gaunt and gray, chewing an unlighted cigar, came shuffling in, his lawyers around him. They nearly filled the well before the bench.

A score of newspapermen formed the next phalanx. Three inadequate rows took care of the few spectators who could get in, including former Congressman L. R. Brinks and Julius Stein, assistant postmaster.

After eight months of sparring in grand jury rooms and judges' chambers, the trial was about to begin.

Here again the reporter sets the scene and introduces the characters in pungent, colorful words:

The attitude of the two youths accused of shooting down an aged grocer differed like day and night.

Jaunty and carefree, young Jameson nodded to his friends and chatted with his attorney as nonchalantly as though watching a baseball game. He seemed to enjoy his sudden rise to notoriety.

Across the table sat his friend and alleged accomplice, Bentley, presenting a sharp contrast. His face pale and tense, one hand gripping the edge of his chair, he resembled a statue most of the time. He looked at no one, staring straight ahead as though acutely aware of the glances in his direction.

At 9 a.m., despite a drizzling rain, the courtroom was jammed with spectators, many of them fellow students of the boys, who filled the first rows of seats.

REPORTING THE EVIDENCE

As a trial reaches the witness stage the task of the covering newsman becomes more complicated. From the day's proceedings he needs to draw a telling lead, present atmosphere and color, and boil down to limited space testimony that occupied hours in the courtroom.

In this opener the reporter withheld names, addresses and places in order to clutch the drama of the testimony:

> A terrified boy sat in the witness chair in Timber County Court yesterday and tried to explain to a jury of grownups how his best pal and playmate met his death—a death for which the State of Centralia will ask that the boy spend the rest of his life in prison.

Again the writer vividly presents scenery and drama together with testimony:

> Biting her lips and fighting back tears at every word, blonde Lucy Perkins sobbed from the witness stand yesterday that she did not remember firing the shot that brought death to her sweetheart, Robert Deal.
>
> The 22-year-old stenographer broke down completely when she took the stand to testify in her own defense against a first-degree murder charge.
>
> After a 20-minute recess ordered by Circuit Court Judge John R. Roper, she was able to answer the questions of Defense Attorney Kenneth Parsons.
>
> "Do you remember shooting Robert?" Parsons asked.
>
> "No," was Lucy's whispered reply.
>
> Lucy was on the stand for 45 minutes. The defense rested shortly after her testimony.
>
> The young woman is accused of shooting Deal to death in an automobile parked near the Two Corners Tavern the night of May 13. The state charges she used her father's .38 caliber pistol to "get even" with Deal for dating another girl.
>
> There was a dramatic hush in the high-ceilinged old courtroom when Parsons summoned the girl to the stand. Her pallor was emphasized by an absence of makeup . . . . . .

Indirect quotation is the form generally adopted in presenting the bulk of the testimony. However, some testimony is so crucial that it should be quoted directly, occasionally at considerable length. When more than two questions and answers are used consecutively, the catechism form is advised, as follows:

> Frank Ditmars, another salesman for the Midland Fruit Co., proved to be the surprise witness of the day. He testified that the night of the shooting Johnson called at his house and visited with him and his wife. He said Johnson did not appear to be worried.

ALTERNATE ARRANGEMENTS OF
QUESTIONS AND ANSWERS

On cross-examination the defense attorney questioned Dr. Sayre as to her state of mind, as follows:

Q.—What she did was not to save her uncle from suffering?

A.—Yes, it was.

Q.—Did she know that what she was doing was to save her uncle from suffering?

A.—Yes.

Q.—So she did know the nature of her act, didn't she? Yes or no.

A.—(After getting a rereading of the question) Yes, she did.

Q.—About an hour ago you told the jury she did not know the nature of her act. Now, is it not a fact that she knew just exactly what she was doing?

A.—No, sir.

Q.—When she pointed that gun at his heart it was not because she had the comprehension to understand she was putting him out of his suffering?

A.—She had the comprehension to know she was putting him out of his misery—yes.

Q.—She did it for a perfectly logical reason—to put him out of his suffering?

A.—She was not conscious of the full consequence of her act.

Q.—But she knew it would cause his death?

A.—Yes.

Q.—Isn't that the full consequence?

A.—No.

Q.—The other consequence was that she would be arrested?

A.—Yes.

For an hour the defendant fought a battle of words with the prosecutor over a statement Lowe had made after his arrest.

Assistant County Attorney Spencer quoted from Lowe's statement: "I pulled the gun and let her have it."

Lowe denied saying this and insisted the gun went off after his wife tried to knock it out of his hand.

Lowe, a 23-year-old accountant, said that after the shooting in the Last Chance Tavern, the gun dropped on the floor. The statement Spencer read had Lowe admitting he had thrown it there.

"Do you deny saying you meant to shoot your wife?" Spencer asked.

"I do," said Lowe.

"Was the safety off?"

"Yes."

"Was the hammer pulled back?"

"Yes, but I didn't pull the trigger."

"And you claim that someone changed the answers you gave in your statement?"

"I certainly do," said Lowe. "Somebody changed them."

Lowe admitted that he bought the gun in a local pawnshop last October but insisted that he expected to use it only to protect his home.

"What do you have to protect at your home?" asked Spencer.

"I keep all my valuable papers at home."

"Did you have any reason to think that you might be robbed?"

"Yes, there had been several burglaries in our neighborhood."

How the News Writer Handles Testimony

"He came to your house at 9:30 p.m. to visit you?" asked Defense Attorney John Sullivan.

"Yes, sir," Ditmars answered.

Q.—What did you do while he was there?

A.—Oh, we talked business for a while and then played cards.

Q.—What time did he leave?

A.—About midnight, I think.

Q.—Do you know where he went?

A.—Yes, he said he was going home—that he had a trip the next day and wanted to get home.

At this, Assistant County Attorney Ewan was on his feet objecting that the question was improper as the witness did not know where Johnson went. The objection was sustained.

There follows another transcript of testimony effectively handled:

Edward Peters, a chubby little boy, 6 years old, mounted the witness stand with grave dignity and was questioned on his qualifications as follows:

Q.—Eddie, do you know where you are?

A.—Sure, Midland.

Q.—Do you know what it means to tell the truth?

A.—Yes, sir.

Q.—What happens to little boys who do not tell the truth?

A.—God will kill me if I don't.

Q.—Do you know what it means to tell a lie?

A.—I never tell my mother lies. When I hit somebody or do something bad, I always tell my mother. . . . .

Reporters transcribe their notes in various ways. Occasionally it is necessary to obtain a record of the evidence from the court stenographer, but most of the time brief memorandums—with fuller notes on certain parts of the testimony worth quoting verbatim—will be quite adequate. Too many notes, hastily scrawled, cause confusion at the typewriter.

At important trials two reporters may work together—one assigned to write successive leads and the other a running account of the proceedings. From time to time the men relieve each other. When only one of the pair is working he keeps two sets of notes, one complete and the other a summary of the important lead facts.

THE CLIMAX OF THE TRIAL

Courtroom reporters face their stiffest test when a criminal trial draws to a conclusion, with the closing arguments, judge's instructions, retirement of the jury, deliberations, the jury verdict, motions for appeal or a new trial, and the sentence often following in quick succession. These events furnish separate or composite stories depending upon the speed of the trial and the paper's deadlines. Frequently developments come rapidly and so close together that they must be handled as a running story containing bulletins, new leads, inserts and adds, with a complete composite story later.

Bulletin

William Worth, just before noon today, was sentenced to life in the penitentiary by Judge Frank Holcomb.

Bulletin

A verdict of guilty of second-degree murder was returned by the Worth case jury at 11:20 a.m. The verdict carries a life prison sentence. The jury was out two hours.

Bulletin

At 10:40 a.m. the Worth jury was reported to be standing 10–2 for a verdict of second-degree murder. Two jurors were said to be holding out for a manslaughter verdict.

Headline

Twelve men and women filed into the jury room of the Timber County Courthouse at 9:20 a.m. today to weigh evidence for and against William Worth, and to decide whether he is guilty of the murder of his sister-in-law, Violet Pond.

The first count of the indictment against Worth, that of murder with premeditation, already was nolled at the request of County Attorney Howard Ford. Worth is charged only with murder while attempting to assault Miss Pond.

In his final argument to the jury, A. S. Howell, senior defense counsel, admitted he believed his client guilty of manslaughter but not of a more serious offense . . . . .

When molding the verdict lead the problem is to combine facts, action and human interest into a compact package:

Paul R. Stevenson smiled wanly and his wife cried this afternoon as he was convicted of the slaying of his wife's admirer, Lester Lattimer, in her bedroom last November.

Wild cheering from a packed courtroom greeted a jury's verdict at midnight last night acquitting Amos Ronson, 32-year-old insurance salesman, of slaying the Ronson family physician.

Be careful with hastily written verdict bulletins and leads, especially with *not guilty*. *Not* is always a dangerous word because *w* is close to *t* on the typewriter and *not* can easily become *now*. Because of the danger of omitting the word *not,* some style sheets require *innocent* for *not guilty.*

The verdict story often follows the multiangled or composite structure. A standard form is this: Lead with the verdict itself and its immediate effect in the courtroom. Then trace the earlier events in descending order of importance—the jury's deliberations, the judge's instructions, the closing arguments. A brief history of the trial may be appended like a prepared obituary.

At some trials sentencing follows a verdict immediately, but more often it comes several days or weeks later and a follow-up is called for. Appeals may ensue thereafter, but as these go to the higher courts the stories usually move out of the hands of local staff reporters.

SHOP TALK

1. Explain why the courts always have been sources of strong public interest. Give examples of the news elements developed in the courts.
2. Discuss in detail the system of courts in your community. What types of news does each produce?
3. Give your definitions of the words listed under "Training for Court Reporting." Add and define others.
4. Discuss the difference between civil and criminal trials.
5. Outline the procedure in a criminal trial in your state, commenting on the news possibilities at each stage.

CHAPTER 29

Sex in News Stories

SKILL IN SEX REPORTING

It is an old saying among newspapermen that you can never succeed in making sex unpopular with the people. In whatever form it takes—and it takes many—sex is a vital part of life and living and, as such, a major element in the news.

As we shall see, certain types of specific stories involving sex are written and displayed quite differently in individual newspapers but in all of them the emotional and physical relations between men and women motivate columns of copy every day.

Sex and its ramifications thread through news of beauty, fashions, society, romance, marriage and divorce. Sex extends deeply into news of crime and the courts. It penetrates probably a third of the general news in an average paper and, in some, frequently emblazons the front page under top headlines.

Deplorable as it may seem to many observers, the journals which value most highly stories of love, courtship, marital misdeeds and sex crimes—to use a shop expression, stories with "the old whambozambo"—usually rank well in circulation comparisons.

Public interest in sex is reflected not only in the impressive circulation figures of the so-called sensational papers, some in tabloid format, but in comparable mass sales of magazines and books centering on the love, romance or confession theme. Not only literature but art, music, sculpture, the stage, screen, radio and television are replete with sex in its various forms.

It is a strange fact that such a subject receives so little attention in the training of young reporters who often enter the newsroom unprepared mentally or technically to handle stories of sex—especially those concerning misconduct—with anything approaching competency. Every city room is acquainted with the naïve neophyte eager to interpret for his readers the finer points of diplomacy, politics, economics and science, only to find on his helpless hands a seamy story of incest or rape.

He finds it difficult to gather pertinent information objectively. And, to make matters much worse, he suddenly discovers that he is unable to translate it into acceptable news copy. He gropes for words. Vainly he draws upon his literary resources, only to dredge up biological terms unintelligible except in a clinic or vulgarisms unfit to print.

It is perhaps small wonder that he flounders. Taboos and restrictions on the discussion of sex at home and in the classroom have limited his learning. He has never written an English composition or even a personal letter about sodomy or indecent exposure. He may be confronted with them during his first week at work.

If instructors and students include sex news as an essential topic for study and practice, such training will be a boon to city editors, who are seeking men and women with a practical knowledge of reporting. Skill in sex reporting is wanted.

HOW NEWSPAPERS TREAT SEX

Sex has been a controversial topic since the Garden of Eden. Its nature has placed it in an area of dispute and indecision in groups of every age and kind, including the managers of modern newspapers.

No editor with sound faculties would consider a total blackout of sex on his pages. Such an order would be to omit a topic which is a mainspring of human activities. Nor can any newsman ignore the fact that sex news sells newspapers and the products they advertise. It is wanted by the public. The disagreement concerns the point at which the press should stop giving the public what it wants.

Some papers systematically temper and minimize the more exciting aspects of sexual behavior and misbehavior. They pay scant attention to the café society and swimming pool sets, subdue stories of marital mix-ups, play down tales of wild parties, and wastebasket pictures of Broadway bosoms and Hollywood legs.

Other papers dramatize, embellish and illustrate the romances of Miss Universe and Miss America. They candidly play up the amorous exploits, sizzling love letters or spicy testimony of screen stars, socialites and other somebodies in the limelight. These papers appeal directly to the sexual impulses of the reader with news selected, written and placed so as to give him or her vicarious pleasure.

Between the extremes are found the majority of newspapers, taking a middle ground and treating sex news as it comes without either lurid detail or puritanical omission. These papers conform generally to public taste in the communities they serve.

The wire services, going to many newspapers, recognize the policy variations and try to be neutral. One method is to warn that certain sections or passages in a dispatch may be considered objectionable, thus giving individual editors the choice of printing, discarding, editing or rewriting the questionable material.

It should be made clear that all policies yield when news pressure is strong enough. If the characters or issues involved are prominent, the *hush-hush* newspapers drop their barriers and print explicit details pertinent to the telling of the news. On the other hand, if all news elements are lacking, even *face-the-facts* newspapers will not deliberately drag in pornography, thereby risking public condemnation and legal restraint.

What is the attitude of his own paper concerning the treatment of sex news? That the reporter can find out by studying its contents. He should then govern his course of action accordingly.

THE CHOICE OF WORDS

Animals—even those like apes which most closely resemble human beings—are completely uninhibited in matters of sex. So were our primitive ancestors.

However, when writing was invented there already were established in family and tribal groups many social customs and taboos. These, through sympathetic magic, were closely associated with the first hieroglyphic symbols, later with letters and finally with words.

In Britain before the Norman conquest, Anglo-Saxon words were used freely in all levels of society. After it the language of the French victors was adopted by the ruling classes, while the short, crude words of the conquered were relegated to the speech of the serfs. They exist now only in the argot of the uncouth and the scrawls on washroom walls.

In our own Colonial era the Puritans and again in the Victorian era of the eighteenth century words once acceptable were submerged in polite conversation because of their association with sex or other bodily functions.

For example, the words *breast* and *leg* became too brazen for the dinner table and we substituted *white meat,* and *dark meat.* Consider the evolution of *shirt* to *smock,* to *shift,* to *slip.* Underwear tends to become *lingerie;* nightgown, *negligee;* and corsets, *foundation garments.*

The giving of nice names to unpleasant things is known as euphemism, a word which is derived from the Greek meaning "to use fair words." Euphemism is aimed to dignify many things, such as occupations. Undertakers become *morticians;* garbage collectors, *sanitation men;* dogcatchers, *canine control officers;* and press agents, *public relations counselors.*

In every area of life there are never-ending changes in the acceptability of words and expressions, and newspaper copy reflects them all.

IT CAN BE WRITTEN

The proficient news writer is an expert in the art of selecting words which are meaningful but not offensive to the readers of his paper. No matter how shocking the facts of a sex story may be, he can reveal them with euphemisms suitable to the policy of his paper.

The key to good taste lies in the flexibility of the writer's vocabulary. It is not necessary to resort to the four-letter words of the washroom. An adult reader is perfectly capable of understanding living room synonyms and filling between the lines if the lines are well written.

For example, the word *naked,* although used freely in some newspapers, may be objectionable in your own. But it can easily be changed to any one of a number of less objectionable words such as *nude, disrobed, undraped, unclad, unclothed, not dressed,* or more breezily, *in her birthday suit, like Lady Godiva,* or *à la September Morn.* Not a single reader will miss the point.

To specify infidelity or adultery a writer can employ such terms as *violation of the marriage vows, marital misconduct, common-law marriage,* and *without benefit of clergy.* Or, if his paper insists that even these are too bold, he may say *misbehavior* or *indiscretion.* Should he need to write about a child born to unmarried parents he may refer to it as *born out of wedlock* or omit any descriptive term, merely mentioning the child's birth without linking it to the parents' nonmarital status. Readers will provide the link themselves.

In America, during the decades between and after two World Wars, there has been a distinct trend toward realism in sex writing, as there has been in public conversation. This is a swing of the pendulum away from the "nice-Nellyism" of the Victorian period.

A word in point is *syphilis.* Not too long ago newspapers referred to it as a *social disease* or *vice disease.* The specific word *syphilis* became commonplace in wartime and now is sensibly accepted in newspaper usage.

A comparison of terms used half a century ago and now reveals striking changes:

FORMER	PRESENT
a delicate condition	pregnant
statutory offense	rape
intimacies	sexual relations
white slave	prostitute
abnormal person	homosexual
affair	seduction
extramarital relations	adultery

The trend in sex news treatment away from verbal camouflage has resulted in more clarity. It is clearer and certainly less absurd to say a woman was beaten and raped than to say she was bludgeoned with a hammer and then criminally attacked or assaulted.

Despite the acceptance of more plain-spoken language, it must again be pointed out that the extent to which it may be used by a newspaper writer is governed by the standards of his own newspaper by which he is obliged to abide.

SOURCES OF SEX NEWS

Although it permeates much of the news of the day, sex cannot be oriented as a type of secondary news such as sports or identified as a specialty such as politics. There are no sex news specialists as such.

In an effort to show where sex news arises and which reporters handle it, let us arbitrarily divide it into three main divisions:

Love: courtship, romance and marriage; "happily ever after" news.

Strife: separation, annulment, divorce; other premarital, marital and nonmarital mishaps.

Crime: prostitution, rape, perversion; other sex and sex-connected crimes.

Variations of the old but ever-young theme of love, of feminine charms and masculine chivalry, of romantic idylls from high school elopements to golden wedding anniversaries come from many sources. Most important of these are marriage license bureaus, justices of the peace and clergymen. Much news of courtship flows to reporters covering the stage and screen, often with the enthusiastic aid of press agents and tipsters. Informants in society circles contribute, as well as correspondents in colleges and other institutions where young men and women mingle.

INCREASING VALUES IN
SEX NEWS

NEWS
One man . . . . one woman . . . . one romance
NEWS
One man . . . . one woman . . . . one engagement

One man . . . . one woman . . . . . one wedding

One husband . . . . one wife . . . . one baby born

One husband . . . . one wife . . . . one anniversary

NEWS
One man . . one woman . . one breach of promise suit

One man . . . . . one wife . . . . . one divorce suit

One husband . . . one wife . . . one alienation suit

One husband . . . two wives . . . one bigamy arrest

One husband . . . . one wife . . . . three babies born

NEWS
One husband . . . three wives . . one polygamy arrest

Two husbands . . . one wife . . . one bigamy arrest

One wife . . . two husbands . . . one polyandry arrest

One husband . . . . one wife . . . . four babies born

Two couples . . . . two divorces . . . . two weddings

Sex in Love, Strife and Crime

Virtually all news in the "strife" and "crime" divisions is privileged and emanates from law-enforcement agencies and the courts. Except in society and Hollywood gossip columns when the principals themselves or their agents supply the information, news of a domestic rift seldom is printed until it reaches the litigation stage. Stories of sex-connected crimes usually come from police records and the courts.

In news of crime *cherchez la femme,* the traditional epigram of the French police, applies also to the reporter. Two men hold up a bank. That's just a bank robbery. But if two men crack the safe and collect the loot while a girl accomplice lures the watchman from his post, and feeds him drugged candy, you have a better story.

Probably the nearest approach to a sex news beat is, in some cities, called the lawyers' beat. It is assigned to a reporter who covers attorneys specializing in lawsuits involving domestic trouble. He writes largely from the complaints and other court documents prepared by these lawyers.

Through the cooperation of attorneys, and despite the ban on premature publication, a court reporter is often able to secure copies of court documents well in advance, thereby giving his paper a chance to get pictures, interview the principals, prepare morgue material and be in readiness with complete coverage when the papers are filed.

Thus it will be seen that reporters covering the city hall, society, drama, schools, police, courts, lawyers and general assignments all help produce the daily output of sex news.

THE LURE OF THE FEMININE

It requires no survey or analysis to show the importance of feminine charm and beauty in all forms of American publicity and advertising. You will find the ever-present pretty girl smiling at you from shopwindows, billboards, calendars and magazine covers. Leg art and plunging necklines—for short, cheesecake—are standard items to news photographers and picture editors.

Any story revolving about feminine allure attracts men and women readers alike. The men read it because they are drawn to loveliness and youth in the opposite sex; the women, because they often see in others the answer to their own desire for perfection.

Note how the writer of this story sought to convey word pictures of beauty:

> A curvaceous blue-eyed blonde who wants to be a model was crowned "Miss Midland Milkmaid" last night at a contest conducted by the League of Dairymen.

Lola Larson, 19, coed who coyly confessed that she cannot milk a cow, won a judges' decision over brunette runner-up Jane Trevor, 18, a real farm girl from Twin Forks.

The winner will represent Midland in the state finals to be held in Capital City in connection with the League's state convention June 10.

Ten beautiful finalists attired in milkmaids' scanty costumes paraded across the stage in the local contest at Walker Hall.

Lola, a honey-haired sophomore at Midland College, and Jane, a home girl with flashing dark eyes and dimples, tied in the first voting. Then the judges took to their tape measures. Lola, weight 120, waistline 23, bust 35, emerged two points ahead of Jane, weight 123, waistline 24, bust 36. Both girls were 5 feet 5 in height.

"I'm happy to be the winner but I don't think I'd make much of a milk-maid," said Lola. "I want to be a model."

Frederick Horner, secretary of the League of Dairymen and one of the judges, said Lola's capabilities on the farm didn't matter. He added: "We think she'll win the state contest and that will help point up Midland as the leading dairy center in Centralia."

The more conservative papers pay little attention to such yarns as this and frown on spicy adjectives, but writers for lighter-vein papers are well stocked with such terms as:

curved and contoured	eyeful from Broadway
lissome lass	luscious bachelor girl
shapely show girl	raven-tressed beauty
siren of the screen	willowy armful
strawberry blonde	winsome stage star

Sex appeal phraseology tends to turn into stereotypes, as some of the foregoing examples indicate. The writer with an inventive term of mind who can create new picture terms in feminine beauty copy is likely to increase his value if he works for a newspaper that likes it.

THEY LIVED HAPPILY

Perhaps they didn't, but just the same the time-tested duologue of the prince and the princess, the king and the commoner, the millionaire and the chorus girl, the football hero and the coed, the matinee idol and the society deb—pair them as you will—never loses its spell of enchant-ment for ordinary newspaper reading folk.

Everybody loves a lover and by the alchemy of imagination the dowager, young wife and school girl, the grandfather, middle-aged busi-nessman and youth become principals in reports of romance. Although routine engagements and weddings seldom get beyond the society page, love becomes lively news if elements such as prominence, conflict or oddity are added.

In this example, prominence removes the romance from the ordinary:

> A modern Cinderella story ended as it should yesterday with a luxurious private honeymoon plane replacing the magic pumpkin coach-and-four.
>
> In a ceremony at First Presbyterian Church attended by a score of notables Miss Helen Reed, 21, a waitress at the Municipal Airport Restaurant, became the bride of Felix Brand Jr., 27, son of the president of the Skyway Co. After a brilliant reception at the Rex Hotel the couple left for New York in a Brand plane piloted by the bridegroom.
>
> "It was love at first sight and it's for keeps," Brand told reporters at the airport. His bride nodded agreement.
>
> "It's all too wonderful to be real," she said happily.
>
> One of the city's wealthiest and most eligible bachelors, Brand surprised Midland society recently with the announcement of his engagement. He said he became acquainted with Miss Reed while lunching at the restaurant where she worked a short distance from his office . . . . .

Conflict and oddity both energize this typical story of love-above-all:

> "I love him!"
>
> This phrase was fervently uttered by Sally Morton at the Timber County Courthouse yesterday. The 21-year-old brunette with appealing brown eyes declared that more than anything else in the world she wanted to marry Jack Hewitt, her childhood sweetheart.
>
> There isn't much future in it. For the next five years or so, the most she can look forward to is a hasty kiss and lovers' whispers through a wire mesh. Jack is going to State Prison today.
>
> Convicted on a charge of burglary, Hewitt was sentenced to five to ten years by Judge Edward Smith. Sally sat with her fiancé throughout the trial.
>
> "I'll wait for him no matter how long it is," she said. "He's not bad. He just made a mistake and must pay for it. But there never will be anyone else except Jack for me . . . . ."

Romance provides many a nutshell drama with a surprise ending to give the reader a chuckle as he peruses the heavier news of the day:

> Norman Ramsey appeared before Judge George H. Mather today on a charge of stealing a diamond ring from Beatrice Kennedy.
>
> "Do you wish to testify, Miss Kennedy?" Mather asked.
>
> "No, your honor, I don't," she replied. "The defendant and I were married last night."
>
> "Case dismissed," the judge said.

ROMANCE ON THE ROCKS

Because normally there is nothing unusual about marriage unless it goes wrong, marital rifts are newsier than marital peace. Divorce and domestic relations courts therefore are closely covered by most newspapers.

It was news for the Midland *Times* when a wealthy socialite married a waitress, but an even bigger story started like this:

> Felix Brand Jr., scion of one of Midland's wealthiest families, and his wife, the former Helen Reed, have agreed to give up trying to make their rags-and-riches marriage work.
>
> Attorneys for both announced yesterday that Mrs. Brand is in Reno . . . . .

Other leads indicate the wide range of sex strife stories that reach the papers through the courts:

> Under the romantic spell of a Florida moon, Merwick Masters, insurance broker, disregarded his 70-odd years and proposed marriage to a dark-haired beauty he had met for the first time. But the spell, Mrs. Donna Masters said in County Court today, didn't last.
>
> Out of a welter of threatened suits and cross-suits by three widows of Josiah X. Lampier, all claiming his estate, wife No. 2 emerged today with $100,000.
>
> "Brokenhearted" but still placing chivalry above father love, a 31-year-old husband yesterday renounced all claim to his 14-month-old son born out of wedlock and called off his custody fight to spare the boy and his mother "public shame and ridicule."
>
> The most discussed young woman in Midland today is Mrs. Elliot Carman, who disclosed in court that she requires $1,000 a month to clothe herself and spends $100 a month in a beauty shop.

With no attempt to disguise emotional appeal, writers for less conservative papers popularize such combinations as *Reno widow, domestic dissolution, heart balm, shattered romance, matrimonial casualty, purloined love, pilfered affection* and *the end of the honeymoon trail.* Seldom do the more conservative newspapers permit writers such freedom with their literary paintbrushes, preferring instead a more matter-of-fact approach. However, regardless of policy, all editors relish marital mix-up stories if the human interest element is strong. An example:

> A code for husbands, in five sections, made its appearance today in a divorce suit before Judge John R. Roper in Circuit Court.
>
> The code was produced by Paul Evart, a mechanic, whose divorce action is being contested by his wife, Edna Evart. He said she told him he must abide by it or "we're through."
>
> Its provisions were:
>
> 1. One night a month out for lodge meetings only.
> 2. No liquor or tobacco in any form.

3. Seven dollars a week allowance from his pay check.

4. Mother must have a permanent home with us.

5. Give up all women but me.

"Now, I ask you, your honor, could any man live up to that and still be a man?" Evart pleaded from the witness stand. The judge reserved decision.

SEX-CONNECTED CRIME NEWS

Once again we must point out the all-important influence of policy upon the reportorial function, for it vitally affects the treatment of sex crime news. While the trend is toward bolder and blunter writing, there remain sharp differences among papers as to the number, display and style of such stories.

Here are two leads on the same story, one printed in a highly conservative paper, the other in a sensational one:

CONSERVATIVE

John S. Royce, vice president of the Midland National Bank, charged yesterday that his wife sought the company of other men, in answer to the separation suit complaint of the former Penelope Perry.

SENSATIONAL

You're in your stateroom on a honeymoon cruise, all alone with your bride. She has red hair and her build is something to set a man ga-ga. Outside is the velvet night of the tropics. A perfect night for love. And she senses it. She sighs and remarks that she'd like to be in the arms—of another man!

To illustrate further, let us look at two versions of exactly the same news as printed by two papers, noting the contrasting styles:

RESTRAINED

Taking the witness stand in his own defense, Eric Joyce, Midland grocer, yesterday pleaded justifiable homicide in the slaying of Donald Torrence last July 30.

Joyce, charged with murder, admitted that he twice shot Torrence, a Clay City businessman, in a Crossroads tourist cabin but did so, he declared, because Torrence took advantage of his wife, Leona Joyce.

Under Centralia law it is justifiable homicide for a husband to kill a man in an act of indiscretion with his wife.

The 45-year-old defendant testified that he and Mrs. Joyce stopped at the cabin for the night. They became acquainted with Torrence in a porch conversation. Later, the witness said, he visited a nearby tavern and upon his return found the other two in a compromising position.

"I had my old service revolver in my car as protection against hitch-hikers and I shot him twice," Joyce testified.

HEADLINES OF TYPICAL
SEX STORIES

Girl, 19, Raped, Slain;
Cabbie Questioned

MARRIAGE OF HEIRESS ANNULLED

Quintuplets Fight for Life In Wash Basket

Engaged 10 Years, Wed 33 Days, Now Wife Wants a Separation

TEST TUBE TWINS BORN

Beau Stabs 5 In Cafe Brawl Over Woman

Married 69 Years

A Great-Grandpa, He
Weds Mail Love, 20

Sex News in the Press

The case is being heard before Circuit Court Judge Edward Smith. The defense is expected to rest this morning and the case may go to the jury before the end of the day.

FRANK

Eric Joyce, Midland grocer, testified yesterday that he shot and killed Donald Torrence after finding his blonde wife and the Clay City merchant in bed together.

The 45-year-old self-styled "man with honor" swore that he walked into a tourist cabin room and saw his wife, Leona, in the act of adultery with Torrence, a casual acquaintance. Centralia law makes it justifiable for a husband to kill a man under such circumstances.

"We met Torrence on the porch of our cabin the night of July 30," said Joyce. "Then I went up the road for a drink.

"When I came back I pushed open the door. I found my wife and Torrence naked in bed. I ran back to my car and got my service revolver."

While Torrence still was unclothed and before the horrified eyes of his wife, Joyce said he pumped two bullets into Torrence's body. Joyce then related how he ordered his wife to dress and they fled in their car.

With only one more witness to be heard, Defense Attorney Henry Yates said he expected to rest his case tomorrow morning.

It will be observed that in structure the stories are identical. They are alike in style except that the first writer preferred *took advantage of, act of indiscretion* and *compromising position,* whereas the second writer preferred *in bed together, act of adultery* and *naked.* A trained news writer has little trouble veering his story one way or the other—spicing it up or toning it down—once he learns the alternate terms available and knows what his paper desires. The best way to determine that is to read and analyze your own paper.

DANGERS IN SEX NEWS

While news of romance and marriage—that is, reports of conventional and accepted behavior—is harmless, virtually all sex news of strife and crime must be privileged. Seldom, if ever, does a newspaper print a derogatory charge involving any kind of unconventional sex behavior without a clear-cut official record to sustain it.

A thin line of demarcation between strictly private affairs and those which a newspaper can make public with impunity may be found cutting across the thresholds of the police station and the courtroom.

Some states, for example, have statutes forbidding the publication of the name of a female victim of criminal assault. In most states reporters are given access to court papers in civil actions for divorce, separation, breach of promise and similar actions. In a few states restrictions are in effect. His own state laws should be known to every newspaperman.

In treating danger-laden data the reporter must be positive that his basic information is correct. He should think twice before writing any accusation which he would resent if applied to himself or members of his own family.

Paradoxically, the writer for a *hush-hush* paper may be in greater peril than the writer for a *face-the-facts* paper. The former may be lulled into a sense of security because he discloses indelicate material through a camouflage of phraseology. An idea conveyed by implication is fully as libelous as one set forth by a bald, unvarnished assertion. Damages are often sought and won on the basis of an impression given to readers even though there is no direct statement.

As a case in point there is the story about an article circulated to rural folk during a political campaign which read: "Are you aware that Candidate Smith is known all over the capital to be a *shameless extrovert?* Not only that, but this man is reliably reported to practice *nepotism* with his sister-in-law; and he has a sister who was once a *thespian* in wicked New York. Worst of all, it is an established fact that before his marriage Smith habitually practiced *celibacy.*"

Smith, of course, was in a position to sue the author for libel. Although every word written is innocent truth, the courts decide on the basis not of what the writer writes but of what he causes the reader to believe.

SHOP TALK

1. Is it true that young reporters are unprepared to handle sex stories?
2. As a publisher, would you operate a *hush-hush* or *face-the-facts* newspaper?
3. Add more stock phrases used in stories of feminine beauty.
4. Define the following: divorce, separation, breach of promise, bigamy, polygamy, alimony, annulment.
5. As a newspaper publisher, would you print the names of victims of sex offenders?

CHAPTER 30
Politics and Elections

WHO COVERS POLITICS?

The answer to that question is just about every newspaper reporter in the land. Certainly it is one of the subjects every young newsman dips into almost immediately and he is more or less in touch with it throughout his career.

We speak of politics here in the broad sense as the science or art of government. As such its ramifications, like the roots of a tree, extend deep into the life of every community, large or small. It plays a part in public affairs from international diplomacy down to doings of the township treasurer and the village postmaster.

As we have seen, the inherent nature of news makes it difficult to departmentalize all of it neatly. Fairly clear limits bound such specialties as farming and finance. Politics, like sports, news for women, crime, courts, and sex, overlaps and blends into the routine work of all reporters from rural stringers to correspondents in Washington and abroad. Particularly close to politics the year round are beat reporters, such as city hall and courthouse men, covering the activities of officeholders.

In the more restricted sense politics consists of news that precedes and is climaxed by an election—local, state or national.

Elections are widely spaced and political news between them is thin. During the lull periods small papers pay scant attention to politics, then draw in nonspecialists to handle a campaign and the voting. Only the larger papers can afford to employ purely political specialists, and in off-election periods even these are subject to assignments which carry them into allied and diversified fields of public affairs and governmental operations. Even the metropolitan press and the wire services shift their Washington staffs to national conventions and election-night headquarters, then back to their regular beats in the capital.

In order to bring our study to a focus let us again enter the local room of the Midland *Times* and meet Howard Robinson, who covers politics and heads the election reportorial staff for our mythical but typical newspaper. Robinson is a 10-year veteran, one of the best-trained and highest-paid men in the office.

While in school he excelled in geography, civics, history and political science as well as English and journalism. He worked on police, then general assignments, schools, city hall, county building and the courts. From year to year he participated in covering elections. Now he devotes all his time to politics during campaign and election periods. Between these periods he covers the legislature at Capital City and occasionally goes to Washington for a Midland story. When available he draws top assignments—such as explaining a new charter—and other stories involving governmental agencies beyond the reach of the beat man.

In the political métier Robinson is an expert. He knows intimately the personalities that control party machinery and operate government. He understands the currents and crosscurrents in political maneuvering. And finally he is a fast, colorful, effective stylist at his typewriter.

POLITICAL NEWS SOURCES

Purely political news divides itself on the basis of election-period chronology into three main types:

1. Preelection *dope* stories.
2. Campaign *speech* and *statement* stories.
3. Election *result* stories.

Early in a campaign the political writer watches closely party alignments and realignments, possible candidacies and personalities—in short, the drift of politics. This is an easy stage of work for the seasoned man. He seems to be the staff idler, both in and out of the office. The assignment editor permits him to go and come as he pleases and he may be found strolling about government buildings and party headquarters chatting casually with this or that politician, perhaps puffing on a gift cigar.

He seldom hurries or becomes excited. In the office, when his fellow reporters are perspiring over last-minute stories, he often has produced his sheets of early *think* copy and closed his desk for the day.

If working means rushing to fires, flashing wreck bulletins and quizzing pretty divorcées, Robinson during this period does little work, for political dope does not manifest itself in dramatic fashion. Most of it trickles out

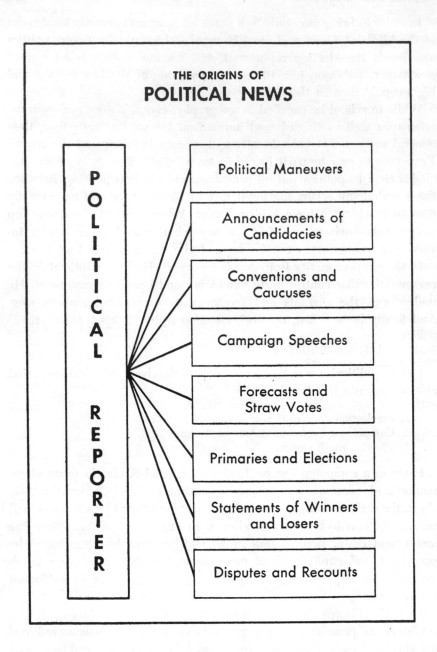

THE ORIGINS OF
POLITICAL NEWS

P O L I T I C A L   R E P O R T E R

Political Maneuvers

Announcements of
Candidacies

Conventions and
Caucuses

Campaign Speeches

Forecasts and
Straw Votes

Primaries and Elections

Statements of Winners
and Losers

Disputes and Recounts

Sources of Political News Copy

of a situation, and the political writer, like a sponge, absorbs its significance. His acquaintances are numerous, his ears open, his mind retentive and capable of close reasoning. A bit of conversation here and a morsel of fact there, pieced together and interpreted in the light of previous information, give him his dope stories. He obtains this kind of news in what is a most practical and effective way—an odd kind of osmosis.

As a campaign gets under way, candidates take the stump and issue propaganda in the form of statements, interviews and prepared publicity. The speech assignments go to the political writer and the publicity material comes to his desk. He moves at a faster pace now, for speeches, meetings, caucuses and conventions call for traveling and produce spot stories with speed competition.

The climax of a campaign requires heavy coverage in the last few days before election. On election day the political writer not only handles the lead story or stories but assists the desk men in organizing other members of the staff who are brought into play. All his experience and skill are put to the test as he analyzes returns, writes and rewrites for each edition, shrewdly calling the turn on vote counts before they are completed.

THE POLITICAL "THINK" PIECE

A "think" piece is a story written out of a reporter's head, perhaps with the aid of a few clippings but minus a strong action or immediacy element. Most preelection dope stories are of this variety.

In writing dope stories political and sports writers are brothers under the skin in matters of style—rebels both, for the reason that each must concoct advance stories requiring to some extent artificial action and synthetic immediacy.

In both sports and political stories the conflict element is strong. Without strife, politics indeed would be a dull business. Yet no blows are struck, no shots fired. Nor are there any physical manifestations of combat in the weeks before election day. To inject the element of struggle, the reporter must rely heavily upon figurative words and expressions. Hence his frequent employment of political journalese which approaches slang.

Observe the synthetic conflict phraseology in the following dope story:

> With the biennial Council election still three months away, party leaders yesterday were *whetting their scalping knives* and *beating their tom-toms* preparatory to what promises to be one of Midland's *hardest-fought* city campaigns.

Ten councilmen—six Republicans, two Democrats and two Independents—whose terms expire April 15 will *make the race* to regain their posts. Four *tossed their hats into the ring* this week. The others are expected to follow soon.

Early reports from the scouts of the GOP have it that the Republicans will boom their public improvement program during the years they have been in City Hall. They will spotlight the record of Mayor Nelson, expected to be a third-term candidate next year.

The Democratic chieftains are *powwowing* over plans to *attack* from a platform demanding economy and lower taxes.

There are *smoke signs arising* from the Independents which may *spell trouble* this year for both the old-line parties. The Independents will *hit in both directions, assailing* the Nelson spending record and *blaming* the Democrats for supporting the state and national party policies.

It will be a *battle* of slogans. The *rallying cry* of the GOP will be: "Don't swap horses." The Democrats will demand: "Turn the rascals out." And the Independents, seeking to put "a plague on both their houses," will declare that "Midland must have a municipal house cleaning.". . . .

In the foregoing story, after using the phraseology of Indian warfare to inject the combat element, the writer picked up several familiar political phrases which originated in national campaigns of the past.

Theodore Roosevelt was the author of the first. In 1912 he announced he would be a candidate by saying: "My hat is in the ring." "Turn the rascals out" was coined by Charles A. Dana in 1872 when Horace Greeley was running against President Grant. Abraham Lincoln in 1864 said: "It is not best to swap horses while crossing the river."

Here are some other handy words and phrases, each with an equally interesting origin, which are repeatedly used in political copy: *bolt, boom, caucus, draft, platform, stump, band wagon, dark horse, favorite son, grass roots,* and *smoke-filled room.*

COVERING A CAMPAIGN

As a campaign progresses, the political reporter moves gradually from announcements of candidacies and occasional dope stories into day-to-day accounts based largely on speeches and publicity material emanating from office seekers and their publicity men.

Now his job is not so much to pick up bits of information here and there, detect trends, and create in his stories his own fight phraseology as to winnow out fresh developments, get rid of buncombe and avoid repetition.

In covering a political speech a good reporter tries to present the points that the candidate thinks are important, if he hasn't made the same speech before. He is careful with crowd estimates and wary of passing judgment on the cheers or boos of an audience. He remembers that the laws of libel are not suspended during a political campaign.

Out of a welter of material the political writer must be able to choose particulars that have real news value. He understands the game of politics and how it is played. Although seldom a moralist or reformer, the political reporter is in no sense a dunce. He instantly detects empty grandiloquence. Stripping away the camouflage he lays bare the facts— not only the surface facts but the circumstances and motivations underlying them.

Consider a statement like this: "On that issue, my friends, I take an unequivocal stand. I have said, and I repeat, that the rates should be lowered to the minimum consistent with good service. On the other hand, they should not be confiscatory. The bus riders, the straphangers, if you please, must be accommodated and the investors must be protected. My pledge is to give both a square deal."

Would an experienced reporter take this statement at face value? He certainly would not. His story, if it mentioned the statement at all, would probably point out dispassionately that the candidate dodged the rate issue.

The veteran reporter will sit up straight when a candidate takes a stand for the first time on a sharp issue or coins an incisive comment, but he will yawn and not take a single note when a political speaker advocates peace, prosperity, liberty, respect for the Constitution, the Stars and Stripes or motherhood, more spending with lower taxes, two autos in every garage, and fair weather every day. So does everybody else!

All sorts of persons and organizations take straw votes. Some are floated deliberately as propaganda. Here is part of a prepared story of the type often handed out to political writers in the hope of securing publicity. What is wrong with it?

Democratic leaders here are jubilant over results of straw votes which indicate overwhelming sentiment in Meade County for Governor Boland.

So enormous is the indicated plurality of Boland over his GOP opponent that the Republicans are expected to open their moneybags wide and send thousands of dollars into the county between now and the election in an effort to turn back the Democratic sentiment.

Despite the assertions of Republicans in the press that they are afraid to spend much money this year because of the campaign fund scandal, it is believed by Democratic leaders here that the present outlook will so alarm the party chiefs upstate that they will take big chances in order to stem the Boland tide . . . . .

One of the constant problems of newspapermen covering political campaigns is how to avoid the banality of the twice-told tale. The ordinary office seeker prepares one speech which he repeats every day and would like to have printed every day. But to the reporter the address loses its news value almost immediately. He must watch unceasingly for new issues, or at least novel slants on old issues.

POLICY IN POLITICS

Newspaper policy manifests itself more definitely and consistently in politics than in any other news topic for the obvious reason that politics and public affairs are inseparable. Few editors whose papers presume to influence public opinion fail to take a keen interest in political activity.

Like a politician, a newspaper in a given locality usually bases its policy upon the prevailing sentiment in that region. A paper in a rural community, for example, would differ diametrically from its metropolitan neighbor over shifting the tax burden from the farmers to city dwellers, just as one in a community with a large foreign-born element would differ from one that serves a native-born population of similar political faith.

Newspapers of the nineteenth century made no pretense of being anything but out-and-out partisan organs, glorifying the Republicans and damning the Democrats, or vice versa. Political stories "pointed with pride" and "viewed with alarm" in good old-fashioned editorial phraseology. Those days are gone. As shown in another chapter, modern policy writing, if not more ethical, certainly is more subtle; at least it disguises itself under a news cloak. Both sides are printed, but at the same time the political writer may be expected to emphasize certain candidates or aspects in the campaign in line with the policy of his publisher.

Note here how newspapers in two cities with differing attitudes toward the candidates treat the same set of facts:

Midland *Times*

More modern roads and continuation of his economy program will be the main issues in the campaign of Gov. George Boland for renomination at the April primary, the Governor indicated in an interview today following the announcement of his candidacy.

The Democratic administration under his leadership the last four years, Boland believes, has hung up a record on these two activities which should send him under the wire again, an easy winner.

"In the last 18 months alone, we have constructed 1,857 miles of throughways, parkways and highways, an average of 100 miles a month," the Governor said, discussing the road program. "We have 340 miles under construction and another 637 miles under contract."

Although the state budget has increased slightly over that of the preceding administration because of the big highway program, Boland pointed out that in other departments expenditures have been slashed to a minimum.

In the public works division, for example, the payroll shows 400 fewer jobholders than a year ago.

Other planks the Governor will nail in his platform, his friends say, will include a bigger state police force, more fish and game preserves, development of the Timber River water-power project and more home rule for the smaller cities.

Word has gone the rounds in political circles here that Martin S. Handley, state treasurer, and former Congressman T. M. Sikes of Capital City have gubernatorial aspirations, and that one of them may be groomed by the Democrats as Boland's opponent. Sikes may make his announcement within a few days.

Capital City *Sun*

Thaddeus M. Sikes of Capital City, former Congressman from the 2nd District loomed up today as a dark horse in the race for the Democratic nomination for governor.

Talk of Sikes as a candidate came close upon the heels of Governor Boland's formal announcement that he will run again.

With the former Congressman as their color-bearer, some of the Jeffersonian leaders believe they can make a clean sweep of the state offices at the November election, especially in view of the rising flood of anti-Boland feeling in the eastern parts of the state over discrimination in the present road-building program.

"Voters in the eastern counties are in no mood to tolerate longer domination by the downstate Boland crowd," one influential Democrat commented. "Sikes would carry the eastern half of the state by a 2–1 vote."

The recent legislative inquiry revealing four members of Boland's family on state payrolls, and the 13-million-dollar boost in the state budget last year, according to the political wiseacres, are going to cut a big figure in the campaign regardless of the Republican choice.

Despite the hostility in the Capital City district over expenditure of a lion's share of the road fund downstate, Boland in an interview today asserted that "more modern highways and strict economy" will be his principal campaign planks. He said that 1,857 miles of highways have been laid in the past 18 months. His figures, however, did not point out that more than 1,000 of them are in the Midland district.

Two incidental pointers particularly applicable to policy in political writing may profitably be remembered. Keep your cause or your candidate on the offensive, carrying the fight to the enemy. Never, if you can help it, depict your favorite as defending himself. Be optimistic. Everybody likes to ride on the band wagon. A newspaper, actively interested in promoting a candidate, never takes him off the band wagon and never admits defeat until the decisive votes are in.

ELECTION DAY AND NIGHT

As the day arrives when voters go to the polls in a local, state or national election, the political reporter becomes the kingpin of the local staff.

If he is employed by an afternoon paper he must write before the polls close and without any actual returns. He exploits in his story or stories of the day every morsel of fact that bears on the election up to the point of a straight-out guess by himself as to the outcome. Among the points which make copy are:

1. *Turnout of voters.* Is the voting heavy or light? In what districts? What is the effect of the weather?

2. *Interviews with candidates.* As they cast their own ballots candidates usually deliver quotable comment.

3. *Violence or fraud.* Trouble of any kind at the polling places is spot news. It may be major news if there is violence, theft of ballots or charges of fraud.

4. *Forecasts of participants.* Both candidates and their managers are prone to make victory claims. They are all included in the PM election day story.

Within minutes after the polls close, the morning newspapers are geared to go into action as the first returns come in. The moment the first figure comes in all dope, speech, statement and other preliminary stuff is forgotten. An ounce of ballots counted outweighs a ton of prophecy.

How the local staff is mobilized to cover and write all phases of a sectional story, of which a major election is one, will be discussed in the next chapter. Here our interest is in the main story prepared by the political reporter. While other staff men, usually helped by press association reporters, gather the returns, the political writer finds himself confronted with column after column of figures. They are just figures, but to him they are meaningful, exciting, as full of significance as play-by-play details in a baseball or football game are to a sports reporter.

It is the task of the writer to translate the figures into trends, pluralities, majorities, and finally victories and defeats. Lead stories on election night are replete with such stock phrases as these:

> forged out in front in the first scattered returns
> led by a scant 1,000 votes at the halfway mark

BOX TREATMENT OF
ELECTION RESULTS

COMPLETE RETURNS

MAYOR

Lawson (Independent)	42,902
Nelson (Republican)	21,699
Bishop (Democrat)	14,007

CITY TREASURER

Masters (Independent)	38,179
Betts (Republican)	18,576
Flanagan (Democrat)	3,928

CITY ATTORNEY

Sparks (Republican)	36,602
Howe (Independent)	28,717
Dorsey (Democrat)	2,236

MUNICIPAL JUDGES

Snyder (Independent)	32,228
Buhl (Independent)	28,727
Wilkins (Republican)	17,724
Jones (Republican)	14,614
Parker (Democrat)	5,706
Quantrill (Democrat)	1,966

BONDS

	For	Against
Street lights, $500,000	10,016	27,629
Park improvements, $300,000	9,681	29,004

Statistical Work for Reporters

steadily widened the gap as the votes were counted
held a commanding lead at the halfway mark
polled the highest total of his political career
clung to what appeared to be a decisive margin
was snowed under by a blizzard of ballots
won renomination easily after a vigorous campaign
swept in on a tidal wave of votes

MOVEMENT IN STATISTICS

The phraseology of an election story is remarkably like that applied by a sports writer. More examples chosen at random follow:

To be close: *bitterly-fought, battle of give-and-take, nip-and-tuck race, dizzy seesaw fight, ran neck and neck, outcome remained in doubt.*

To lead: *held a slim margin, forged ahead, closed the gap, rolled up a lead, looked like a victor, race turned into a rout.*

To lose: *conceded, admitted defeat, suffered a major blow, trailed, gave up his seat.*

To win: *edged out, beat off, squeaked through, nosed out, barely brushed by, captured the seat of, scored a startling upset, ousted, toppled his opponent, wrested from, overwhelmed, rode roughshod, carried, smashed the bid of, buried, clinched control, thumping plurality, swept into office, landslide victory, grandstand finish, scored a record-breaking triumph.*

As his phraseology indicates, the political writer is more likely to follow the touchdown runner down the field than to dwell on the misfortune of the man who made the fumble and lost the ball.

Action verbs energize the election result stories from edition to edition, from the first return to the final decision. Observe the life and movement in this one:

Piling up decisive majorities in the outlying residential districts, W. C. Lawson, Independent candidate for mayor, was *swept into office* and almost the entire Independent ticket with him on the face of fairly complete returns available this morning.

The election results came as a *crushing defeat* for Mayor Nelson, regular Republican candidate, who has held office for two terms, and for the entire Tollman-Jenks faction. Out of four major city officers who have been in the saddle under the Nelson regime, only City Attorney Gerald Sparks survived.

With 132 out of 150 precincts heard from at 1 a.m., the mayoral vote stood: Lawson, 36,902; Nelson, 18,611. Eugene Bishop, Democratic candidate, had received only 12,436.

The Independents, after *trailing* in the early returns from the downtown district, began *picking up* shortly after 10 p.m. as reports *flowed in* from the 11th and 12th Wards. At midnight their *victory was assured* and Mayor Nelson *conceded defeat*. The 11th Ward, comprising the East

Side suburban area, *handed Lawson a 3–1 vote,* as did the 7th, 10th and 13th.

Mayor-elect Lawson will take office on Jan. 1. Those going in with him will be Martin Masters, city treasurer; Gerald Sparks, city attorney; R. T. Snyder and Clarence F. Buhl, judges of the Municipal Court.

Yesterday's election *climaxed one of the bitterest campaigns* in Midland's history, *swinging around* charges of waste and corruption under the Nelson administration. Lawson's slogan was: "A municipal house cleaning for Midland." In the last few days of the battle he *hammered* the present mayor personally as "a disgrace to the Republican party." Among other pledges, he promised an immediate cleanup of the police department . . . . .

On election night the high point of the coverage is when the political writer, on the basis of the figures before him, writes first a bulletin and then a lead story naming the victor in the main contest and thus commits his newspaper on the outcome. Usually he is able to do this by projecting from one-fourth to one-half of the votes counted. In rapid succession thereafter there are likely to follow a victory claim from the winner, then a concession and congratulatory statement from the loser. These are often treated as bulletins, then as inserts in the main story and finally as separate stories in later editions.

There is little rest for the political writer when the last election day edition has gone to press on election night even if the result story is wrapped up and finished. There are important follow-ups the next day and for several more days thereafter. Interest turns quickly from post-mortems to the plans of the winners, who are covered closely between election and inauguration day.

Once the new regime is installed and its appointments made, its coverage goes back to the beat man. The political reporter turns his attention to special assignments in the public affairs and governmental fields until the next campaign gets under way.

SHOP TALK

1. By what methods does a political reporter obtain his news? Is he really an idler?
2. What does the political writer cover in off-seasons between campaigns and elections? Tabulate a few of his assignments.
3. In what respects do political articles differ from conventional news accounts? Why does the political writer enjoy more reportorial freedom?
4. Discuss the place of policy in political news. Do you prefer modern policy writing to old-fashioned editorializing in political stories?
5. Do you feel that more or less space in your local newspaper should be given to news of politics and elections?

CHAPTER 31

Teamwork by the Staff

MOBILIZING FOR A BIG STORY

The first flash on a story recorded in Midland history as the *Mermaid* disaster came from Fred Maxwell at police headquarters at 4:20 p.m. At the foot of Front street, near the Carson Coal Co. dock, the *Mermaid*, a small pleasure steamer plying the Timber River between Midland and Belleview Park, three miles downstream, was reported to be sinking.

"Keep her on the wire," Harry Baxter ordered a copy boy. General assignment reporter Alice Nestor had just telephoned from a settlement house in the Front street neighborhood. Baxter turned to the other phone. He told Miss Nestor briefly what had happened and hung up with: "Grab a cab and get down to the Carson dock."

Photographers, with Fred Markham and George Donnelly, then free in the office, and two copy boys, had already started in both of the *Times* radio cars when the woman reporter called back with word that the boat, loaded with passengers, apparently had rammed a coal scow and was sinking in mid-stream.

"Okay . . . if you can hire a boat for a photographer . . . Markham and Donnelly will be there directly . . . Markham goes out with the fotog . . . Donnelly covers the shore . . . Can you sew up this telephone? . . . give me the number . . . stay close to it until a radio car gets there . . . copy boy'll have change to take it over . . . then you help Donnelly with witnesses and survivors."

Baxter swung around to a copy boy. "Round 'em up," he ordered. "Get Levison and Wilson. Give me Kemp and McCauley when they call. Wheeling too."

The clock said 4:35. Within 15 minutes Baxter had marshaled his main forces for crash coverage and deployed them to their posts. The assignment editor, like a commanding general, was a master in logistics —the maneuvering of manpower in an emergency.

His strategy followed a time-tested pattern. His tactics were those credited to a Confederate general, "Get there fustest with the mostest men," in other words, deploy the forces in the field first. The second tactical move—organization behind the lines—followed fast. Already, overhearing the phone conversations, Jefferson Harris, rewrite man, Frank Fenwick, business and labor reporter, and David Jordan, science and aviation writer, had hurried toward the desk. Baxter swung around to them.

"How are you fixed, Fenwick?" Baxter asked. "Okay, get on the phone to the Carson Coal people. Find out all you can about the scow, its crew, cargo, everything."

Then to Harris: "Try the morgue on the *Mermaid*. A-matter for Markham. Separate piece on other sinkings if you can find the stuff."

Finally to Jordan: "Dave, get set to handle the casualty list. Better start a card index. We'll box it."

A fresh sheet in the city desk typewriter began to accumulate assignments:

NESTOR: On scene.
MARKHAM: Cover the main story.
DONNELLY: Interviews with survivors; rescues; human interest stuff.
KEMP: Work with Donnelly.
MAXWELL: Police and fire department angles.
FENWICK: Coal barge angle.
HARRIS: Historical stuff; get up early matter for Markham.
JORDAN: Box on dead and injured.

The clock now said 4:50. The office force was in motion—the whole tactical action under way.

At 5 p.m., when Mark Mason arrived at the city desk, he found more than half the local room staff at work on some angle of the *Mermaid* disaster, with the first copy already clattering out of the typewriters. The Midland *Times* would have complete coverage on a big sectional story in its Early edition.

NEWS OF THE FIRST MAGNITUDE

You will not hear such terms as "news of the first magnitude" in the city room, nor do workers speak about "sectional" stories. Newsmen do not talk in formal language. They call a big story a big story, perhaps adding a bit of picturesque profanity for emphasis.

TYPICAL TOPICS FOR
SECTIONAL STORIES

HURRICANE

WRECK

CONVENTION

ELECTION

TOURNAMENT

RIOT

News Requiring Staff Teamwork

However, in a textbook it is necessary to use some academic expressions and definitions in order to analyze and understand newsroom operations. With this apology let us then say that news stories may be placed in one of three classifications:

1. One-incident stories.
2. Composite stories.
3. Sectional stories.

Probably 70 per cent of the average day's news consists of simple one-incident stories, each concerned with an isolated event covered and written by one reporter. Twenty-five per cent, perhaps, goes into composite news accounts, each dealing with several associated events or one event with several angles and likewise written by one reporter, although others may assist in gathering the material. The remaining five per cent appears in the form of sectional stories.

Earlier discussions have dealt fully with both one-incident and composite or multiangled narratives, thus preparing the way for practice with the weightier and more complicated sectional variety.

A sectional story is not a single article but rather a series of articles clustered around one major news event, each appearing under its own headline. Thus it always engages two or more reporters and occasionally every available member of the staff.

A sectional story deals with events that command the best part of page one and a good deal of additional space on the inside pages.

As a general practice any news event broken into phases so important and interesting that the whole carries appeal to all classes of readers is handled in divisions by a group of reporters. Some of the most typical are:

Calamities of nature. Floods, earthquakes, exceptionally severe storms.
Industrial disasters. Wrecks, explosions, widespread fires; mine, air and sea calamities.
Assemblies. Fairs, conventions, celebrations, mass meetings; other gatherings of wide general interest.
Political events. Elections, political conventions, diplomatic conferences; extraordinary Congressional and Legislative sessions.
Sporting events. Championship baseball and football games and boxing bouts; tournaments of regional or national significance.
Lawlessness. Riots, lynchings, other forms of disorder involving many persons; unusual crimes and important trials.

Any type of story may climb into the sectional class whenever it possesses the requisite combination of factors to make significant news.

Even the death of a prominent man, or a business transaction if it affects enough people, may merit sectional treatment. Briefly, then, the distinguishing mark of a sectional story is that it is important enough to divide into two or more parts, each under a separate headline.

HOW THE STAFF OPERATES

Organization, discipline, partition and specification of duties and coordination—these are the watchwords of the local room when a momentous sectional story thrusts itself into the news schedule. Each reporter has a definite job and all work together like an advancing army.

As commander in chief the city editor directs the activities of his troops—the general assignment, beat and special reporters, the leg and rewrite men. From his headquarters in the local room he shifts his men into action to meet news demands, dividing the assignments so that resultant stories adequately cover the situation but do not overlap.

Re-examine the typical sectional stories listed and you will see that they fall into two classifications—expected and unexpected. Assemblies, sports and political events are anticipated and prepared for in advance. Stories of lawlessness, calamities of nature and disasters such as the *Mermaid* sinking, break suddenly without warning.

Whatever the nature of the sectional story, the effectiveness of the coverage—planned or crash—depends upon the leadership of the city editor and the resourcefulness and energy of his assistants and reporters.

A businessman may spend weeks planning a sales campaign, a scientist months experimenting to establish the validity of a theory, and a historian years perfecting and polishing his manuscript, but the reporter and the news-gathering organization have little time for prolonged consideration and leisurely procedure. At best the deadline looms only a few hours away and often minutes determine the fate of an important sectional story. Organization means speed plus volume, and these are important factors in the making of a modern newspaper.

Working on a sectional story the reporter acts as both a subordinate and an executive. Although he must confine himself strictly to his assignment, at the same time the value of his service to the organization depends largely upon his own initiative.

SECTIONAL STORY ASSIGNMENTS

The city editor's plan of campaign depends, first, upon the size and availability of his staff when a sectional story breaks and, second, upon his own organization of assignments.

Take a case in point: January in Midland was mild until yesterday, when a blizzard swept in from the north and gripped the city. Today snow buries the streets and sidewalks, the mercury stands below zero and a further drop is expected. With this situation at hand, the Midland *Times* assignment sheet reads as follows:

Storm Schedule

DONNELLY: COLD. Lead storm story. General local and state conditions. Temperature, forecast. Any relief in sight?

NESTOR: SUFFERING. How many deaths? What about the poor? Charity activities. Better visit tenement district. If three or more deaths, get up list for box. Also give list to Donnelly.

WHEELING: TRAFFIC. General traffic tie-up. Buses stalled, trains late, wires down, etc. See Wilson on snow removal. How many shovelers? How do new motor plows work?

WILSON: FIRES. Superior Milling Co. burned. Any other big fires? See chief for number of alarms. New record? See street commissioner and give stuff to Wheeling. Health Department to Nestor.

KING: SCHOOLS. Will the schools close? If not, classes dismissed, etc., to Donnelly.

DILLARD: SKATING. Skating season should open. How's the ice? Anyone on lake or river? Sleighs out?

BRANSFIELD: CROPS. How do the farmers like it? Snow help the wheat? Are the mail carriers stalled? Give to Donnelly early.

From these assignments an idea may be gathered as to the necessity for coordination among the staff members. Not only must each man cover his own section of the story thoroughly, but he must give willing assistance to his teammates. Should he obtain an angle properly belonging in another's story his duty is to turn it over to his associate. Adopting a program of "One for all and all for one," the staff works in unison and the outcome is comprehensive coverage—a collection of stories, each complete in itself, but none encroaching upon another.

Two passenger planes crash at the outskirts of Midland, killing 17 persons and injuring 20 others. It constitutes a sensation, with only an hour to spare before the early deadline. The city editor quickly organizes his staff. There is no time for written assignments, so the chief delivers them orally as follows:

HARRIS: Write the main crash story, with plenty of action. Handle bulletins and flashes. Keep it coming.

BURKE: Get up the casualty list. Keep in touch with Schafer at the hospitals. Have a list for a special box and give the summaries to Harris.

LOVELACE and WHEELING: Go to the scene. Get everything in sight. Phone to Harris and Burke.

ASSIGNMENTS SHOWING

TEAMWORK BY THE STAFF

The Midland Times
SPECIAL ELECTION SCHEDULE

MASON—Handle all election copy.

BAXTER—Handle all other copy.

ROBINSON—Write the main election story, leading with mayor.

WILSON—Write separate story city treasurer, city attorney and judges.

LOVELACE—In reserve.

McCAULEY—Cover county offices.

KEMP—Interview wives of candidates.

LEVISON—Telephone returns.

McCONNELL—Telephone returns.

WHEELING—Bond issue propositions.

SHAW—Hillview offices.

SCHAFER—Crestwood offices,

DONNELLY—In reserve.

FENWICK—Prepare tables.

Election Night Organization

McConnell with Lovelace and Wheeling: Help with the dead and injured list.

Nestor: Eyewitness stuff. Interview survivors.

Donnelly: Try for a statement from company officials. Get the lowdown on what happened. Play up the new airport policy angle. Will there be an investigation?

Wilson: Give us a half column on previous crashes in Midland. Is this the worst? Dig into the morgue.

Schafer: Cover all the hospitals. Check often with Burke on names and addresses.

A typical example of staff teamwork on an expected sectional story takes place on election night.

Midland voters have gone to the polls for an election of new county and city officials, including five county commissioners, a mayor, 10 city councilmen and several lesser officials. State officers are to be chosen at the same time, and two local bond-issue propositions are on the ballots.

How does the Midland *Times*, going to press within a few hours after the polls close, present detailed stories covering each phase of such a complicated event? Again the answer is organization.

Robinson, political reporter, takes care of the general lead story. McCauley covers the county offices; Wilson, the city offices; Wheeling, the bond-issue propositions. Miss Kemp interviews the candidates' wives. Shaw checks up on the suburban vote. Levison and McConnell, the leg men, telephone the returns from the counting places, and Donnelly and Simpson remain in reserve to help Fenwick compile statistics and prepare tables, and to step into a breach should something unexpected develop.

With such an organization an election becomes a comparatively simple problem. Swiftly and smoothly the copy flows in, catches the deadlines and is converted into print with the least possible delay.

We saw in the preceding chapter an illustration of a general lead election story. Let us now look at examples on other topics.

SHAPING THE MAIN SECTION

The main or lead sections of the sectional story, usually placed under the banner page one headline, carry the heaviest news load and consequently are the most difficult to write. The major over-all section is assigned either to a seasoned rewrite man or to the reporter familiar with the topic involved.

Not only must the main story bring to the fore the strongest points of the news, but it should also epitomize the other stories, setting forth in swift, compact phrases the high spots of each. The reporter on the main story, in fact, writes as though his contribution alone is to be printed, on the presumption that some readers will not dig deeply into the more detailed accounts. In short, he produces a comprehensive composite article.

Observe the sweeping scope of this, the lead story in a tornado schedule:

> Four persons, three of them pupils of the George Washington School, were killed, 10 others injured, and a dozen Midland homes laid in ruins yesterday by a tornado which swept down the Timber Valley and across the southeast corner of the city, leveling every building in its path.
>
> The tornado ripped asunder the two-story school building, strewing wreckage for a hundred yards.
>
> Those killed were Irene Johnson, 14, 1903 Polk Ave.; John Pace, 12, 1261 Poplar St.; and Maxine Morris, 12, 209 Lake St. All were buried in the debris. The bodies have been recovered.
>
> Arnold Jameston, 42, a carpenter living at 2281 Weston St., two blocks from the school, was the other victim. He was crushed by a falling roof when the tornado demolished the workshop in the rear of his home.
>
> The tornado, one of the most violent which has ever visited this section, struck Midland at 1:15 p.m. without warning. Although heavy black clouds had overcast the sky for several hours, a dead calm prevailed just before noon. Persons living south of the city said they saw a funnel-shaped cloud dip down and swing northward along the valley with great velocity.
>
> The funnel swirled down near 29th and Poplar Sts. and swept northward, doing its worst damage between 7th and Poplar. Seven homes on Poplar were unroofed or smashed. The George Washington School is at 28th and Poplar, in the center of the stricken area.
>
> The total property damage in Midland was estimated at between $750,000 and a million dollars. . . . .
>
> Mayor Lawson, who took personal charge of relief work, called for volunteers to help police and firemen dig into the ruins of the school building. At 3 p.m. all were accounted for. The injured children were in Haven Hospital, several in critical condition. A full list of the injured appears in another column. The three bodies were identified by parents.
>
> The tornado struck the school just after the children had entered it from the midday recess. Ten teachers and about 250 pupils were in the classrooms.
>
> "We had just started classes after the noon recess when I saw the storm coming up the valley," Miss Elizabeth Richmond, one of the teachers, said. "The cloud alarmed me but I said nothing to the pupils, not wishing to cause uneasiness. The wind velocity increased rapidly with a loud howling noise. I was on the second floor. I suppose it was only a few moments after I really became alarmed before our part of the building collapsed with a great crash."
>
> Floyd Noblin, principal, and the other teachers told similar stories.

The wind tore out a section of the east wing, ripping off the roof. Part of the wall collapsed. A small fire broke out in the wreckage, but nearby residents who reached the scene were able to smother it.

Several stories of the heroism of teachers in rescuing children were being told last night, the outstanding one that of William Severs, eighth-grade instructor, who, with one leg crushed, managed to extricate three children and push them out to the rescuers before he himself was removed. Miss Edna Thompson saved one first-grade pupil by shielding him with her body as bricks fell around them. She was seriously hurt.

Plans were being rushed last night by R. E. Johnson, president of the Chamber of Commerce, for the collection of a relief fund to care for the victims of the storm. More than $10,000 had already been subscribed. The money will be handled by the local Red Cross, in charge of relief work.

Although many telephone and telegraph wires were down, scattered reports coming in last night indicated that the storm damage was heavy all over the south part of Timber County. At Booneville three persons were reported to have been hurt, and at Southfield one person. Crops were badly damaged everywhere . . . . .

The main section lead of another teamwork story shows a similar breadth of treatment:

With a fanfare of colorful ceremony, a parade, and thousands of visitors thronging the city, Midland opened its 12th annual Commercial Progress Exposition yesterday. The exposition will last for 10 days.

Through the brilliant lanes of exhibits in Central Auditorium, focal point of the celebration, between 10,000 and 11,000 persons crowded during the afternoon, and 50,000 viewed the opening-night carnival parade on Main street, according to the estimates of Mark R. Cooper, chairman of Mayor Lawson's management committee.

The climax of the day's festivities came at 7 p.m. when 500 new lamps along Main street were flashed on, transforming the thoroughfare into a radiant white way flanked by scintillating shop windows dressed with special displays.

An extra $250,000 will clink through the cash registers of the city's merchants during the exposition, Cooper predicted.

Long before the doors of the auditorium with its $300,000 worth of exhibits opened at noon, lines of spectators waited at the ticket offices. First through the main entrance was George Falkner, 12, who had arrived at 5 a.m. to be No. 1 in line. The first hundred women visitors received free souvenirs . . . . .

THE SECONDARY STORIES

The tornado in Midland without doubt would have been handled sectionally, with possible separate stories scheduled as follows: (a) detailed casualty lists; (b) eyewitness accounts of the school disaster; (c) the tragedies in the victims' homes; (d) details of damages other than to the school building; (e) the relief program; (f) what the tornado did to surrounding regions; (g) comparison with previous storms. In addition there might have been a column of side bars or paragraph items headed *Freaks of the Tornado* or *Side Lights on the Storm.*

A similar grouping of divisions would have been used to cover various phases of the exposition story: (1) a crowd story; (2) a description of the auditorium exhibits; (3) prize winners in the carnival parade; (4) side lights and feature paragraphs.

At a major sports event, such as a championship baseball game, one man handles the lead story. Another concentrates on plays, a third on strategy and breaks. There may be a man doing crowd and color and still another assigned to the dugouts and dressing rooms.

It will be noted that the main story swiftly summarizes each of these blocks of facts and paints a word picture of the general scene, but leaves fuller details to the other sections.

In order to set forth the high lights of a composite story more effectively the editors may order a *box* set either above or within the article, possibly in an adjacent column. Material most frequently framed includes casualty lists, speech excerpts, chronologies of similar events. In connection with both composite and sectional stories boxes will often be found most useful for summaries of striking facts and for statistics.

In style and structure there is little to distinguish the secondary or supporting divisions in a sectional story from ordinary news accounts except, as previously explained, that they must not trespass on adjacent fields. The reporter should stay strictly within his own assignment, being constantly concerned with developing what legitimately belongs to him but at the same time be willing and ready to pass on to his colleagues other information that chance may steer into his hands.

It is this sort of legwork, plus headwork, plus teamwork, that makes the American newspaper a swift and well-laden courier of current events.

SHOP TALK

1. Explain the distinguishing features of one-incident, composite and sectional stories. Cite examples of each.
2. Discuss staff coordination in covering a sectional story. How does the city editor prepare for an election or an important convention?
3. Prepare on the blackboard a list of assignments for a heat wave story.
4. Outline the facts to be included in the main section of a graduation day story in your school paper and for three or four secondary stories.
5. Discuss the advantages of sectional treatment as compared to the presentation of all the news about an important event in a single composite story.

CHAPTER 32

The Newsmen of the Future

A LOOK BACK AND AHEAD

You are reaching a milestone as you come to this, the final chapter in *Modern News Reporting*. You have not read this book, or even scanned it, without purpose. If you have used it through a course of study the chances are that you seriously contemplate becoming a newspaper reporter and are taking the first steps in that direction.

It is well, then, to pause, look back at your introduction to reporting and look forward with a view to mapping more thoughtfully your own pathway into the future.

Even if you should move in another direction, one thing is certain— you have not wasted your time up to this point. To the extent that you have learned to find factual data, to assess its validity and to arrange it logically you have acquired skill vital to every trade and profession as well as to everyday living.

More important, if you can write news you can express yourself clearly. The one characteristic which successful people have in common above all others is the ability to speak and write good English.

The scientist must describe his discoveries; the doctor must win the confidence of his patients; the lawyer must plead his case; the executive must talk and write to run his business and enlist the loyalty of his employes; and the teacher must engage the minds of his students. In private and social life, too, the art of speaking and writing well spells the difference between superiority and mediocrity.

It is established that journalism students and newsmen as a group rank high in their ability intelligently to appraise and discuss, orally or in writing, the happenings around them.

So far, so good. The questions now arise: Where do I go from here? Shall I be a general reporter or a specialist? Shall I aim for a newspaper

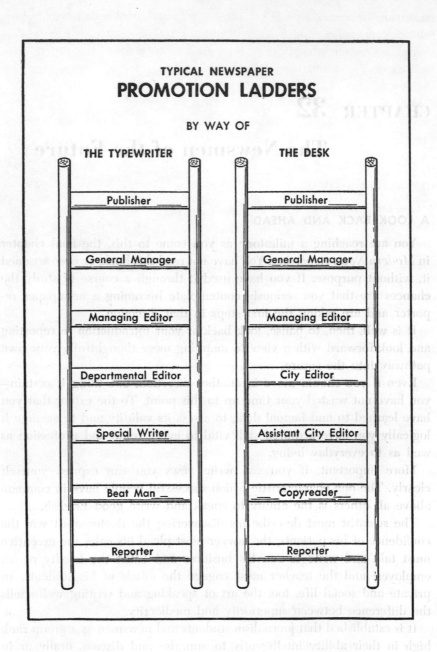

Ways to Go Up

editorship or ownership? What about radio and television news, public relations, magazine and book writing?

And, above all, what tides of the past and currents of the present are bearing on these vocations? Which ship may take me to what shore over the sea of time?

Without pretending to prophesy, let us survey these possible advancements both within and without the newspaper office in order to broaden the perspective of the young man or woman about to enter a reporting career.

NEWSROOM PROMOTION LADDERS

Leaving other fields for later discussion, let us examine the opportunities within a newspaper editorial department itself, likening them to ladders with each rung representing a promotion. One may be called the desk ladder whereby a reporter may become an executive. The other may be called the typewriter ladder whereby he may become a news specialist or departmental editor.

If a reporter has a bent toward the organization and supervision of others rather than a flair for writing, he is likely to be drawn toward the desk ladder. In that case it is to his advantage to serve apprenticeships as both reporter and copyreader and then seek a position as an assistant on the city desk. Thereafter he can reach the city editor's chair and be promoted into that of the managing editor who is in charge of the entire editorial department.

If the reporter is strong as a writer and becomes interested in a special kind of news he may climb the typewriter ladder. As an example, if he writes well about public affairs he may be assigned to a beat such as courthouse or city hall and advance to become a political reporter.

For his own or a larger paper he may be sent to the state capital and on to Washington as a correspondent. Thus he may be in a striking position to join the corps of wire service or metropolitan newspaper correspondents abroad.

Travel and distance lend no enchantment to others who prefer their home towns, perhaps in rural areas. Now and then a city newsman fulfills a long-cherished ambition to run a weekly or small daily, while a newsman from a smaller place replaces him in the city.

Special writers on the larger papers also have a chance to become departmental editors in charge of sports, news for women, business news or one of the other classifications of news that require experts. And both departmental and managing editors may hope to become the general manager of all departments and finally the publisher of the paper.

Thus within the newspaper business there is plenty of room for the youthful jobholder to make his way into the particular position which suits him best.

THE WRITING SPECIALIST

The ideal reporter is one who knows everything about everything. That ideal stands unfulfilled in a world moving toward more and more specialization.

All newspapers to some extent are departmentalized and scores of writers are specialists. Specialization corresponds roughly to the size of the newspaper. Even a small town weekly separates general, sports and society news. Medium-sized papers use from two or three to a dozen specialists. Metropolitan papers, especially in their Sunday editions, split into multiple sections and pages devoted to every topic from stamps and bridge to the care of pets, each calling for expertness. Syndicates and news bureaus serving many papers specialize even more.

The number of specialists and degrees of specialization thus hinge directly upon their cost, and they always will be few in comparison with utility men who cover beats and general assignments. Nevertheless, if you choose to become a byline expert—a true interpretive writer in a particular field—you can, through preparation and persistence, find and grasp the opportunity to become one.

During the course covered by this book we have entered only the special fields of reporting which interest major blocs of readers and interlace so closely with the general news of the day that the beginner is drawn into them from the start. These include sports, news for women, crime, the courts, business and labor, and politics.

Reporters who become Washington and foreign correspondents, editorial writers and critics of books, music, the theater, movies, the arts, radio and television are among those in the specialist ranks.

Because of rapidly increasing public interest in recent years, two new subjects warrant special attention. These are science and religion.

Science in all its forms is fast becoming a part of everybody's life. During and since the World War periods millions have realized that they personally are affected by the advances in military methods, atomic and nuclear energy, space exploration, medicine and public health, the industrial application of science, new inventions for the home, and the products of engineering, physics and chemistry. There is an urgent need for more writers who can convey this significant news to laymen in their own language.

A DOZEN FIELDS OF
NEWS SPECIALIZATIONS

 **SCIENCE**

 **RELIGION**

 **TRAVEL**

 **REAL ESTATE**

 **PETS**

 **FOOD**

 **FASHIONS**

 **HUNTING AND FISHING**

 **BOATING**

 **PHOTOGRAPHY**

 **GARDENING**

 **ENTERTAINMENT**

Opportunities for Reporters

Wars and rumors of wars have stimulated interest in religion and what it has to offer suffering and scared humanity. Half the population is affiliated with some religious group. Religious organizations have become more public-relations conscious. From Saturday church announcements news of religion is often moving into page one position.

The list of specializations can be carried into almost every phase of human activity in which substantial numbers of people are engaged. To mention a few more: *antiques, boating, bridge, child care, gardening, housing, hunting and fishing, pets, photography, real estate, stamps, teen-age activities, travel.* Each of these topics and many more open doors to the newsman who has learned the rudiments of reporting and has the desire and skill to become an expert in his own right.

The man or woman with general reporting background usually is the one who graduates into one of the specialties. It is not often that an expert nonreporter does so, for there seldom is one can express himself well in words. Even if he can he is so steeped in the fine points of his field that his copy is likely to be too technical for the average newspaper reader.

THE ALLIED ACTIVITIES

The notion that superior newspaper reporters tend to shift into other areas of work or into allied fields is not borne out by fact-finding surveys. At least three-quarters of them and probably more remain reporters or move into executive or specialist jobs for life. Nevertheless, perhaps one-fourth use their reportorial skills and experience as a springboard into allied activities.

Many ex-newsmen with aptitude as educators become part-time or full-time teachers of journalism, thereby performing the invaluable service of guiding new recruits into the field.

More go into advertising and public relations. While advertising demands skills other than writing, it always is in the market for men and women trained in the use of words. Many of these people are drawn from the ranks of reporters.

Virtually all publicity experts can say: "I'm an old newspaperman myself." Indeed, newsroom training is almost indispensable to the publicity man, for he must know reporters and their techniques if he is to win space for his clients in the newspapers. You have noted the publicity man walking in and out of the pages of this book, for he works in close and constant association with his former colleagues.

Other professional cousins of newsmen are writers for magazines, especially periodicals of the news variety. Often starting as a contributor a reporter finds the magazine field lucrative and moves into it to his profit.

Not infrequently a newsman becomes a book author. Perhaps he expands his own news specialty into a book or a series of books or branches out from magazine contributions into book authorship. In fact on becoming proficient as a writer he has an opening wedge into any industry or occupation that produces printed pages.

Nor is his future confined to ink, type and paper. During recent years there have appeared on the scene newer methods of communicating ideas—motion pictures, radio, television. Primarily a medium of entertainment, the movies have only indirectly touched the press. But the broadcasting media *do* affect it because they are conveyers of news. Questions concerning them which are uppermost in the minds of reporters are: How will they influence newspapers? Will they hurt my job? What opportunities do they open to me?

THE CONVEYERS OF NEWS

From the time movable type was invented to the turn of the 20th century the printing press was the chief vehicle of mass communication. Then in rapid succession came motion pictures, radio, facsimile, news magazines and television.

Motion-picture newsreels and news magazines are too lacking in the immediacy element to compete with newspapers. Facsimile, a method of transmitting print and pictures via the air waves, has proved practical only as an interoffice conveyer and even in that field is overshadowed by the Teletype and Teletypesetter.

Radio at first was looked upon as a plaything. Then, as it entered the news field, it was viewed by the press as a dire threat. This threat proved to be empty. Radio won out as a speed medium, all but eliminating extra editions, but newspaper circulations continued to grow.

Television entered the scene as a news medium in the late 1930s. To the speed of radio it added sight and motion through the TV and newsreel cameras. Here indeed seemed to be a formidable competitor of the newspapers. Again the threat faded out.

What has happened? Radio and television are thriving and so are the newspapers. Why?

To understand, one must keep in mind a basic fact. That fact is that, while an improved mechanical device supersedes one less efficient, we add new cultural attainments without discarding the old.

In warfare the clenched hand was outmoded by the club, the club by the thrown stone, the stone by the bow and arrow, the bow and arrow by gunpowder and gunpowder by nuclear energy. Steam put sailing ships off the seas and automobiles sent buggies to the museums.

But did the modern theater put Shakespeare out of print? Did Rembrandt lose value when we learned to print color pictures? Did movies destroy the legitimate stage? Did we discard the violin when the phonograph arrived? No, none of these things happened. Nor will any medium of intelligence go into complete eclipse when another is introduced.

People accept one layer of culture on top of another, keeping the old as they enjoy the new. The old-*to*-new mechanical advances not only parallel but abet the old-*plus*-new cultural advances because the former give people more and more leisure time for entertainment and the pursuit of knowledge. For example, the housewife with machines that sweep, wash and iron is freer to read newspapers or watch television.

Newspapers, radio and television—the present conveyers of spot news —are all partly mechanical, partly cultural. To estimate their future let us separate and analyze their component assets.

QUALITIES IN NEWS MEDIA

Man has five senses. He can see, hear, taste, smell and feel. He does not taste, smell or feel news. He can only see and hear it. Therefore each of the three conveyers is a medium of sight or sound, or both.

Mechanically the newspaper reaches only the eye. Radio reaches only the ear. Television reaches both. It would seem then that mechanically television might replace the other two. But this reasoning is too simple. There are other all-important factors involved in news distribution. These we will call *speed, motion, convenience, retention* and *volume,* defining them as follows:

> *Speed*—Quickness in delivery from source to senses.
> *Motion*—Transmission of moving as against static images.
> *Convenience*—Availability with little effort.
> *Retention*—Permanent form which can be retained and perceived at will.
> *Volume*—Variety and completeness, giving the recipient wide selectivity.

In these five factors will be found the reasons for the continuance of newspapers as the major distributors of news, with radio and television in second place.

Radio and television have both strengths and weaknesses as news media. Both have speed unchallenged by the press. Radio is more convenient than television because its range is greater, sets are more portable and cheaper. People can listen to it while doing other things like sewing or driving a car. But radio reaches only the ear, whereas both television and newspapers reach the eye. Moreover, television can transmit not only printed type and still pictures but newsreels and living action pictures as well.

Why, then, does not the newspaper succumb to television as a news medium? The three-word answer is: *convenience, retention, volume.*

People have other and more urgent things to do than sit with their ears, or their ears and eyes, glued to an electronic box. There are jobs to work at, trains to catch, children to care for, meals to eat, friends to visit, places to go, and a multitude of other things demanding attention. You can do some of these things, but not all, and listen to the radio. You can't do any of them well while watching television. Nor can you switch off your radio and television set, do something else, then return to the newscast or ball game at the point where you left it. In the electronic media time is the only dimension and news must be presented sequentially.

Further, there are only 24 hours in a day and there is simply not enough time in a broadcast day to treat in detail the full panorama of news. Talking at the rapid clip of 175 words a minute a newscaster in 15 minutes speaks only 2,625 words, less than those on a single page of a newspaper. There is no such thing as a personal item in radio or television news.

Turn now to the newspaper. It is convenient, retainable, comprehensive. It will wait for you on the newsstand or at your doorstep. You can carry it in your pocket or lay it on the table, keep it as long as you like, read it as much as you like, turn back a page and reread it, return to it again and again at *your* choosing. You can be interrupted and pick it up again. You can divide it into parts, pass it on to other people or save it. You can clip it and mail the clipping or paste it in your scrapbook. You can do none of these things with news not on paper.

In a newspaper you can read *when* you want to read *what* you want to read in a place *where* you usually can find it—far more of it than is presented by any other medium. One Sunday newspaper makes available to you a volume of information greater than that in a solid week of broadcasting or telecasting. Completeness in the sense of detailed coverage is a monopoly of the press. Thus the newspaper gives you a wider range of news in a more convenient, larger-sized package usable over a longer period of time than radio or television.

It is technically possible that television may attain the important asset

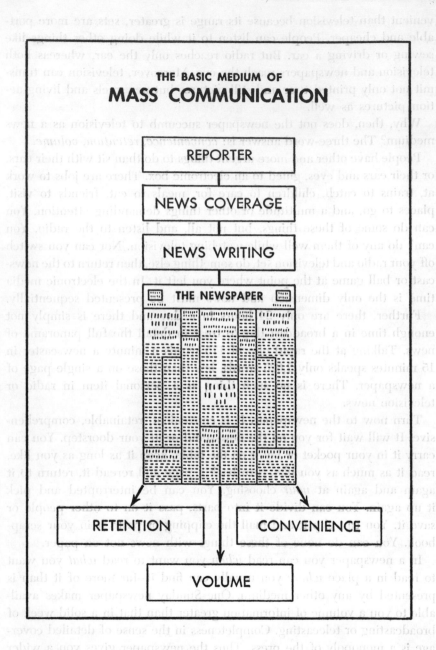

THE BASIC MEDIUM OF
MASS COMMUNICATION

REPORTER

NEWS COVERAGE

NEWS WRITING

THE NEWSPAPER

RETENTION

CONVENIENCE

VOLUME

Why Reporting Is Fundamental

of retention whereby its images may be obtainable at will, but this improvement is not now even in an experimental stage. Even so, a portable electronic plate with push buttons to tune in a front, sports or financial page would be, in fact, a newspaper minus the paper. Only
the mechanical printing process would be altered.

While they are competitors mechanically, culturally the news conveyers to some degree tend to supplement—even assist—one another.
Having heard a brief radio news item you want to read more about it
in your paper. If you have seen a live event on television you will turn
to an account of it in print, just as you read about the parade you witnessed or the wedding you attended. And if a newspaper article interests
you in a current news topic you will follow its developments as reported
by radio or television.

As each medium improves technically, making a larger variety of news
available, there is no doubt that its consumption will increase in accordance with the law that cultural capacity is cumulative.

NEWS REPORTING IS BASIC

The foregoing discussion makes it clear that there will be no drastic
upset in the methods of disseminating news until entirely new discoveries
and technical improvements are made.

Such discoveries and improvements are not at all impossible. But
even if they come they will still constitute *publication* in the broad
sense of that word. Whether news is conveyed via chiseled stone, clay
tablets, papyrus or parchment, the town crier, carved wood or handset
type, the printing press, facsimile receiver, radio loud-speaker, television
screen or some other vehicle it is publication. The printing press, the
microphone, the TV camera, and so on are but mechanical links between
news sources and the senses.

Somebody must gather news and somebody must put much of it into
words. These are basic and everlasting occupations. It is true that a
television camera can cover a fixed news event such as a boxing bout.
But will the stealthy murderer call the TV mobile unit to telecast his
crime? Or can the electronic camera penetrate invisible thoughts and
emotions that make news? A radio or television newscaster can speak
a few lines of news from memory, but can he go on for long without
using accurately written copy?

No. The gathering and writing of news must continue regardless of
changes in publication media. And so far the techniques of both skills
have been developed by the newspaper and merely adapted to the other

media. Moreover, many newspapers, radio and television stations have interlocking ownerships or close associations which make it easier for reporters to enter the new fields if they choose.

You need have no fear for the future if you start your journalistic career as a news reporter. Newspapers will be printed for decades to come; television and radio simply add to your opportunities to use your basic skill in covering and writing news. There will always be news and there will always be a demand for men and women to get it and write it.

To those who plan to go forward and make their livings as reporters the future promises opportunity, satisfaction and security.

News reporting always has been and always will be a game of eternal youth. It wants open minds, clear heads and sharp wits. It reflects the growing, changing world. To record the news and to present it to a free people who are seeking the truth from a free press is an exciting and challenging lifework worthy of the best of us.

SHOP TALK

1. Compare the opportunities for advancement in an editorial room with those in a bank; in a store; as a teacher; as a lawyer.
2. If you had to become a news specialist, which field would you choose and why?
3. If you were a successful reporter, would you go into public relations or advertising at a substantial pay increase?
4. Do you agree with the author's theory of mechanical and cultural progress? Debate it.
5. Are the opportunities in news reporting greater or less than they were 25 years ago?

Appendixes

I. Practice and Assignments

CHAPTER 1: THE REPORTER AND HIS JOB

Practice. Ask each student to write a 300-word article on "Why I Am Taking This Reporting Course." Criticize the logic, lucidity, clearness and neatness of the articles written.

Assignment. Study the eight elements which give an event news value. Then analyze the front page of a newspaper. Give each story a one-word title and list the news factors you find in it.

CHAPTER 2: WHAT IS NEWS AND WHY?

Practice. Have each student write a 250-word monograph explaining in pithy, concise terms the characteristics of news as distinguished from history, fiction and drama.

Assignment. Assume that you are the city editor of a local newspaper. Go through several papers. Clip and mount 10 stories for a future file. Date each item and note why it might be of value on that date.

CHAPTER 3: INSIDE THE LOCAL ROOM

Practice. Take the students on a tour of a newspaper building, paying special attention to the local newsroom.

Assignment. Prepare a comprehensive list of news sources in your city, such as police headquarters, city hall and hospitals, ranking them in order of importance and explaining the types of news emanating from each one.

CHAPTER 4: GO AND GET A STORY!

Practice. Ask each student to prepare imaginary assignment sheets, with three to five items on each, for general assignment, beat and special assignment reporters. Then make up a schedule sheet from these assignments. Practice the preparation of properly titled, spaced, indented and closed sheets of copy.

Assignment. Tear off the front pages of two newspapers. Underscore every word and phrase in each story which you believe is not clear to the average reader. Mark at least a dozen. Type each one and under it a substitute which is clear.

CHAPTER 5: WRITING THE NEWS CLEARLY

Practice. Give the students a list of 25 long, abstract and elegant words and phrases. Ask them to substitute for each one another which they would use in news copy. Compare and discuss the substitutes.

Assignment. Go through each story on the front pages of two newspapers. Underscore with a red pencil words, passages and paragraphs which are colorful and personalized. Write 250 words scoring the two papers on these counts, citing examples.

CHAPTER 6: THE SECRETS OF STYLE

Practice. Have the students rewrite several flowery, bromidic and dull articles taken from small country newspapers. List on the blackboard every stereotype used. Contrast these with accepted slang.

Assignment. Clip from the newspapers 10 summary leads. Analyze each of them to show how they answer the questions: Who? What? When? Where? Why or How? Break each one into parts, each part representing an answer to one of the five questions.

CHAPTER 7: HOW TO START THE STORY

Practice. Present to the students the major facts in several news stories in haphazard order. Have them single out the main facts and write summary leads. Choose and compare the best ones.

Assignment. Clip from current newspapers a half dozen types of news story leads other than the five-W variety. Classify and paste up at least two of each type.

CHAPTER 8: NOVELTY IN NEWS LEADS

Practice. Present a set of facts for a news story. Ask each student to write at least three different types of leads. Compare the leads and select the best of each type.

Assignment. Clip from the newspapers a fact story, an action story, a quote story. Using the charts in Chapter 9, diagram each with a pencil. Explain briefly how each story conforms to the diagram.

CHAPTER 9: THE STORY STRUCTURE

Practice. Ask the students to rewrite material taken from the body of an ordinary news story. Give them the lead as printed, and other data orally at random. Practice with fact, quote and action stories.

Assignment. Clip from the newspapers a personal item, a birth notice, an illness report and a funeral story. Comment briefly on the style, structure and content of each. Explain if and how you would order any of them re-covered, rewritten or edited.

CHAPTER 10: NEWS OF THE NEIGHBORHOOD

Practice. Give to the students the partial facts for a birth story and the remaining facts when brought out by their questions. Repeat with illness and funeral stories. Criticize the style and structure of the specimens they write.

Assignment. Clip a story of an automobile smashup, a plane crash, a train wreck or a fire, containing a casualty list. Chart it by the diagram in Chapter 11. Clip and criticize a suicide story.

CHAPTER 11: ACCIDENTS, FIRES AND SUICIDES

Practice. After they have developed the data through questions, have the students write short fire, accident and suicide stories. Assign them then to write a plane-crash story containing the names of a half dozen or more persons killed and injured.

Assignment. Prepare a 250-word paper defining and explaining the handling of advance and follow-up stories. Clip from an afternoon paper the follow-up of a story previously printed in a morning paper, and vice versa.

CHAPTER 12: FORECASTS AND FOLLOW-UPS

Practice. Using the data from a speech or meeting story, have the students write an advance, the story proper and a follow-up. Practice with new leads and tie-ins.

Assignment. Clip and diagram a speech story, commenting on the summary-quote-summary-quote arrangement. Also clip a statement story and explain how it resembles the speech story. Clip a third story containing direct quotations from a debate or discussion. Underline the synonyms for the word *said*.

CHAPTER 13: FROM PLATFORM TO PRESS

Practice. Read to the students one or two speech manuscripts and have them write the stories. Criticize leads and structure.

Assignment. Interview some person of news interest on the campus or elsewhere in your community or watch a news panel program on television. Write a 200- or 300-word interview story in newspaper style.

CHAPTER 14: INTERVIEWS AND PRESS CONFERENCES

Practice. Invite to the class some campus or local person of prominence—an experienced newspaperman would be best—and have students interview him and write the story. Criticize their conduct of the interview as well as their copy.

Assignment. In a 250-word paper, quote what your state constitution says about freedom of the press. Explain in your own words the difference between unprivileged and privileged news material, citing examples.

CHAPTER 15: LIBEL WILL MAKE YOU LIABLE

Practice. Have the students rewrite in safe form several articles laden with libelous material. Trap them if possible. Criticize from the standpoint both of dangerous matter used and of safe, privileged matter discarded.

Assignment. Read the next chapter carefully. Write a brief, critical analysis setting forth points on which you disagree with the author and why. Suggest, if you can, one or two taboos which he has omitted and which you would impose as a city editor.

CHAPTER 16: THE TABOOS OF THE TRADE

Practice. Present the facts about an influenza epidemic in your community, speaking as a city health officer. Have students write the story. Posing as a sheriff, let the students interview you on reports that several people have seen what they believed to be a space ship. Analyze treatments of the stories.

Assignment. Clip a composite story with at least three separate angles. Analyze the lead and structure, showing how the units dovetail. Underline the coupling-pin words. Draw a diagram.

CHAPTER 17: COMPOSING THE COMPOSITE STORY

Practice. Have the students weld into a composite story material about three or four occurrences of a similar nature. Practice with various leads and arrangements for the same story.

Assignment. Write a 250-word paper contrasting straight and human interest news. Clip three short human interest stories. Comment on their special appeal and the effectiveness of their preparation.

CHAPTER 18: THE HUMAN TOUCH IN NEWS

Practice. Give the students the unvarnished facts from a human interest story. Let them develop and write it. Practice the rewriting of overdone human interest stories.

Assignment. Clip one long or two or three short suspended interest stories. Write a brief explanation of suspended interest structure.

CHAPTER 19: SUSPENDED INTEREST STORIES

Practice. Have the students practice with suspended interest structure, writing several stories of the narrative and dramatic formula type from data provided by the instructor from actual stories.

Assignment. Clip from a morning paper a story rewritten from an afternoon paper, or vice versa, without any new material. Show how the rewrite man made it appear to be fresh, up-to-the-minute news. Rewrite the same story yourself for a third newspaper.

CHAPTER 20: GIVE IT TO A REWRITE MAN

Practice. Have the class practice rewriting morning paper stories for afternoon papers, and vice versa. Call for speed. Try localizing an out-of-town dispatch.

Assignment. Write a 300-word paper explaining the organization of the Associated Press and United Press International. Go to the library or local offices for material.

CHAPTER 21: NEWS FROM OUT OF TOWN

Practice. Using data from stories appearing in a local paper, have the students write queries, bulletins and wire stories. Put increasing emphasis on speed.

Assignment. Clip a running story with at least one bulletin. Analyze it, marking with a pencil what appears to be inserted, added or A-matter copy. Explain briefly in writing how a running story is compiled.

CHAPTER 22: CATCHING THE DEADLINES

Practice. Let each student be a rewrite man. Set deadlines for three or four editions during the class period. Have the students write a running story with one or two bulletins, a new lead, one or two inserts and adds. Each piece of copy must be ready before the edition deadline. Emphasize speed.

Assignment. In a 250-word paper state your views on opinion in the news columns. Do you think a publisher is ever justified in ordering stories slanted? Clip a story slanted by policy and apply your conclusions.

CHAPTER 23: POLICY, CRUSADES AND EXPOSÉS

Practice. Divide the class into two groups representing the staffs of two papers with divergent policies on a given issue. State the policies, then present material for a practice story. Switch the staffs and have the class write another story involving the same policy issue.

Assignment. Analyze the sports page or pages of a newspaper, tabulating the space given to each class of sports. Clip a sports dope story; also a good baseball, football or basketball story. Type briefly the essential facts in the latter story.

CHAPTER 24: SPORTS FROM THE PRESS BOX

Practice. Give the students unorganized material from a story about a game. Have them write it for the sports page. Have each student prepare a box score or summary.

Assignment. Examine the women's pages of a newspaper. Clip a wedding story and criticize its style. Also clip three other stories with special appeal to women readers and explain why you think they will read them.

CHAPTER 25: WRITING NEWS FOR WOMEN

Practice. By asking questions, let the students obtain the necessary facts for and write engagement and wedding stories.

Assignment. Clip a business story. Comment upon the presentation of figures, free advertising, if any, and the general style and structure. Clip a labor strike story. Comment upon its fairness to both sides and to the public.

CHAPTER 26: THE BUSINESS BEAT MAN

Practice. Have the students write a story replete with lengthy statistics. Emphasize clearness. Practice rewriting handouts, separating legitimate news matter from unwarranted advertising.

Assignment. With a ruler, measure the exact amount of space devoted to crime news in one edition of a newspaper. Write a report. Compare your total with the amount devoted to other news. Examine the crime stories and criticize them as to style and good taste.

CHAPTER 27: THE TREATMENT OF CRIME

Practice. Choose a short murder story in a detective magazine or a chapter in a crime novel. Read it slowly to the students, allowing them to take notes. Have each write it as a news story. Add new developments for a follow-up story.

Assignment. Make a list of all the courts in your state, county and city. Write a line or two describing the kinds of cases handled by each. Clip a court story and state from which court it was obtained.

CHAPTER 28: COVERING THE COURTS

Practice. For practice material give the students the facts that develop in three or four stages of a criminal trial. Have them write the stories with new leads and bulletins on jury retirement, verdict and sentencing.

Assignment. Clip two stories in which the sex element predominates—one written conservatively, the other in racy style. State which treatment you would favor as a city editor, and why.

CHAPTER 29: SEX IN NEWS STORIES

Practice. Present the facts and quotations for a typical divorce story. Have it written, first for a conservative paper, then for a more sensational paper. Repeat with a rape-murder story.

Assignment. Clip a political story. State whether it is a dope, speech or election story. Analyze it as to style. Does it conform to the paper's policy? Underscore words and phrases often used in political stories. Set forth your findings in a 150-word paper.

CHAPTER 30: POLITICS AND ELECTIONS

Practice. Quote copiously from a long political speech. Have the students write a short, condensed story. Using the data from a local election, have them write an election story for the local paper. Let them obtain material, other than figures, by questioning the instructor.

Assignment. Clip or bring to class pages containing a sectional story handled under at least three separate headlines. From the clippings prepare assignments for three or more reporters.

CHAPTER 31: TEAMWORK BY THE STAFF

Practice. Organize the class into staffs of six students each. Appoint one student in each group as city editor, and assign each of the others to one phase of a sectional story. Present material for the story and let each staff handle it, the city editors reading copy and roughly mapping a page layout.

Assignment. Write a 400-word paper explaining why you have taken this course in reporting, criticizing it and appraising its value to you.

CHAPTER 32: THE NEWSMEN OF THE FUTURE

Practice. Have each student write a 300-word paper entitled: "How I Think News Will Be Prepared and Published 100 Years from Today." Read and discuss the papers.

II. Newsroom Glossary

Ad. Advertisement.

Add. Fresh copy added at the end of a story already written.

Advance. A story about an event to occur in the future.

Alibi copy. Duplicates of news copy filed in the morgue.

AM. A morning newspaper.

A-matter. The last part of a story written before the lead.

Angle. A division of a composite story; to slant.

AP. Associated Press.

Art. Pictures, maps and other illustrations.

Assignment. Any news-gathering task allotted to a reporter.

Attribution. Statement of the source of information.

Banner. A headline stretching across a page; streamer, line.

Beat. An exclusive story; a scoop; a reporter's regular run, as city hall beat, school beat.

Beg your pardon. A newspaper's correction, printed as a separate item, of a mistake in an earlier story.

Black sheets. Carbon copy pages of a typewritten story; dupes; flimsies.

Blind query. A query lacking specific information.

Blurb. A publicity or advertising item; a puff.

Box. News material enclosed by line rules.

Break. To become available for publication.

Brightener. A short light item, usually humorous; a smile.

Bromide. A trite, hackneyed expression; a stereotype.

Bug man. A copyreader who makes trifling changes in copy.

Bulldog. The earliest edition of a newspaper, often applied to the Sunday mail edition.

Bulletin. An urgent last-minute news brief.

Bunk lead. A temporary opener for a running story to be replaced in a later edition; a throwaway lead.

Byline. Signature of a reporter preceding a story.

Canned copy. Publicity material.

Caption. Reading material which accompanies art.

City editor. The chief in charge of the local newsroom.

City room. The local newsroom.

Clip. A newspaper clipping.

Columnist. Writer of a departmentalized column, usually bylined.

Composite story. A story composed of several angles.

Copy. All news manuscript.

Copybook. A unit consisting of alternate sheets of copy and carbon paper used for typing news.

Copy boy. A boy who runs editorial room errands.

Copy desk. The desk where copy is edited and headlined.

Copy fighter. A copyreader who changes words and punctuation unnecessarily.

Copyreader. A newsroom employe who reads and corrects copy and prepares headlines.

Correspondent. An out-of-town reporter.

Coupling pin. A transitional word, phrase or sentence.

Cover. To get all the available news about an event.

Crusade. A newspaper campaign to bring about a reform or improvement.

Cub. An untrained reporter; a beginner.

Cut. A metal plate bearing a newspaper illustration.

Dateline. The line preceding an out-of-town story giving the date and place of origin.

Day shift. The daytime working period; day side.

Deadline. The last moment when copy for an edition must be completed.

Deck. A section of a headline.

Desk man. The city editor or an assistant.

District man. A beat reporter.

Dope. Advance news story material, mostly prophecy and gossip.

Double truck. The two facing pages at the center of a newspaper or section that are made up as one page.

Down style. The style favoring lower case or small letters; opposite of up style.

DPR. Day press rate; discounted telegraph charge for press copy.

Dummy. A layout of a newspaper page.

Dupe. Carbon copy; flimsy.

Ear. The small box in the upper corner of a front page, often enclosing the weather report or a slogan.

Edition. Copies of a newspaper printed during one run of the presses, as *Early, Home, Final.*

Editorialize. To inject the writer's opinion into a news story.

Exclusive. A story printed by only one paper; a scoop; a beat.

Exposé. A newspaper exposure of something viewed by it as detrimental.

Extra. An edition other than a regular one.

Feature. The nub or trump fact of a news story; to give prominence to a story; a human interest or magazine type of story.

File. To send news by wire.

Filler. Short minor story used to fill space where needed.

Five W's. Who? What? When? Where? Why?

Flag. The front page title of a newspaper.

Flash. An abbreviated wire service report sent before a bulletin.

Flimsy. A thin-paper carbon copy.

Follow. To cover new developments of an earlier story.

Follow-up. A story presenting new developments of one previously printed; a second-day story.

Fotog. Photographer.

Fudge column. A page one column for last-minute news.

Future. A memorandum about a story likely to develop later, kept in a future file by the city editor.

Galley. A shallow metal tray for holding type when it comes from the composing machine.

Gloomy run. The beat covering hospitals, morgues and funeral homes.

Guideline. A one-word title of a story, as *Fire, Storm, Tax;* a slug.

Handout. A piece of publicity material.

Head. Headline.

Hold for release. News not to be printed until a specified time or under specified circumstances.

Hook. A spike for incoming or discarded copy.

Human interest. Emotional appeal in the news; a story with emotion appeal as contrasted with straight news; H-I.

Insert. New material inserted in the body of a story already written.

Italic. Slanting type.

Jim dash. A short dash used to separate the decks of a headline or short items in a column.

Jump. To continue a story from one page to another.

Jump head. The headline carried over the continued portion of a jumped story.

Kill. To strike out or discard a story or part of a story.

Lead. The introductory sentence or paragraph of a story.

Lead-to-body link. Short segment of a story between the opening and main body, usually attribution or identification.

Leaders. A row of dots or short dashes used to indicate omitted matter or to direct the eye across an empty space in tabular matter.

Leased wire. A telegraph circuit reserved for newspaper use.

Leg man. A reporter who gathers but does not write news.

Libel. Any defamatory matter wrongfully published.

Library. Systematized files of newspaper clips, reference books and other data; the morgue.

Lift. A light or human interest item; to appropriate the facts of a story from another newspaper.

Line. Banner; streamer; headline stretching across front page.

Linotype. A typesetting machine.

Lobster shift. Early morning working hours.

Local. A local news story.

Localize. To stress the local angle of a story.

Local newsroom. The workshop of the city news staff.

Log. Assignment book.

Makeup. The arrangement of news matter and pictures on a newspaper page.

Masthead. An editorial page heading that gives information about the paper.

Matrix. A flat brass Linotype letter mold used in typecasting.

Microfilm. Film used in newspaper libraries to preserve files and save storage space.

More. The word put at the bottom of a page of copy meaning more to come.

Morgue. The library.

Must. A designation on copy ordering it to be printed without fail.

New lead. A new or rewritten item or items replacing a lead already prepared; the fresh development in a follow-up story.

Newscast. A radio or television news broadcast.

Newsroom. A room or office where news is written and edited.

Night shift. The night working period; night side.

NPR. Night press rate; discounted telegraph charge for press copy.

Obituary. A biography of a dead person; a death story; obit.

Off the record. Information given a reporter that is not to be printed.

Opener. A news story lead.

Overhead. To file telegraph copy on regular rather than leased wires.

Overline. The heading over a cut.

Overnight. An assignment to be covered the following day.

PA. Press agent.

Patchwork. Repair or revision of a story already prepared.

Personal. A news brevity about one or more persons; local item.

Pix. Pictures.

Platform. The position of a newspaper on matters of policy.

Play up. To give prominent display to a story or an angle in a story.

PM. An afternoon newspaper.

Policy. The views of a newspaper on a public question.

Precede. Matter intended to precede a news story.

Press agent. A publicity or public relations man.

Press association. A news-gathering organization serving many papers, radio and TV stations.

PR. Public relations.

Primary news. Major news.

Printer. A receiving Teletype machine.

Privilege. The right granted to the press by the Constitution to print with immunity otherwise libelous material.

Proof. An impression of type taken on paper for the purpose of making corrections.

Proofreader. An employe who corrects errors in typesetting.

Puff. A piece of publicity or free advertising; a blurb.

Punch. A surprise lead.

Put to bed. To lock up the forms for an edition.

Q-A matter. Question and answer copy, as in court testimony.

Query. A brief telegraphic synopsis of a story sent to a newspaper by a correspondent.

Quote. Quotation.

Railroad. To rush copy into print without careful editing.

Release copy. Copy that is not to be published until a given date and time.

Replate. To recast a page of type in order to insert an urgent story received too late to catch a deadline.

Rewrite. To write for a second time.

Rewrite man. The staff member who rewrites but does not cover news.

Rim. The outer edge of a copy desk where copyreaders work.

Rim man. A copyreader.

ROP. Run-of-paper color.

Run. The territory assigned regularly to a reporter; a beat.

Running story. A fast-breaking story usually written in sections or takes.

Schedule. The list of assignments or stories for an edition; to prepare such a list.

Scoop. An exclusive story; a beat.

Secondary news. Minor news.

Short. A brief news item.

Slander. Oral defamation as differing from written defamation, or libel.

Slant. To emphasize a phase of a policy story.

Slot. The inside of a copy desk where the chief sits.

Slug. A guideline set in type; the name, title, letter or other notation placed on a story or item as identification or to specify its disposal.

Smile. A short humorous story.

Split-run edition. An edition of a newspaper containing news of a suburban zone not included in other press runs.

Spot news. Live, urgent news, often unexpected.

Spread. The display given to an important story.

Squib. A short minor news story.

Stereotype. A bromide.

Stickful. Two inches of type.

Story. Any newspaper article written by a reporter.

Straight news. A plain recital of news facts written in standard style and form.

Streamer. Banner; headline stretching across page one.

String. Clippings pasted together in a continuous ribbon or scrapbook.

Stringer. A correspondent who is paid by the inch for clippings strung together.

Stuff. Any news; raw material.

Style. Literary quality of writing.

Sub. Substitute.

Subhead. A small headline inserted in the body of a story to break up a long stretch of type.

Summary lead. A lead answering the five *W's.*

Suspended interest. A news story with the climax near the end.

Swing man. Any employe who takes over for another who is off duty for any reason.

Syndicate. A business organization engaged in the distribution of news, feature, art material to newspapers.

Tag. The final part of an item containing the surprise; punch line.

Take. A portion of copy in a running story.

Teletype. A trade-mark applied to a kind of teletypewriter; a transmitter or printer; to send by Teletype.

Teletypesetter. A trade-mark applied to a machine which transmits and sets news into type automatically; TTS.

Think piece. A dope story.

Thirty. The end.

Thumbnail. A cut half a column wide.

Tieback. A tie-in.

Tie-in. Information previously printed and included in a story to refresh the reader's mind.

Tip. Information which may lead to a story.

TR. Turn rule.

Transition. A coupling pin; movement from one scene to another.

Trim. To reduce the length of a story.

TTS. A Teletypesetter.

Turn rule. An instruction to the printer to turn a slug or rule upside down to indicate that a correction or alteration is to be made at that place.

TV. Television.

UPI. United Press International, a wire service.

Up style. The style favoring capitalization; opposite of down style.

Zone coverage. The reporting and printing of news from a suburban zone.

III. Style Sheet

NOTE: This Style Sheet is based on the Associated Press Style Book and Webster's New International Dictionary.

ABBREVIATIONS

Government agencies, military or civil organizations, radio and television stations, time zones and commonly known corporations take initials without periods: UN, FBI, USDA, GI, MIG, ROTC, AP, GOP, YMCA, WABC, WABC-TV, CST, CDT, GM, IBM, AT&T.

Business firms and other groups are abbreviated: Co., Corp., Assn., Inc.

Addresses are abbreviated: St., Ave., Blvd., Sq., Ter., Pl., N., E., S., W., 1119 S.E. 4th St., 461 Park Ave., NW., Grand Blvd. at 47th St., but Grand boulevard will be paved.

Time is abbreviated: 10:30 p.m., but 6 o'clock.

Months are abbreviated when used in specific dates: Oct. 12, 1492, but October 1492. March, April, May, June and July are not abbreviated at any time. With dates, omit *d, nd, rd,* and *th*: June 2, not June 2d or 2nd.

Days of the week are not abbreviated: Monday, Friday.

States are abbreviated when immediately following the names of towns, cities or other geographic terms: Chicago, Ill., but citizen of Illinois. Abbreviations: Ala., Ariz., Ark., Calif., Colo., Conn., Del., Fla., Ga., Ill., Ind., Kan., Ky., La., Md., Mass., Mich., Minn., Miss., Mo., Mont., N.C., N.D., Neb., Nev., N.H., N.J., N.M., N.Y., Okla., Ore., Pa., R.I., S.C., S.D., Tenn., Tex., Va., Vt., Wash., Wis., W.Va., Wyo. Idaho, Iowa, Ohio, Maine, Utah, Alaska and Hawaii are not abbreviated.

Do not abbreviate Christmas as Xmas.

Titles when preceding a name are abbreviated and capitalized: Mr., Mrs., Dr., Rev., Prof., Dist. Atty., Sen., Rep., Capt., Gen. Exception: Spell out when the first name or initials are omitted: President Wrightman.

Lower case abbreviations usually take periods: m.p.h., c.o.d., r.p.m., a.c., d.c., f.o.b., a.m., p.m.

Do not abbreviate first names: James, Samuel, George, Joseph. Caution: Names often are correctly Ben, Alex or Fred. Do not contract Benjamin, Alexander or Frederick unless the person uses one of these forms.

CAPITALIZATION

Titles preceding names should be capitalized. Titles standing alone or following names are lower case, except: President when President of the

United States is meant (not the office), head of any nation as Premier, King, Queen.

Capitalize Congress, Senate, House, Cabinet, Supreme Court, Legislature, Council.

Capitalize special events, holidays, historic events: Battle of Bunker Hill, Memorial Day, National Safety Week.

Capitalize descriptive terms for specific regions, localities or geographic features: Middle East, the West, Midwest, Deep South, Arctic Circle, Orient, South Side.

Calendar divisions are capitalized but not seasons: January, Monday, spring, winter.

Trade names are capitalized but the noun is lower case: Philco radio, Peace rose, Adams store.

Names of all races are capitalized: Indian, Chinese, Negro, Oriental, Occidental, Caueasian; but white, black, yellow, red (not colored).

Wars of historical significance are capitalized: World War I, second World War, the Revolution, Civil War.

Degrees are capitalized when abbreviated, lower case when spelled: B.A., bachelor of arts.

The common noun is capitalized when forming an essential part of a proper name, but lower case when used alone as a substitute: Hoover Dam, the dam; Ohio River, the river; Timber County, the county; Midland College, the college.

Fanciful appellations are capitalized: Empire State, Leatherneck, Old Sol.

Military decorations are capitalized: Congressional Medal of Honor, Silver Star.

Proper names and derivatives of proper names are capitalized except in names of common usage: brussels sprouts, dutch treat, paris green, venetian blind.

Titles of books, plays and songs are capitalized: "The Courtship of Miles Standish."

In titles, ex- and former are lower case: ex-champion Kelly, former Mayor Nelson.

COMPOUNDS

Consolidate two nouns when frequently united to form another: baseball, skyscraper, stockholder, businessman.

A hyphen is used to avoid a doubled vowel: pre-empt, re-echo, semiannual, undergraduate.

A hyphen is omitted in words of common usage: coordinate, cooperate, reinstate, reelect.

NUMERALS

In general spell out figures below 10 and use numerals for 11 and above: five men, seventh day, 12 miles, 380 spectators. Either ten or 10 is proper.

In a series of related expressions treat all alike: He had three horses, sixteen pigs, one dog. He had 3 suits, 12 pairs of socks, 18 shirts.

In a series of related, but doubled numerical expressions, use both figures and spelled numerals: There were three 5-room houses, ninety 4-room houses and six 8-room houses.

Use numerals for ages, scores, odds, dates, time of day, sums of money, percentages, financial and tabular matter, temperatures, dimensions, military ranks and units, highways: 6-year-old; 6 years old; John Doe, 40; 3–1; 5–2; June 1959; June 3, 1959; Sept. 1 to Oct. 15, 1959; Dec. 1–20, 1959; Jan. 1953–59; 4:30 p.m., 4 o'clock; $4.95 shirt; 3½ per cent interest; 32 degrees, 8 by 12 inches; U.S. Highway 117.

Spell out all numerals which start a sentence.

The dollar sign is not used in round sums of millions or billions: one million dollars; 20 billion dollars; $11,657,318; $100.75; $10,000; $1.25.

Spell out titles, historical periods, groups and committees, geographical names: "The Thousand and One Nights," Thirty Years' War, Thousand Islands.

Spell out indefinite numbers and casual figures: twenty-odd, a hundred and one reasons, a thousand times no!

Fractions are confined, in figures, to eighths: ⅛, ¼, ⅜, ½, ⅝. In ordinary reading matter fractions are spelled: three-fourths of the people.

Street addresses, serial numbers, phone numbers, sports scores are printed solid: 7415 Oak St., A12345678, JAckson 4–5481, 21–6.

Roman numerals are used for personal sequences, wars, Popes, royalty, yachts and horses: John Jones III, World War I, Pope John XXIII, Louis XIV, Pancoast III, Hanover II.

Ordinals below 10 are spelled except in classifying orchestra instruments or voices, in addresses or in political or military divisions: 1st Army, 1st violin, 2nd tenor, 1st Ward, first contingent.

Ordinals above 10 carry the *th, nd, rd, st* except in dates: 22nd, 33rd, 54th, 41st, June 19.

Write it: No. 1 man, No. 1 candidate.

PUNCTUATION

Period. The period is used after a letter or number in a series: A. Korean War. B. World War II. Exception: Q.– and A.–. 1. Punctuate correctly. 2. Write simply.

Three periods (leaders) are used for the omission of words within a sentence or at the end of a single incomplete sentence: The combination . . . was secure. They worked seven hours . . . Five periods indicate an incomplete article of more than one sentence.

Comma. The comma is used to set off parenthetic words, phrases or clauses and scores: The work, he said, was exacting. Midland Blue Sox 7, Capital City Oilers 6.

The comma is omitted between the name and abbreviation of persons, before the ampersand, before the dash, in street addresses, telephone numbers, years and serial numbers: John Jones Jr.; Smith, Jones & Co.; LOgan 3–3448; 7415 Elm St.; A1234567890.

Semicolon. The semicolon separates phrases containing commas to avoid confusion; separates clauses when the conjunction is implied but omitted; separates statements of contrast or statements too closely related in meaning to be separate sentences and separates phrases in lists: Frank Bates, Booneville; Ralph Chambers, Midland.

Colon. The colon precedes the final clause summarizing prior matter, introduces listings or statements, and takes the place of an implied *for instance:* He replied: "Go fly a kite." The situation is this: Do we change or don't we?

The phrase before a sentence quotation ends with a colon, not a comma: He replied: "We have already outlined our policy."

Apostrophe. The apostrophe is used in plurals of letters but not in plurals of figures: the ABC's, three R's, late 1950s, 90s, class of '90, John Jones '48.

The official form is to be followed as to use of the apostrophe in geographic, institution and firm or organization name: Harpers Ferry, Johns Hopkins University, Teachers College, Actors Equity Assn., Harper's Weekly, Readers Digest.

Usually the possessive of a singular noun not ending in *s* is formed by adding the apostrophe and *s;* in the plural ending with *s* or *ce* the apostrophe only is added: man's, women's prince's, hostess', princes', Joneses', hostesses', Caution: Family name plurals: the Joneses, not the Jones or the Jones's.

Exclamation Point. The exclamation point is used to indicate surprise, appeal, incredulity or other strong emotion even in an interrogative sentence: How wonderful! "Wow!" Who yelled: "Come here!"

Question Mark. The question mark is used in proceedings of public bodies, dialogue, interview and court report: Q.—Were you there? A.—I don't remember.

Parenthesis. Parentheses are used to set off material which is not part of the main statement, or an identification or grammatical element of a sentence important enough to be included. Parenthetic matter is closely related, differing from matter separated by dashes: Sen. Smith (D-Va) John (Tiger) Smith.

Parentheses are used to set off figures or letters in a series within a sentence: The order of importance will be (a) general acceptance, (b) cost and (c) opposition by leaders.

Dash. The dash marks a sudden or abrupt change in thought. The dash is sometimes used instead of parentheses: He claimed—no one denied it—priority.

Quotation Marks.   Quotation marks enclose direct quotations and some words or phrases in ironical use, political controversy, or use other than true significance. Some accepted sobriquets or misnomers take quotation marks instead of parentheses but nicknames should be in parentheses: "lame duck" amendment, "Fair Deal," "gentlemen's agreement," "Old Guard," Define "neologism," He uses "and-ah" too much in conversation.

The comma and final period are placed inside the quotation marks. Other punctuation marks should be placed inside quotation marks only when they are part of the quoted matter: The coach shouted: "Let's go!" He asked "Why?" Why call it a "gentlemen's agreement"?

Title of books, plays, documents, operas, songs, subjects of lectures and sermons take quotation marks. Names of newspapers, periodicals, ships, airlines, animals, names of characters in books or plays do not take quotation marks.

Hyphen.   The hyphen is one of the most overworked, improperly used punctuation marks. The hyphen should be used only to divide words, in scores and in some cases of abbreviation for clarity.

The general rule for using the hyphen in abbreviations: Like characters are hyphenated, unlike characters are printed solid: A-bomb, 20-20 vision, 3D, B29, 3-2.

The hyphen is used for double occupation or office: poet-artist, secretary-treasurer.

The hyphen is used to separate a prefix ending in a vowel when followed by the same vowel when there may be confusion except where common usage has closed the word: pre-empt, re-echo, coordinate.

The hyphen is used in compound adjectives that precede a noun: old-fashioned song, up-to-date style.

Caution: An adverb ending in *ly* never takes a hyphen when used with an adjective to form a compound adjective: badly mangled, fully informed, newly chosen, widely advertised product.

The hyphen sometimes is used in a compound word which is so long, or unusual, as to be confusing: post-revolutionary, ultra-fashionable.

The hyphen is used to differentiate between words of similar or identical spelling but different meaning: correspondent, co-respondent, recover, re-cover, overall, over-all, resent, re-sent.

The hyphen is used to separate a prefix from a proper name: ante-Christian, un-American.

Non as a prefix is set solid except in proper names: nonfederal, non-Arabic.

Titles taking *ex-* and *-elect* use the hyphen: ex-officio, mayor-elect, ex-champion.

Transoceanic compounds take no hyphen: transatlantic. Trade name, firm name, nation or country take the hyphen: trans-Mississippi, trans-Siberian.

Ampersand.   The ampersand is used in abbreviations and common firm names: Jones & Co., AT&T, A&P.

INDEX